Prologue
At the Shore: The Beginning and End of a Journey
-On the Beach•b-

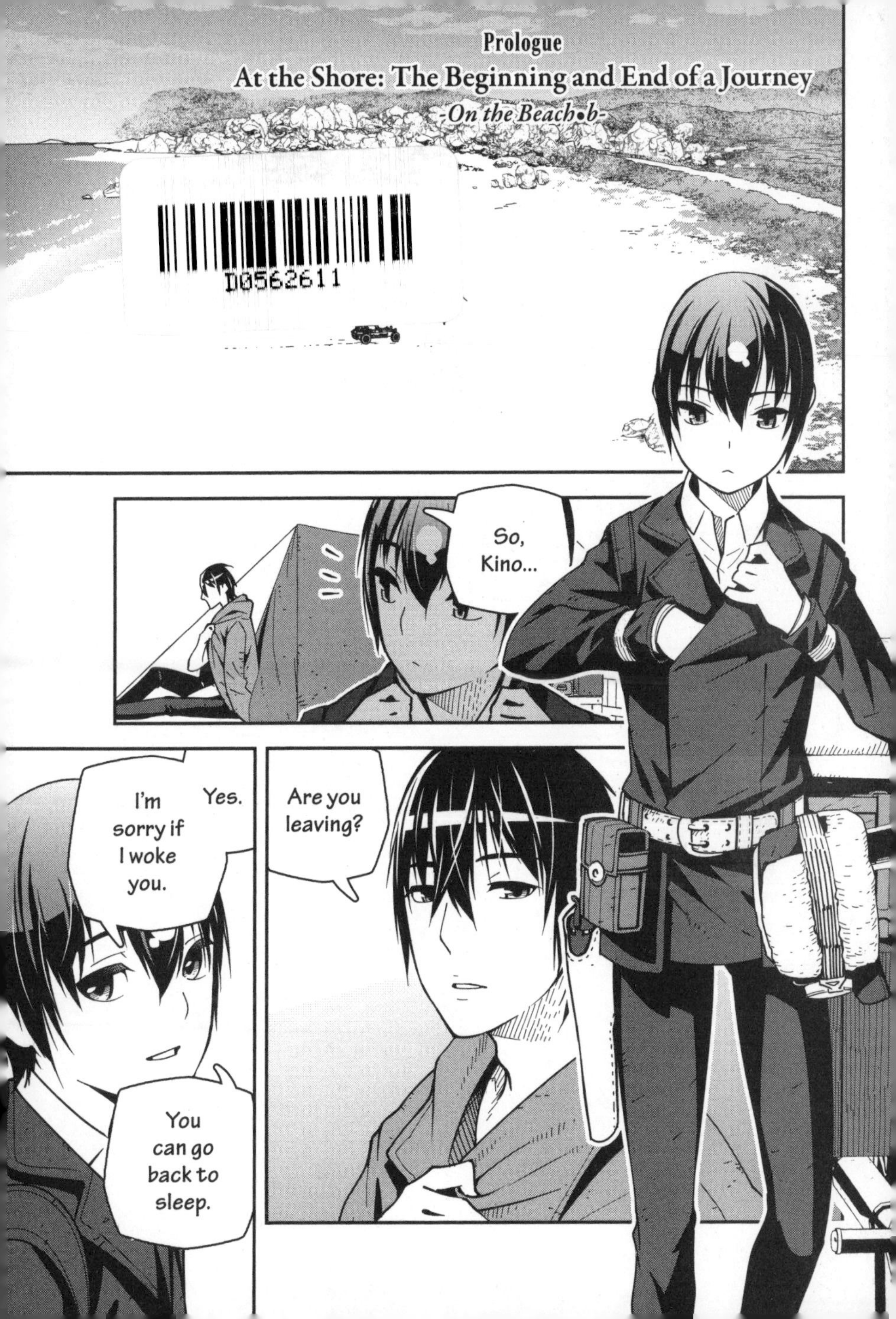
So, Kino...
Are you leaving?
Yes.
I'm sorry if I woke you.
You can go back to sleep.

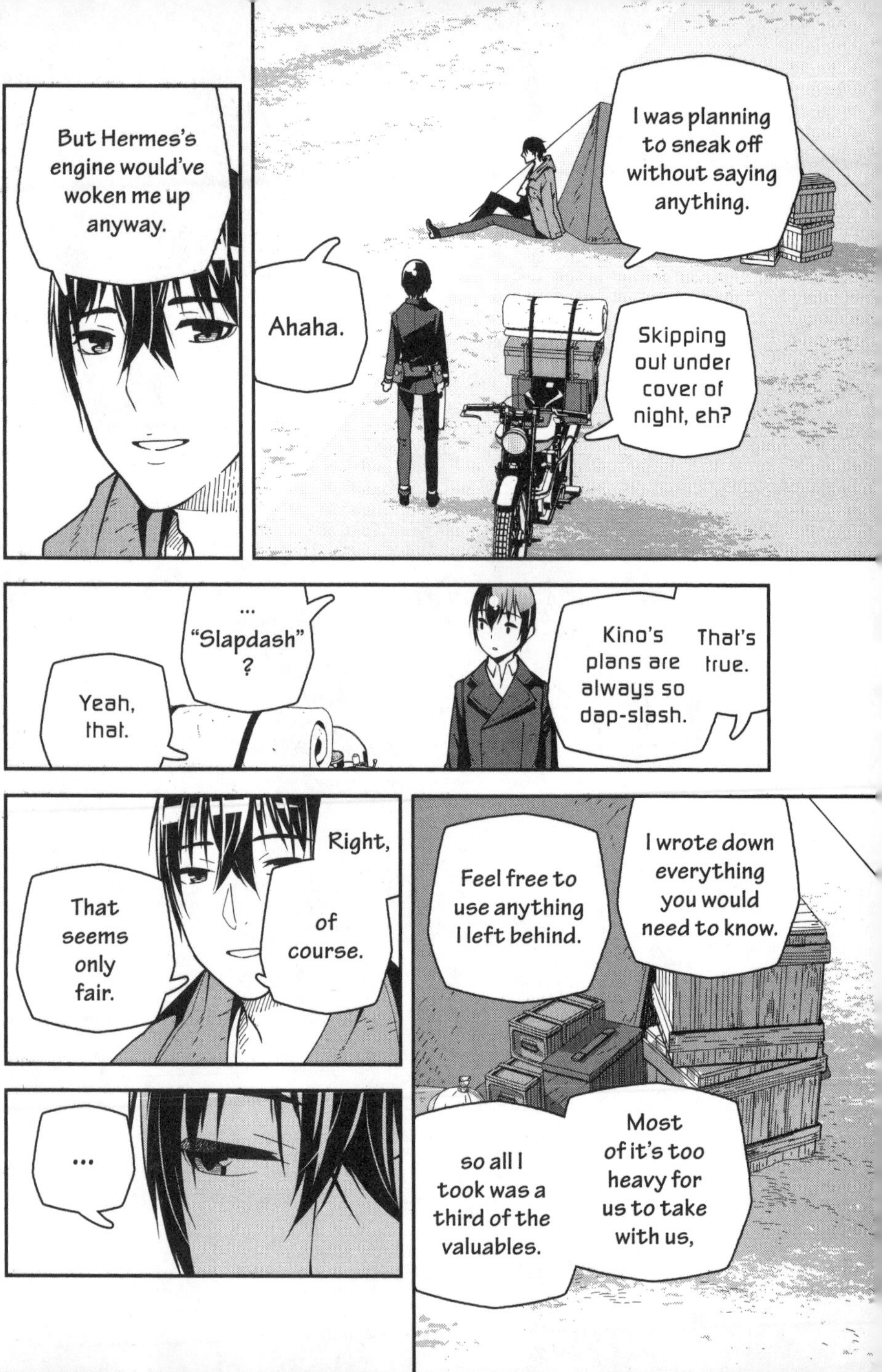
I was planning to sneak off without saying anything.
Skipping out under cover of night, eh?
Ahaha.
But Hermes's engine would've woken me up anyway.
That's true.
Kino's plans are always so dap-slash.
... "Slapdash"?
Yeah, that.
I wrote down everything you would need to know.
Feel free to use anything I left behind.
Most of it's too heavy for us to take with us,
so all I took was a third of the valuables.
Right,
of course.
That seems only fair.
...

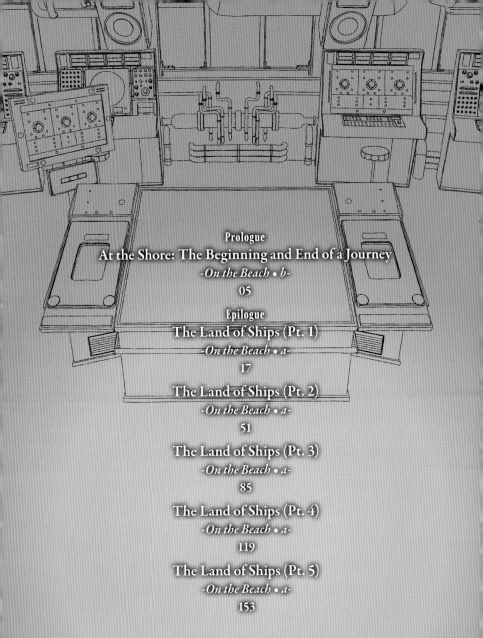

Prologue
At the Shore: The Beginning and End of a Journey
-*On the Beach • b*-
05

Epilogue
The Land of Ships (Pt. 1)
-*On the Beach • a*-
17

The Land of Ships (Pt. 2)
-*On the Beach • a*-
51

The Land of Ships (Pt. 3)
-*On the Beach • a*-
85

The Land of Ships (Pt. 4)
-*On the Beach • a*-
119

The Land of Ships (Pt. 5)
-*On the Beach • a*-
153

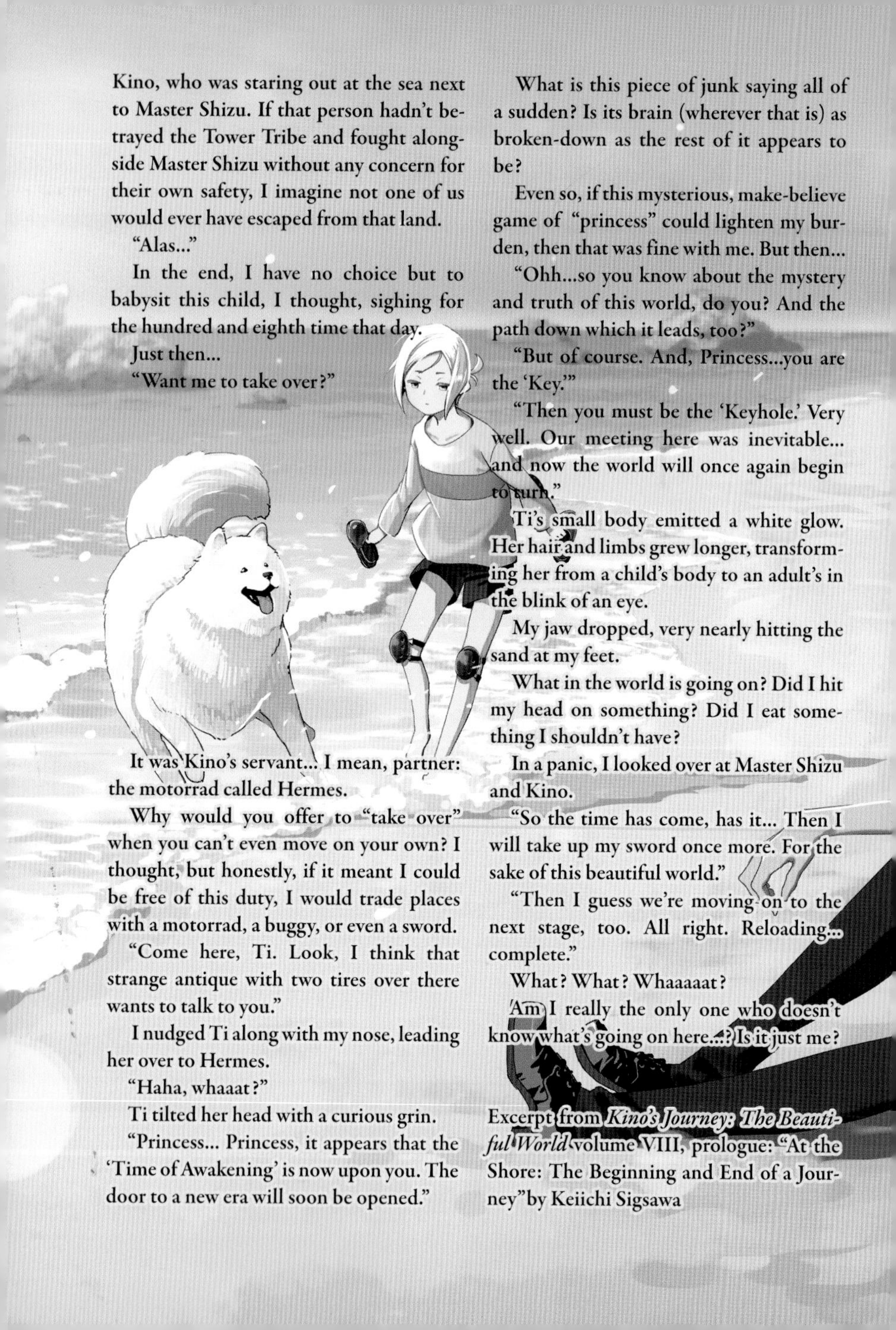

Kino, who was staring out at the sea next to Master Shizu. If that person hadn't betrayed the Tower Tribe and fought alongside Master Shizu without any concern for their own safety, I imagine not one of us would ever have escaped from that land.

"Alas..."

In the end, I have no choice but to babysit this child, I thought, sighing for the hundred and eighth time that day.

Just then...

"Want me to take over?"

It was Kino's servant... I mean, partner: the motorrad called Hermes.

Why would you offer to "take over" when you can't even move on your own? I thought, but honestly, if it meant I could be free of this duty, I would trade places with a motorrad, a buggy, or even a sword.

"Come here, Ti. Look, I think that strange antique with two tires over there wants to talk to you."

I nudged Ti along with my nose, leading her over to Hermes.

"Haha, whaaat?"

Ti tilted her head with a curious grin.

"Princess... Princess, it appears that the 'Time of Awakening' is now upon you. The door to a new era will soon be opened."

What is this piece of junk saying all of a sudden? Is its brain (wherever that is) as broken-down as the rest of it appears to be?

Even so, if this mysterious, make-believe game of "princess" could lighten my burden, then that was fine with me. But then...

"Ohh...so you know about the mystery and truth of this world, do you? And the path down which it leads, too?"

"But of course. And, Princess...you are the 'Key.'"

"Then you must be the 'Keyhole.' Very well. Our meeting here was inevitable... and now the world will once again begin to turn."

Ti's small body emitted a white glow. Her hair and limbs grew longer, transforming her from a child's body to an adult's in the blink of an eye.

My jaw dropped, very nearly hitting the sand at my feet.

What in the world is going on? Did I hit my head on something? Did I eat something I shouldn't have?

In a panic, I looked over at Master Shizu and Kino.

"So the time has come, has it... Then I will take up my sword once more. For the sake of this beautiful world."

"Then I guess we're moving on to the next stage, too. All right. Reloading... complete."

What? What? Whaaaaat?

Am I really the only one who doesn't know what's going on here...? Is it just me?

Excerpt from *Kino's Journey: The Beautiful World* volume VIII, prologue: "At the Shore: The Beginning and End of a Journey" by Keiichi Sigsawa

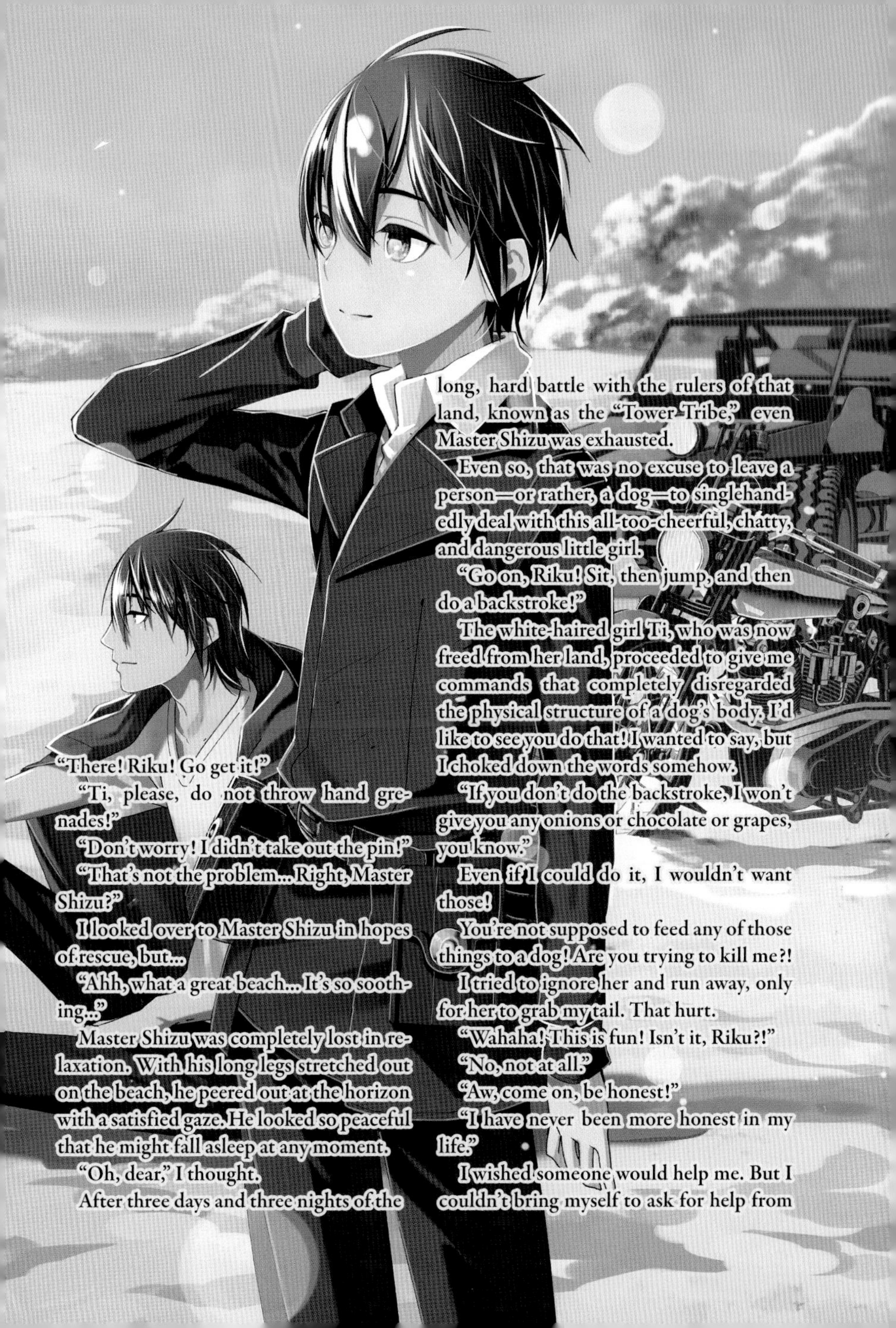

"There! Riku! Go get it!"

"Ti, please, do not throw hand grenades!"

"Don't worry! I didn't take out the pin!"

"That's not the problem... Right, Master Shizu?"

I looked over to Master Shizu in hopes of rescue, but...

"Ahh, what a great beach... It's so soothing..."

Master Shizu was completely lost in relaxation. With his long legs stretched out on the beach, he peered out at the horizon with a satisfied gaze. He looked so peaceful that he might fall asleep at any moment.

"Oh, dear," I thought.

After three days and three nights of the long, hard battle with the rulers of that land, known as the "Tower Tribe," even Master Shizu was exhausted.

Even so, that was no excuse to leave a person—or rather, a dog—to singlehandedly deal with this all-too-cheerful, chatty, and dangerous little girl.

"Go on, Riku! Sit, then jump, and then do a backstroke!"

The white-haired girl Ti, who was now freed from her land, proceeded to give me commands that completely disregarded the physical structure of a dog's body. I'd like to see you do that! I wanted to say, but I choked down the words somehow.

"If you don't do the backstroke, I won't give you any onions or chocolate or grapes, you know."

Even if I could do it, I wouldn't want those!

You're not supposed to feed any of those things to a dog! Are you trying to kill me?!

I tried to ignore her and run away, only for her to grab my tail. That hurt.

"Wahaha! This is fun! Isn't it, Riku?!"

"No, not at all."

"Aw, come on, be honest!"

"I have never been more honest in my life."

I wished someone would help me. But I couldn't bring myself to ask for help from

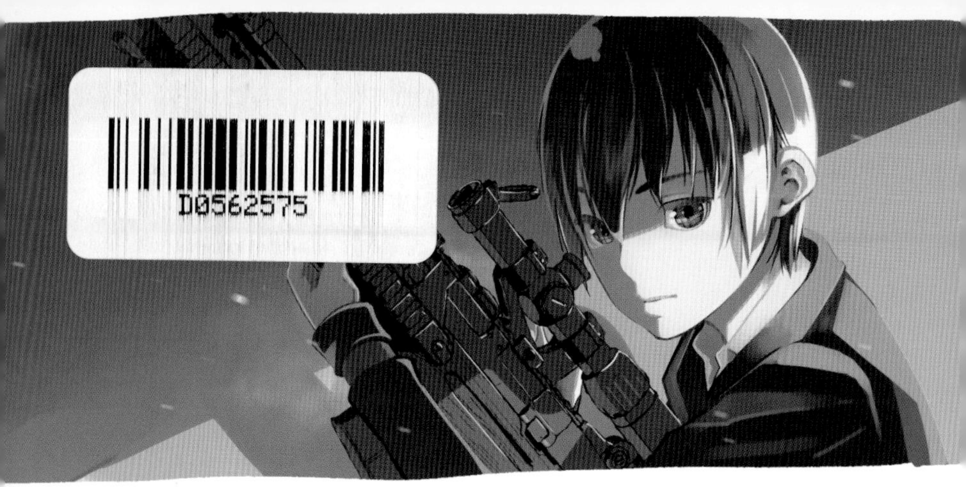

Kino's Journey

The Beautiful World

8

Iruka Shiomiya

Original Story:
Keiichi Sigsawa

Original Character Design:
Kouhaku Kuroboshi

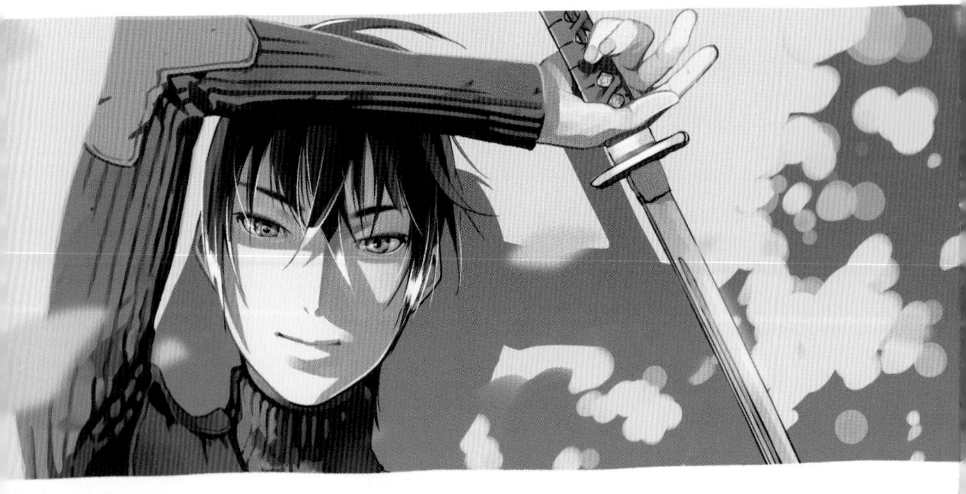

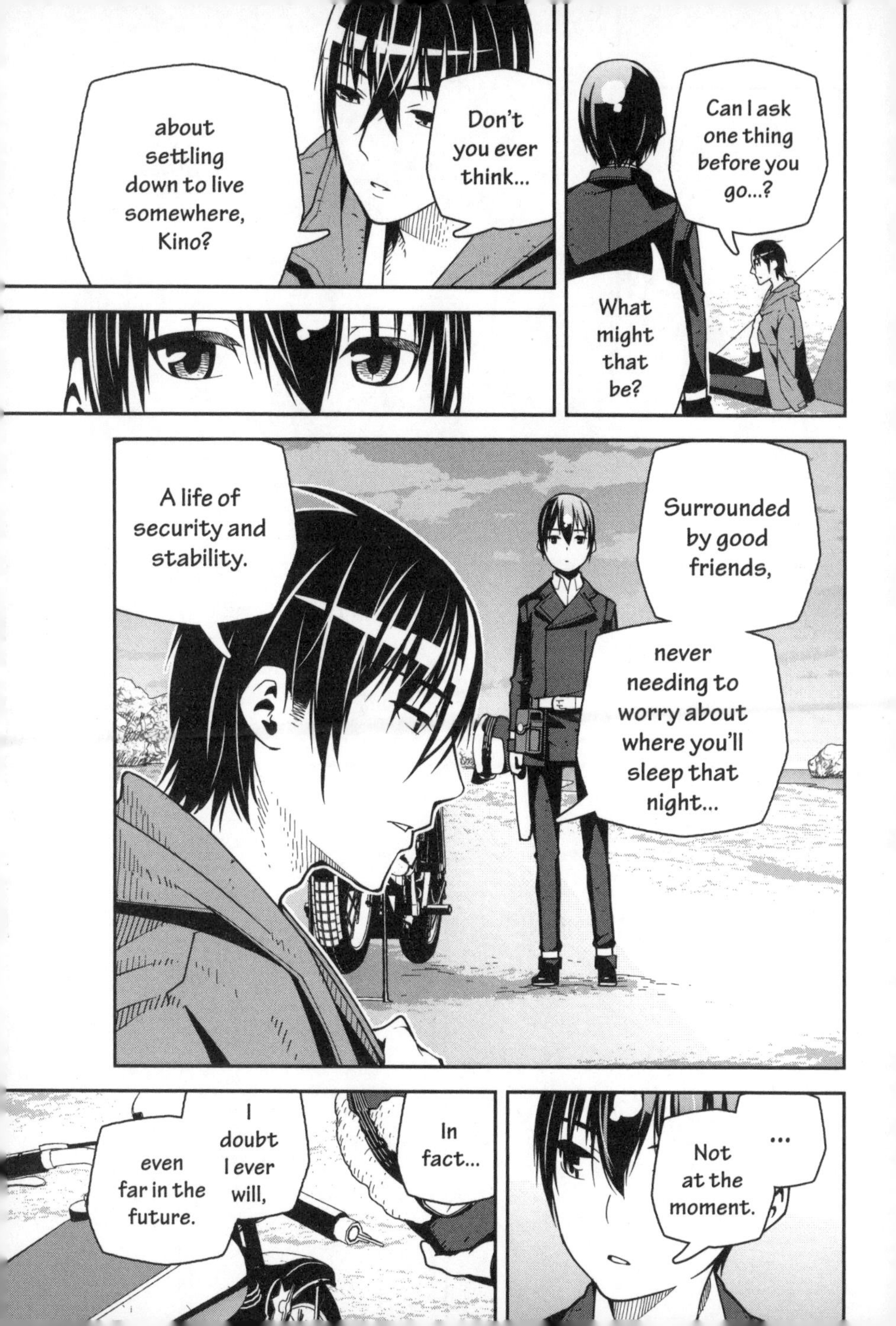

Can I ask one thing before you go...?
What might that be?
Don't you ever think...
about settling down to live somewhere, Kino?
Surrounded by good friends,
never needing to worry about where you'll sleep that night...
A life of security and stability.
...
Not at the moment.
In fact...
I doubt I ever will,
even far in the future.

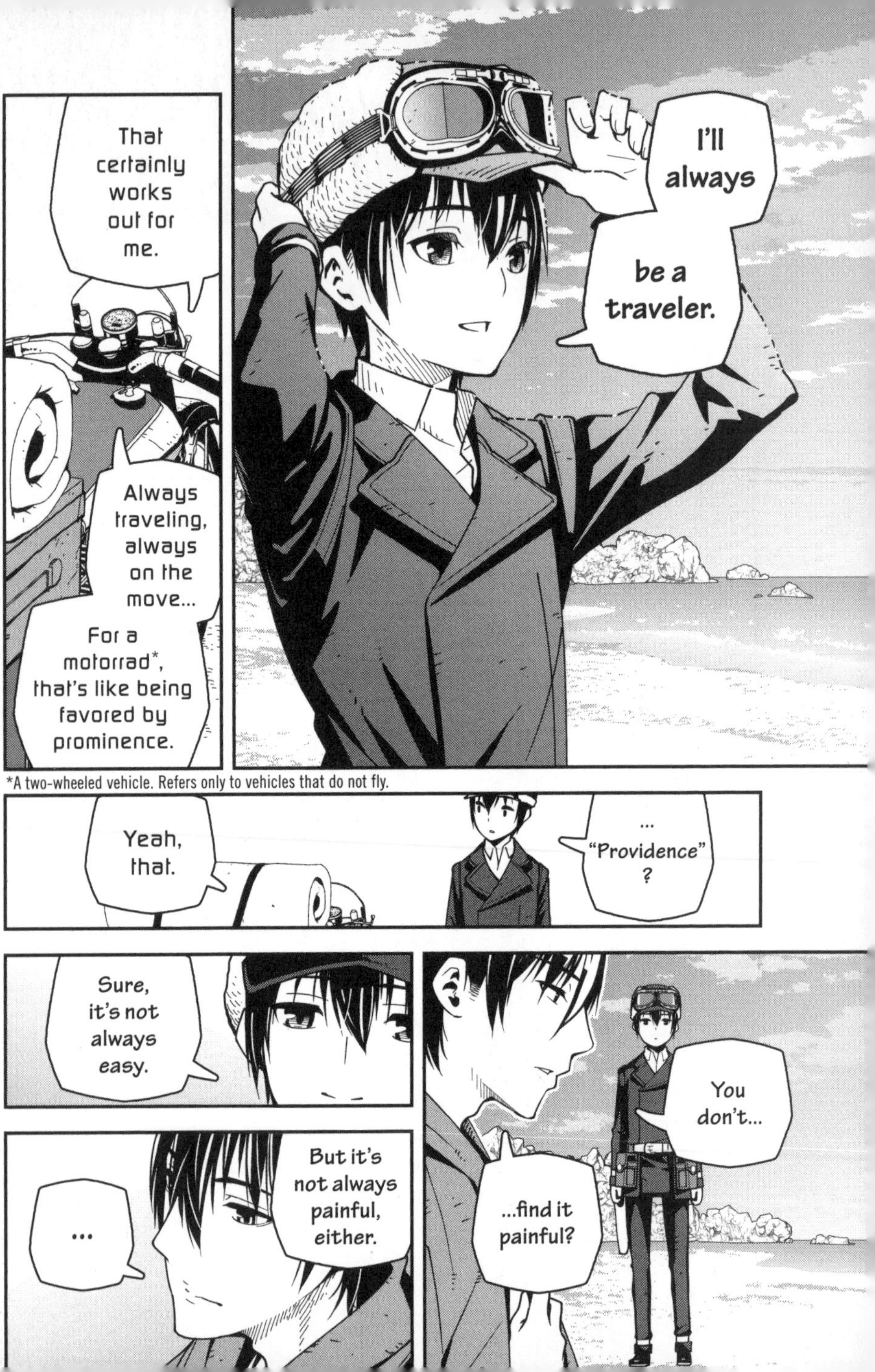
I'll always
be a traveler.
That certainly works out for me.
Always traveling, always on the move...
For a motorrad*, that's like being favored by prominence.
...
"Providence"?
Yeah, that.
You don't...
...find it painful?
Sure, it's not always easy.
But it's not always painful, either.
...

*A two-wheeled vehicle. Refers only to vehicles that do not fly.

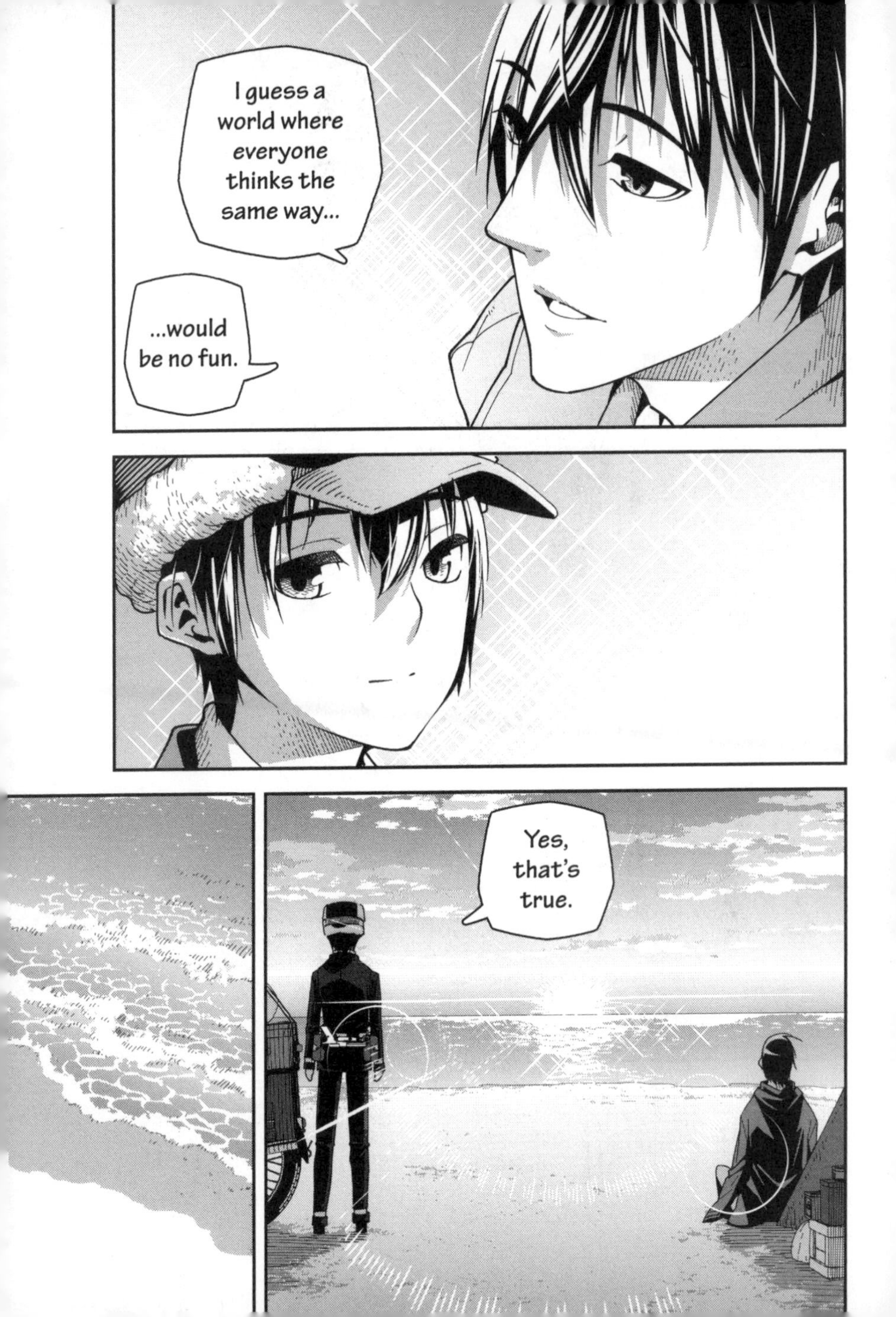
I guess a world where everyone thinks the same way...
...would be no fun.
Yes, that's true.

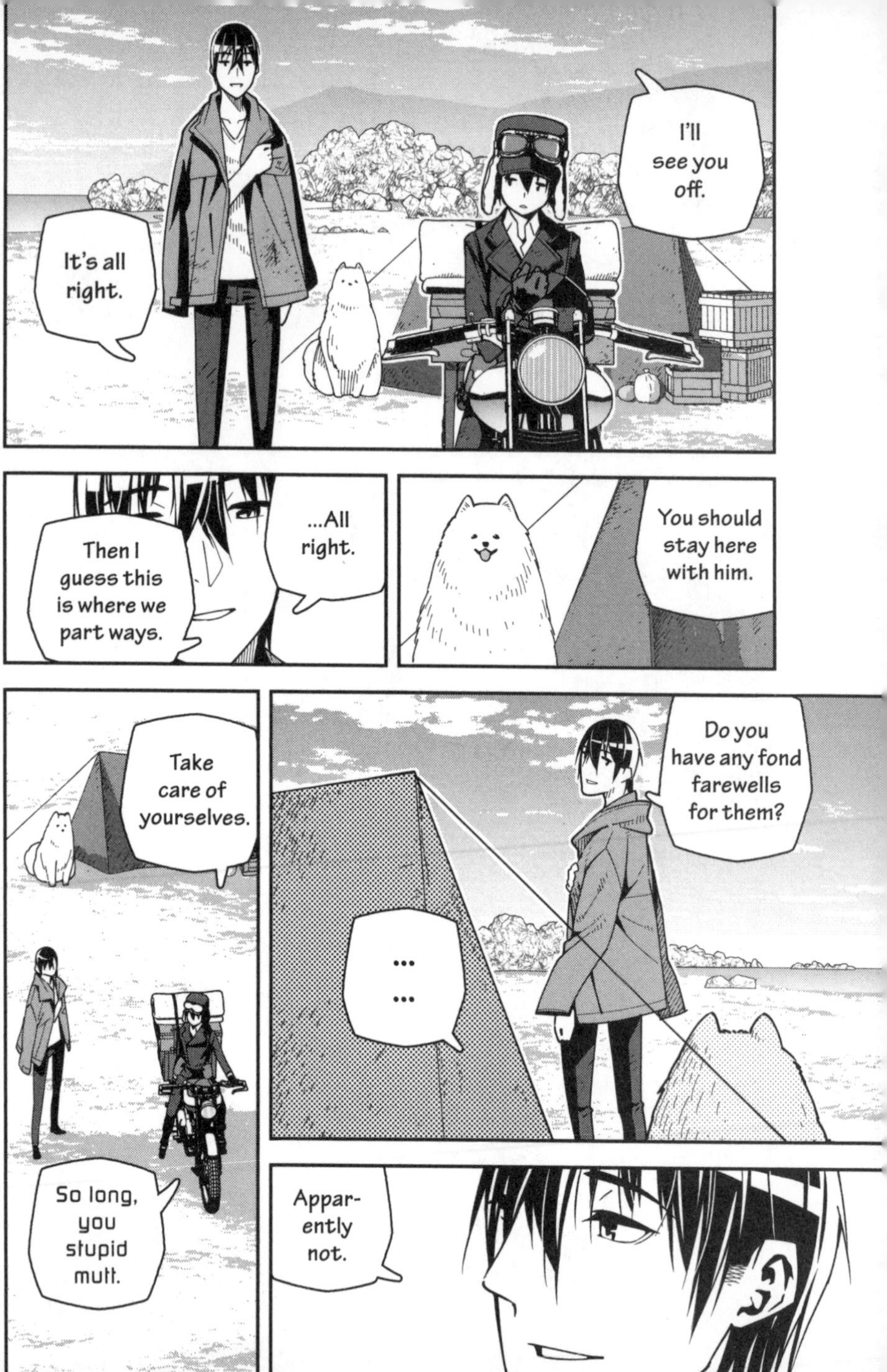
I'll see you off.
It's all right.
You should stay here with him.
...All right.
Then I guess this is where we part ways.
Do you have any fond farewells for them?
... ...
Apparently not.
Take care of yourselves.
So long, you stupid mutt.

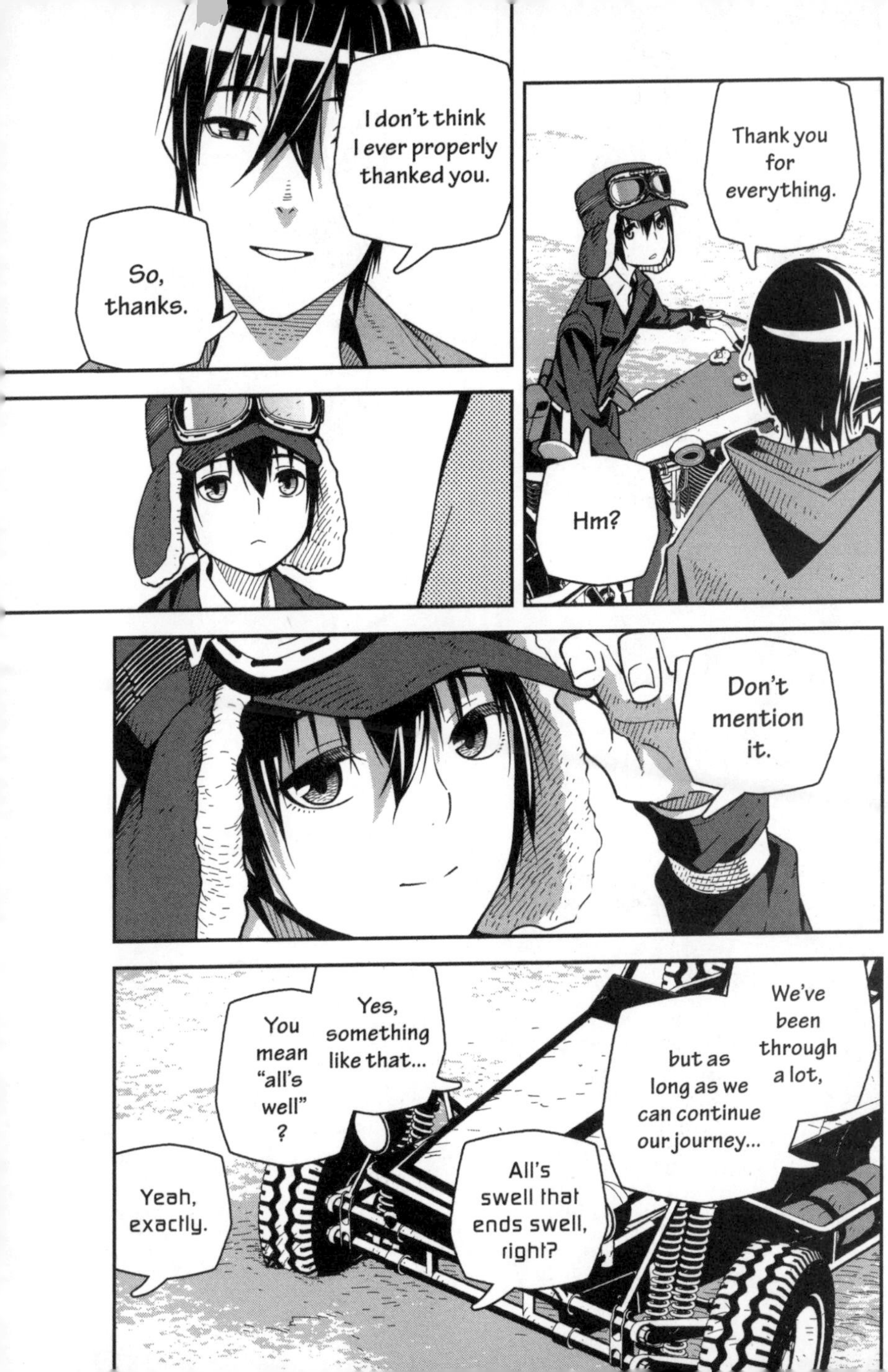
Thank you for everything.
Hm?
I don't think I ever properly thanked you.
So, thanks.
Don't mention it.
We've been through a lot,
but as long as we can continue our journey...
All's swell that ends swell, right?
You mean "all's well"?
Yes, something like that...
Yeah, exactly.

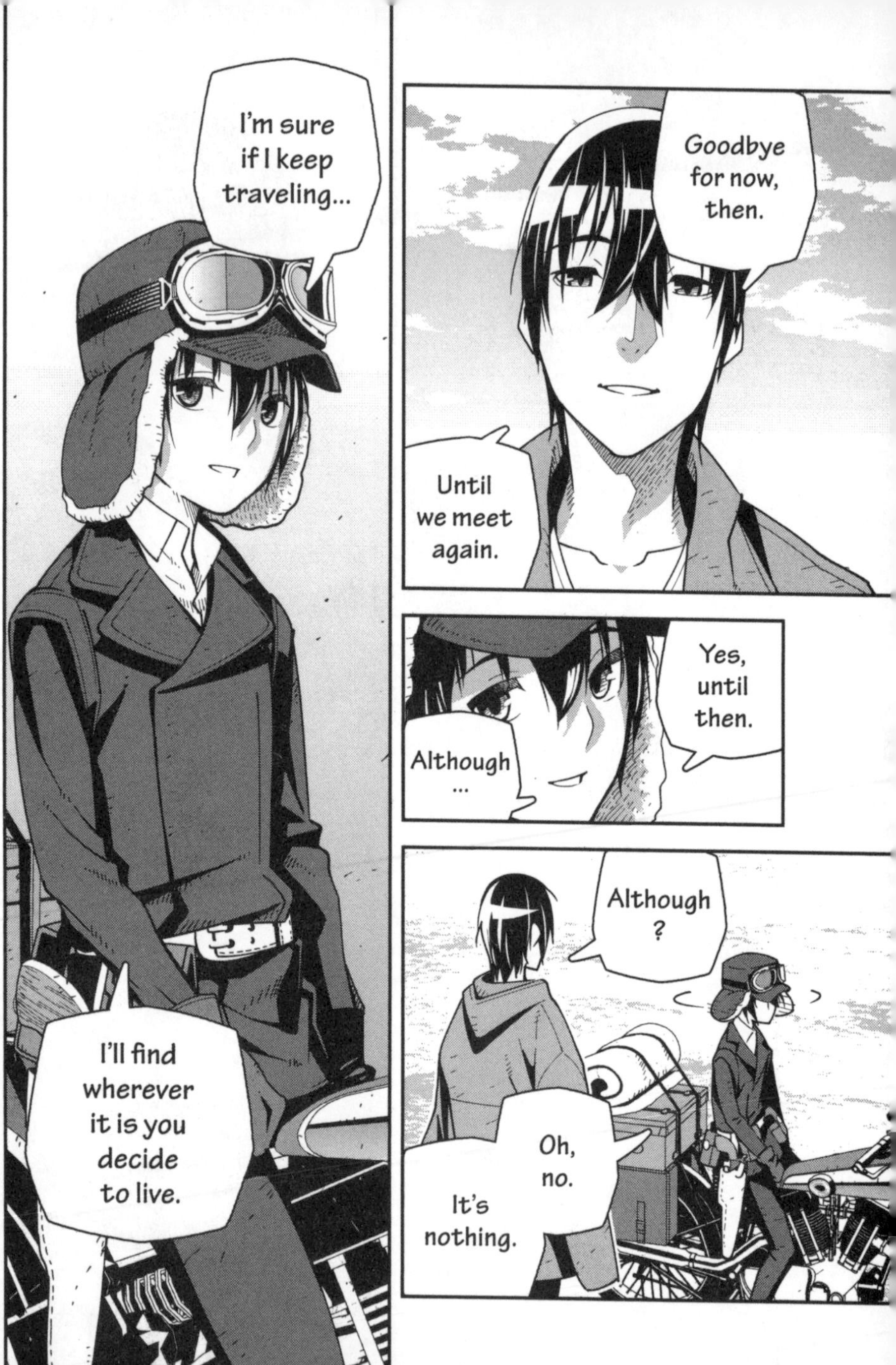
Goodbye for now, then.
Until we meet again.
Yes, until then.
Although ...
Although ?
Oh, no.
It's nothing.
I'm sure if I keep traveling...
I'll find wherever it is you decide to live.

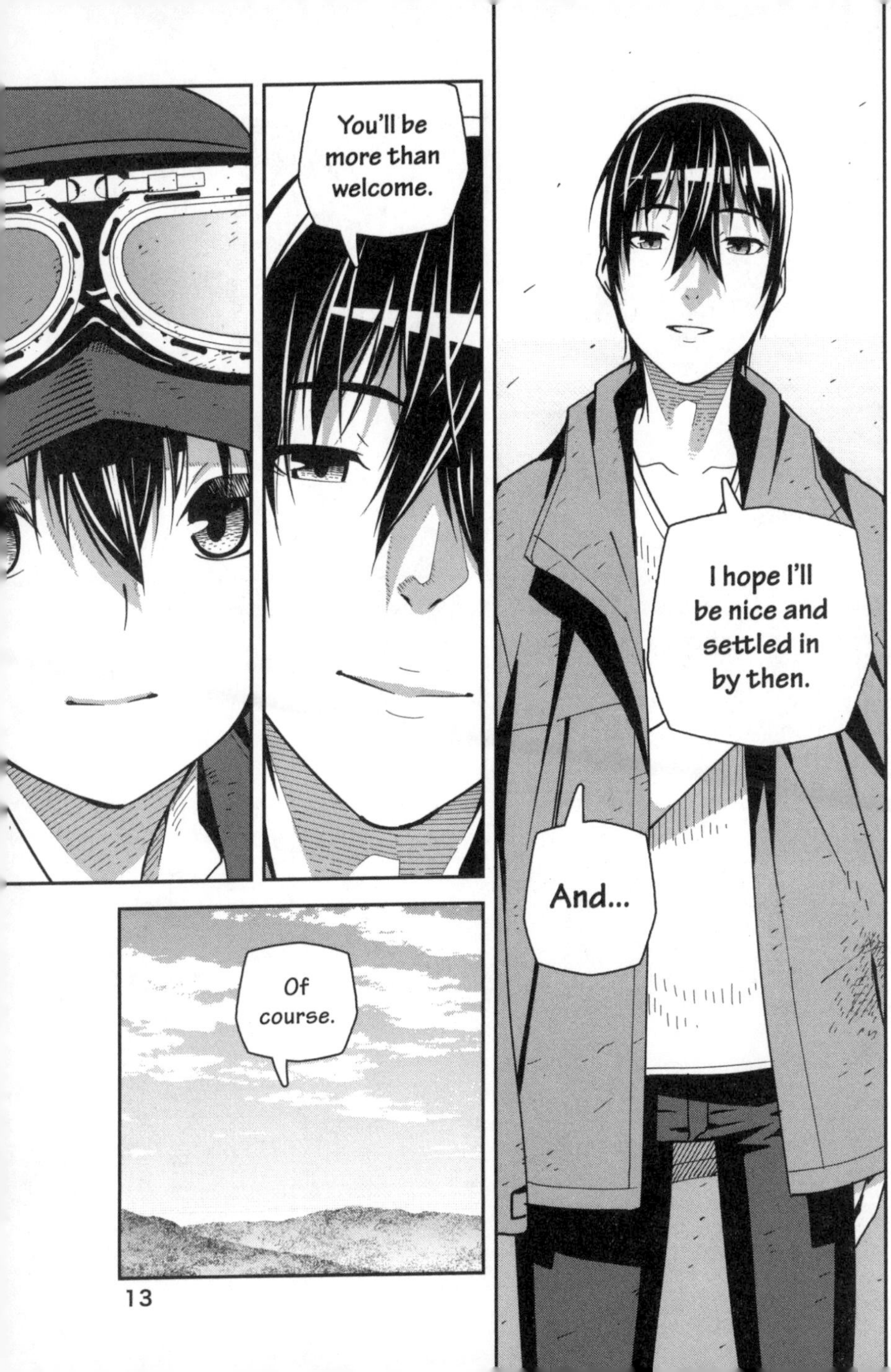
I hope I'll be nice and settled in by then.
And...
You'll be more than welcome.
Of course.

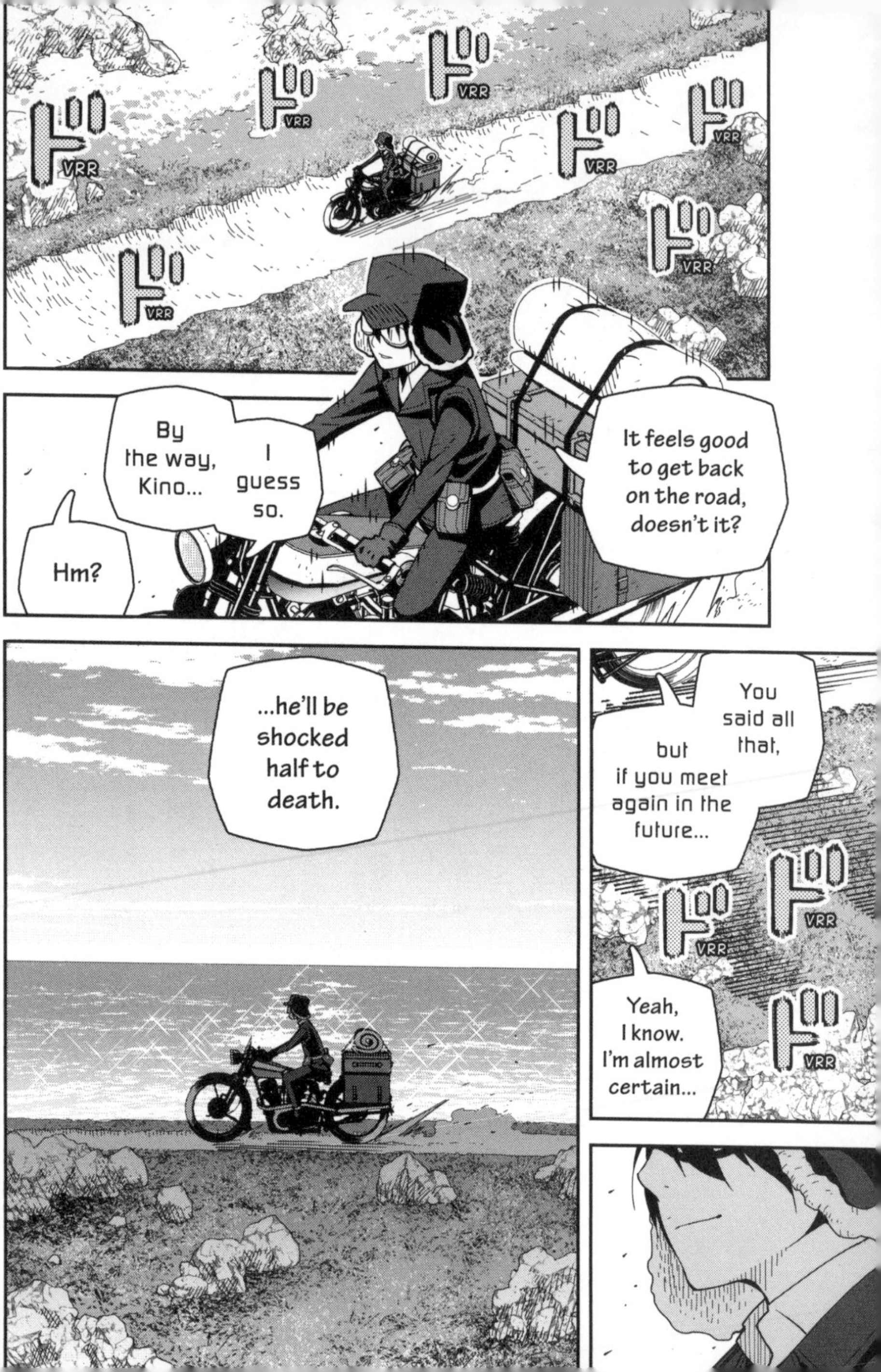
VRR
VRR
VRR
VRR
VRR
VRR
VRR
It feels good to get back on the road, doesn't it?
I guess so.
By the way, Kino...
Hm?
You said all that, but if you meet again in the future...
VRR
VRR
VRR
Yeah, I know. I'm almost certain...
...he'll be shocked half to death.

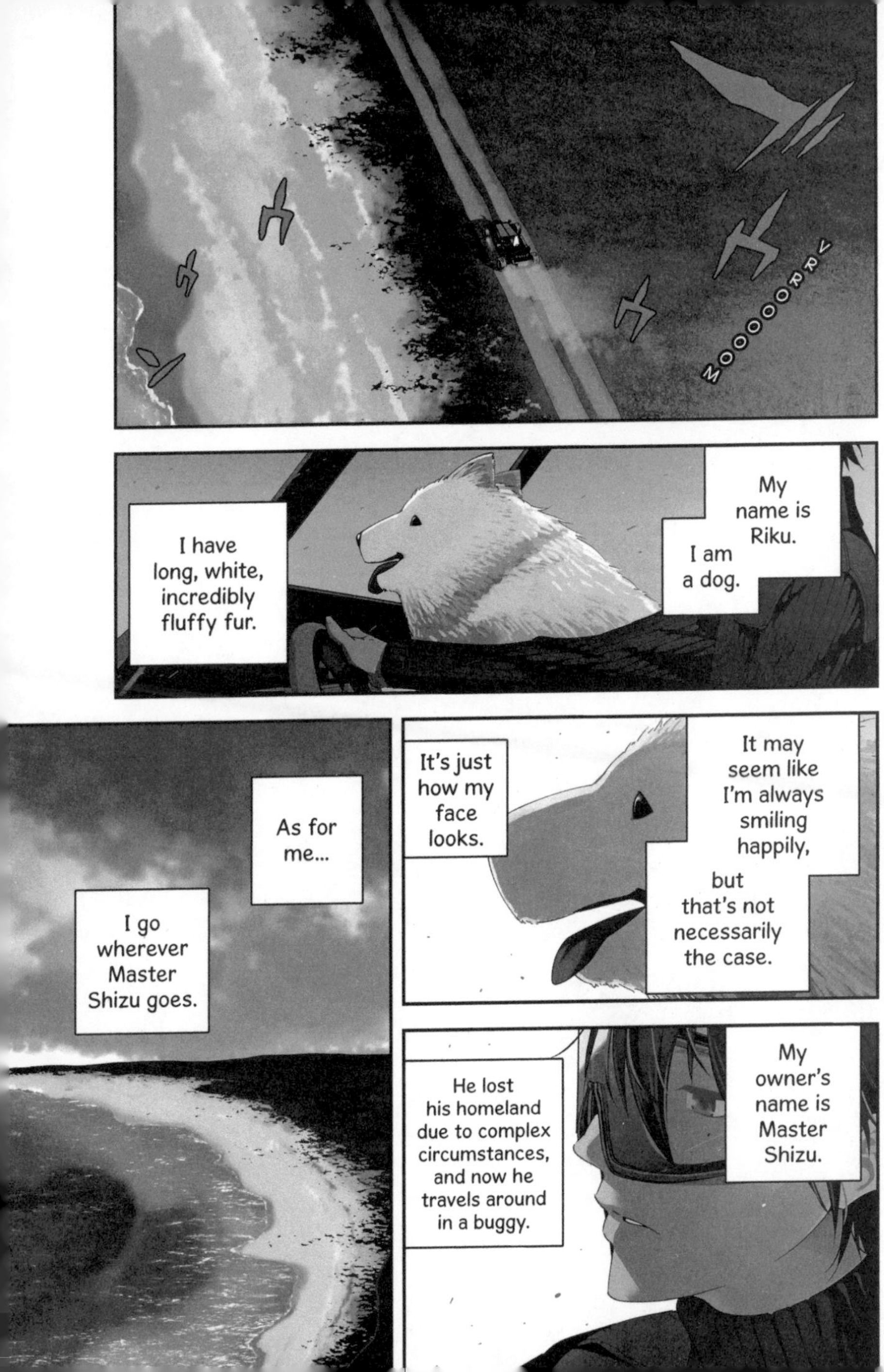
MOOOOOORRV
My name is Riku.
I am a dog.
I have long, white, incredibly fluffy fur.
It may seem like I'm always smiling happily,
but that's not necessarily the case.
It's just how my face looks.
My owner's name is Master Shizu.
He lost his homeland due to complex circumstances, and now he travels around in a buggy.
As for me...
I go wherever Master Shizu goes.

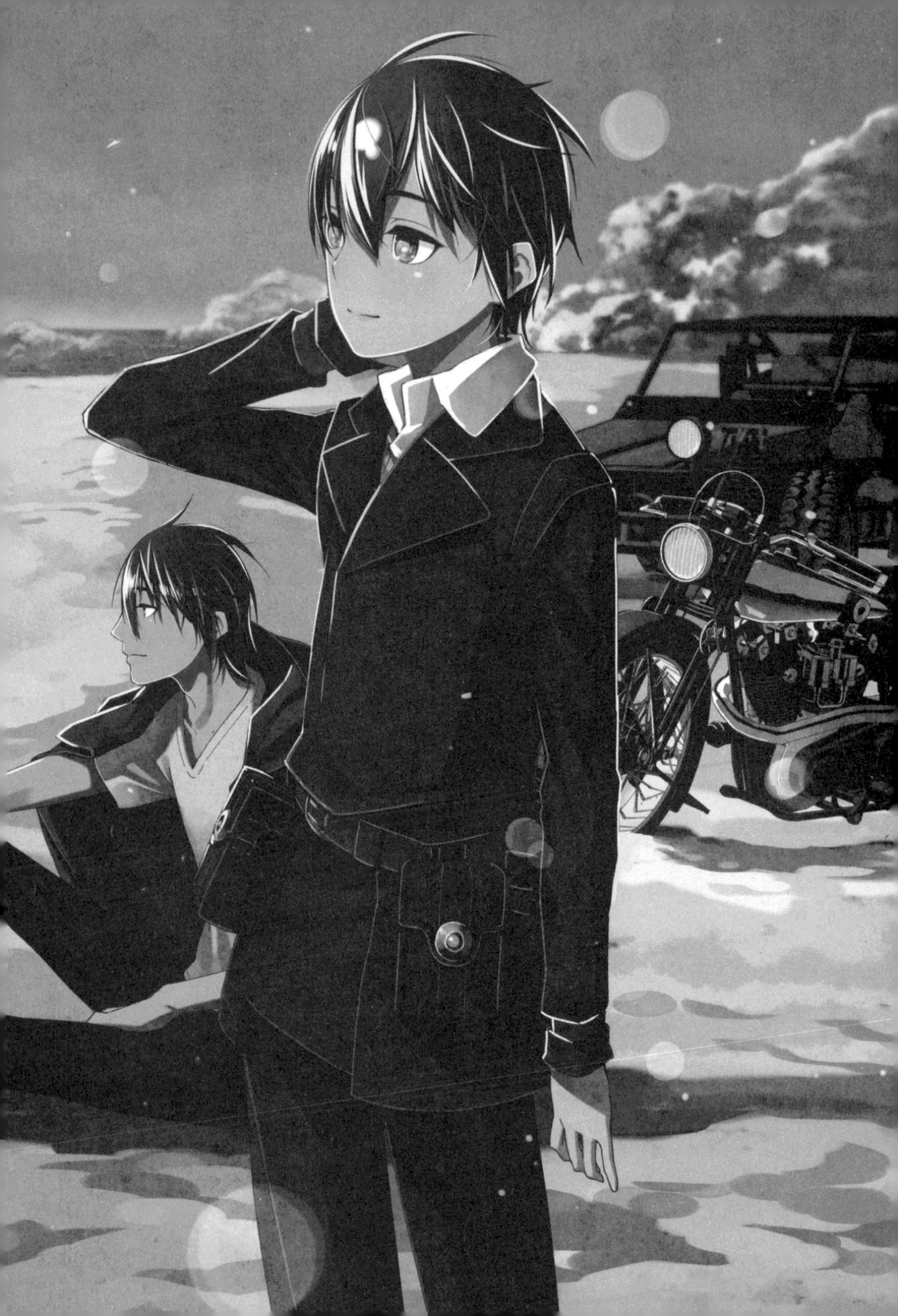

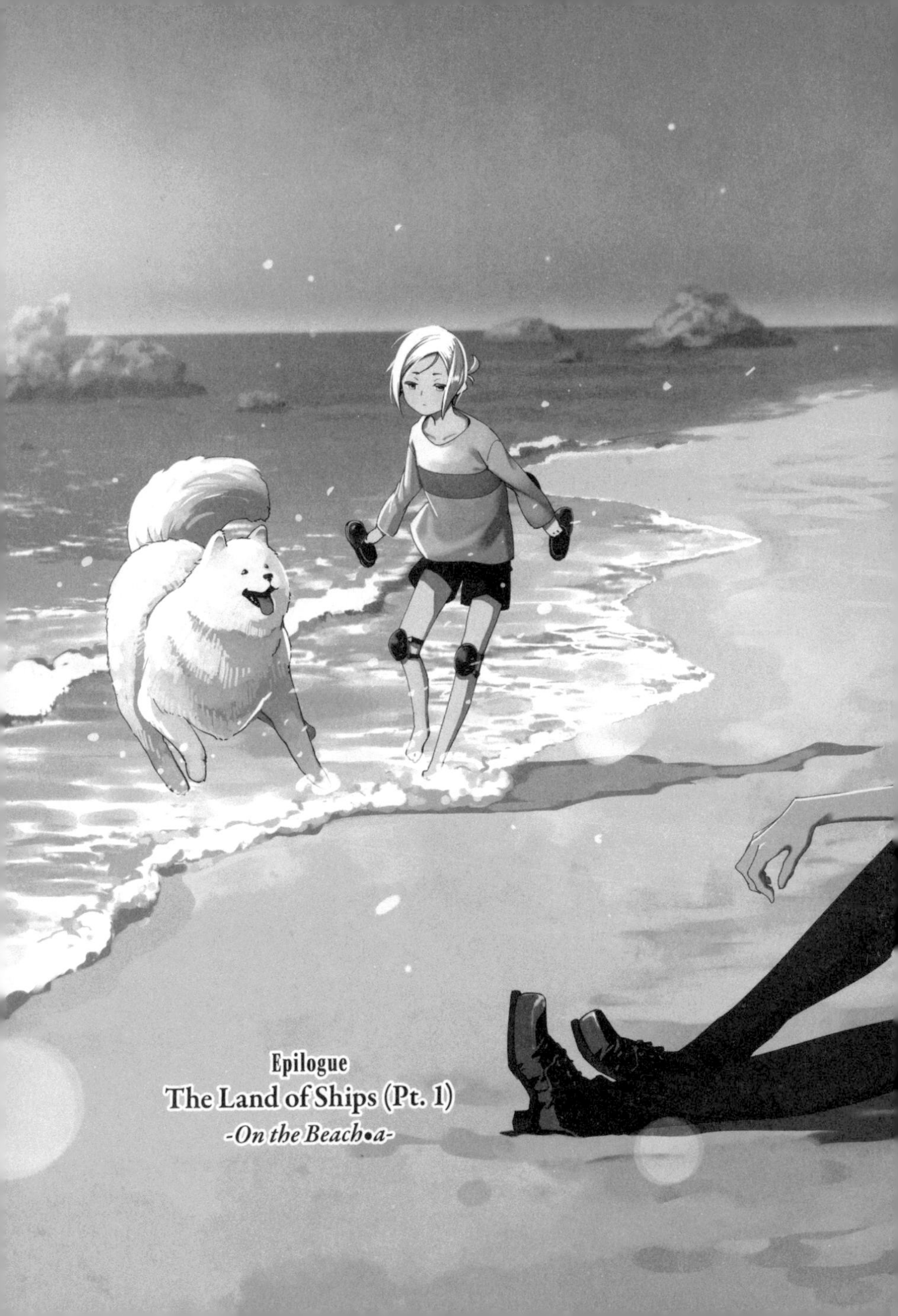

Epilogue
The Land of Ships (Pt. 1)
-On the Beach•a-

Kino's Journey

——➤ The Beautiful World ◄——

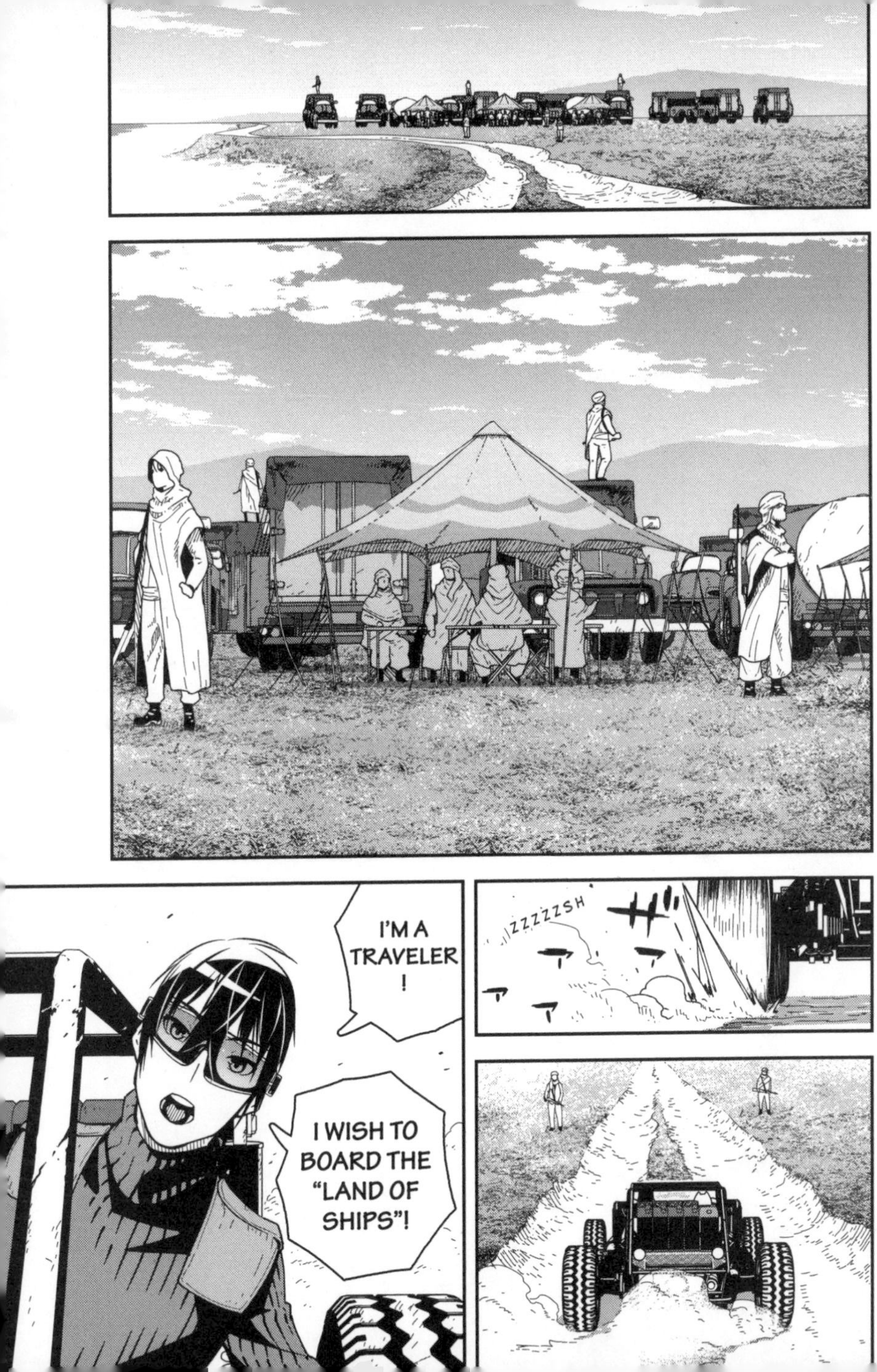
ZZZZZSH
I'M A TRAVELER!
I WISH TO BOARD THE "LAND OF SHIPS"!

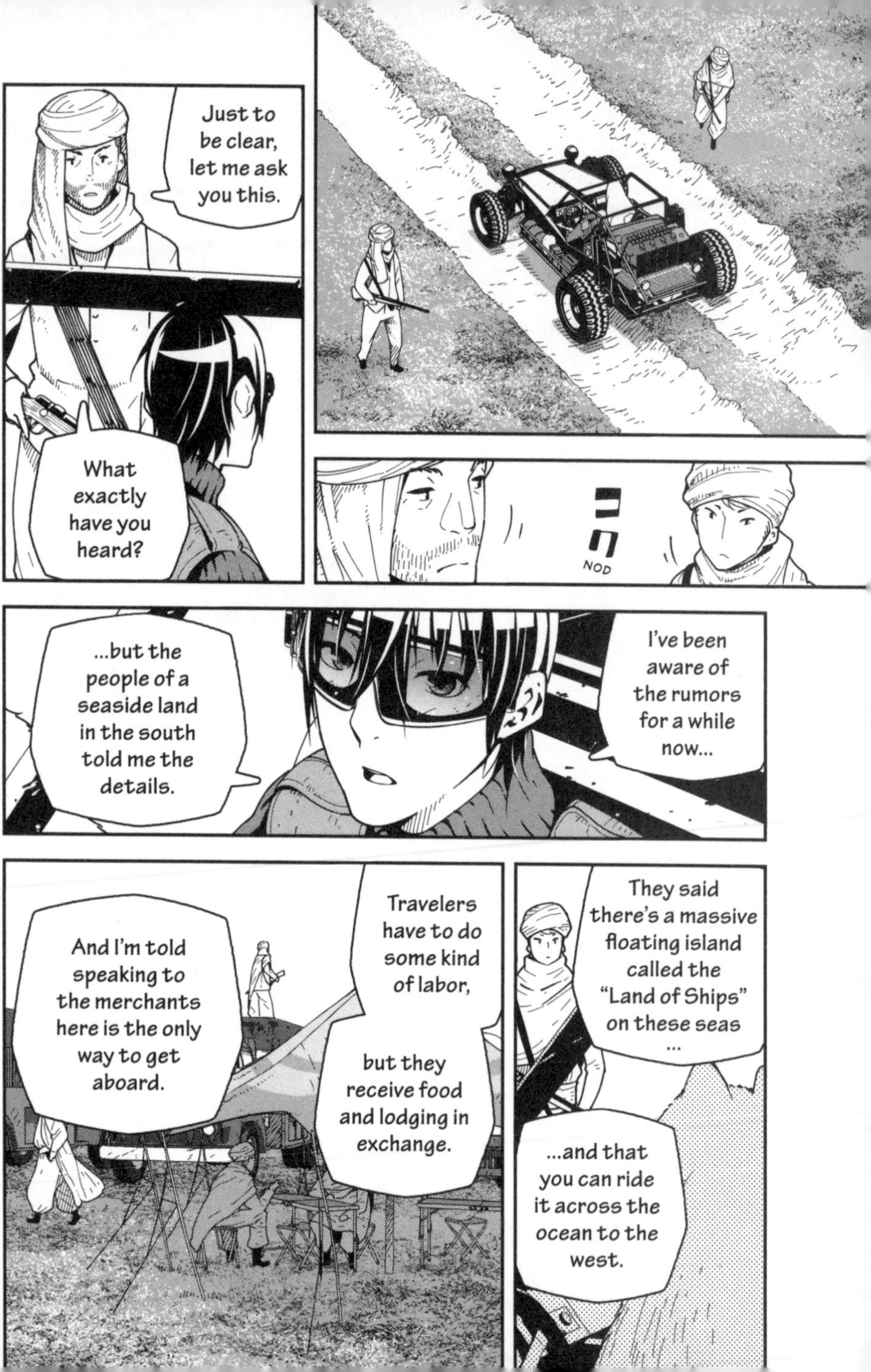
コク
NOD
Just to be clear, let me ask you this.
What exactly have you heard?
I've been aware of the rumors for a while now...
...but the people of a seaside land in the south told me the details.
They said there's a massive floating island called the "Land of Ships" on these seas ...
...and that you can ride it across the ocean to the west.
Travelers have to do some kind of labor,
but they receive food and lodging in exchange.
And I'm told speaking to the merchants here is the only way to get aboard.

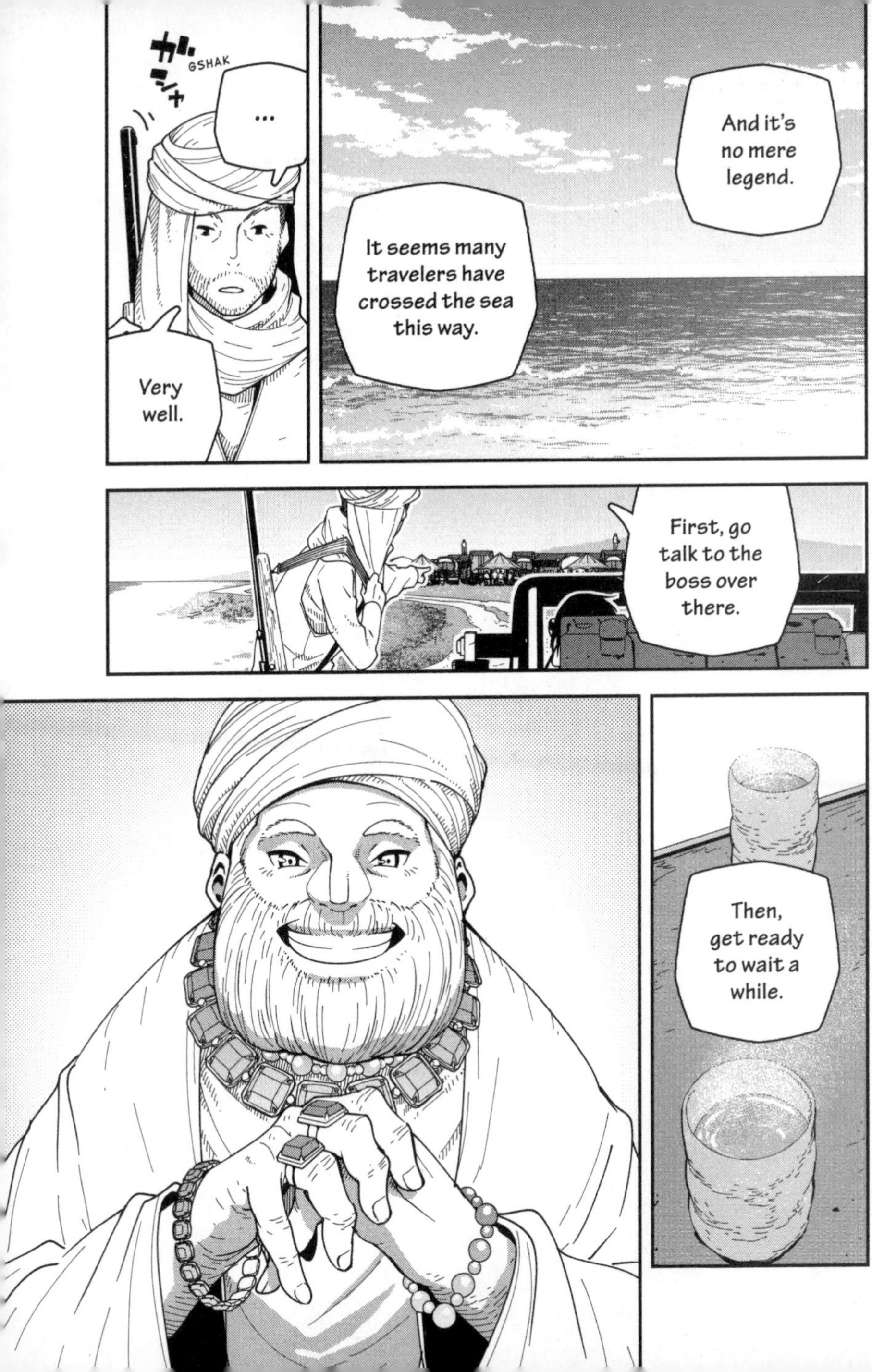
And it's no mere legend.
It seems many travelers have crossed the sea this way.
ガシャ
GSHAK
...
Very well.
First, go talk to the boss over there.
Then, get ready to wait a while.

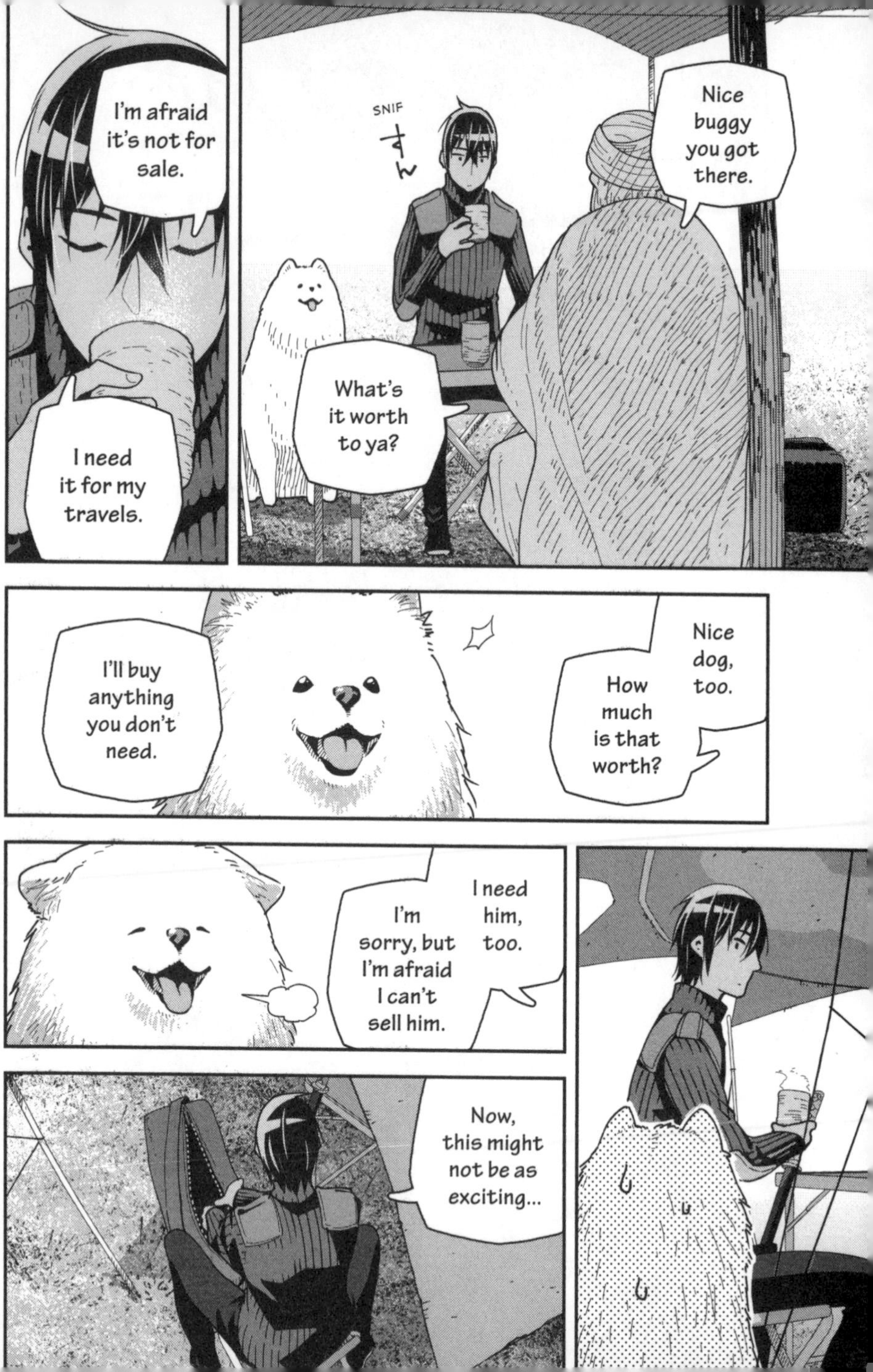
Nice buggy you got there.
SNIF
すん
What's it worth to ya?
I'm afraid it's not for sale.
I need it for my travels.
Nice dog, too.
How much is that worth?
I'll buy anything you don't need.
I need him, too.
I'm sorry, but I'm afraid I can't sell him.
Now, this might not be as exciting...

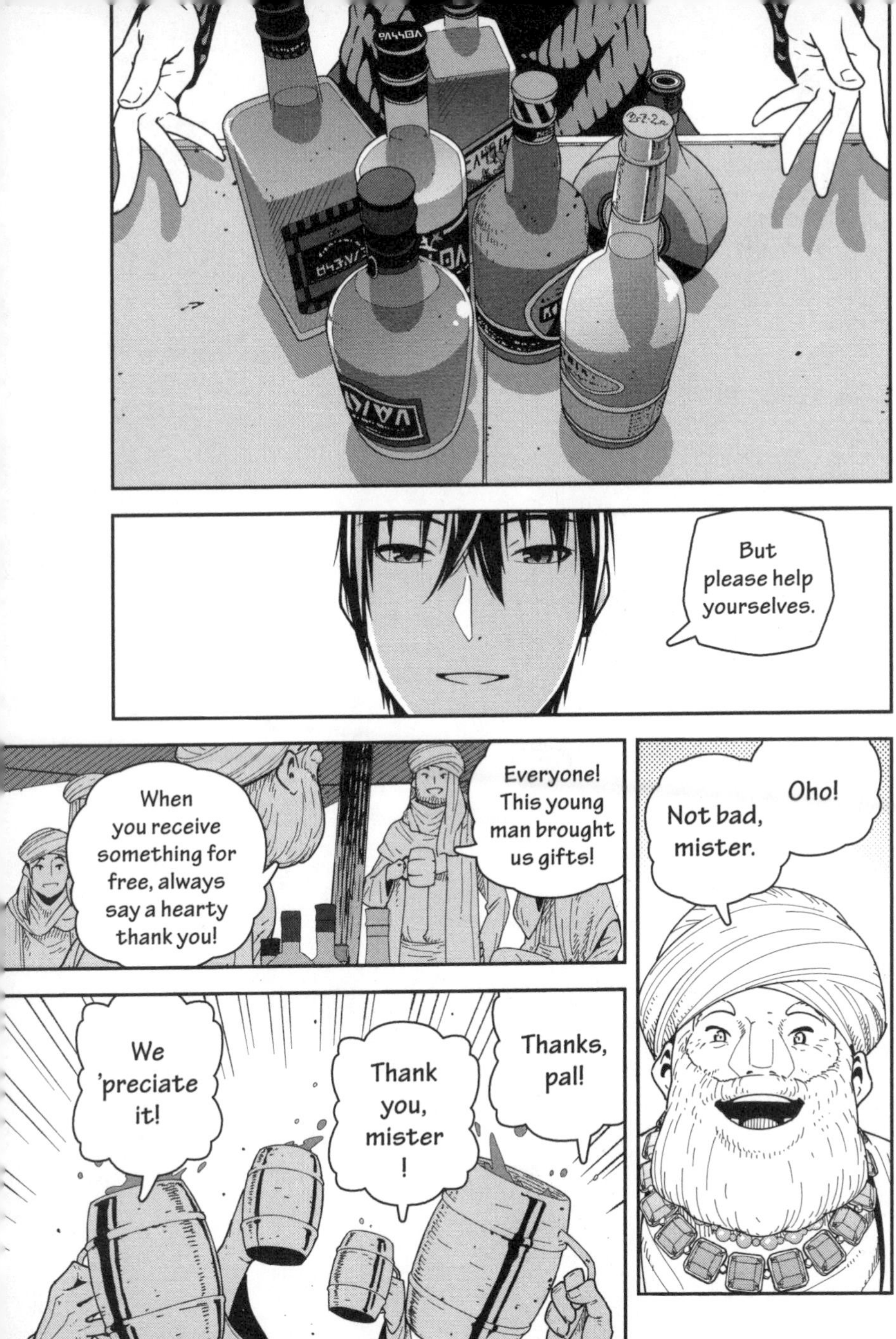
But please help yourselves.
Oho!
Not bad, mister.
Everyone! This young man brought us gifts!
When you receive something for free, always say a hearty thank you!
Thanks, pal!
Thank you, mister!
We 'preciate it!

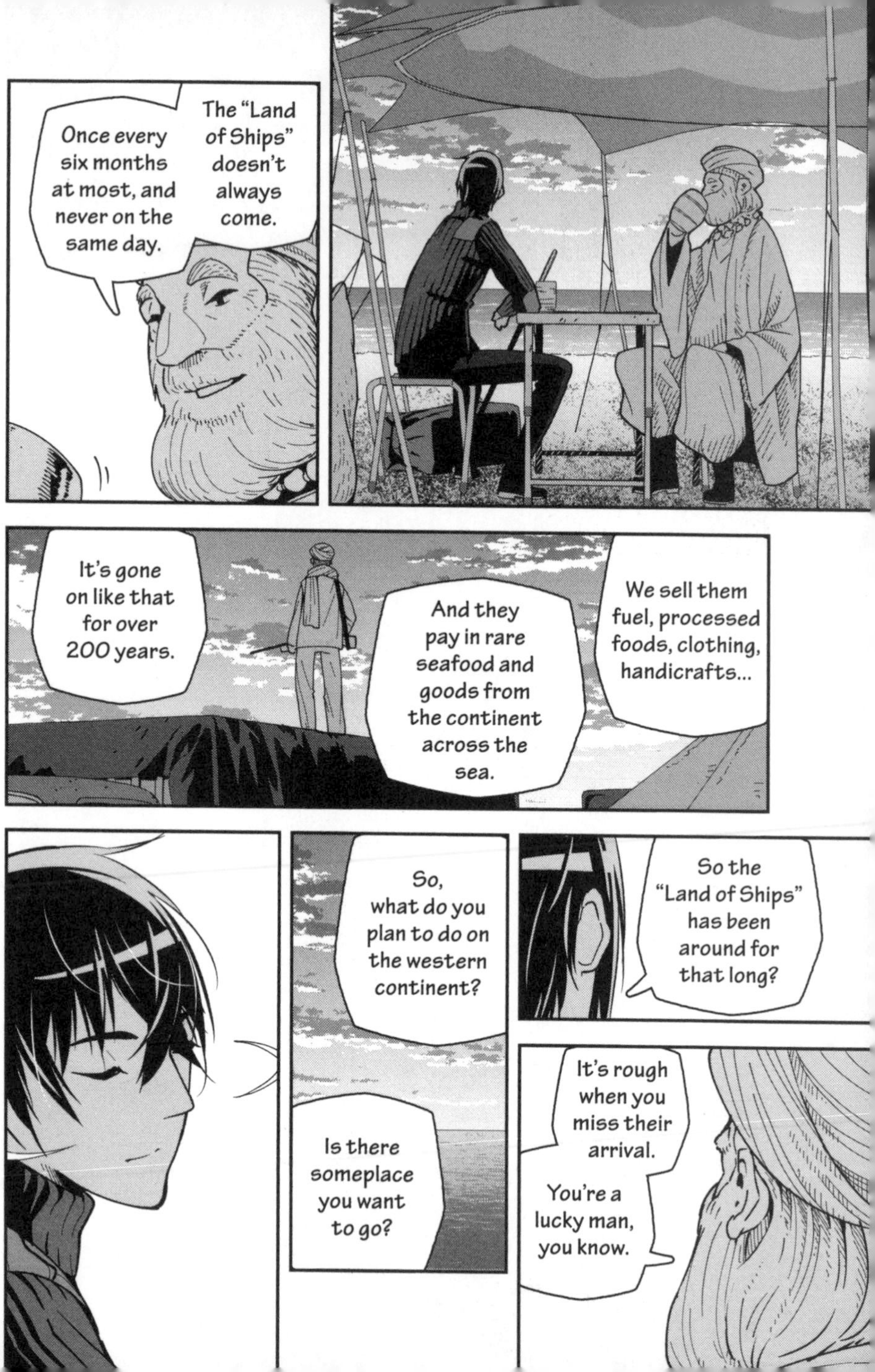
The "Land of Ships" doesn't always come.
Once every six months at most, and never on the same day.
We sell them fuel, processed foods, clothing, handicrafts...
And they pay in rare seafood and goods from the continent across the sea.
It's gone on like that for over 200 years.
So the "Land of Ships" has been around for that long?
It's rough when you miss their arrival.
You're a lucky man, you know.
So, what do you plan to do on the western continent?
Is there someplace you want to go?

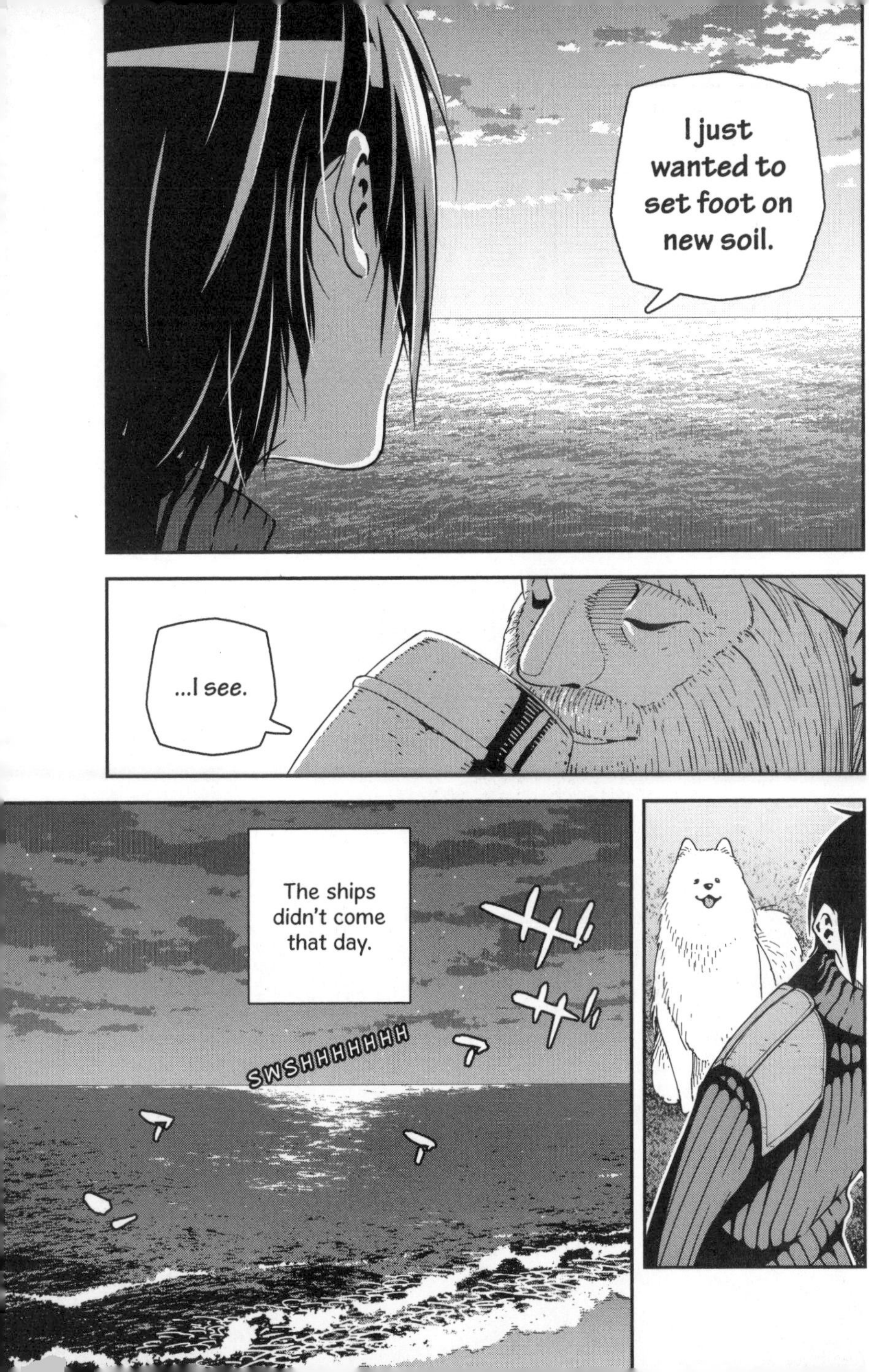
I just wanted to set foot on new soil.
...I see.
The ships didn't come that day.
SWSHHHHHHH

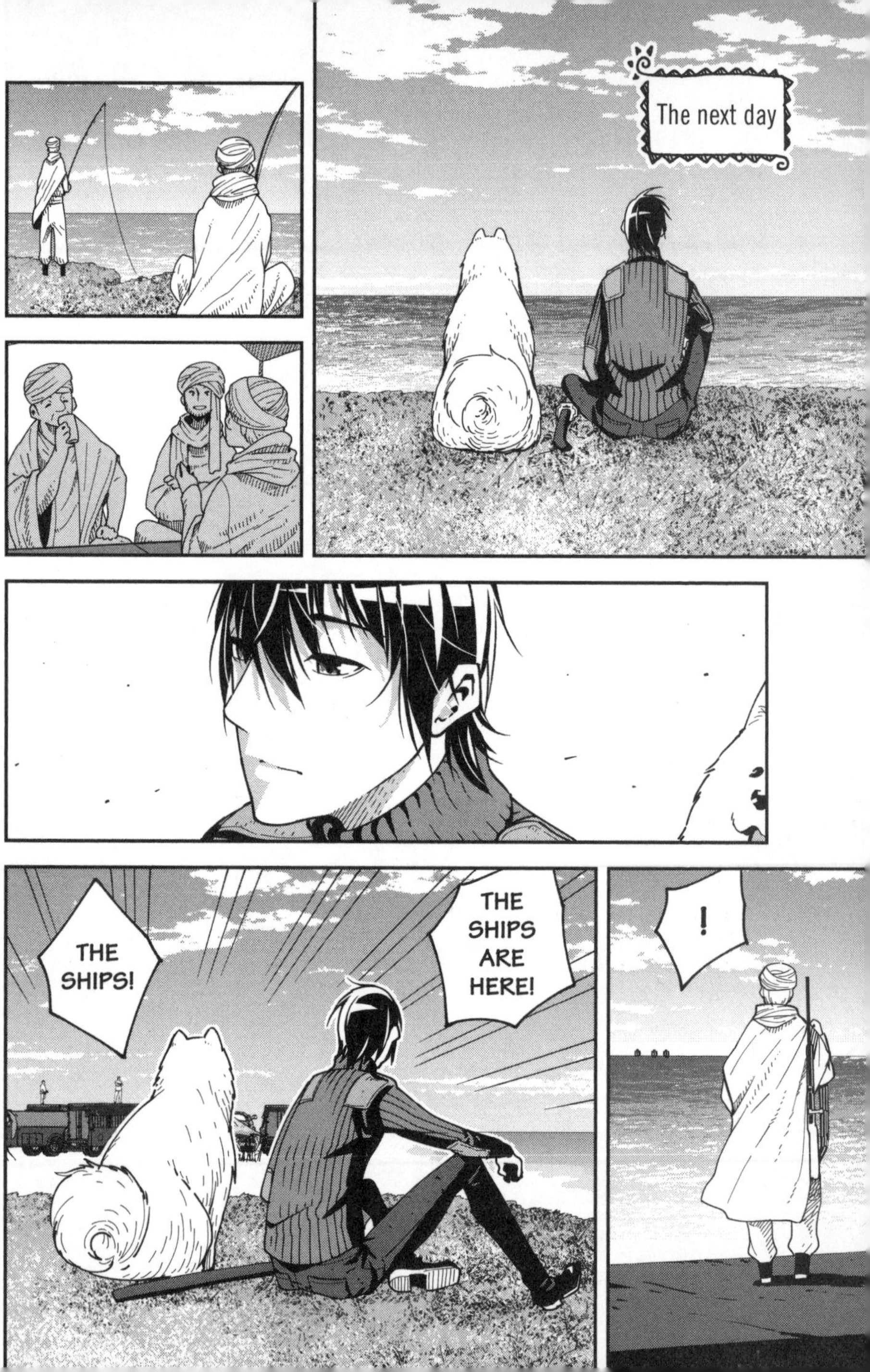
The next day
!
THE SHIPS ARE HERE!
THE SHIPS!

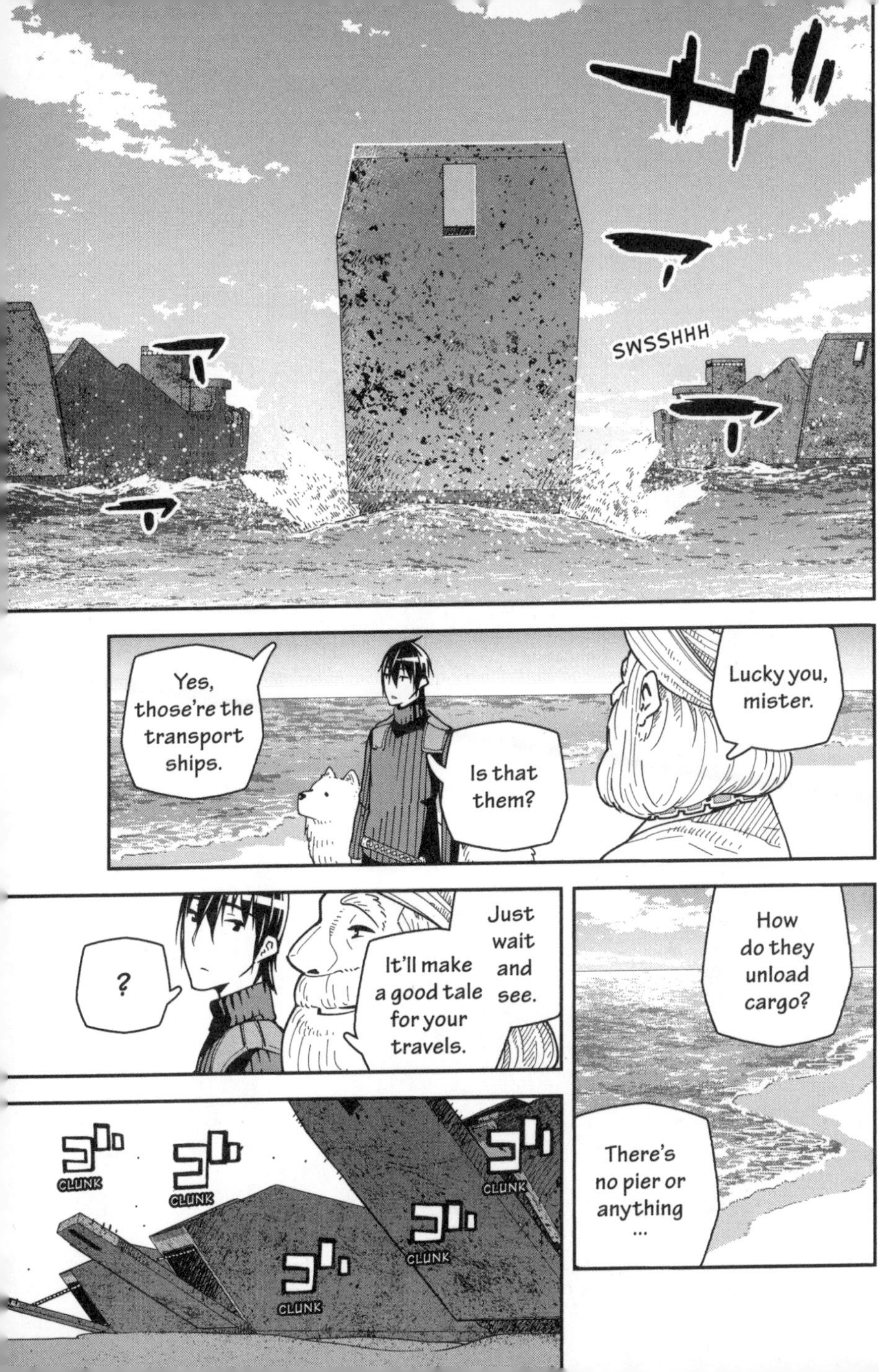
SWSSHHH
Lucky you, mister.
Is that them?
Yes, those're the transport ships.
How do they unload cargo?
There's no pier or anything ...
Just wait and see.
It'll make a good tale for your travels.
?
CLUNK
CLUNK
CLUNK
CLUNK
CLUNK

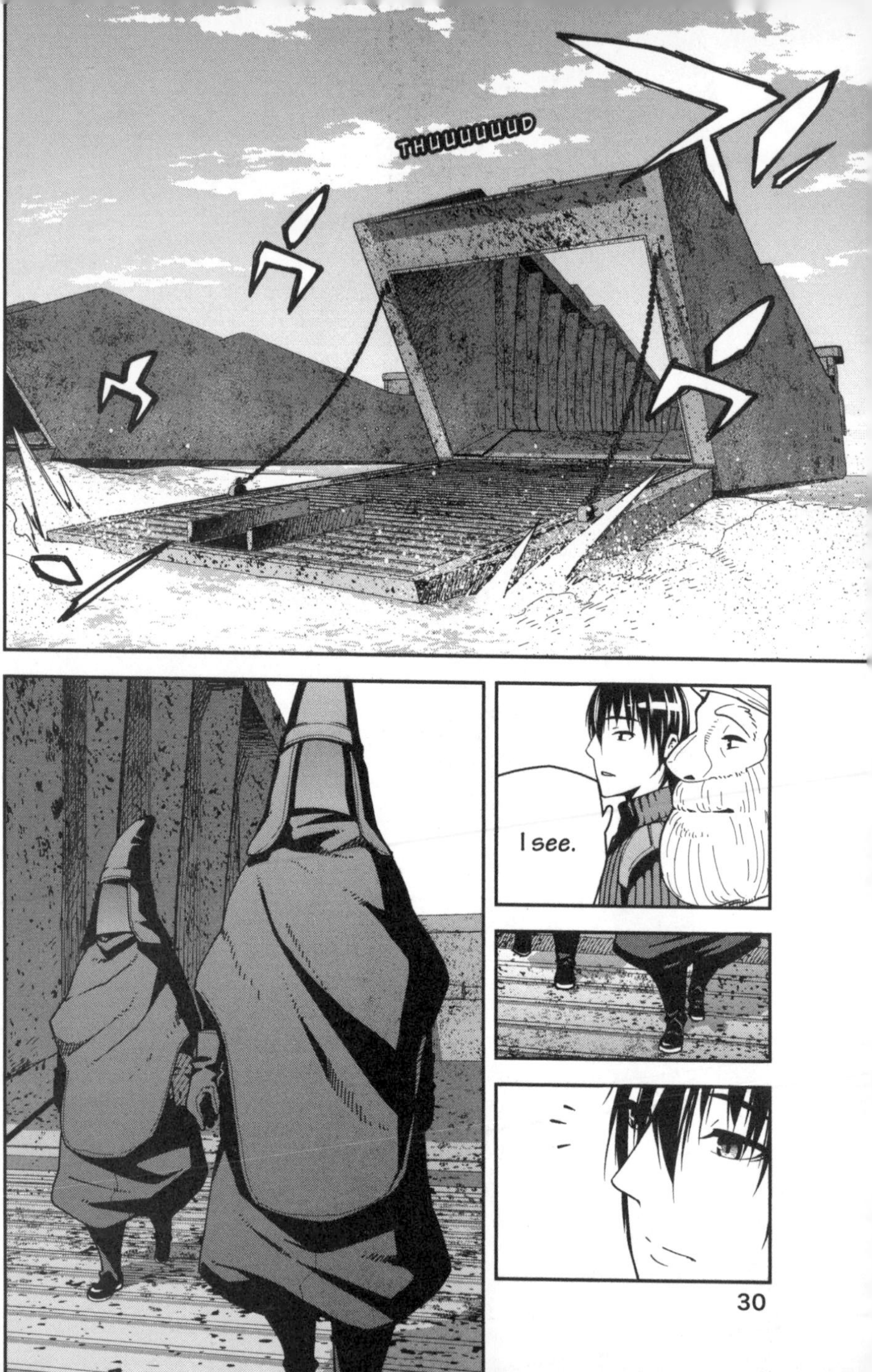
THUUUUUUUD
I see.

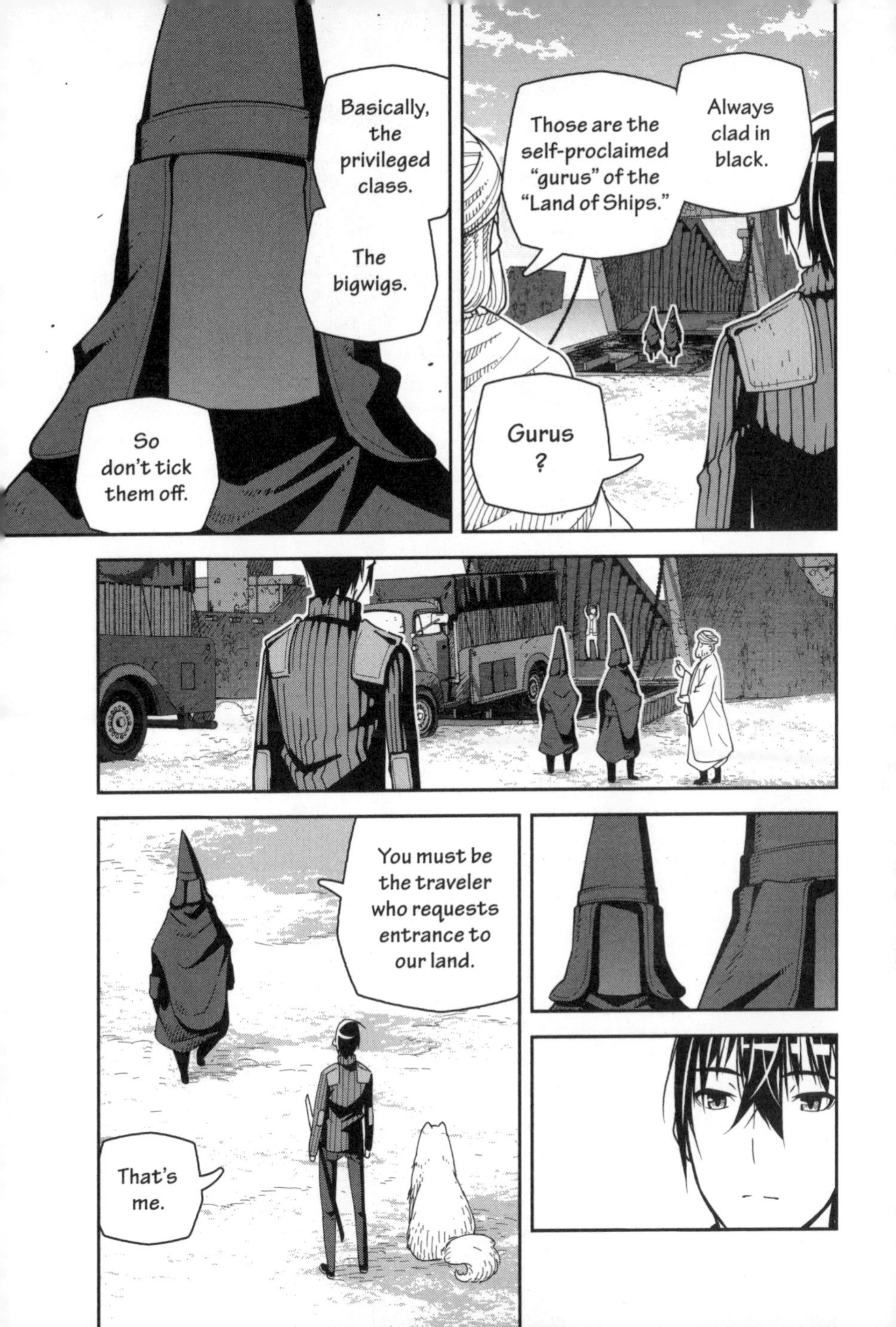
Always clad in black.
Those are the self-proclaimed "gurus" of the "Land of Ships."
Gurus?
Basically, the privileged class.
The bigwigs.
So don't tick them off.
You must be the traveler who requests entrance to our land.
That's me.

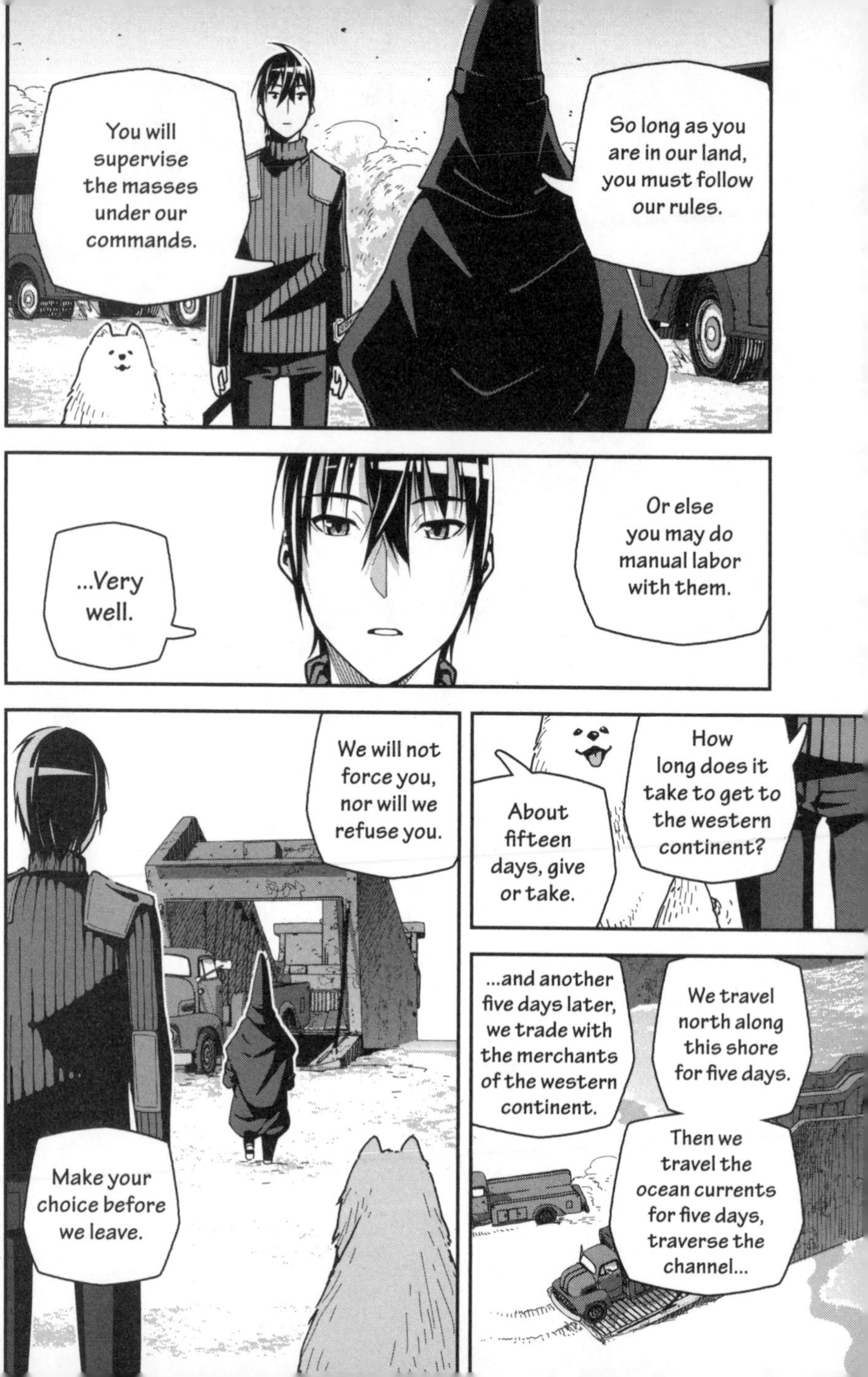
So long as you are in our land, you must follow our rules.
You will supervise the masses under our commands.
Or else you may do manual labor with them.
...Very well.
How long does it take to get to the western continent?
About fifteen days, give or take.
We travel north along this shore for five days.
Then we travel the ocean currents for five days, traverse the channel...
...and another five days later, we trade with the merchants of the western continent.
We will not force you, nor will we refuse you.
Make your choice before we leave.

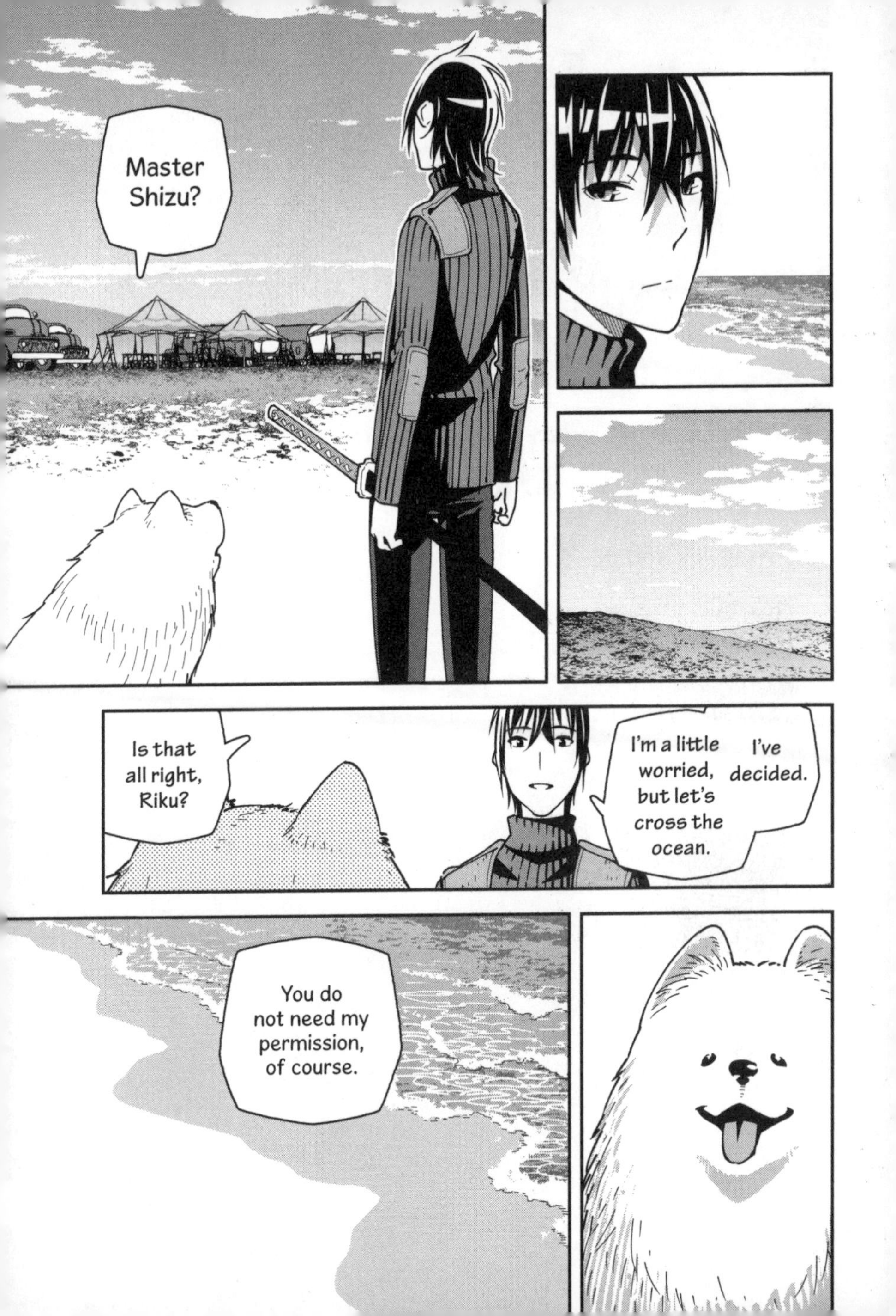
Master Shizu?
I've decided.
I'm a little worried, but let's cross the ocean.
Is that all right, Riku?
You do not need my permission, of course.

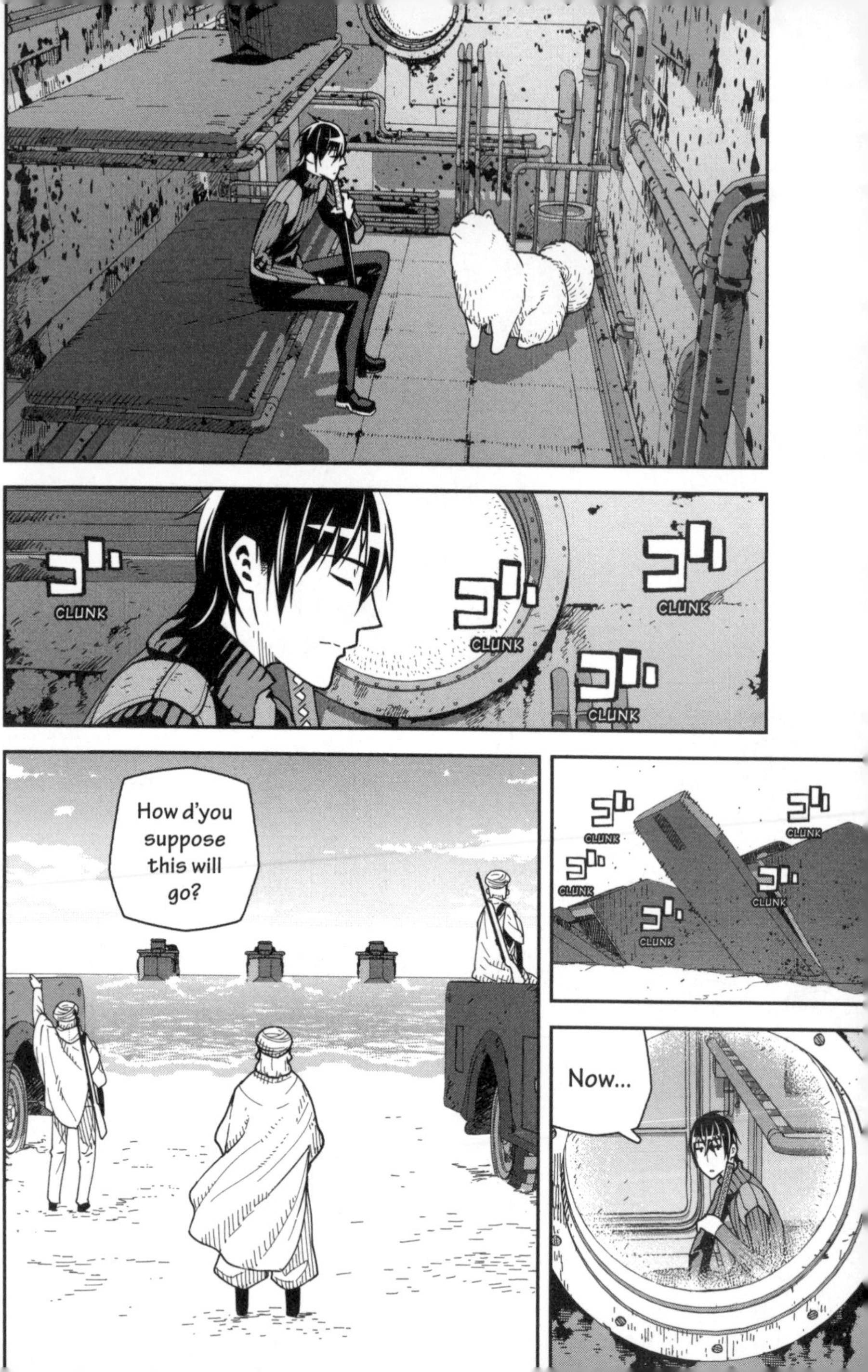
CLUNK
CLUNK
CLUNK
CLUNK
CLUNK
CLUNK
CLUNK
CLUNK
CLUNK
Now...
How d'you suppose this will go?

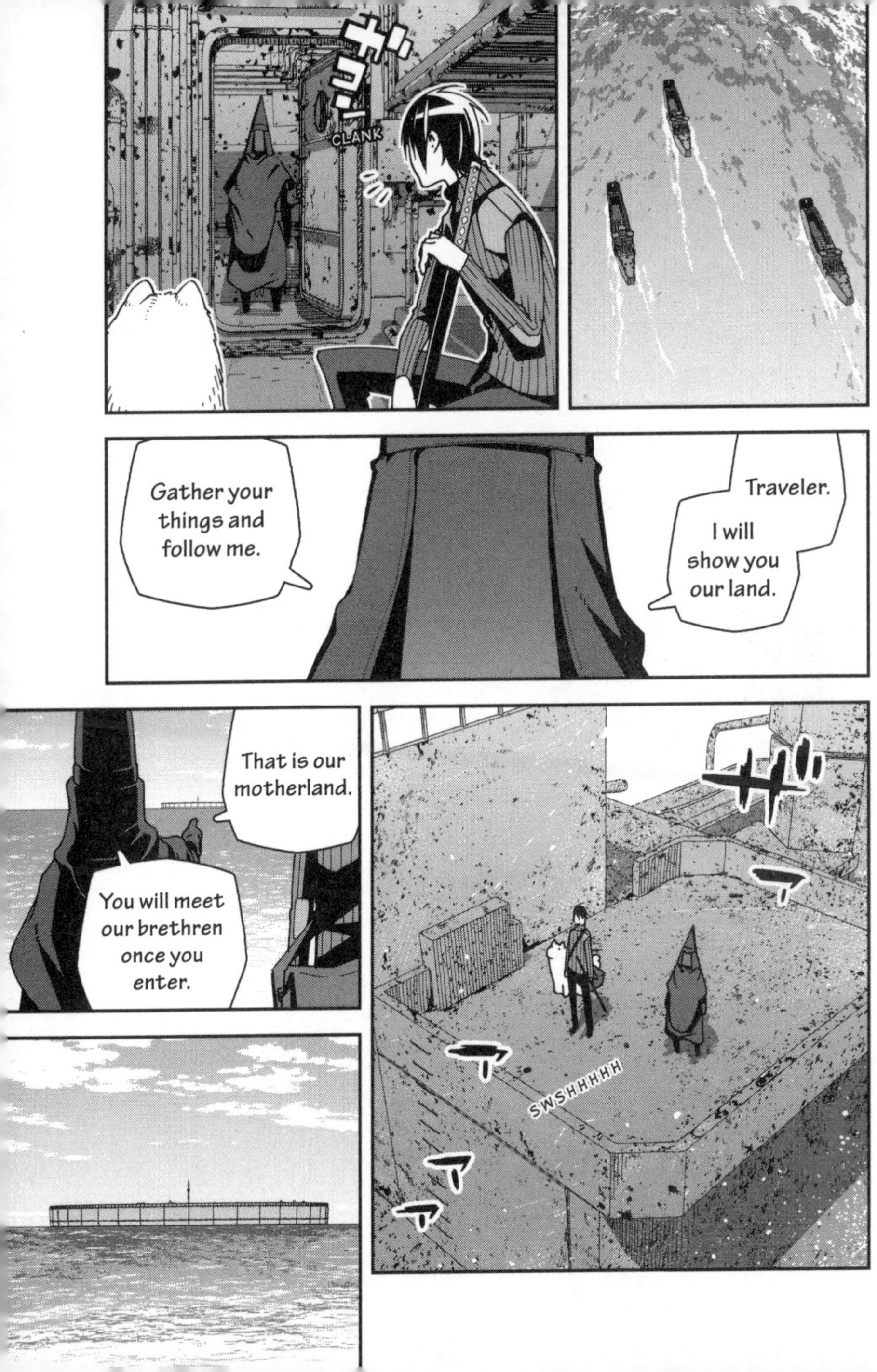
CLANK
Traveler.
I will show you our land.
Gather your things and follow me.
SWSHHHHH
That is our motherland.
You will meet our brethren once you enter.

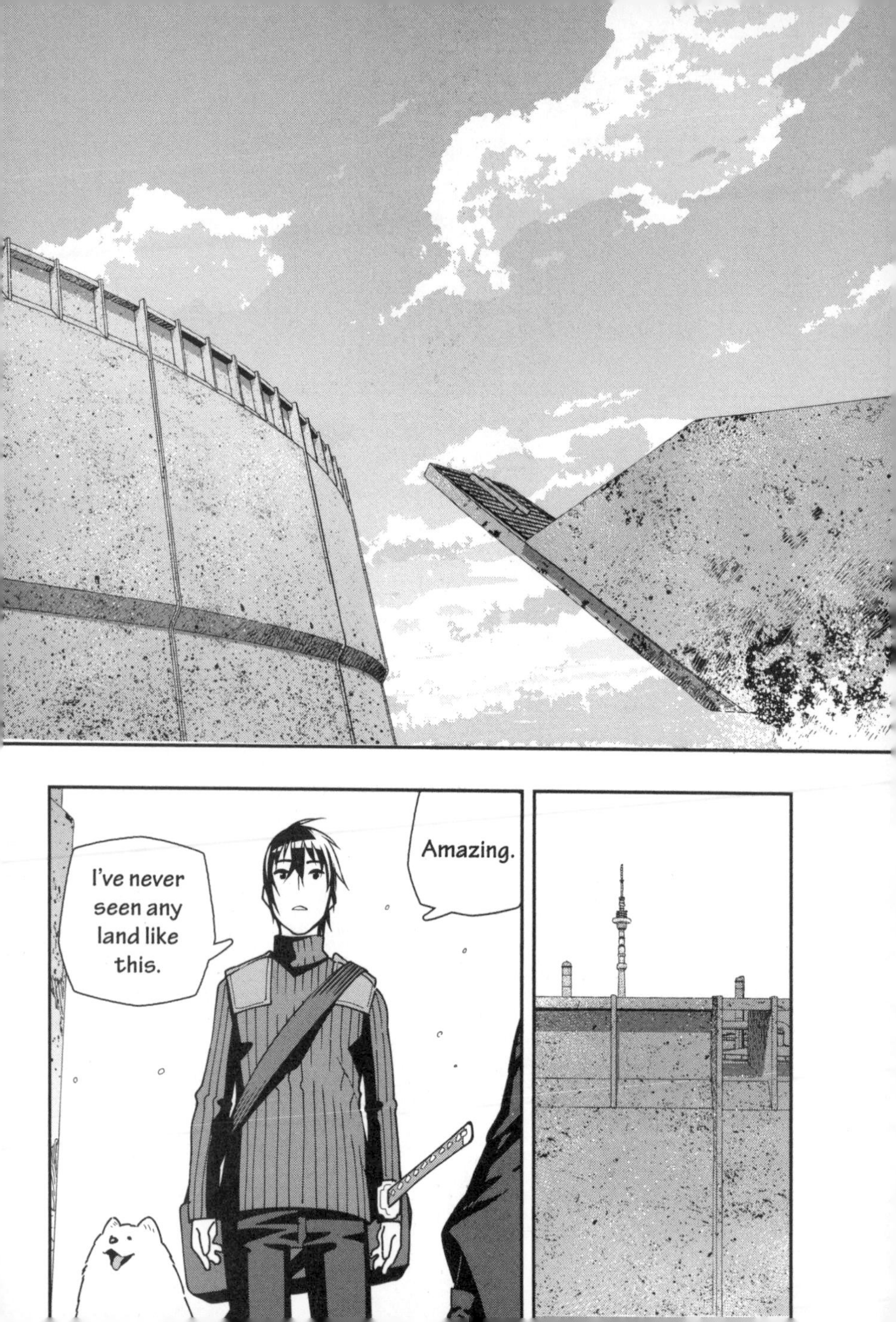
Amazing.
I've never seen any land like this.

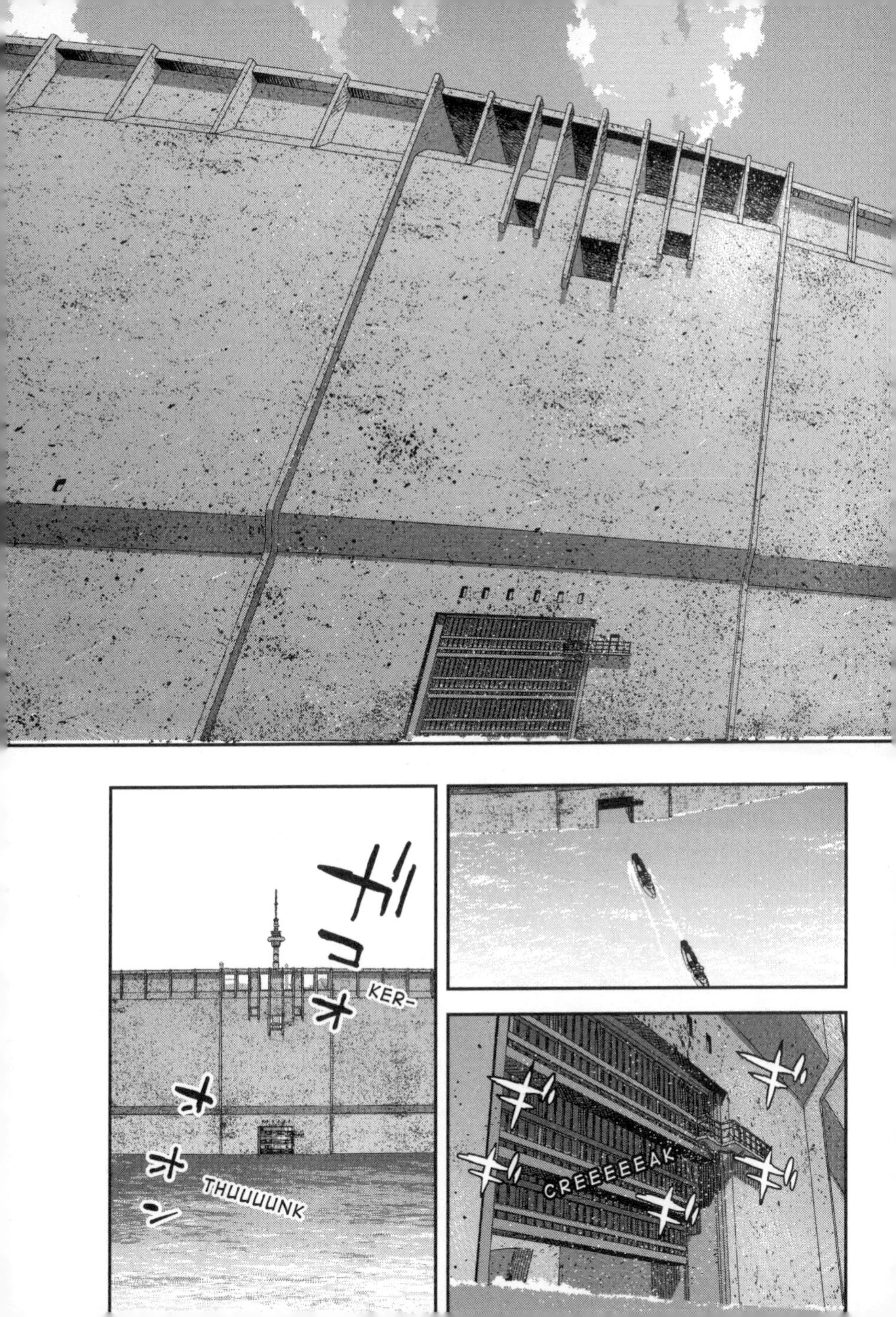
CREEEEEAK
KER-
THUUUUNK

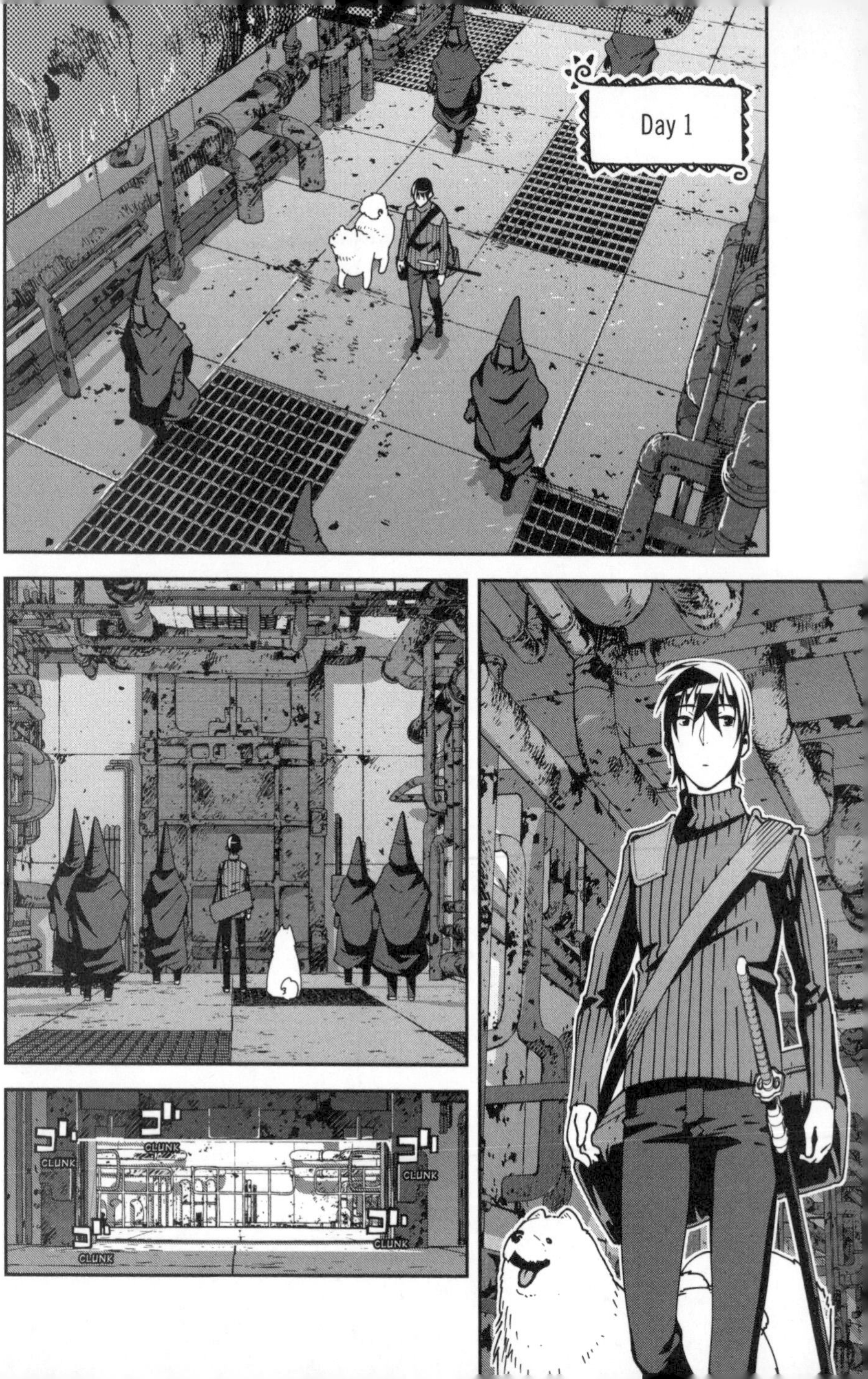
Day 1
ゴッ
CLUNK
ゴッ
CLUNK
ゴッ
CLUNK
ゴッ
CLUNK
ゴッ
CLUNK

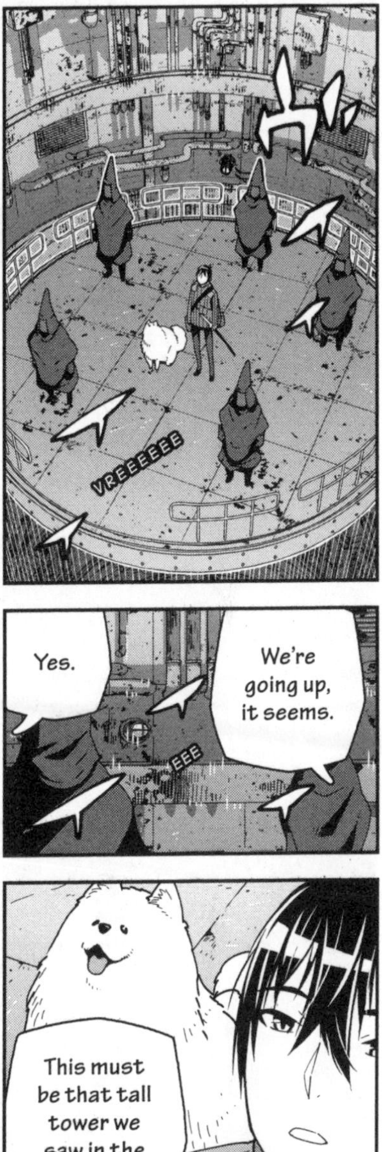
VREEEEEEE
We're going up, it seems.
Yes.
EEE
This must be that tall tower we saw in the center.
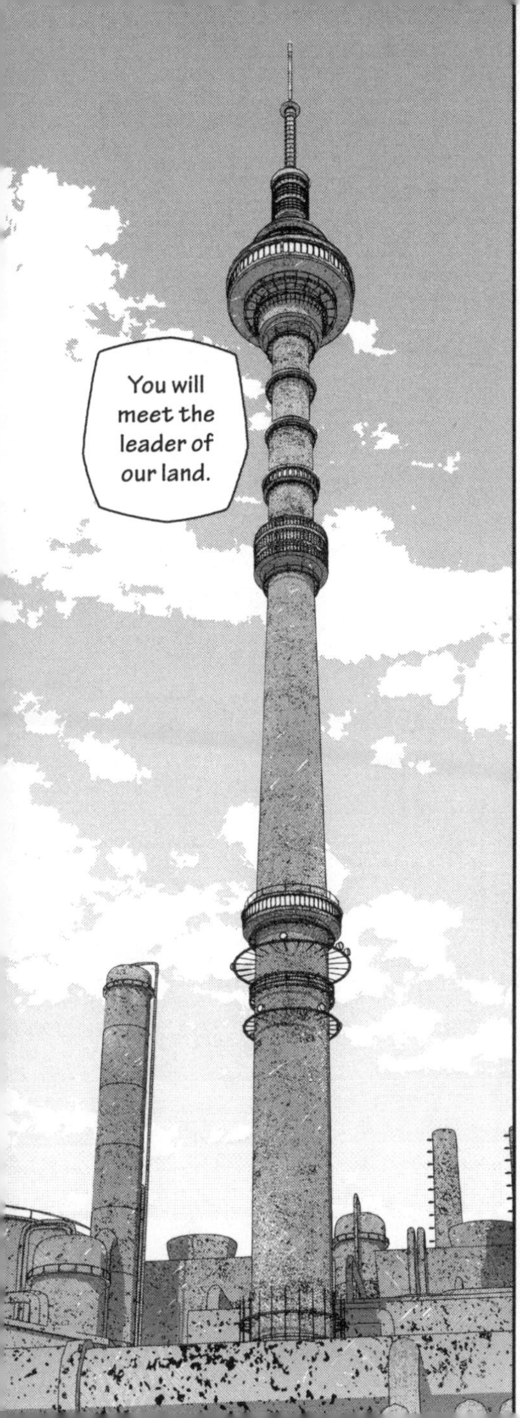
You will meet the leader of our land.

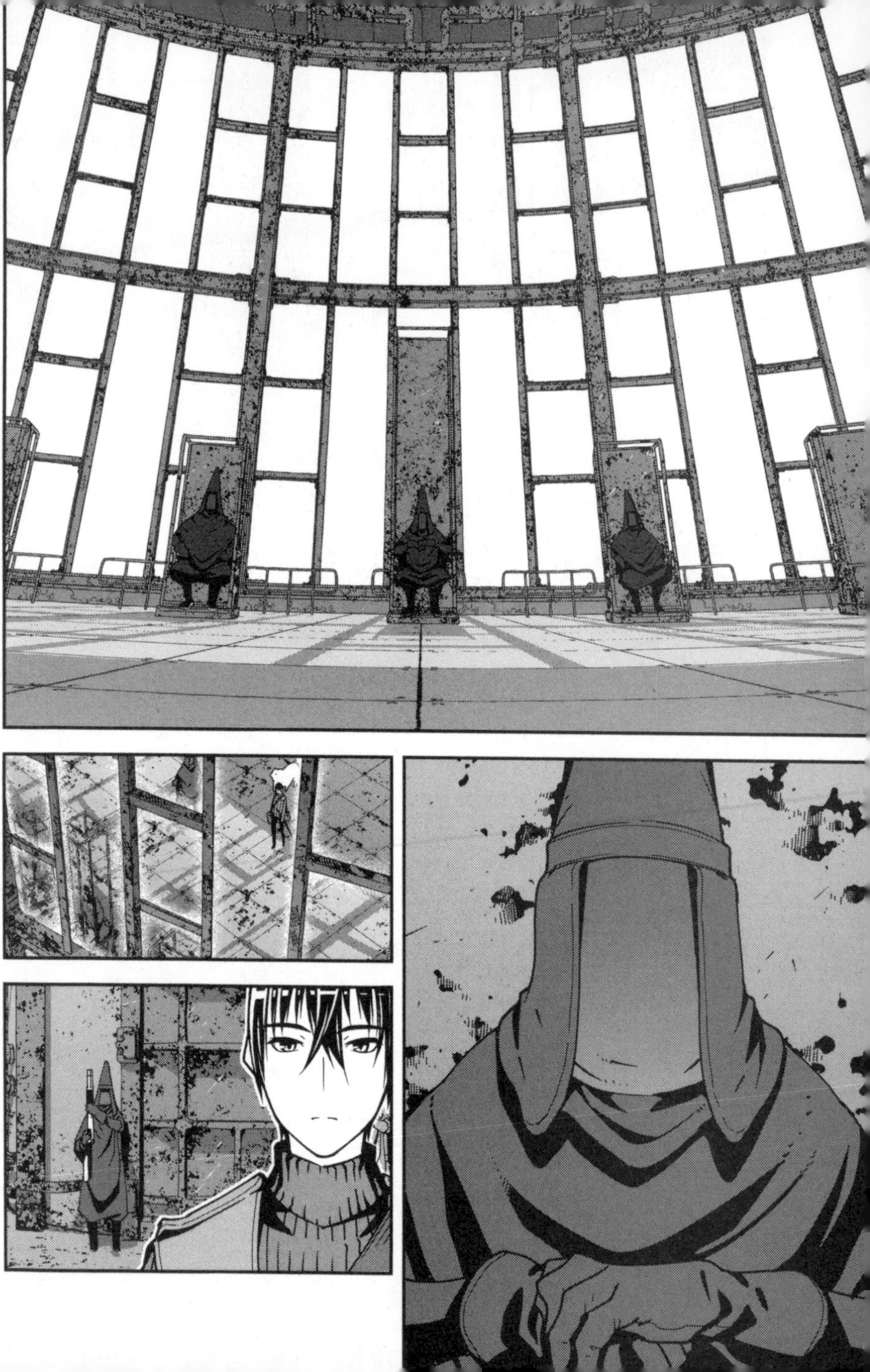

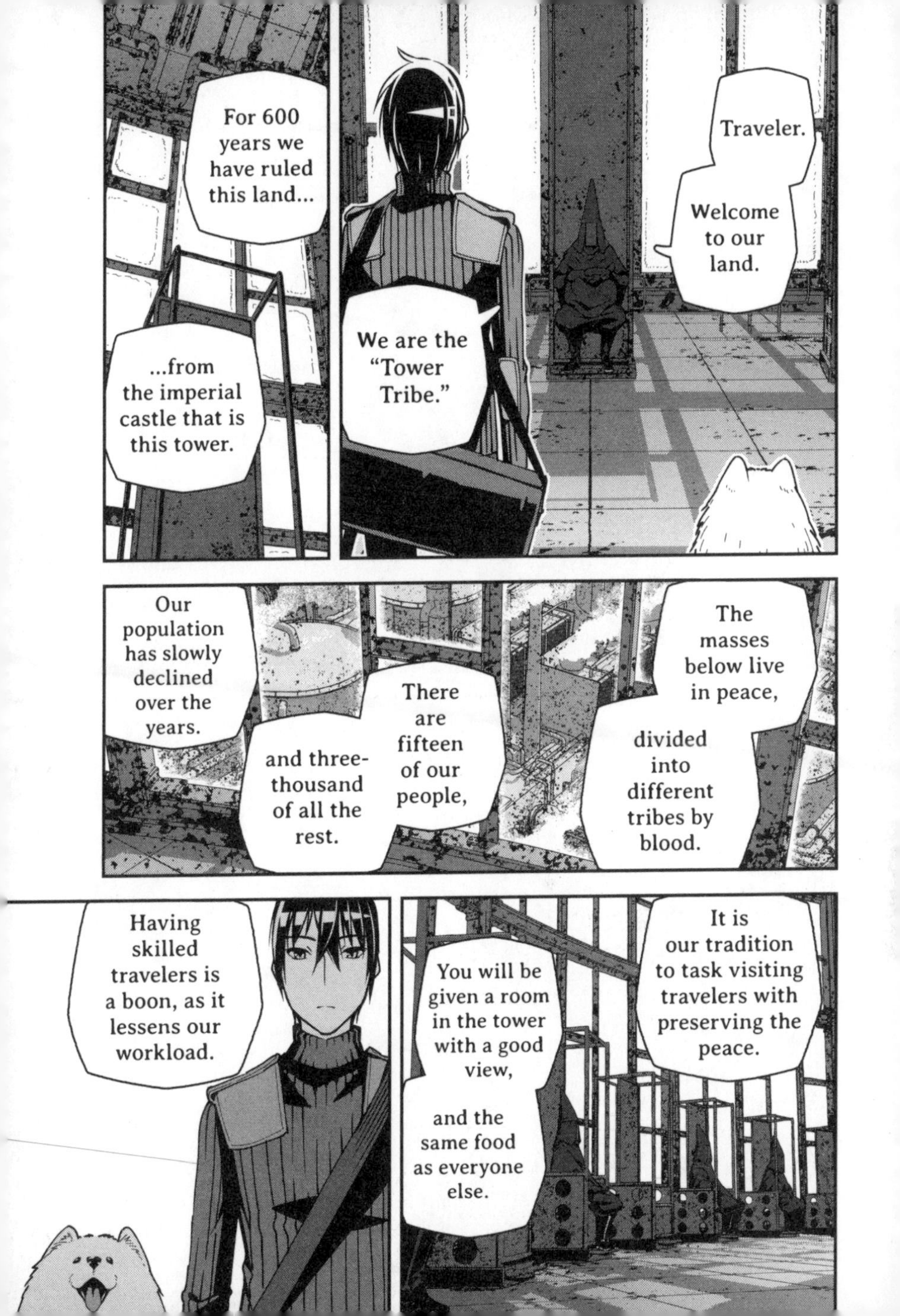
Traveler.
Welcome to our land.
We are the "Tower Tribe."
For 600 years we have ruled this land...
...from the imperial castle that is this tower.
The masses below live in peace,
divided into different tribes by blood.
There are fifteen of our people,
and three-thousand of all the rest.
Our population has slowly declined over the years.
It is our tradition to task visiting travelers with preserving the peace.
You will be given a room in the tower with a good view,
and the same food as everyone else.
Having skilled travelers is a boon, as it lessens our workload.

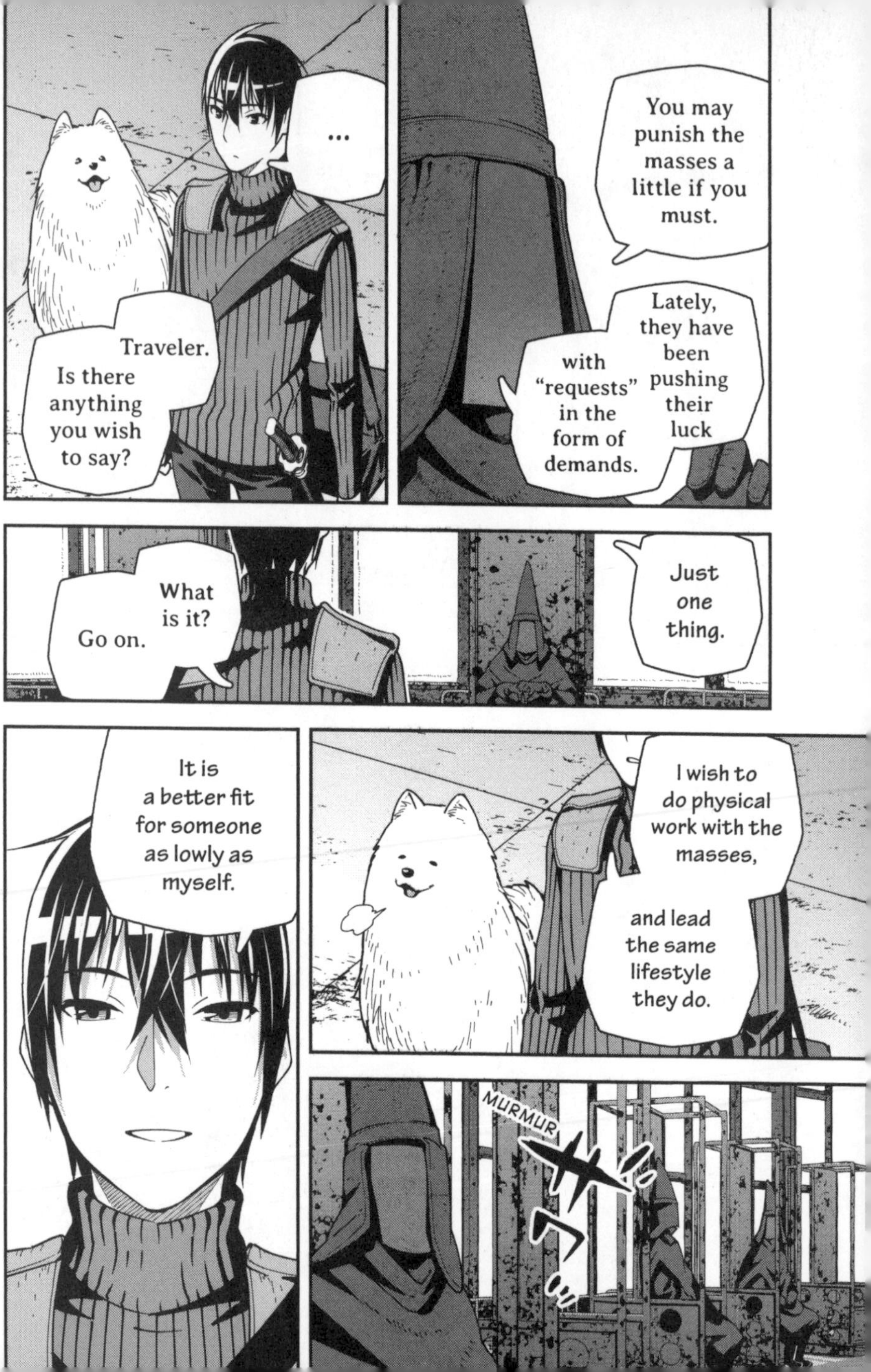
You may punish the masses a little if you must.
Lately, they have been pushing their luck with "requests" in the form of demands.
...
Traveler. Is there anything you wish to say?
Just one thing.
What is it? Go on.
I wish to do physical work with the masses,
and lead the same lifestyle they do.
MURMUR
It is a better fit for someone as lowly as myself.

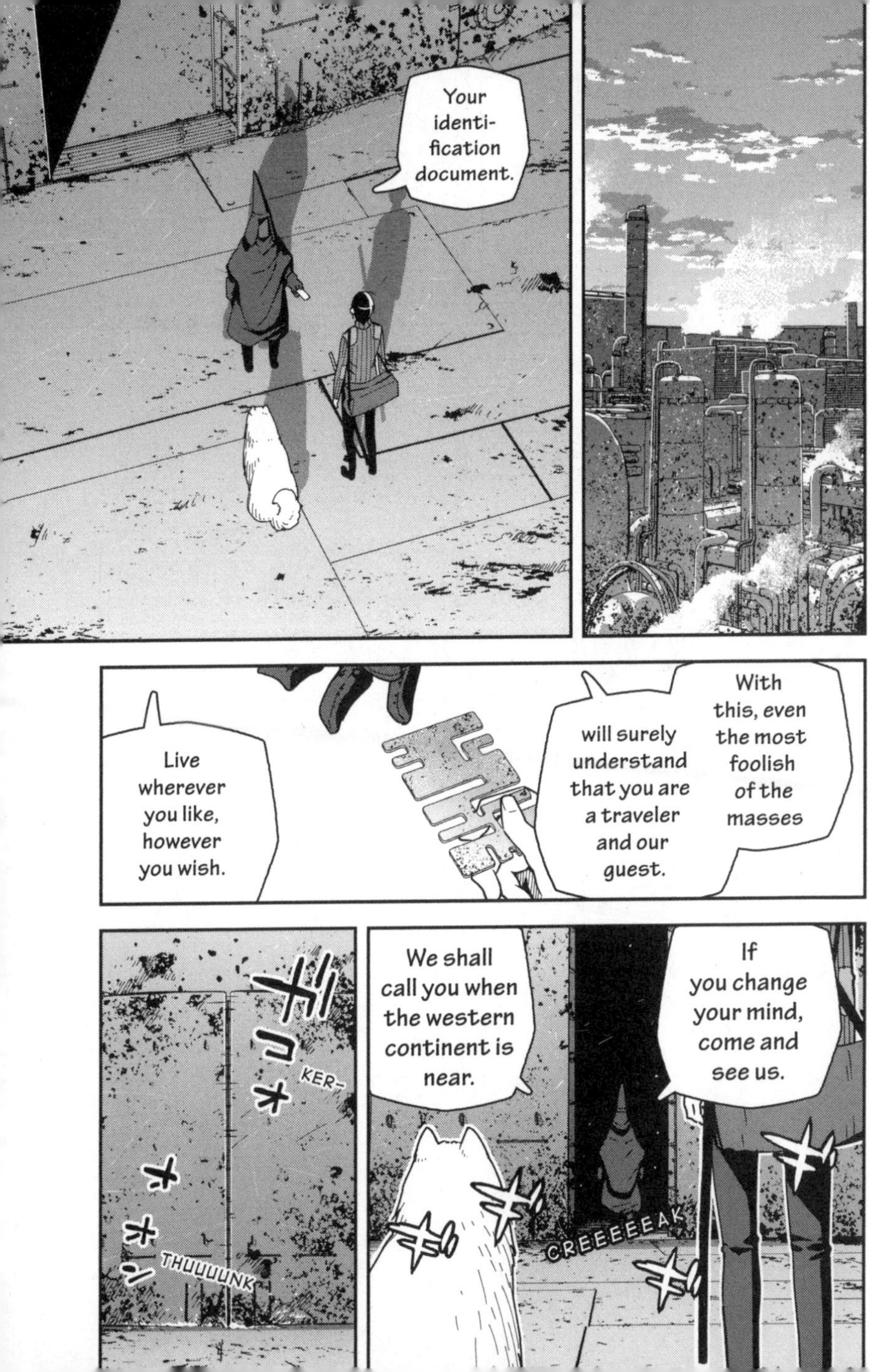
Your identification document.
With this, even the most foolish of the masses
will surely understand that you are a traveler and our guest.
Live wherever you like, however you wish.
If you change your mind, come and see us.
We shall call you when the western continent is near.
CREEEEEAK
KER-
THUUUUNK

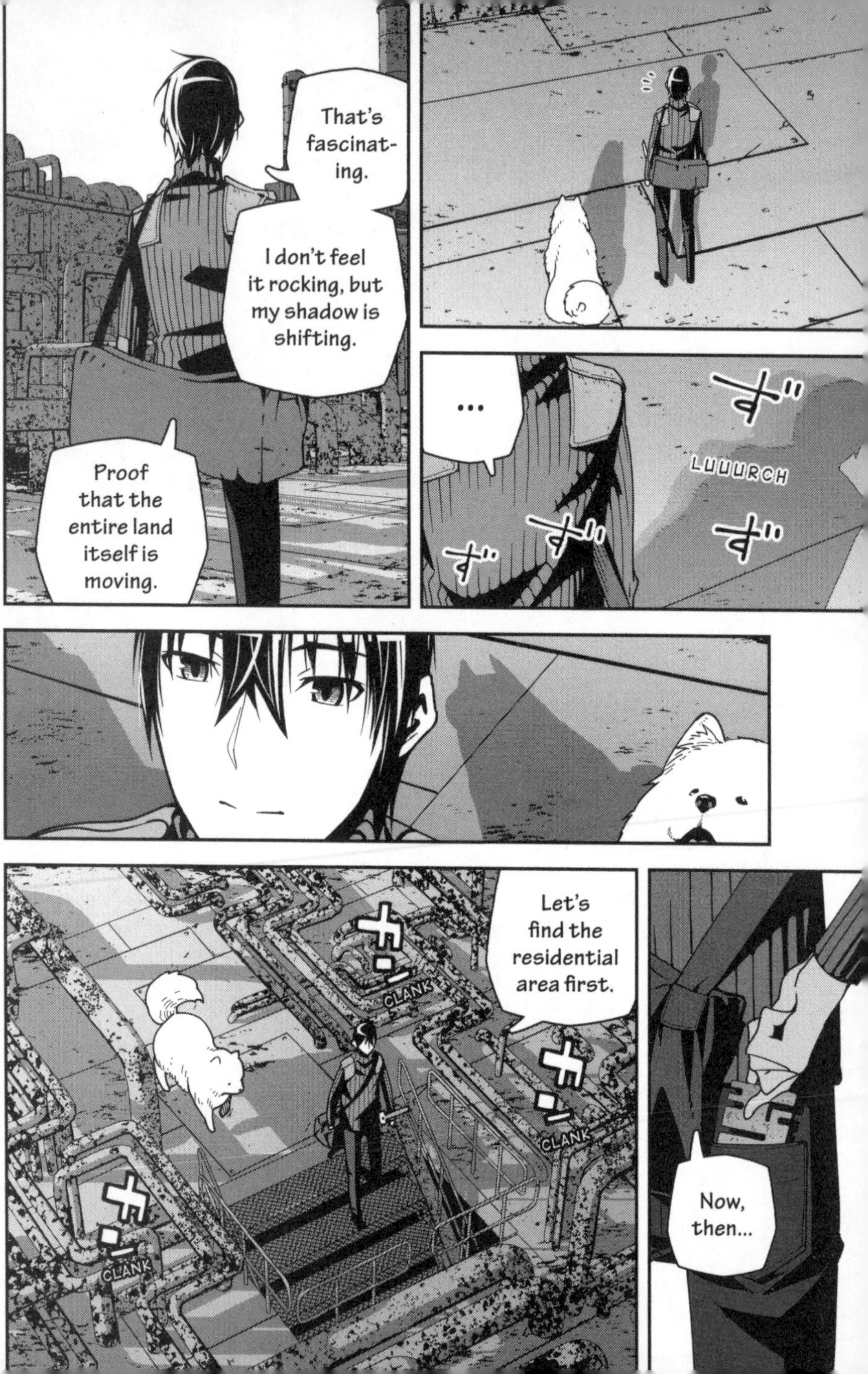
...
LUUURCH
That's fascinat-ing.
I don't feel it rocking, but my shadow is shifting.
Proof that the entire land itself is moving.
Now, then...
Let's find the residential area first.
CLANK
CLANK
CLANK

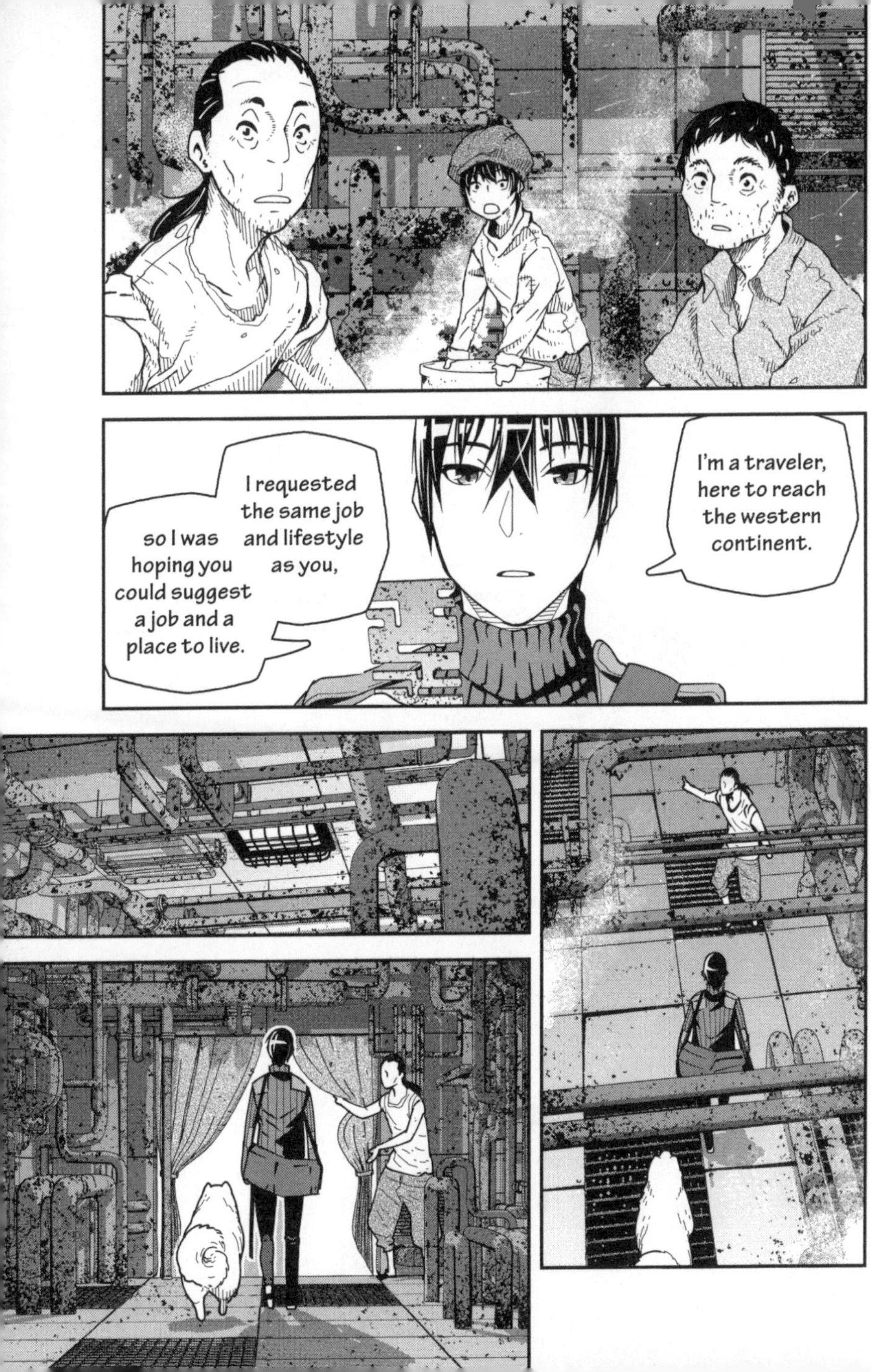
I'm a traveler, here to reach the western continent.
I requested the same job and lifestyle as you, so I was hoping you could suggest a job and a place to live.

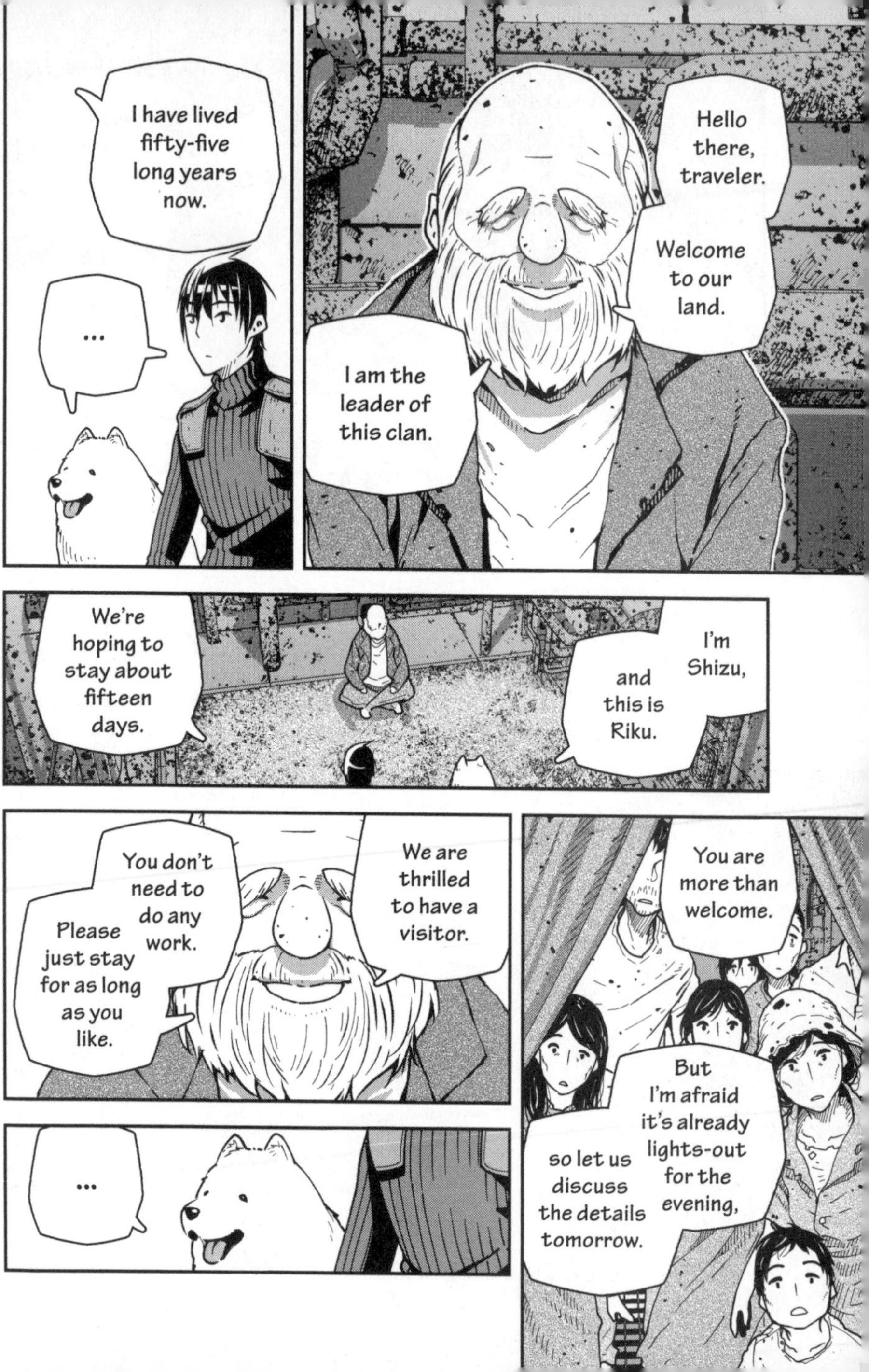
Hello there, traveler.
Welcome to our land.
I am the leader of this clan.
I have lived fifty-five long years now.
...
I'm Shizu, and this is Riku.
We're hoping to stay about fifteen days.
You are more than welcome.
But I'm afraid it's already lights-out for the evening,
so let us discuss the details tomorrow.
We are thrilled to have a visitor.
You don't need to do any work.
Please just stay for as long as you like.
...

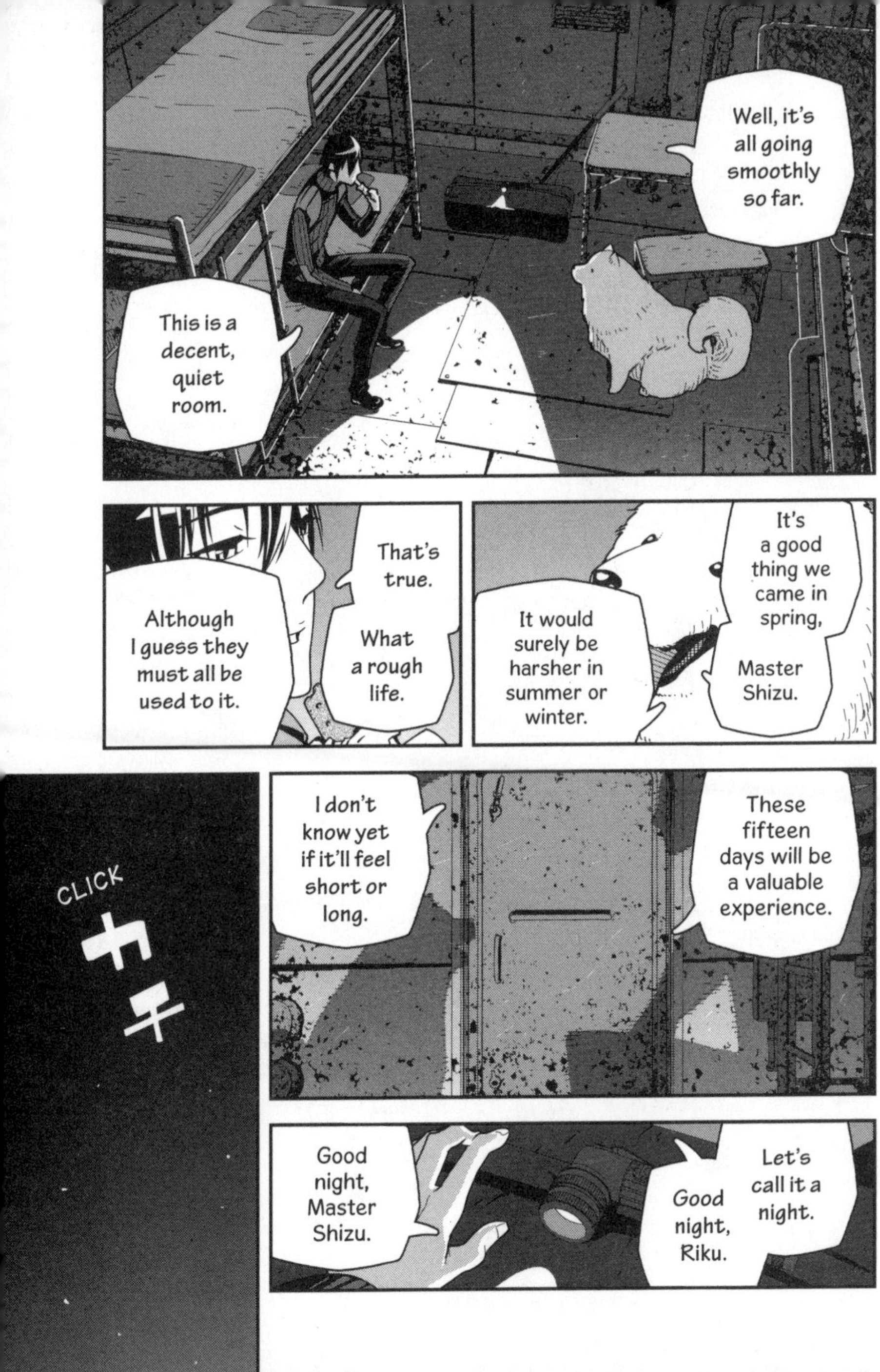
Well, it's all going smoothly so far.
This is a decent, quiet room.
It's a good thing we came in spring,
Master Shizu.
It would surely be harsher in summer or winter.
That's true.
What a rough life.
Although I guess they must all be used to it.
These fifteen days will be a valuable experience.
I don't know yet if it'll feel short or long.
Let's call it a night.
Good night, Riku.
Good night, Master Shizu.
CLICK
カチ

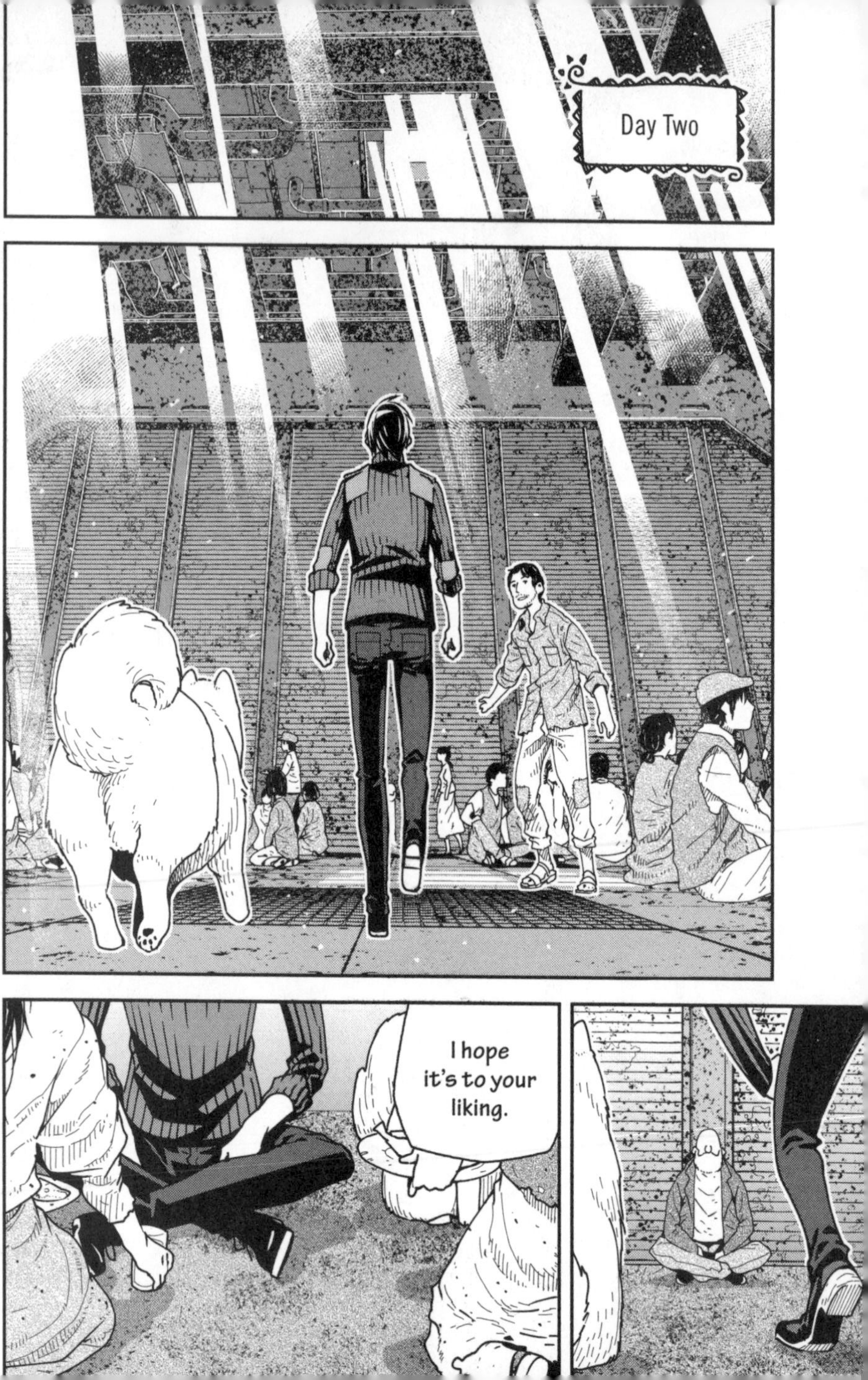
Day Two
I hope it's to your liking.

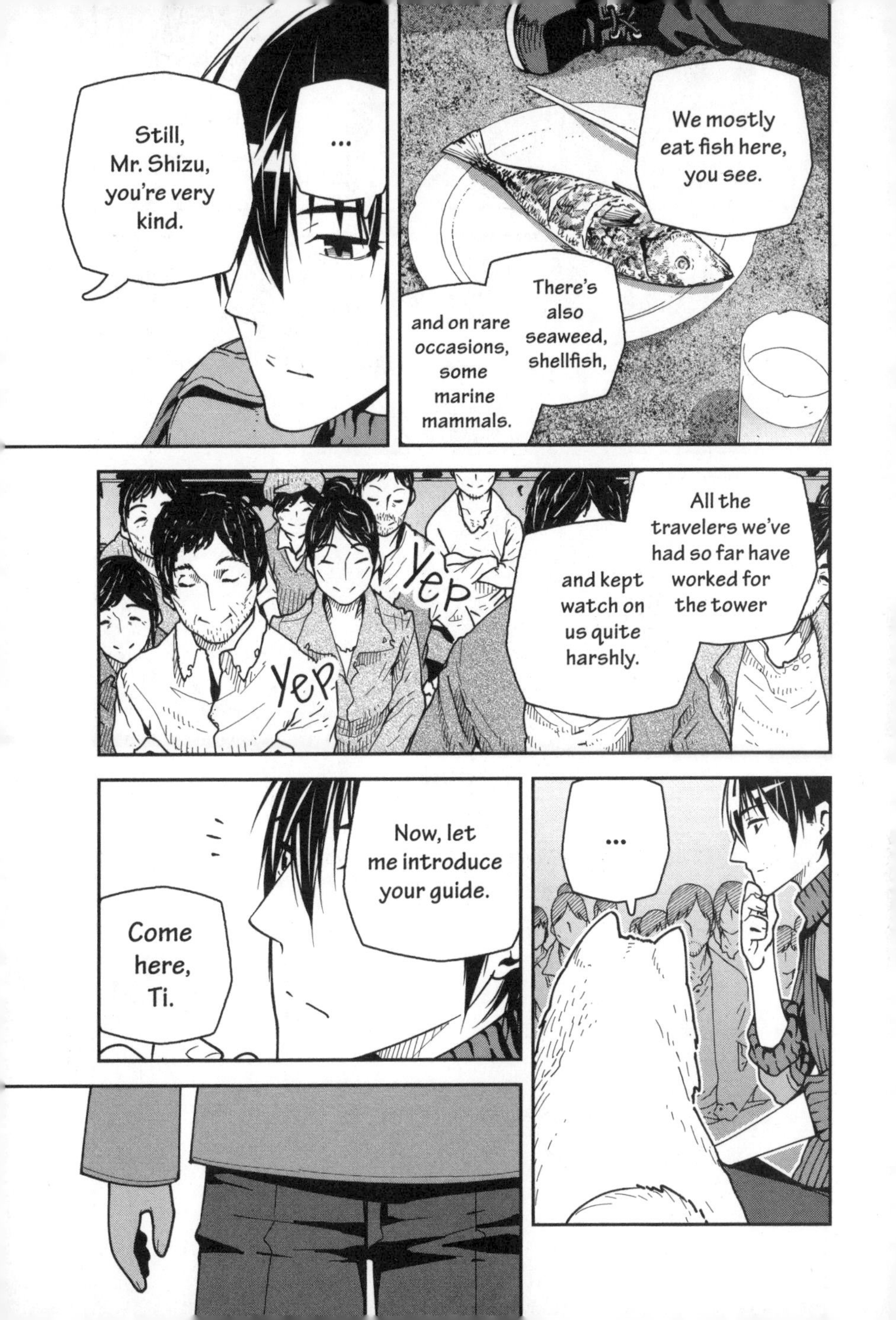
We mostly eat fish here, you see.
There's also seaweed, shellfish,
and on rare occasions, some marine mammals.
...
Still, Mr. Shizu, you're very kind.
All the travelers we've had so far have worked for the tower
and kept watch on us quite harshly.
Yep
Yep
...
Now, let me introduce your guide.
Come here, Ti.

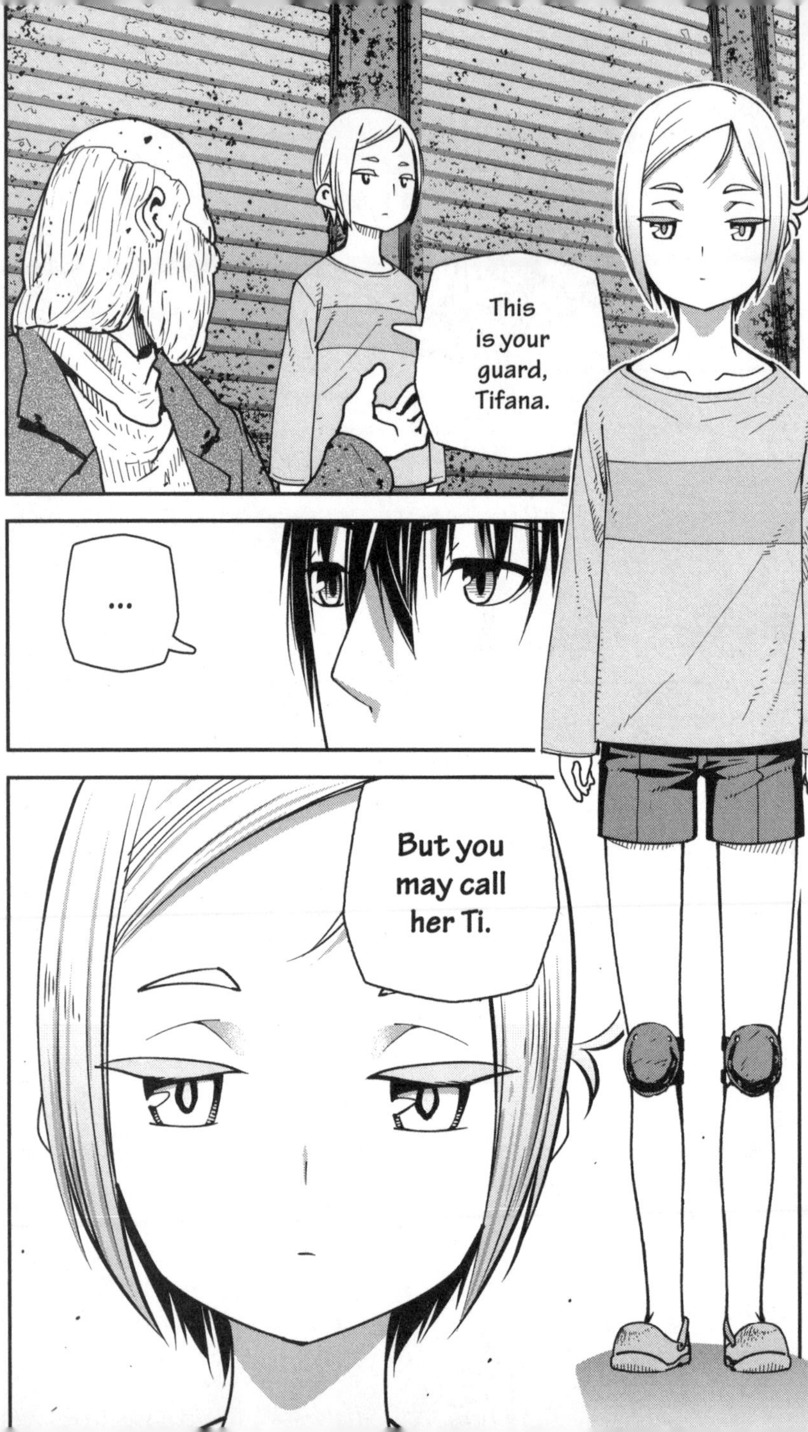
This is your guard, Tifana.
...
But you may call her Ti.

Epilogue (Pt. 2)

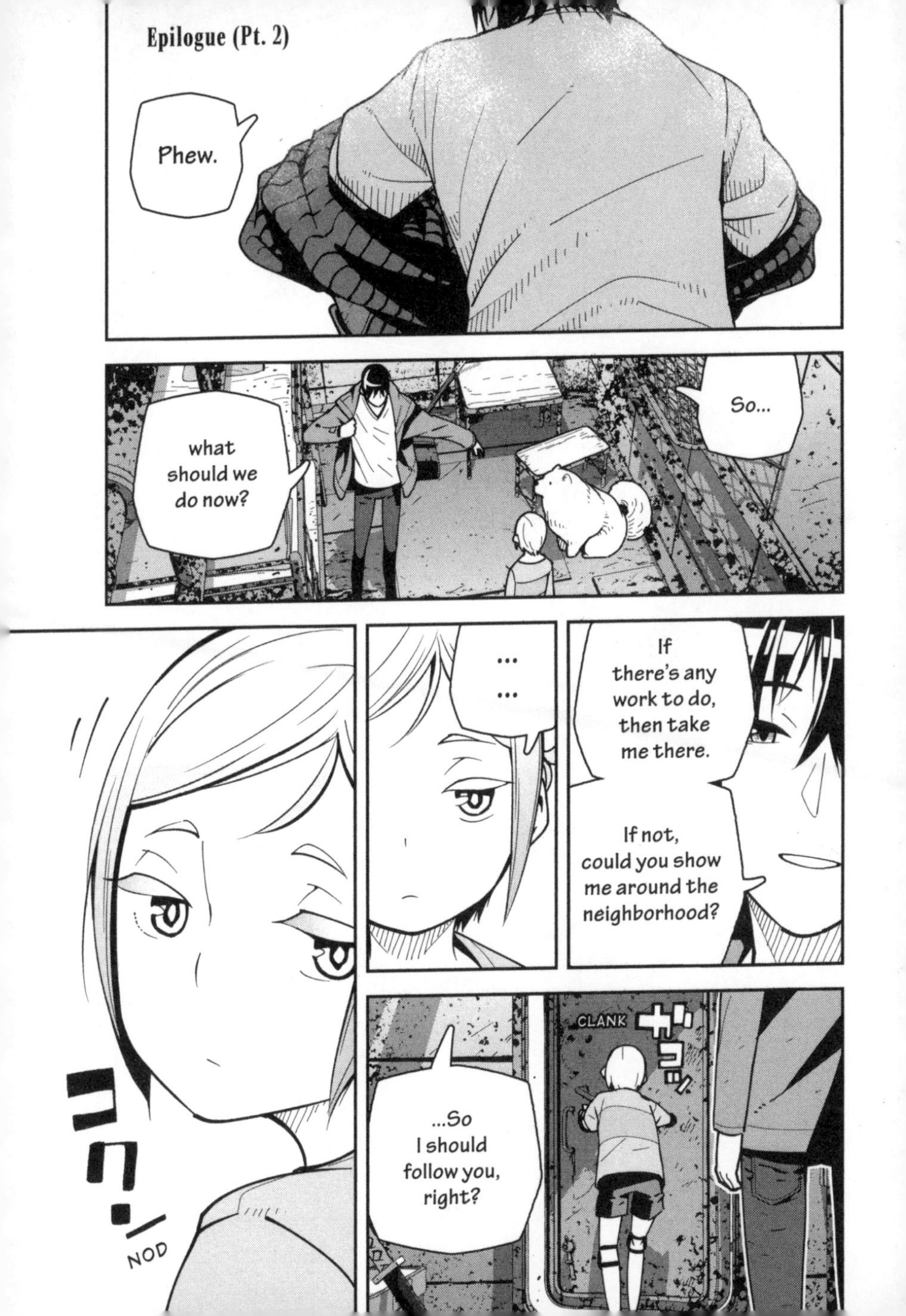
Phew.
So...
what should we do now?
If there's any work to do, then take me there.
If not, could you show me around the neighborhood?
...
...
CLANK
...So I should follow you, right?
NOD

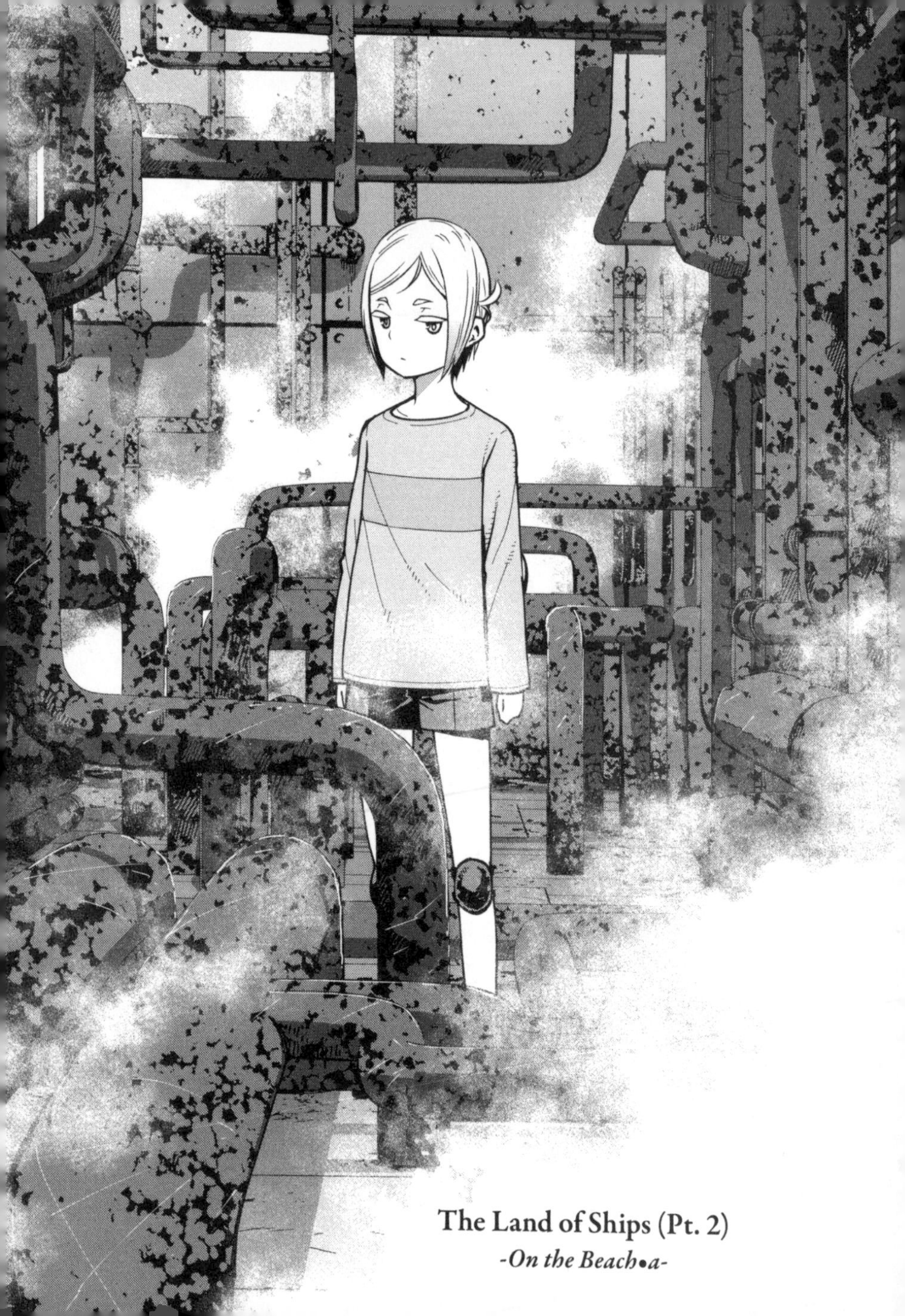

The Land of Ships (Pt. 2)

-On the Beach•a-

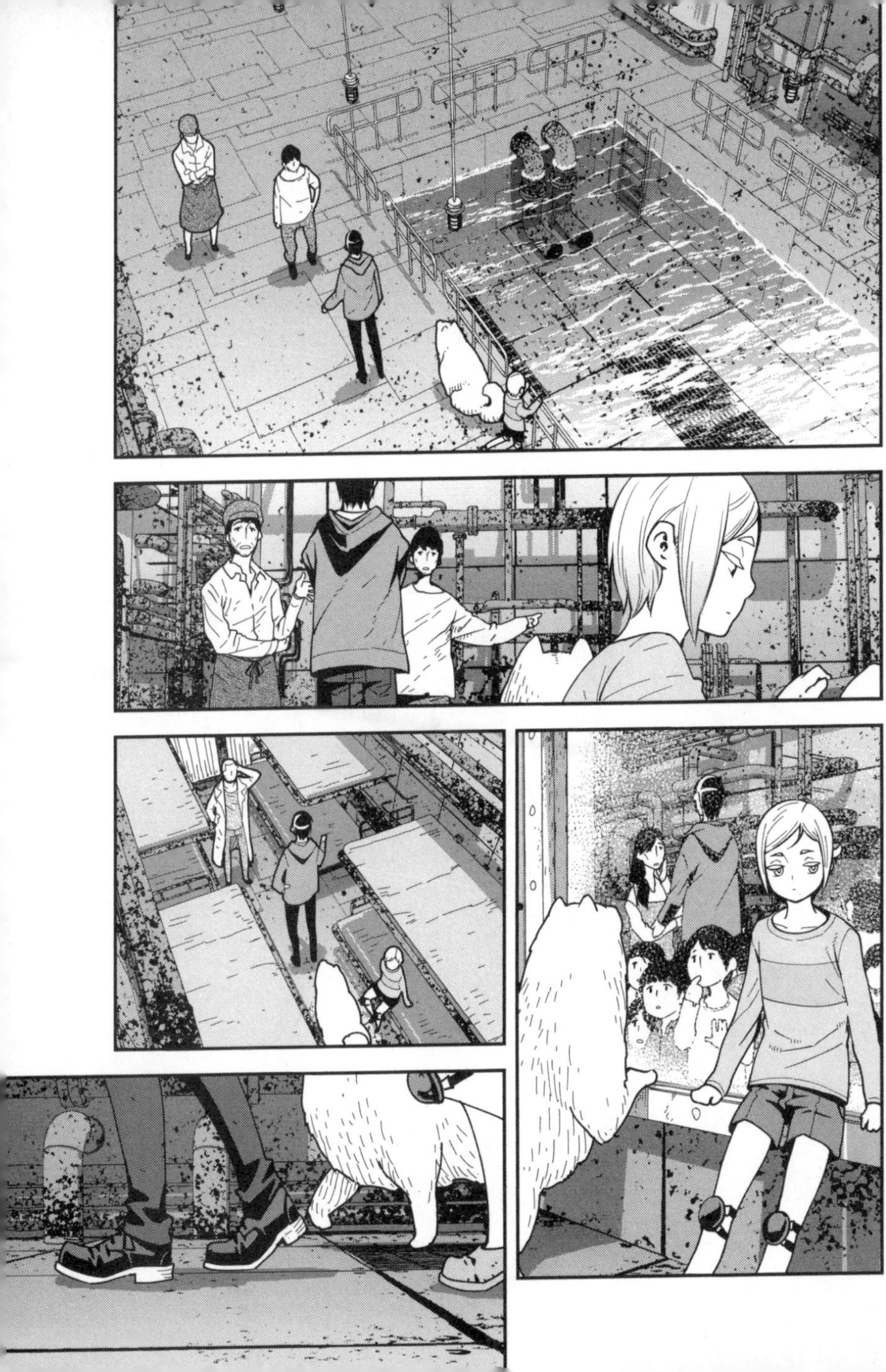

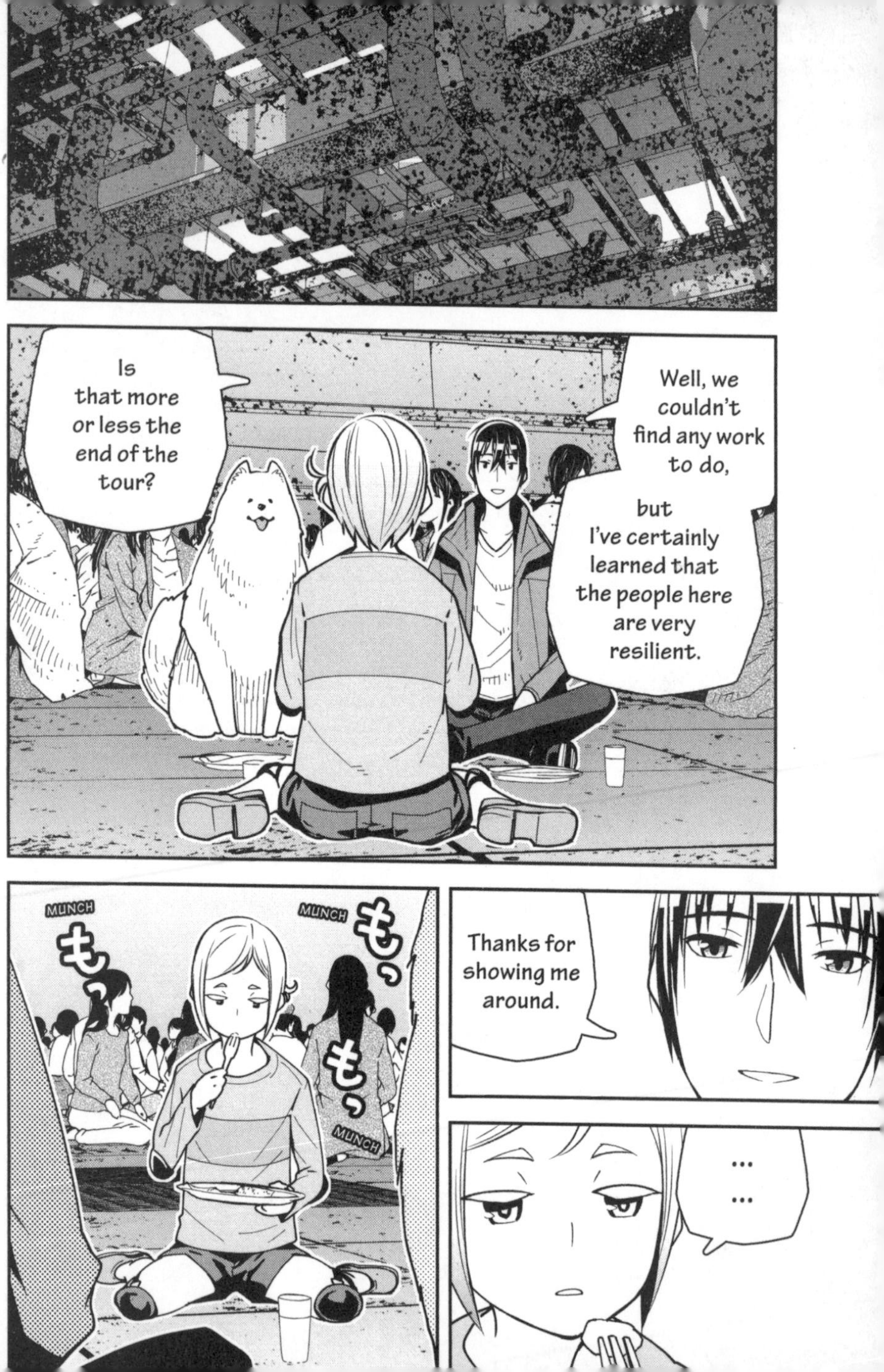
Is that more or less the end of the tour?
Well, we couldn't find any work to do,
but I've certainly learned that the people here are very resilient.
Thanks for showing me around.
...
...
MUNCH
もっ
MUNCH
もっ
もっ
MUNCH

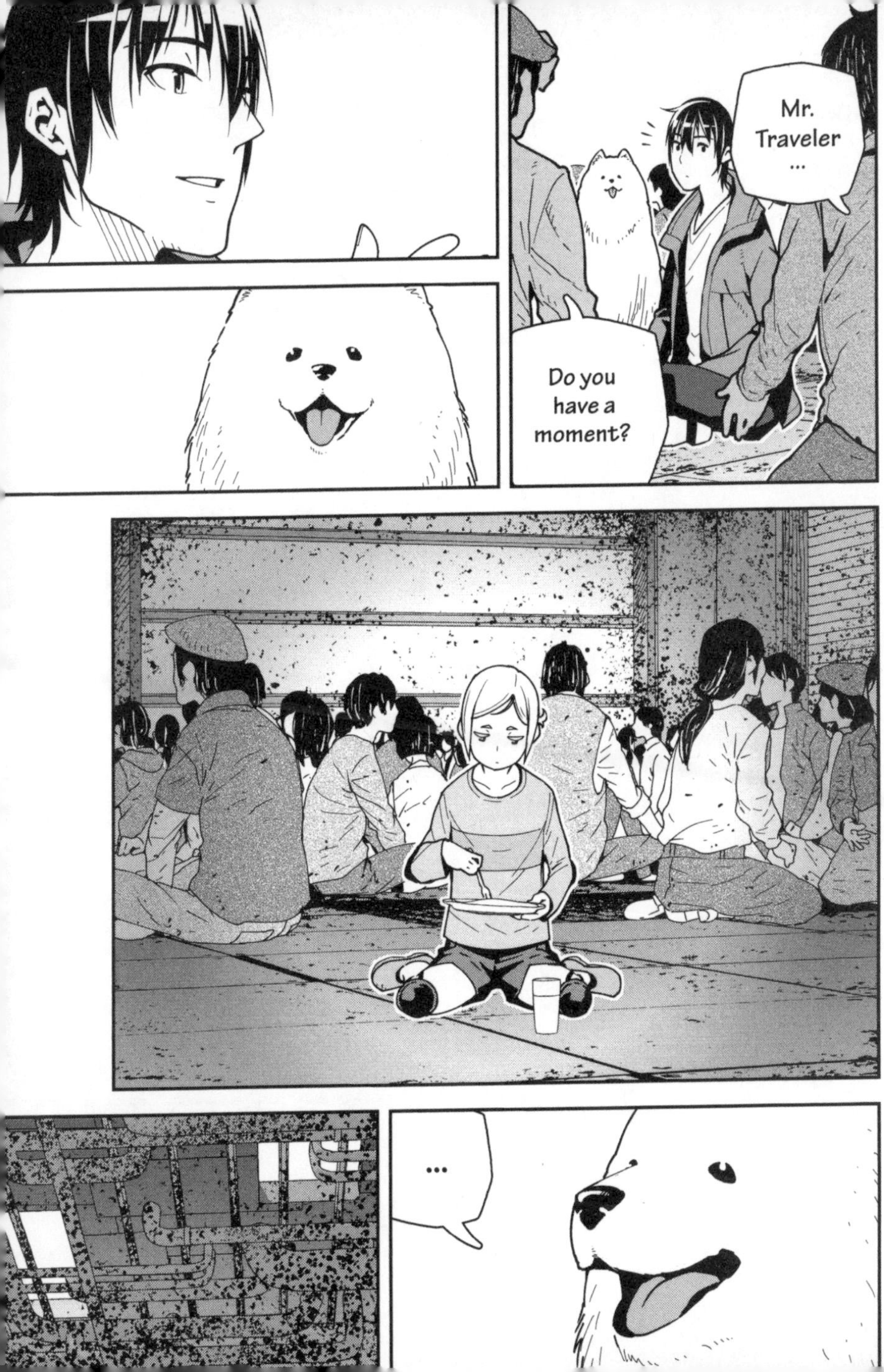
Mr. Traveler ...
Do you have a moment?
...

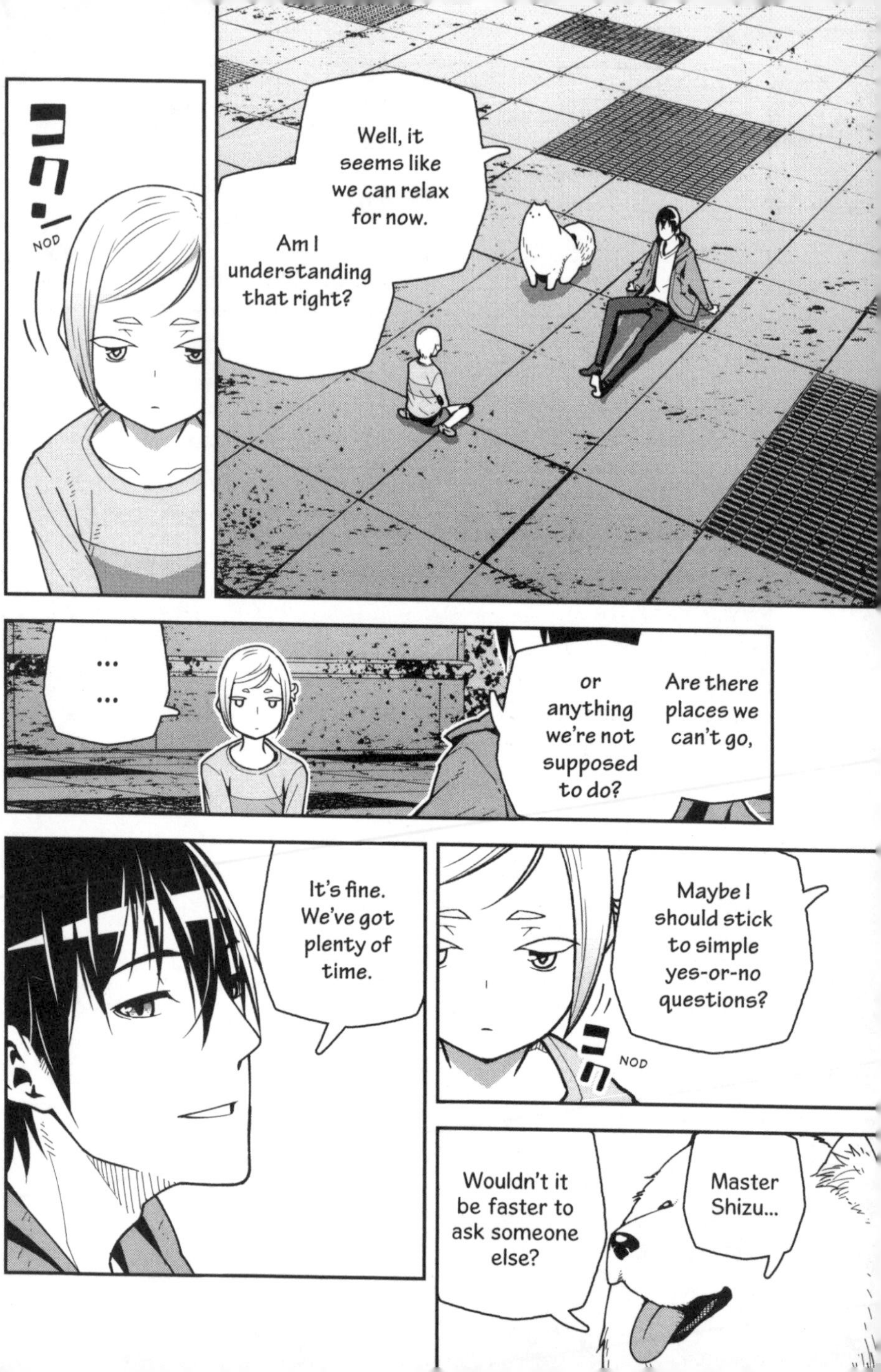
Well, it seems like we can relax for now.
Am I understanding that right?
コクン
NOD
Are there places we can't go,
or anything we're not supposed to do?
...
...
Maybe I should stick to simple yes-or-no questions?
NOD
Master Shizu...
Wouldn't it be faster to ask someone else?
It's fine. We've got plenty of time.

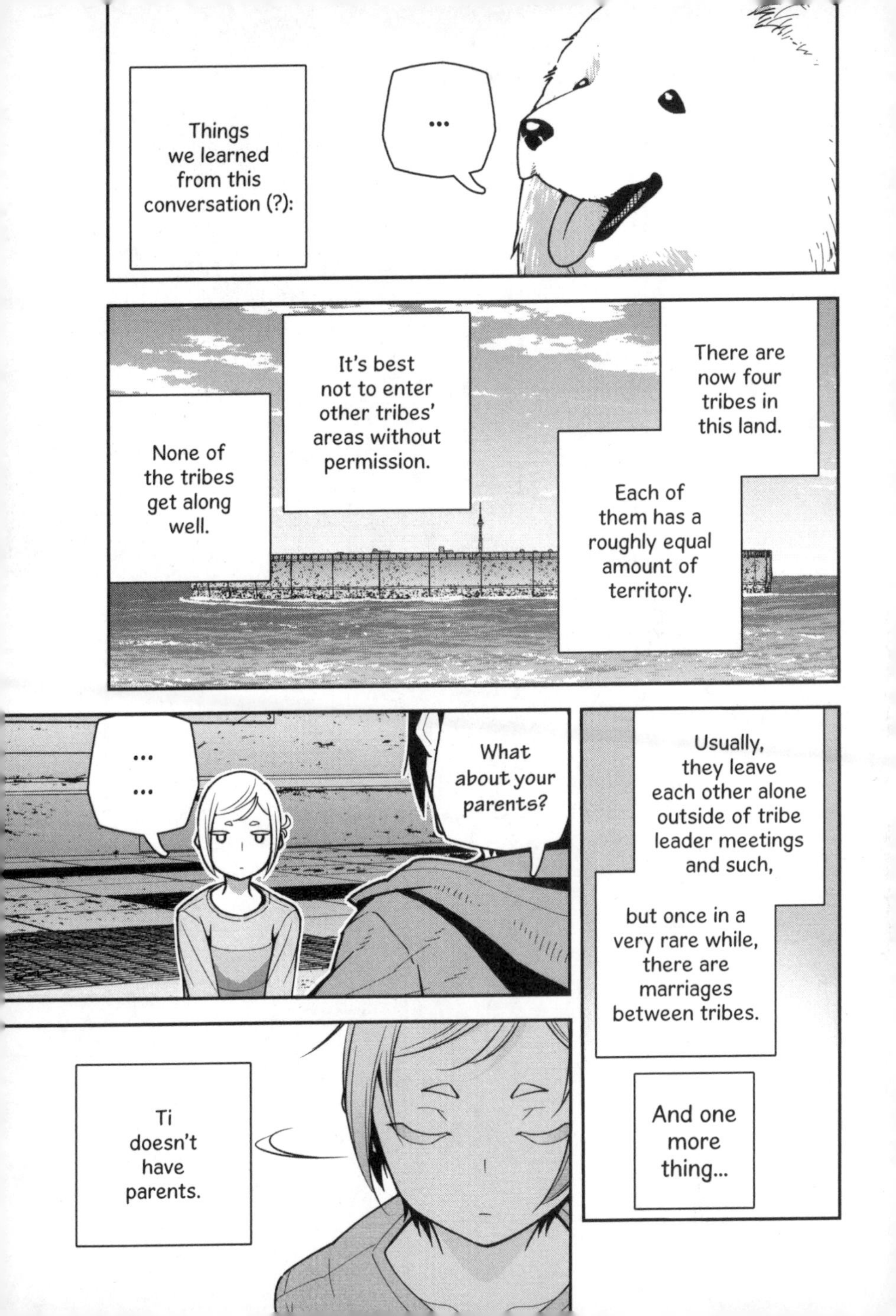
...
Things we learned from this conversation (?):
There are now four tribes in this land.
Each of them has a roughly equal amount of territory.
It's best not to enter other tribes' areas without permission.
None of the tribes get along well.
Usually, they leave each other alone outside of tribe leader meetings and such,
but once in a very rare while, there are marriages between tribes.
And one more thing...
What about your parents?
... ...
Ti doesn't have parents.

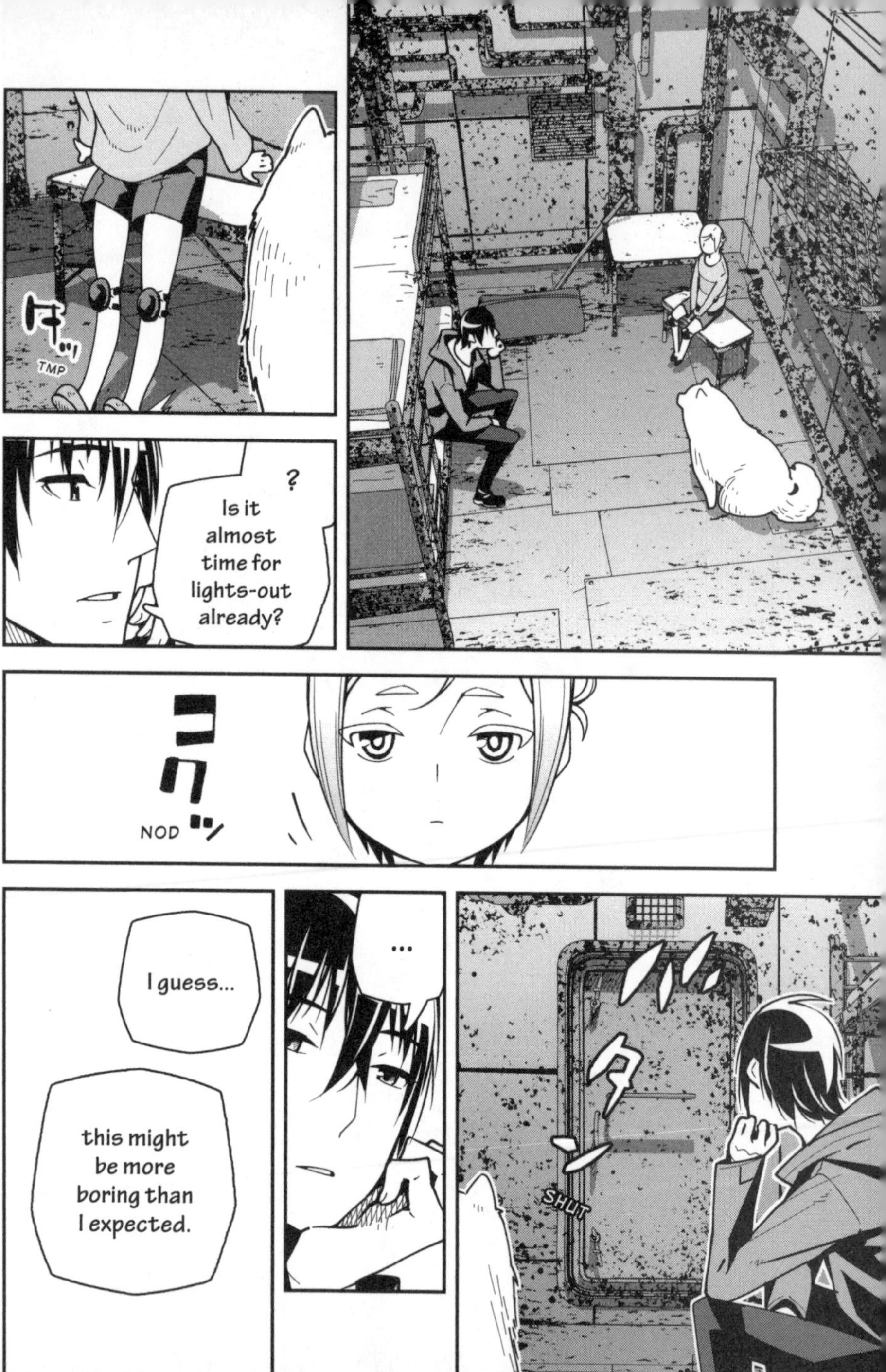
TMP
?
Is it almost time for lights-out already?
NOD
SHUT
...
I guess...
this might be more boring than I expected.

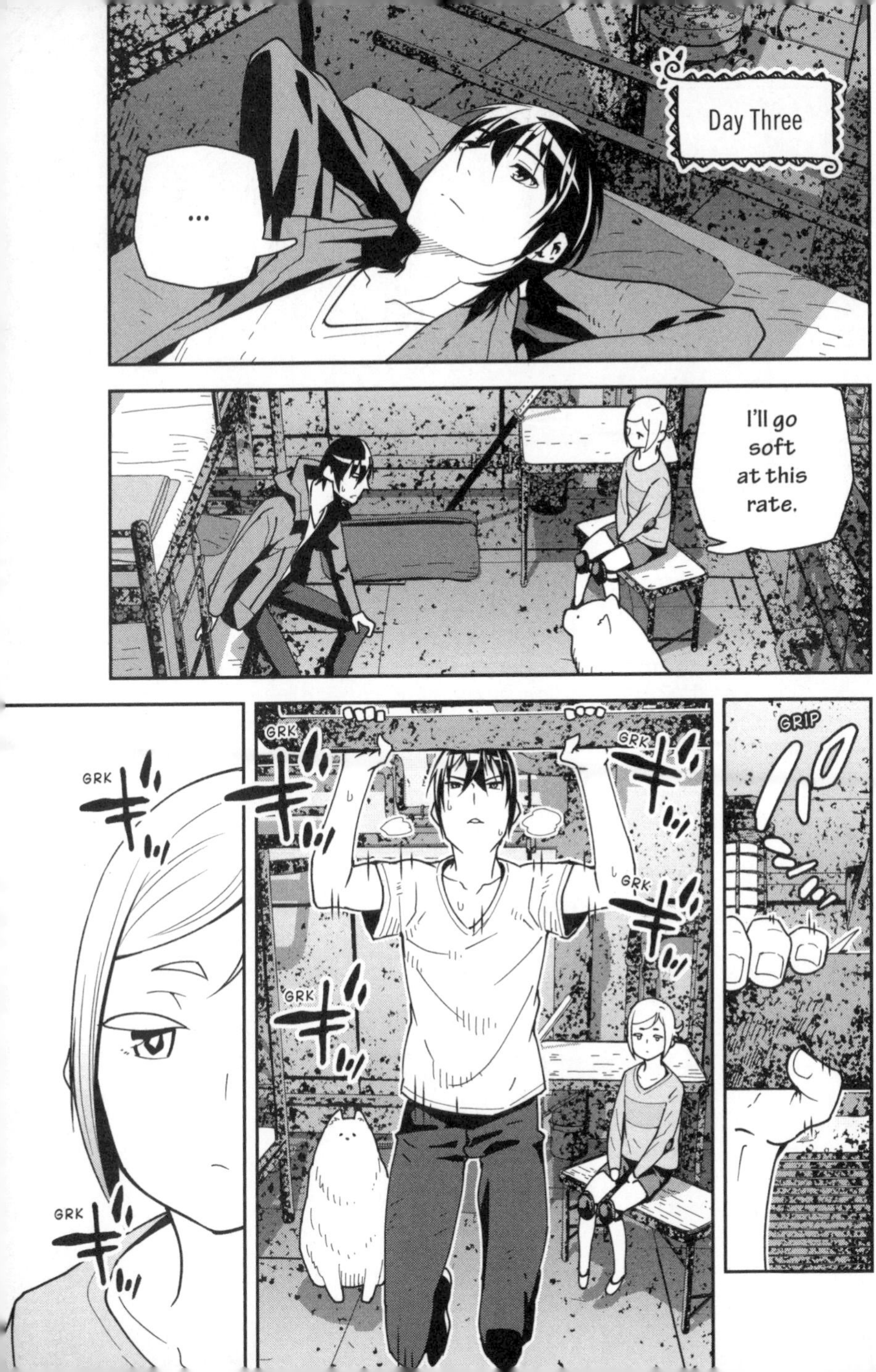
Day Three
...
I'll go soft at this rate.
GRIP
GRK
GRK
GRK
GRK
GRK
GRK

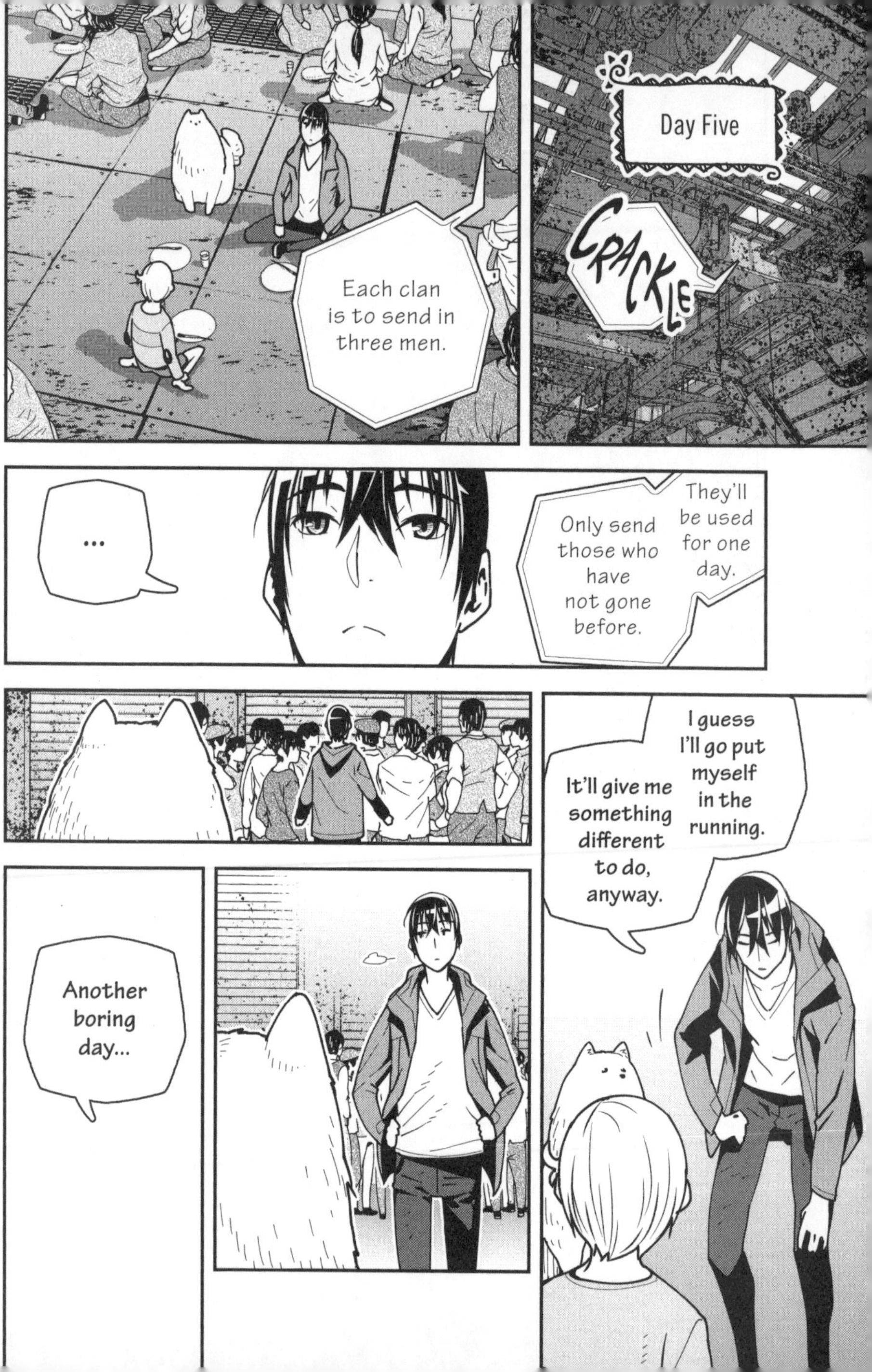
Day Five
CRACKLE
Each clan is to send in three men.
They'll be used for one day.
Only send those who have not gone before.
...
I guess I'll go put myself in the running.
It'll give me something different to do, anyway.
Another boring day...

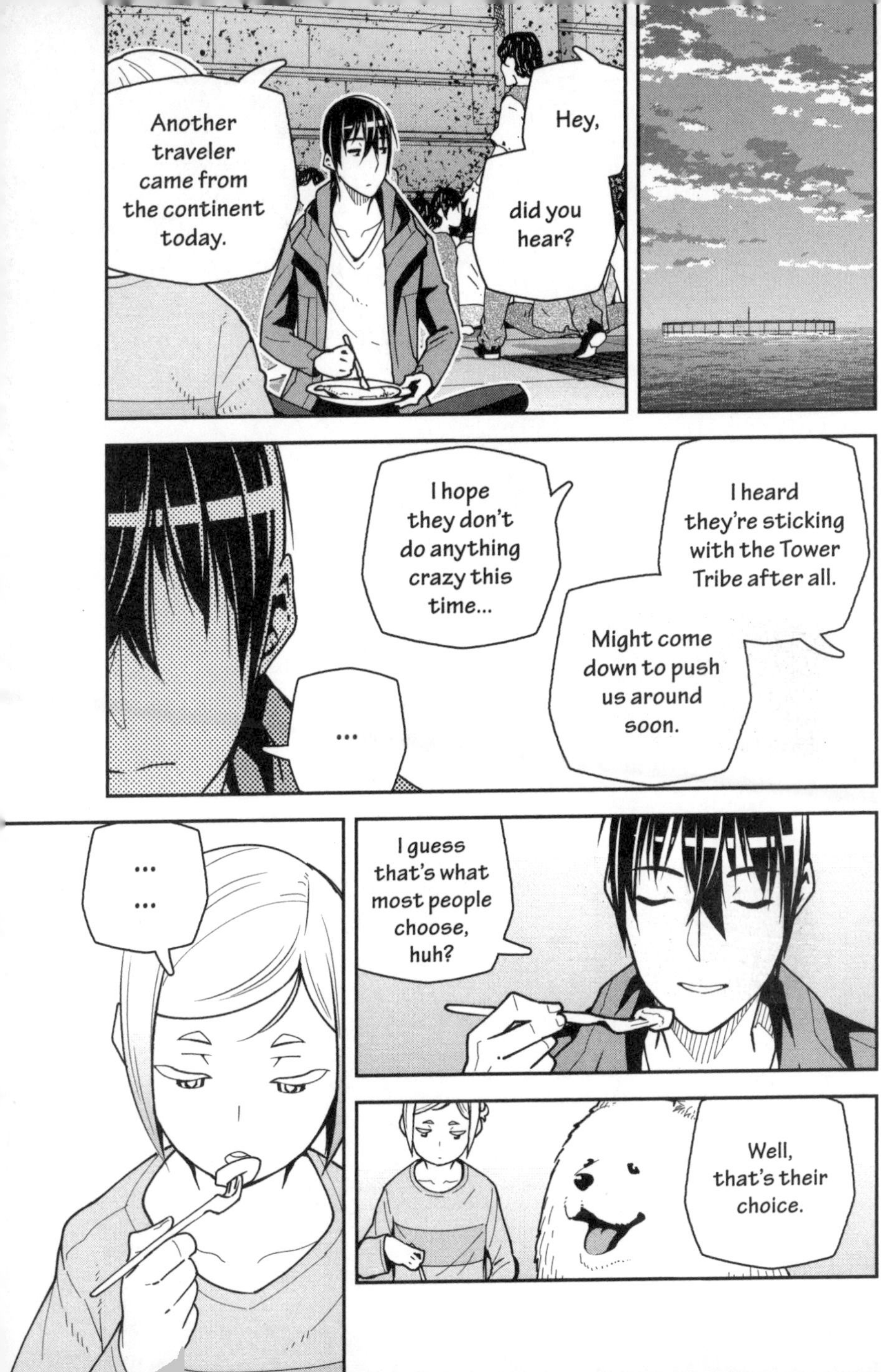
Hey,
did you hear?
Another traveler came from the continent today.
I heard they're sticking with the Tower Tribe after all.
Might come down to push us around soon.
I hope they don't do anything crazy this time...
...
I guess that's what most people choose, huh?
Well, that's their choice.
...
...

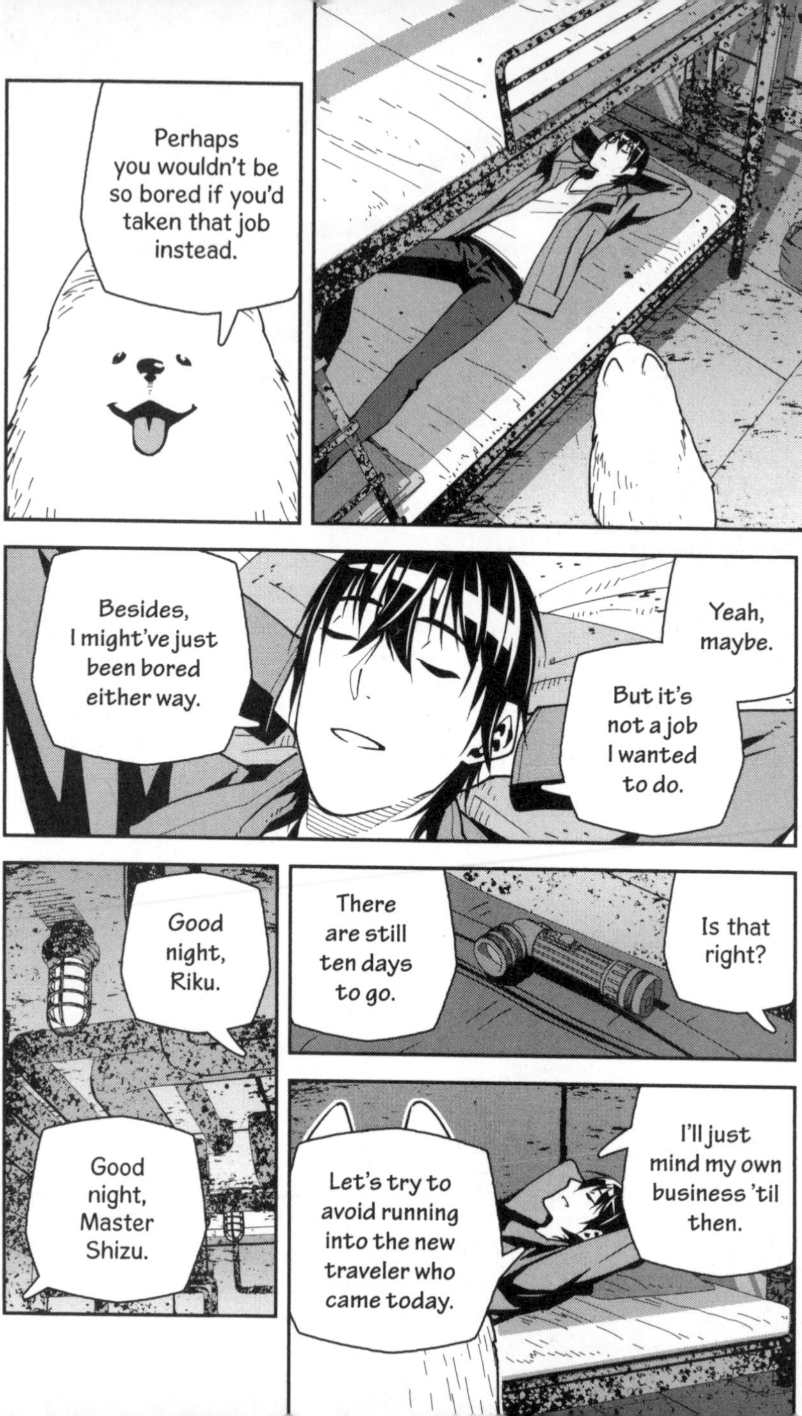
Perhaps you wouldn't be so bored if you'd taken that job instead.
Yeah, maybe.
But it's not a job I wanted to do.
Besides, I might've just been bored either way.
Is that right?
There are still ten days to go.
I'll just mind my own business 'til then.
Let's try to avoid running into the new traveler who came today.
Good night, Riku.
Good night, Master Shizu.

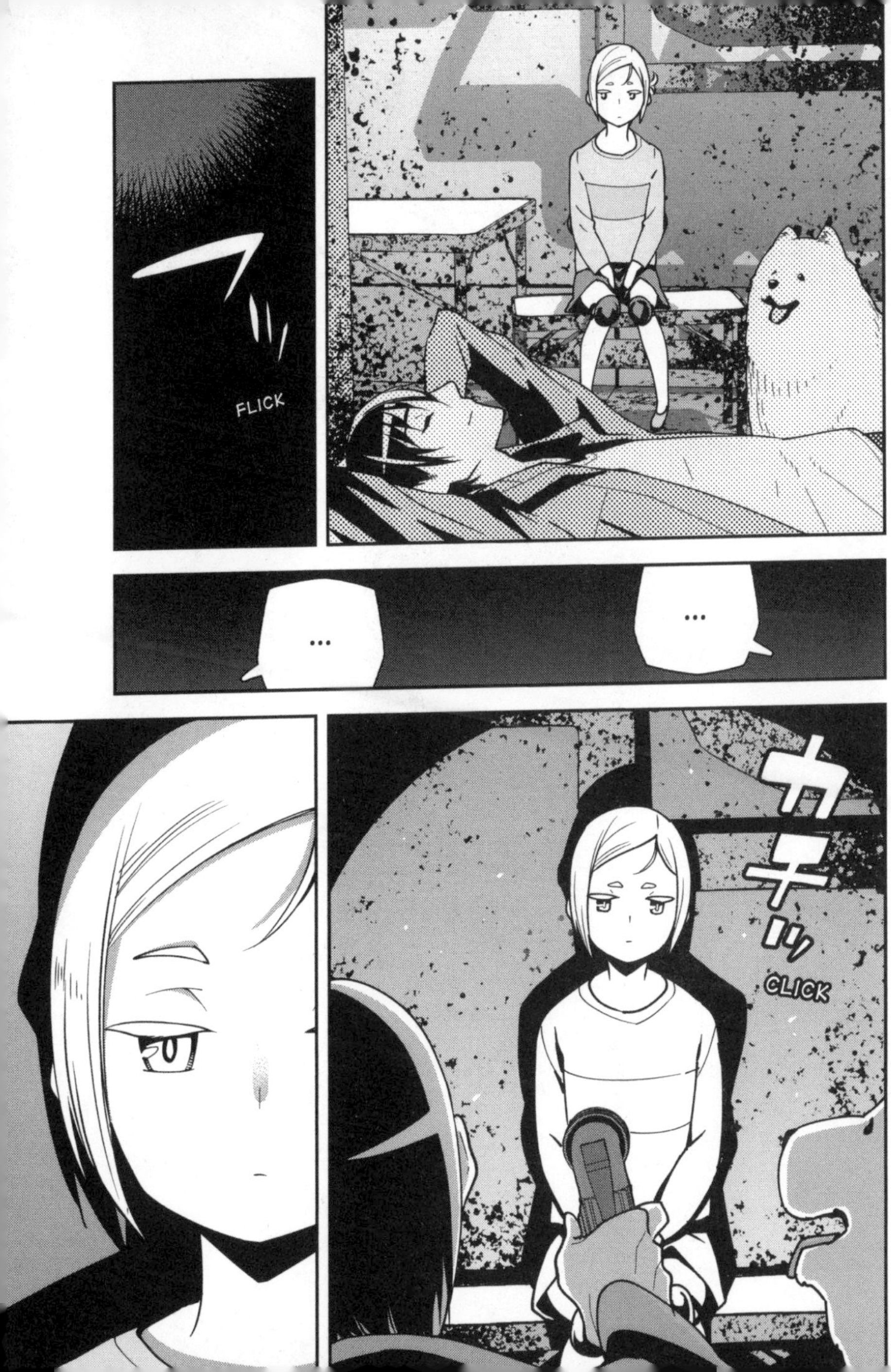
FLICK
...
...
カチッ
CLICK

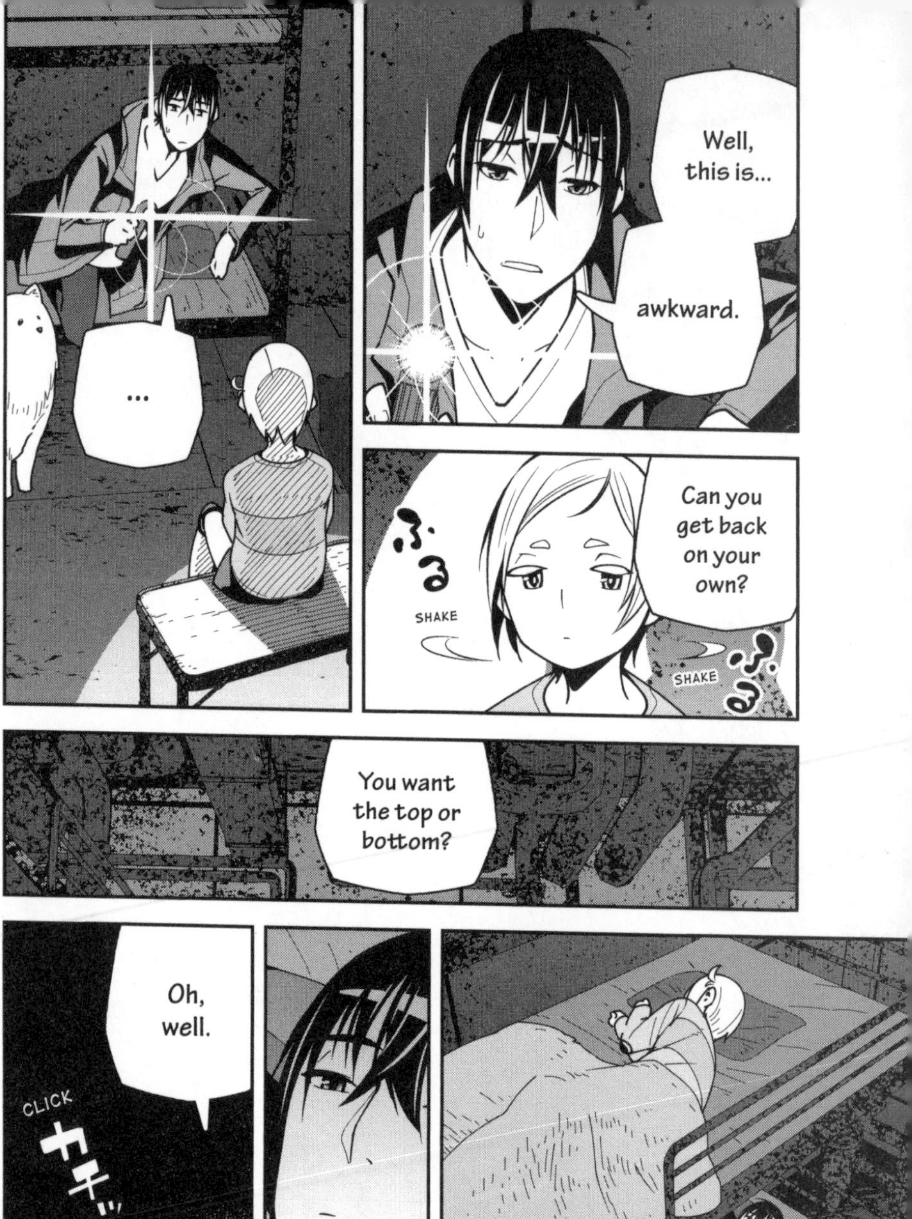
Well, this is...
awkward.
Can you get back on your own?
ふる
SHAKE
SHAKE
ふる
...
You want the top or bottom?
Oh, well.
CLICK
カチッ

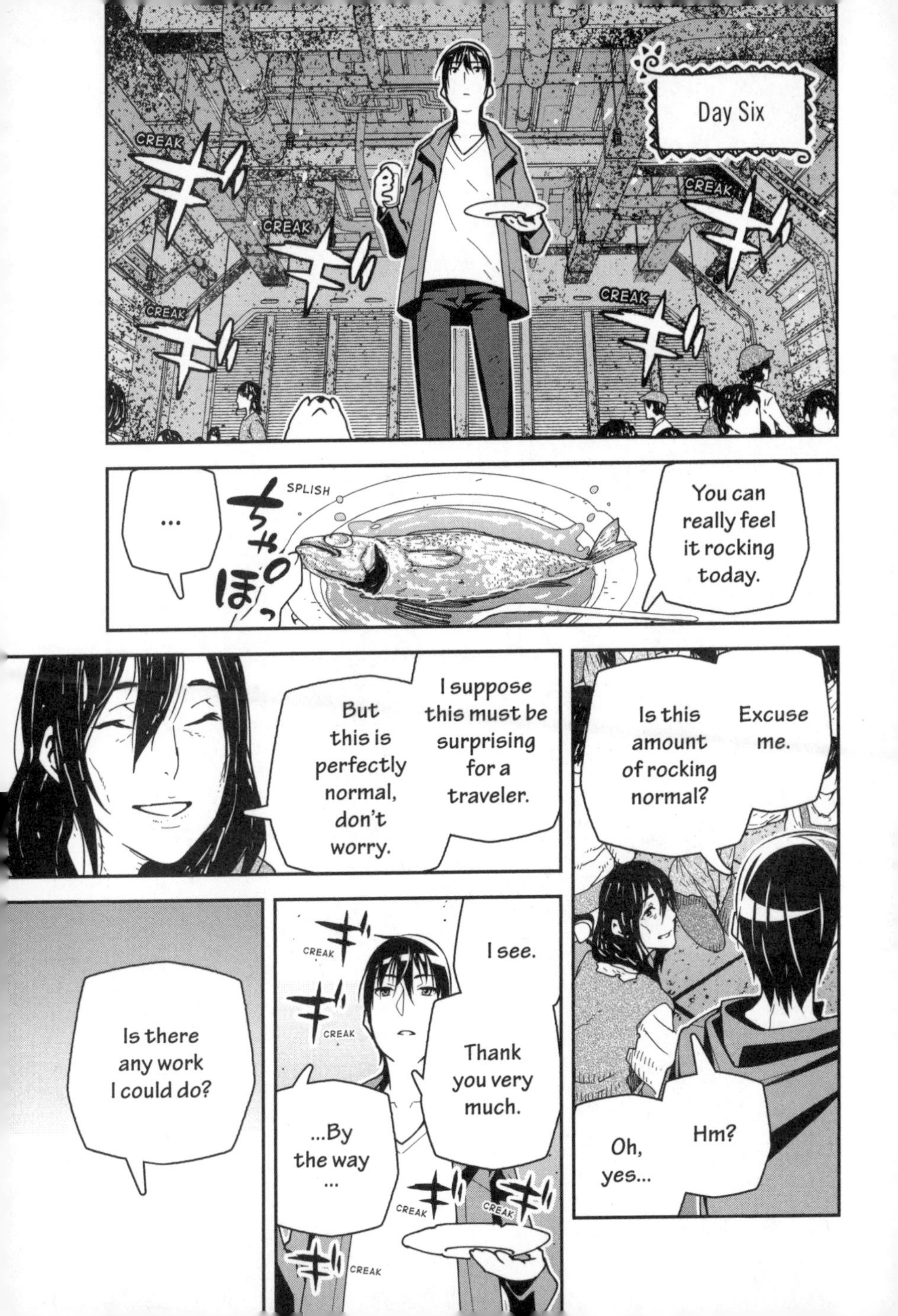
Day Six
CREAK
CREAK
CREAK
CREAK
CREAK
You can really feel it rocking today.
SPLISH
ちゃぽっ
...
Excuse me.
Is this amount of rocking normal?
Hm?
Oh, yes...
I suppose this must be surprising for a traveler.
But this is perfectly normal, don't worry.
I see.
Thank you very much.
CREAK
CREAK
...By the way...
CREAK
CREAK
CREAK
Is there any work I could do?

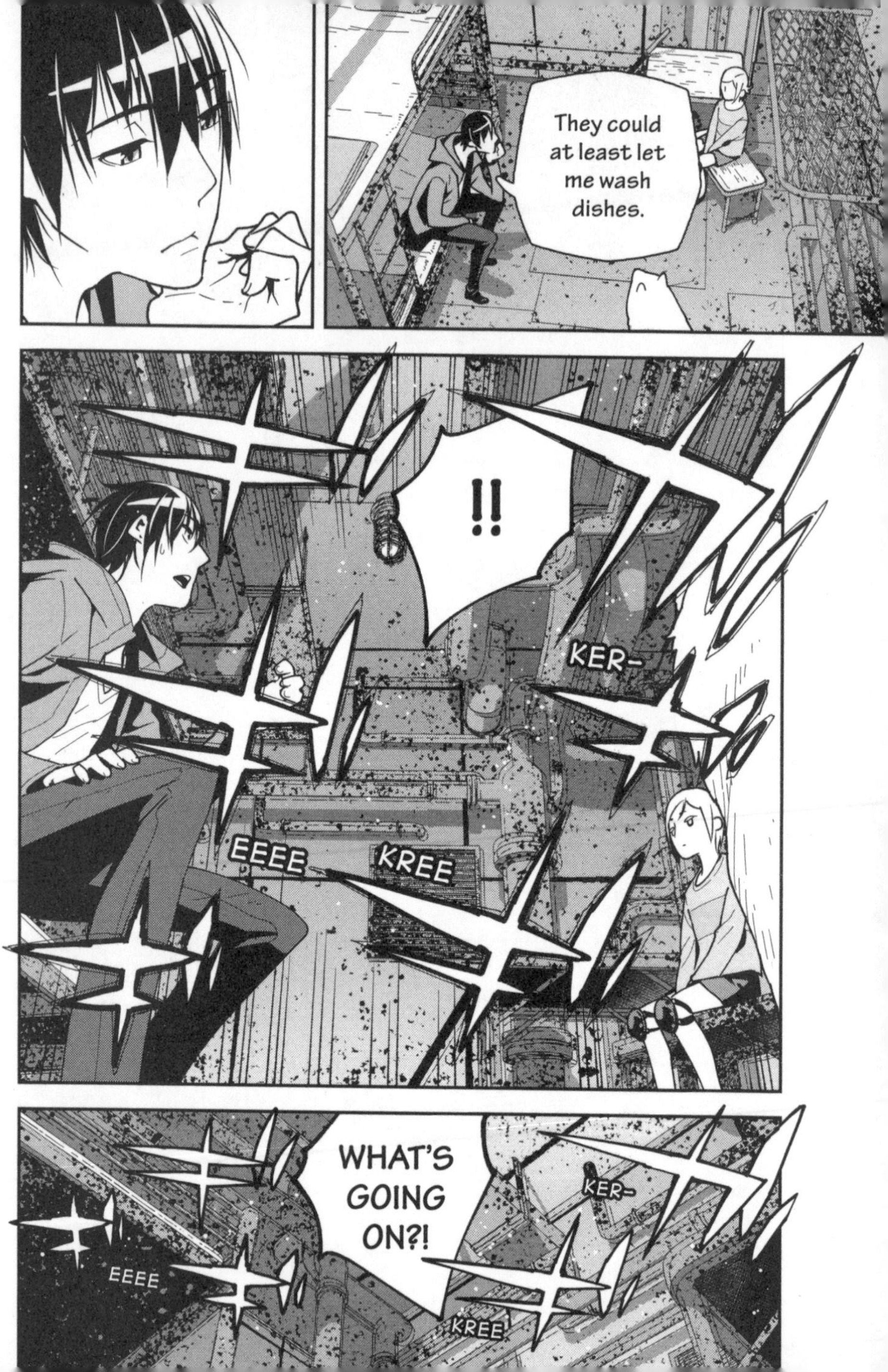
They could at least let me wash dishes.
!!
KER-
KREE
EEEE
WHAT'S GOING ON?!
KER-
KREE
EEEE

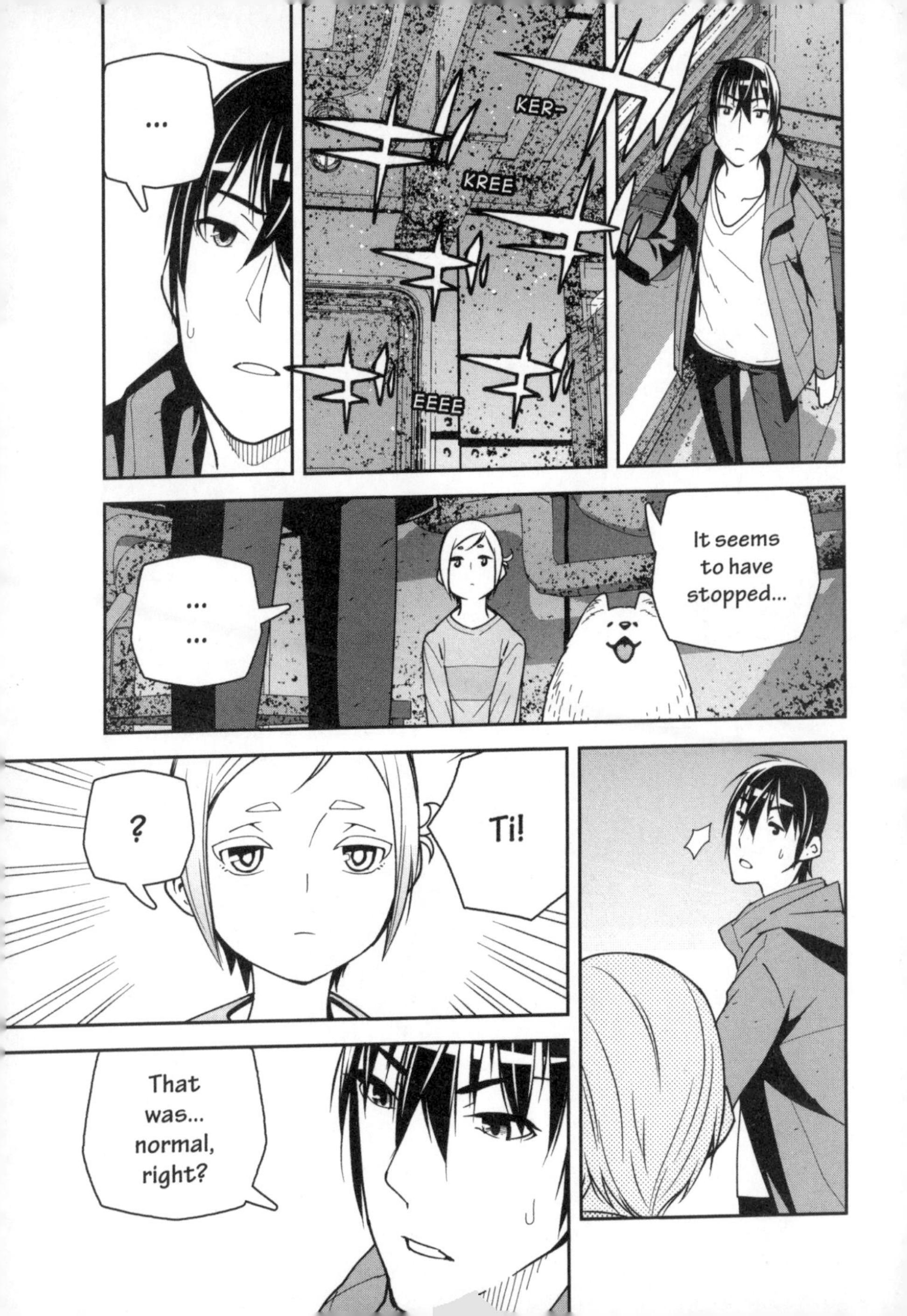
KER-
KREE
EEEE
...
It seems to have stopped...
... ...
Ti!
?
That was... normal, right?

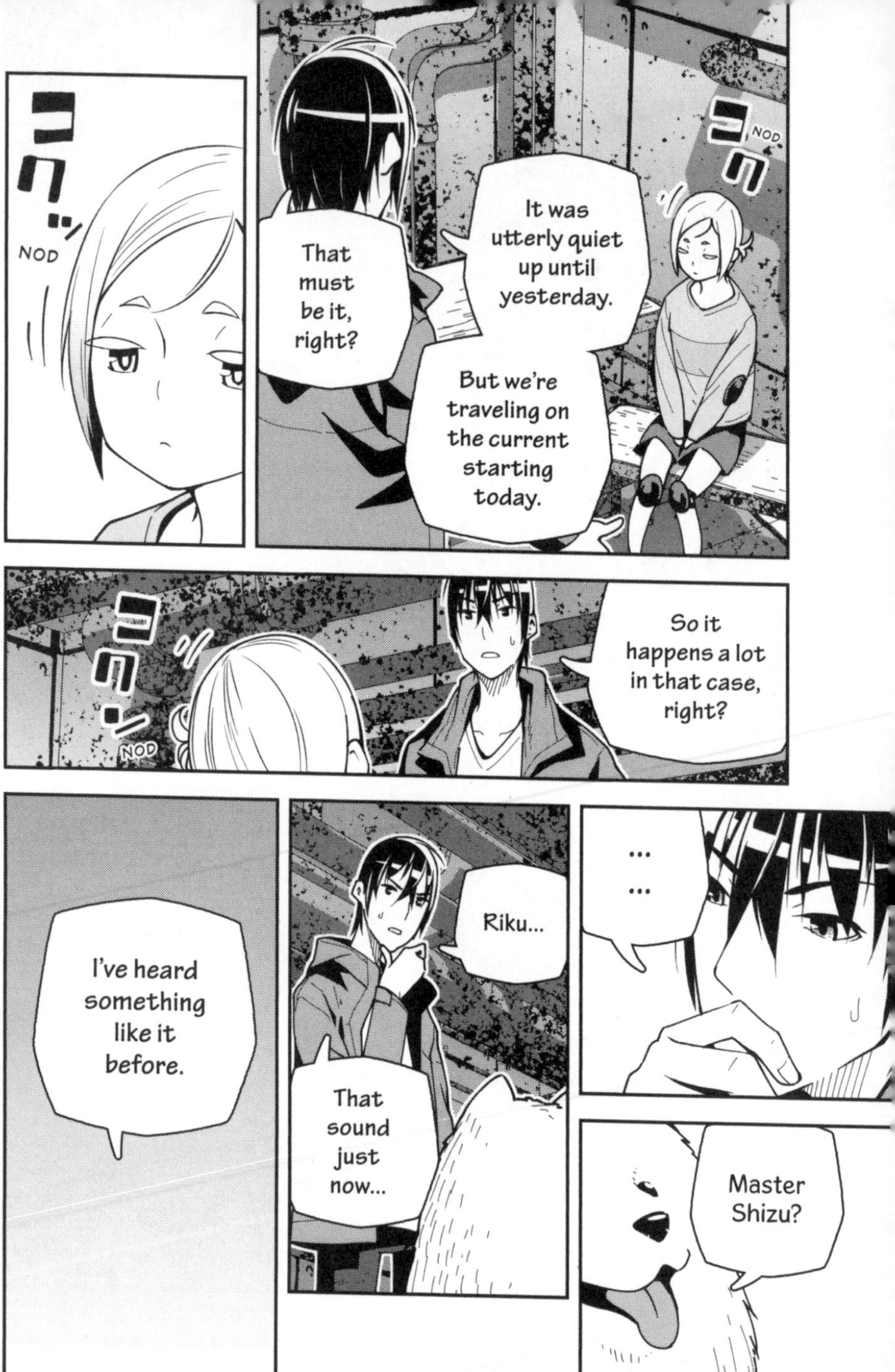
NOD
It was utterly quiet up until yesterday.
But we're traveling on the current starting today.
That must be it, right?
NOD
So it happens a lot in that case, right?
NOD
…
…
Master Shizu?
Riku...
That sound just now...
I've heard something like it before.

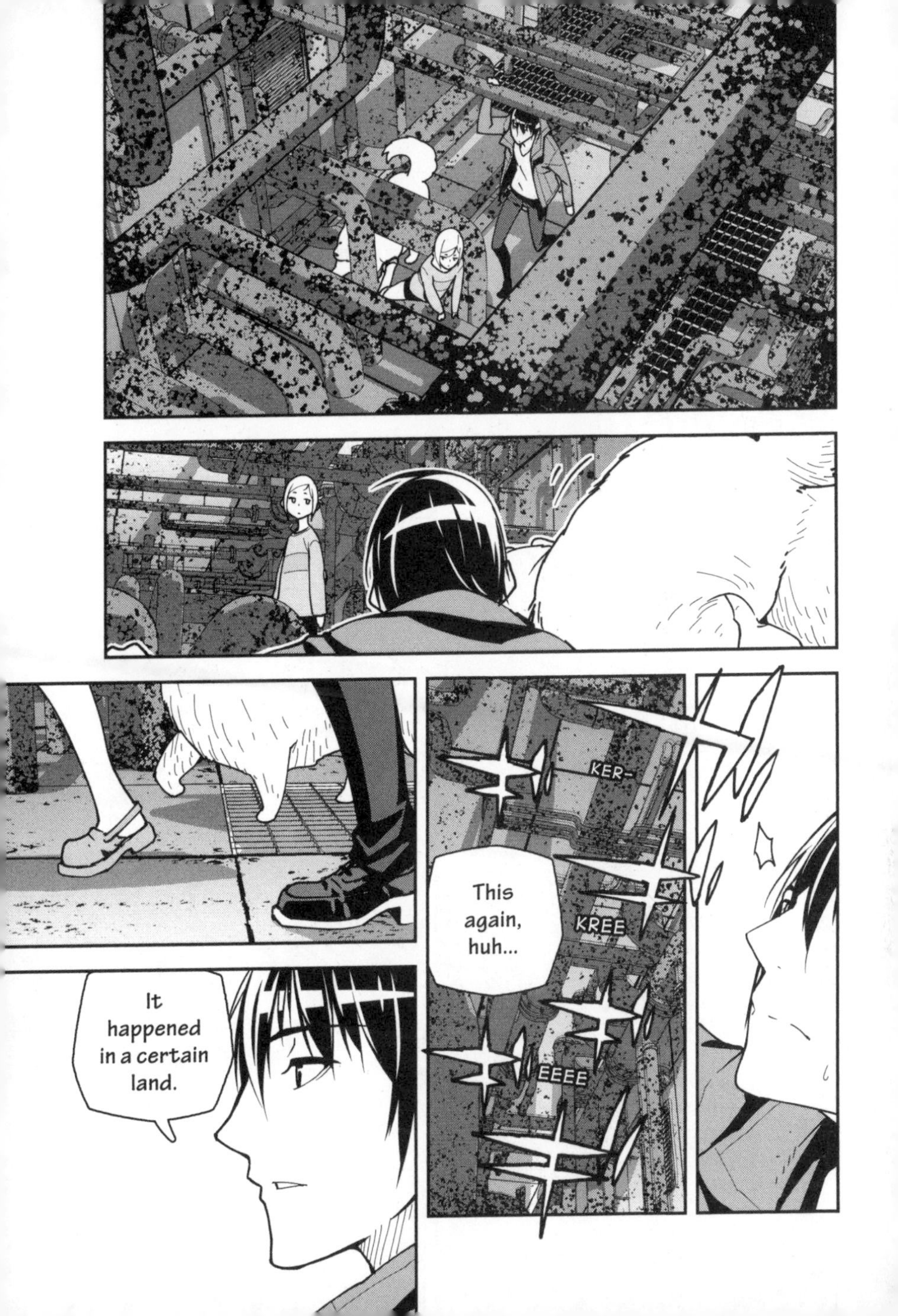
KER-
KREE
EEEE
This again, huh...
It happened in a certain land.

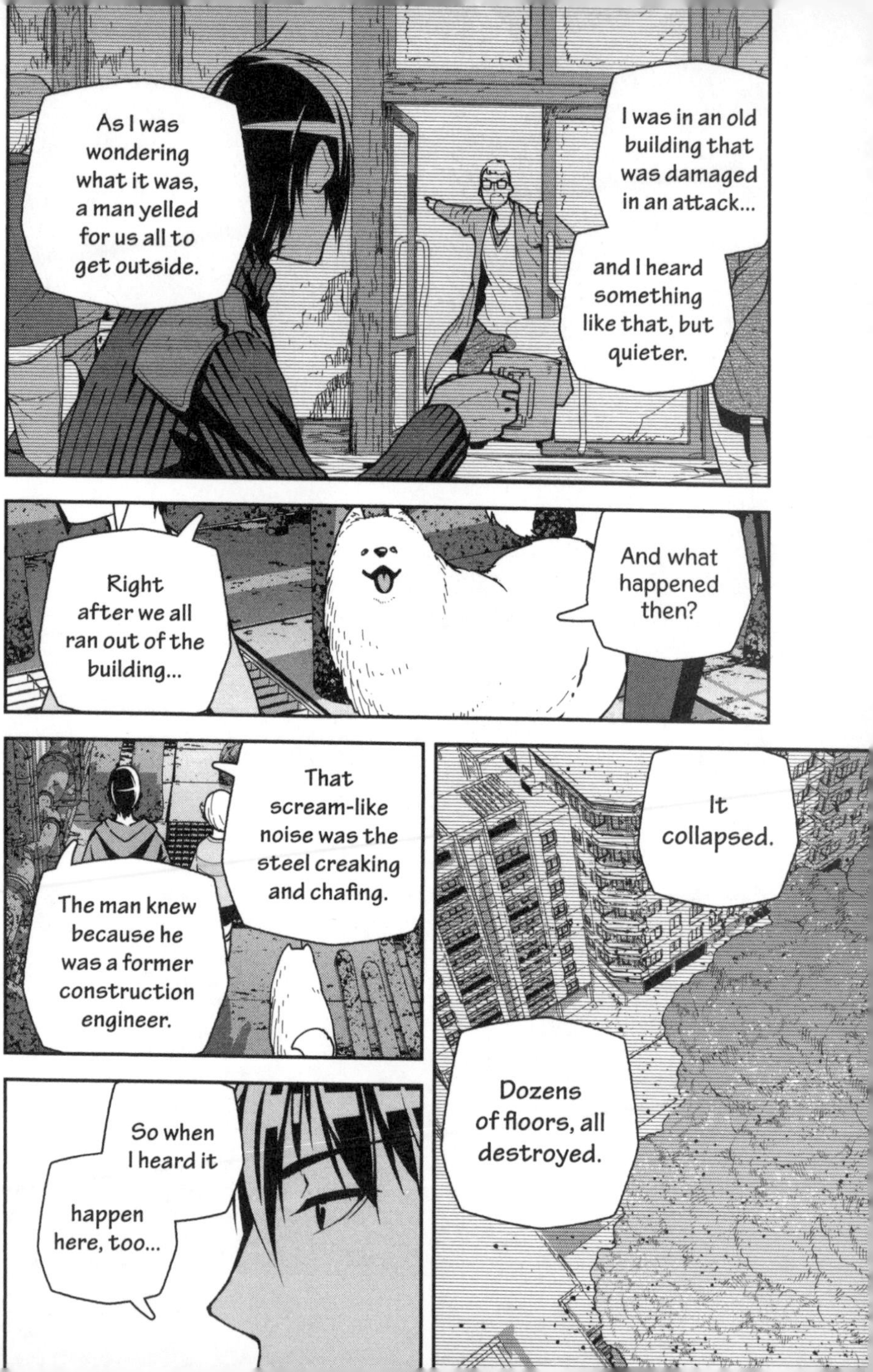
I was in an old building that was damaged in an attack...
and I heard something like that, but quieter.
As I was wondering what it was, a man yelled for us all to get outside.
And what happened then?
Right after we all ran out of the building...
It collapsed.
Dozens of floors, all destroyed.
That scream-like noise was the steel creaking and chafing.
The man knew because he was a former construction engineer.
So when I heard it
happen here, too...

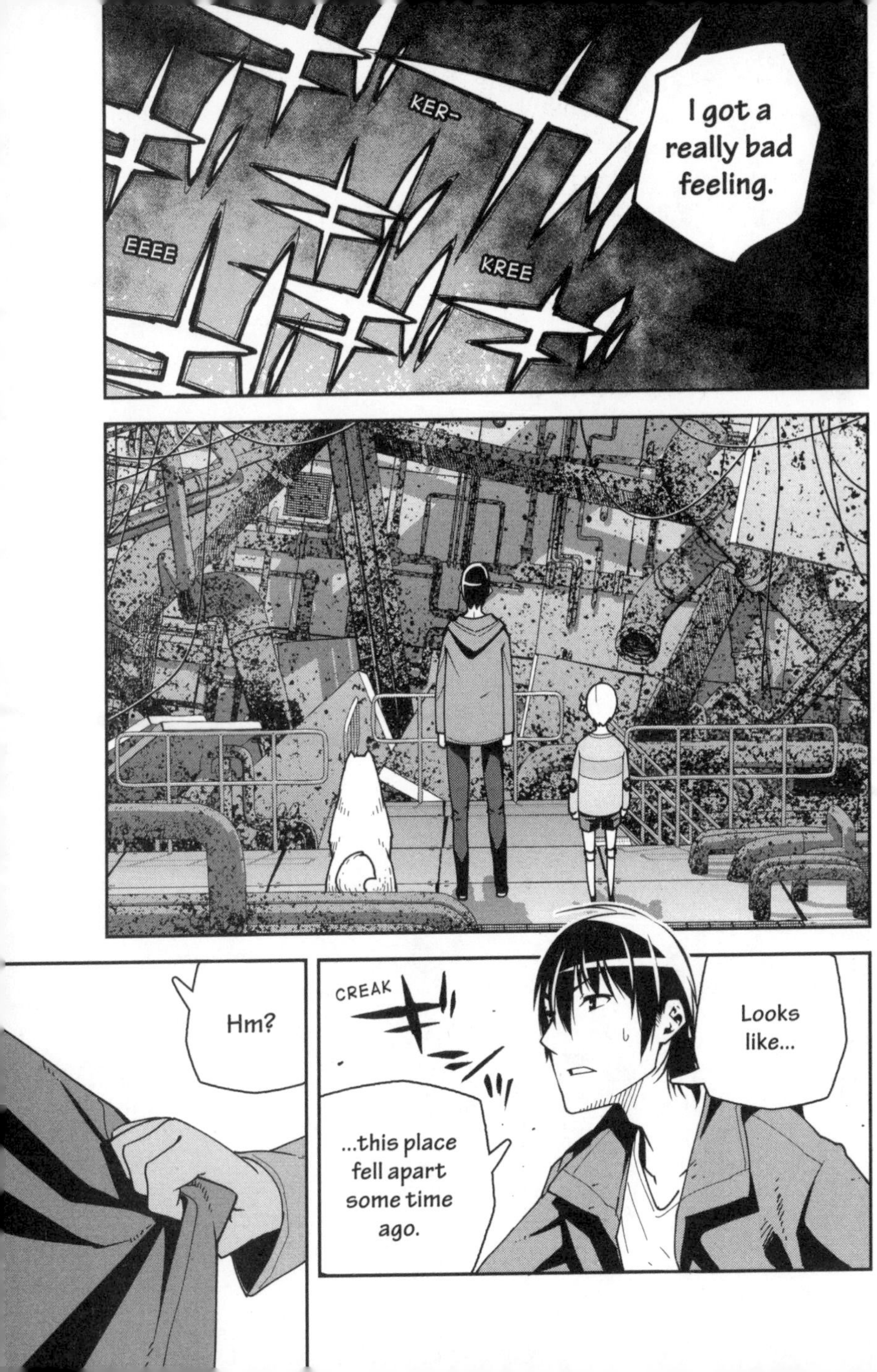
I got a really bad feeling.
KER-
KREE
EEEE
Looks like...
CREAK
...this place fell apart some time ago.
Hm?

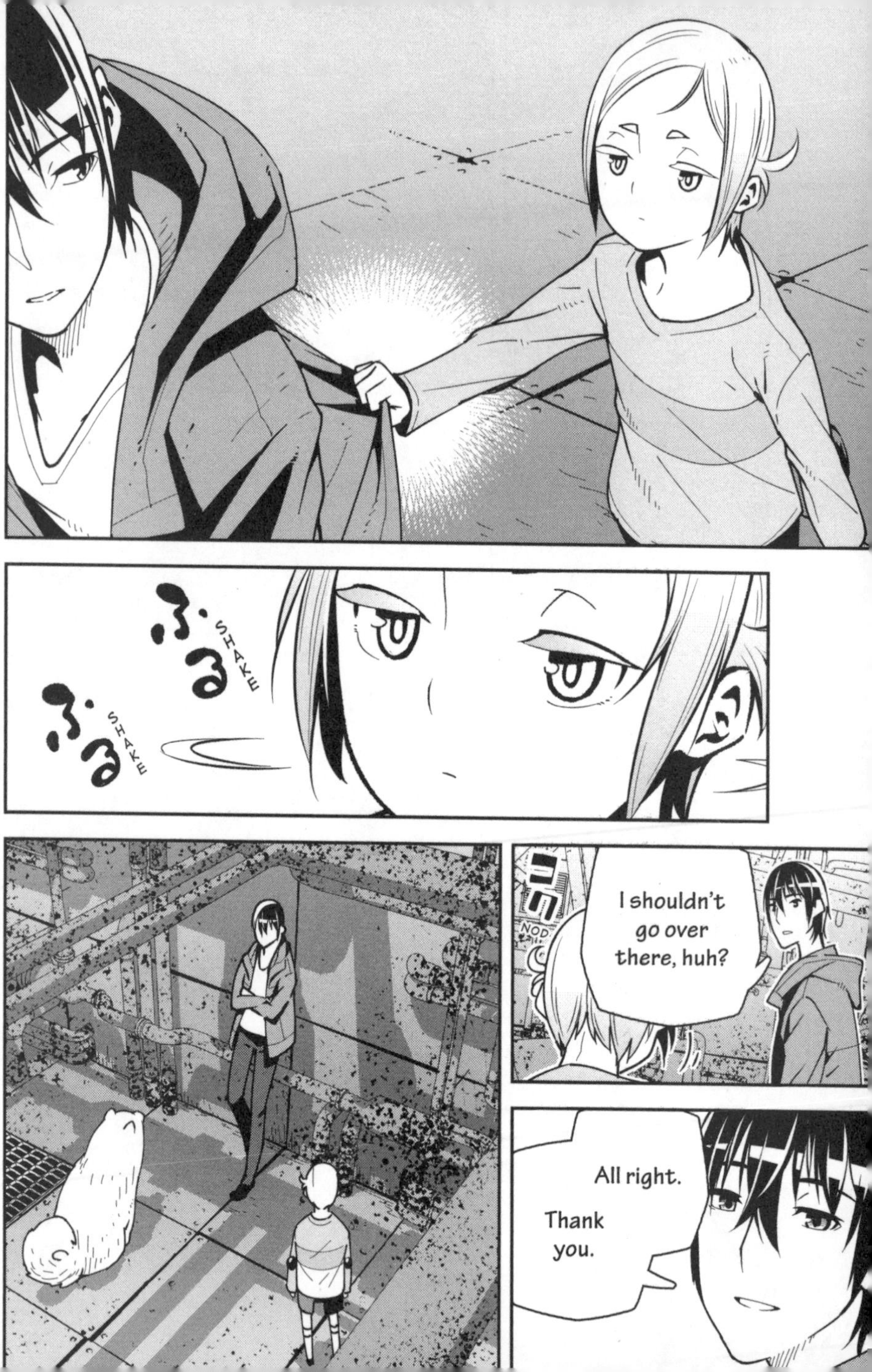
ふる
SHAKE
ふる
SHAKE
NOD
I shouldn't go over there, huh?
All right.
Thank you.

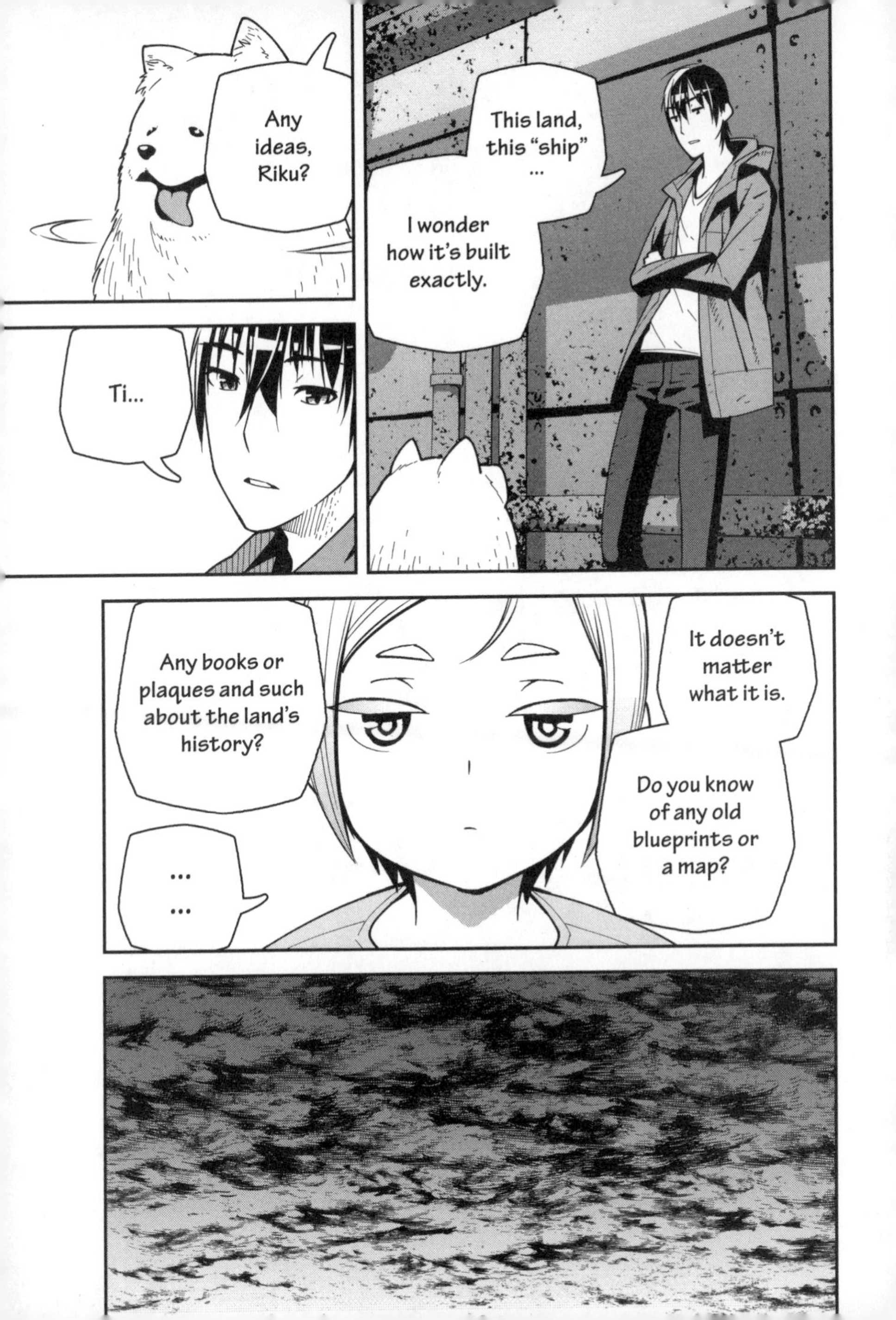
This land, this "ship" ...
I wonder how it's built exactly.
Any ideas, Riku?
Ti...
It doesn't matter what it is.
Do you know of any old blueprints or a map?
Any books or plaques and such about the land's history?
... ...

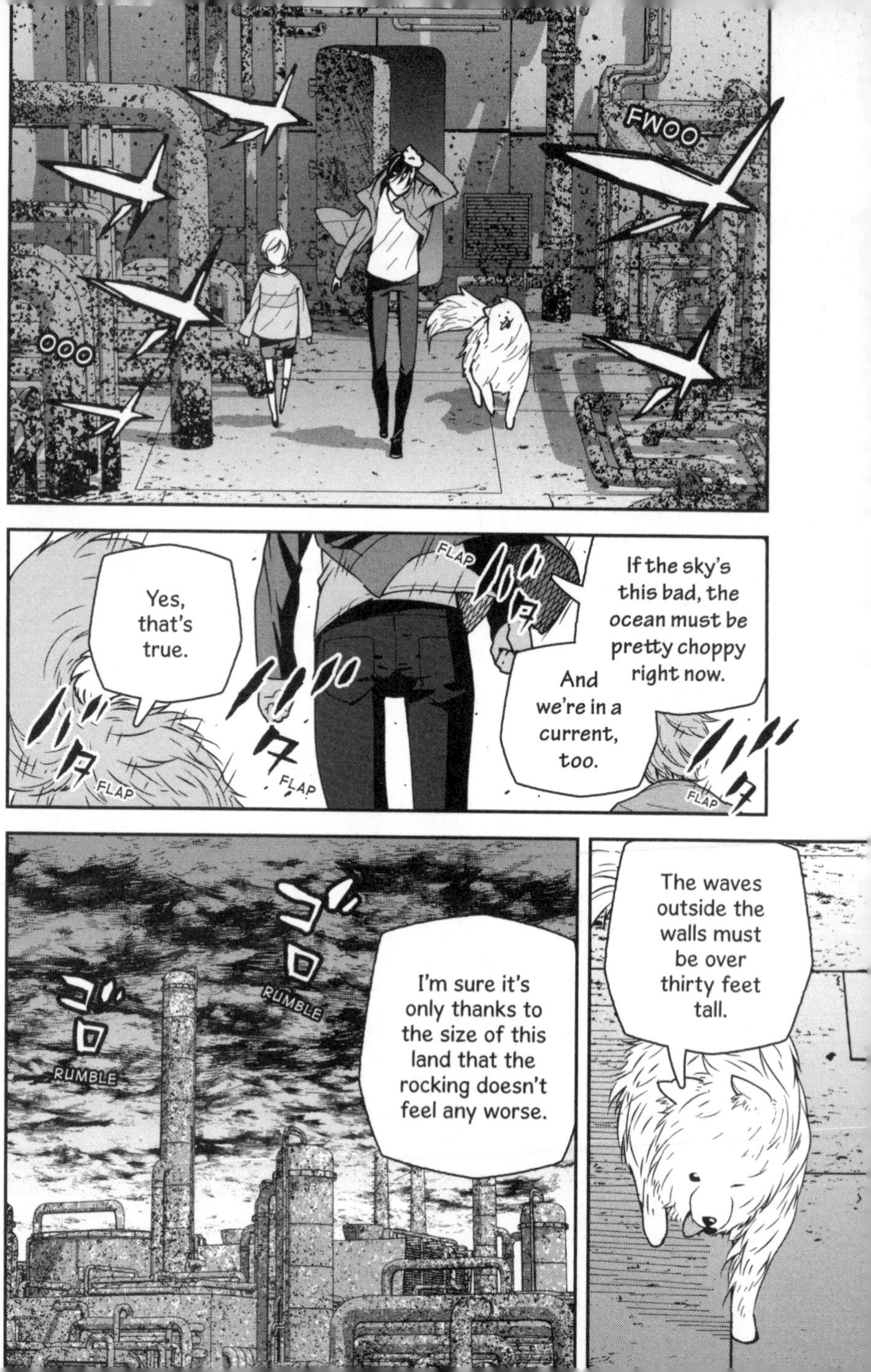
FWOO
OOO
FLAP
If the sky's this bad, the ocean must be pretty choppy right now.
And we're in a current, too.
FLAP
Yes, that's true.
FLAP
FLAP
The waves outside the walls must be over thirty feet tall.
I'm sure it's only thanks to the size of this land that the rocking doesn't feel any worse.
RUMBLE
RUMBLE

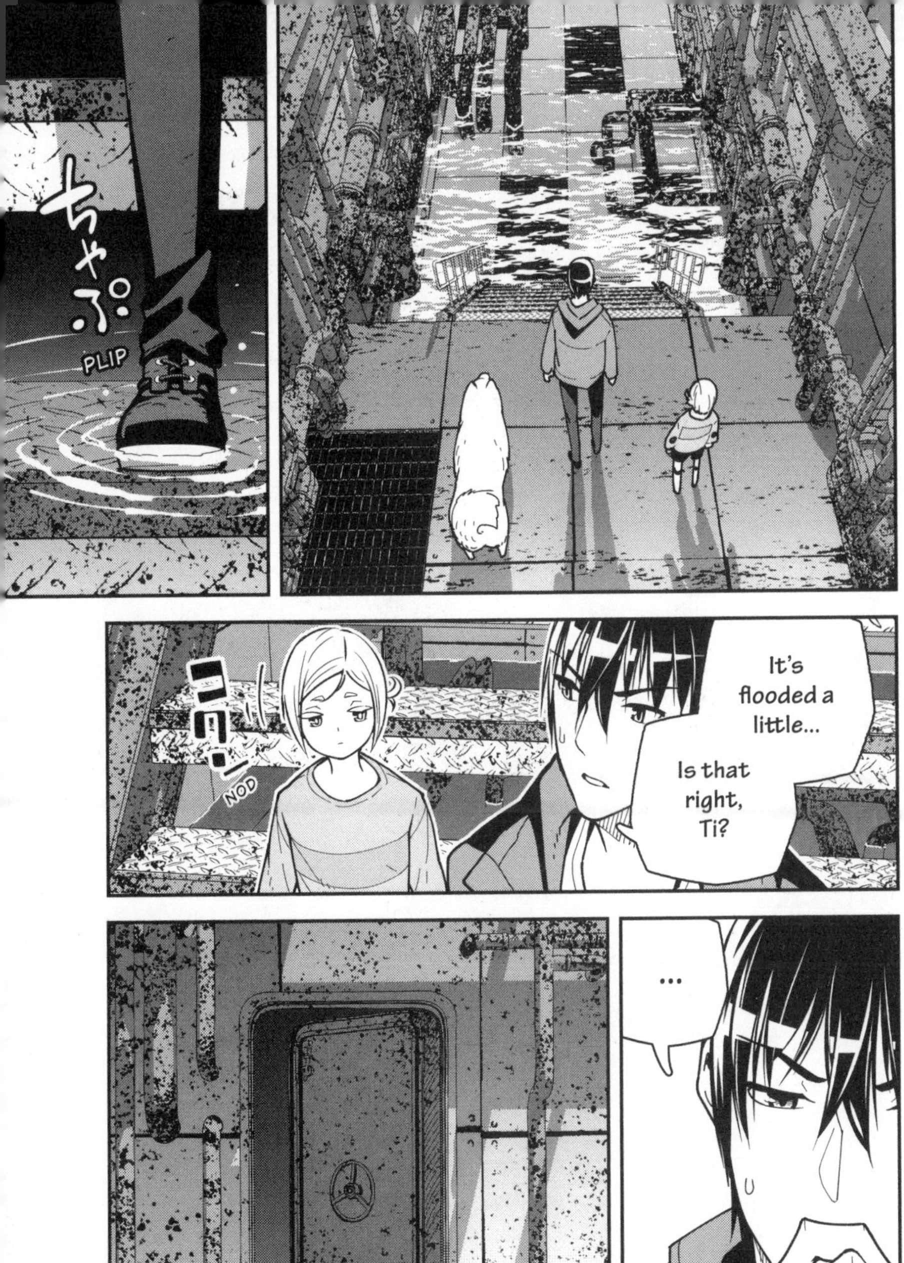
ちゃぷ
PLIP
It's flooded a little...
Is that right, Ti?
コクン
NOD
...

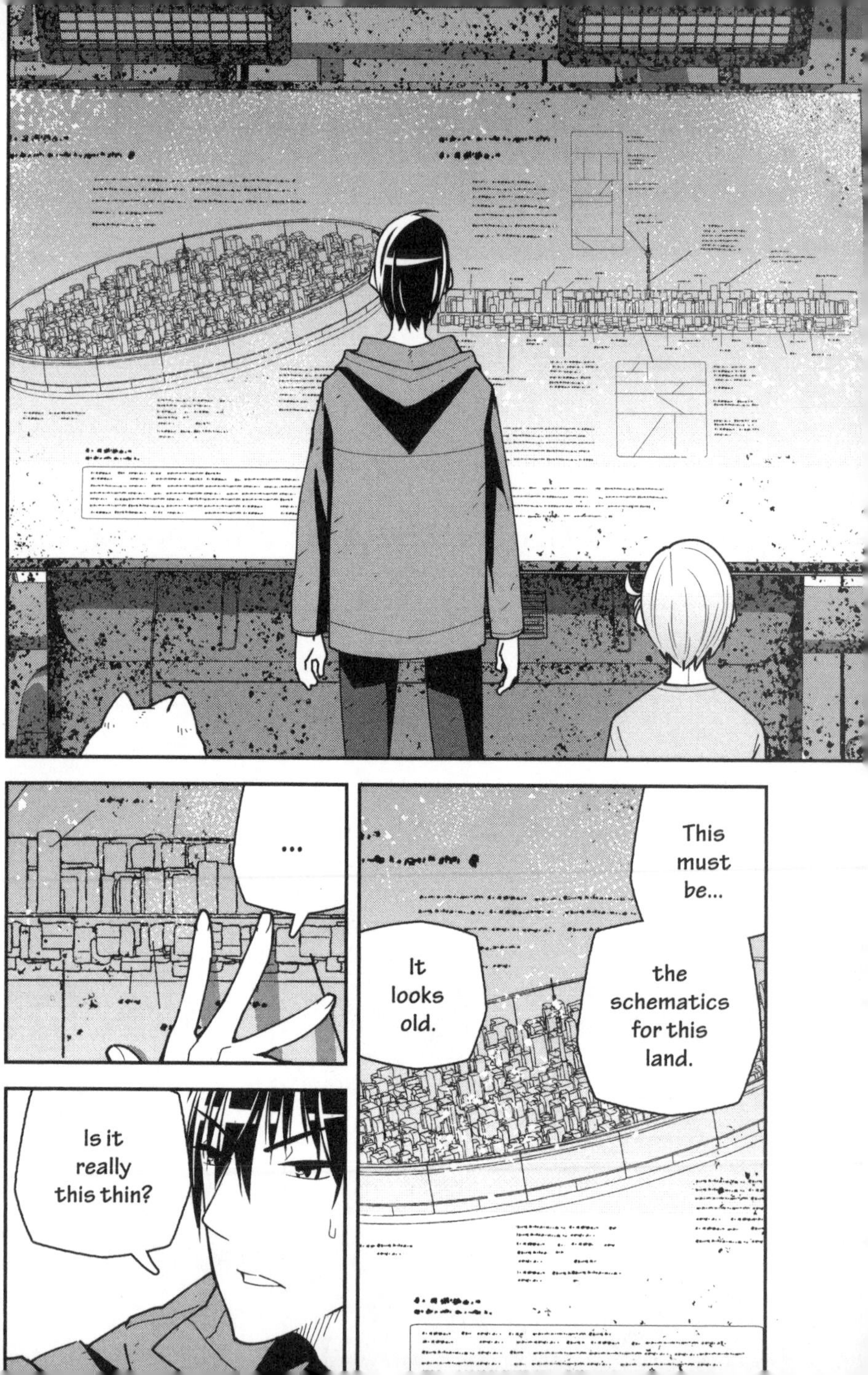
This must be...
the schematics for this land.
It looks old.
...
Is it really this thin?

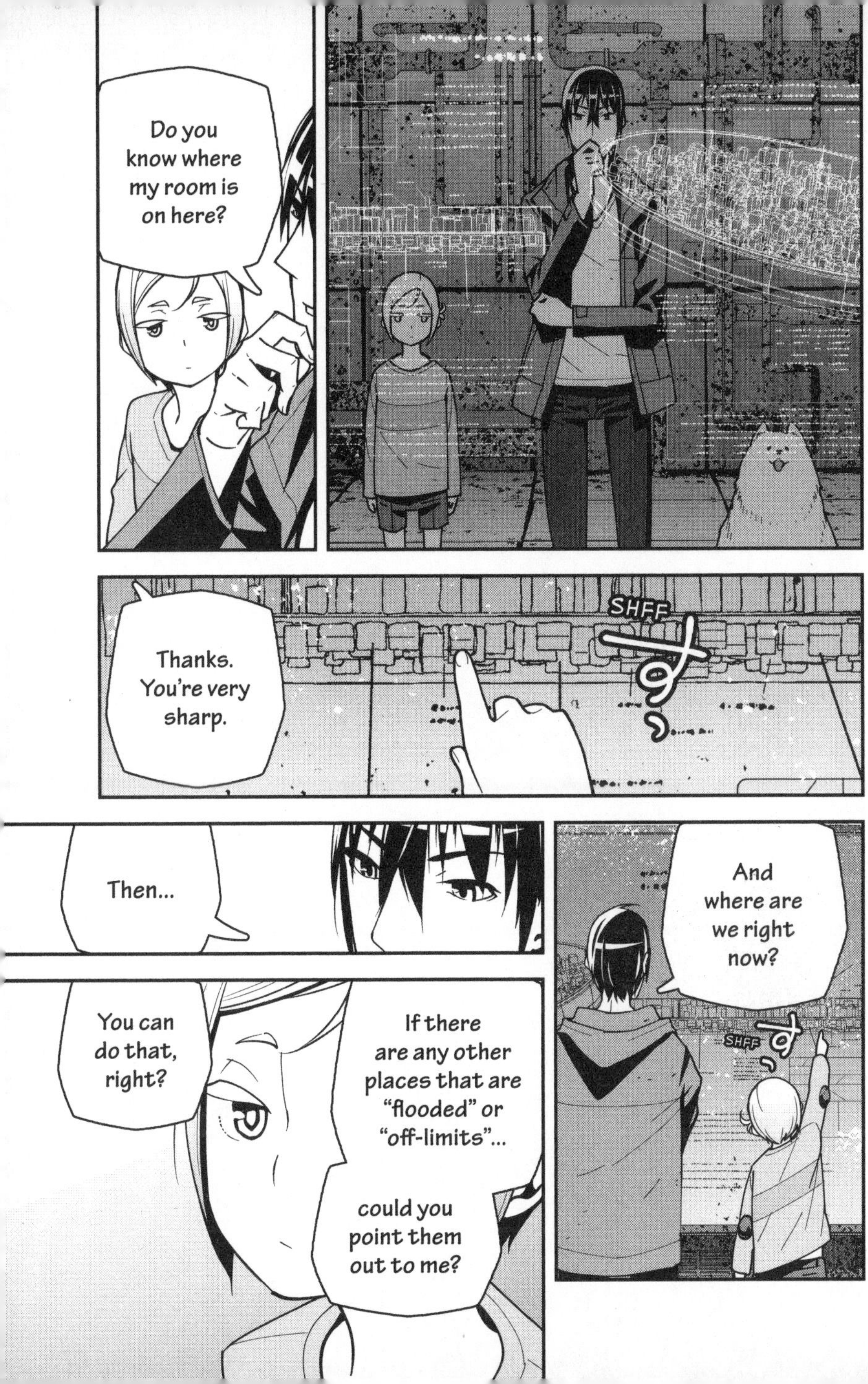
Do you know where my room is on here?
SHFF
Thanks. You're very sharp.
And where are we right now?
SHFF
Then...
If there are any other places that are "flooded" or "off-limits"...
could you point them out to me?
You can do that, right?

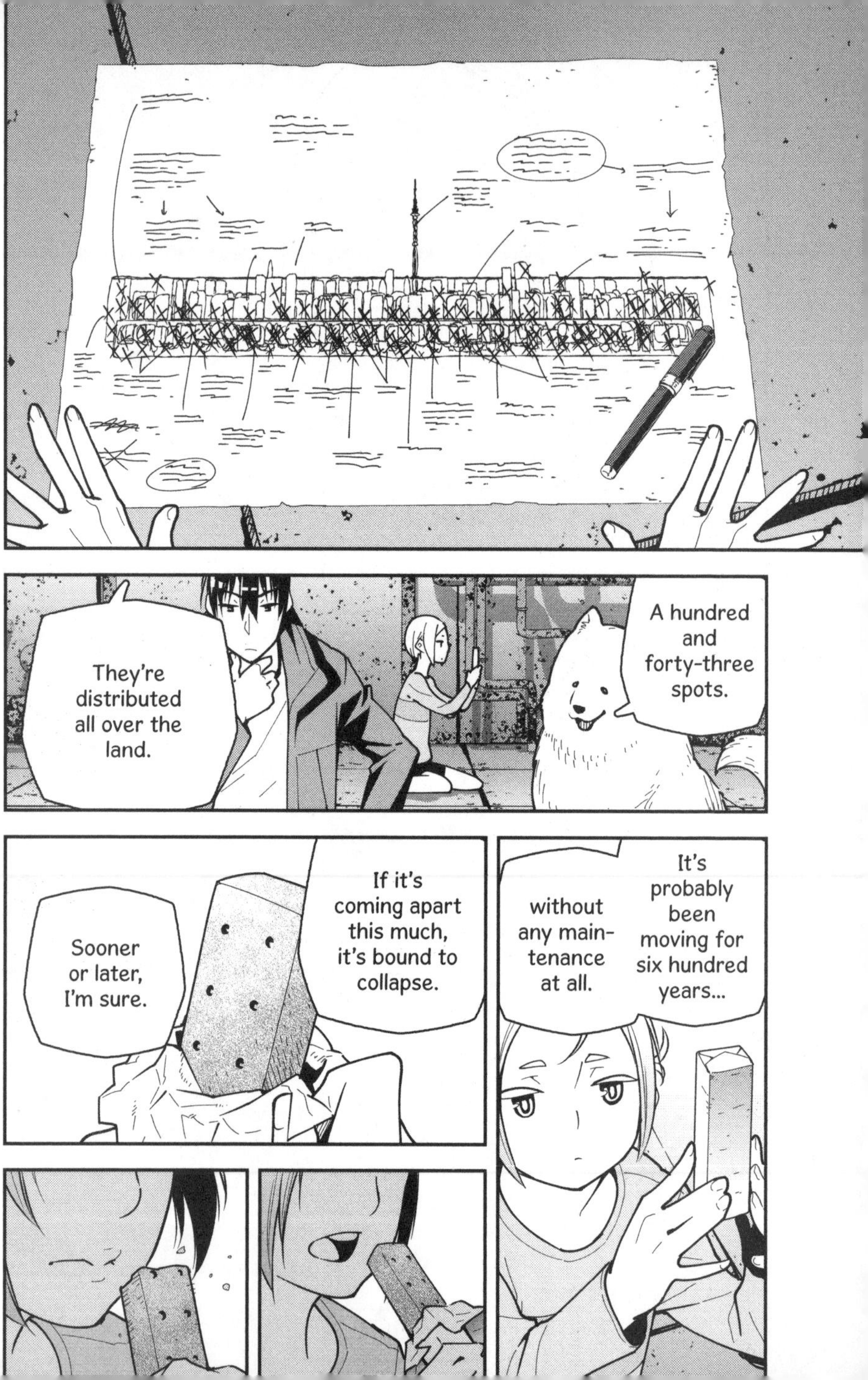
A hundred and forty-three spots.
They're distributed all over the land.
It's probably been moving for six hundred years...
without any maintenance at all.
If it's coming apart this much, it's bound to collapse.
Sooner or later, I'm sure.

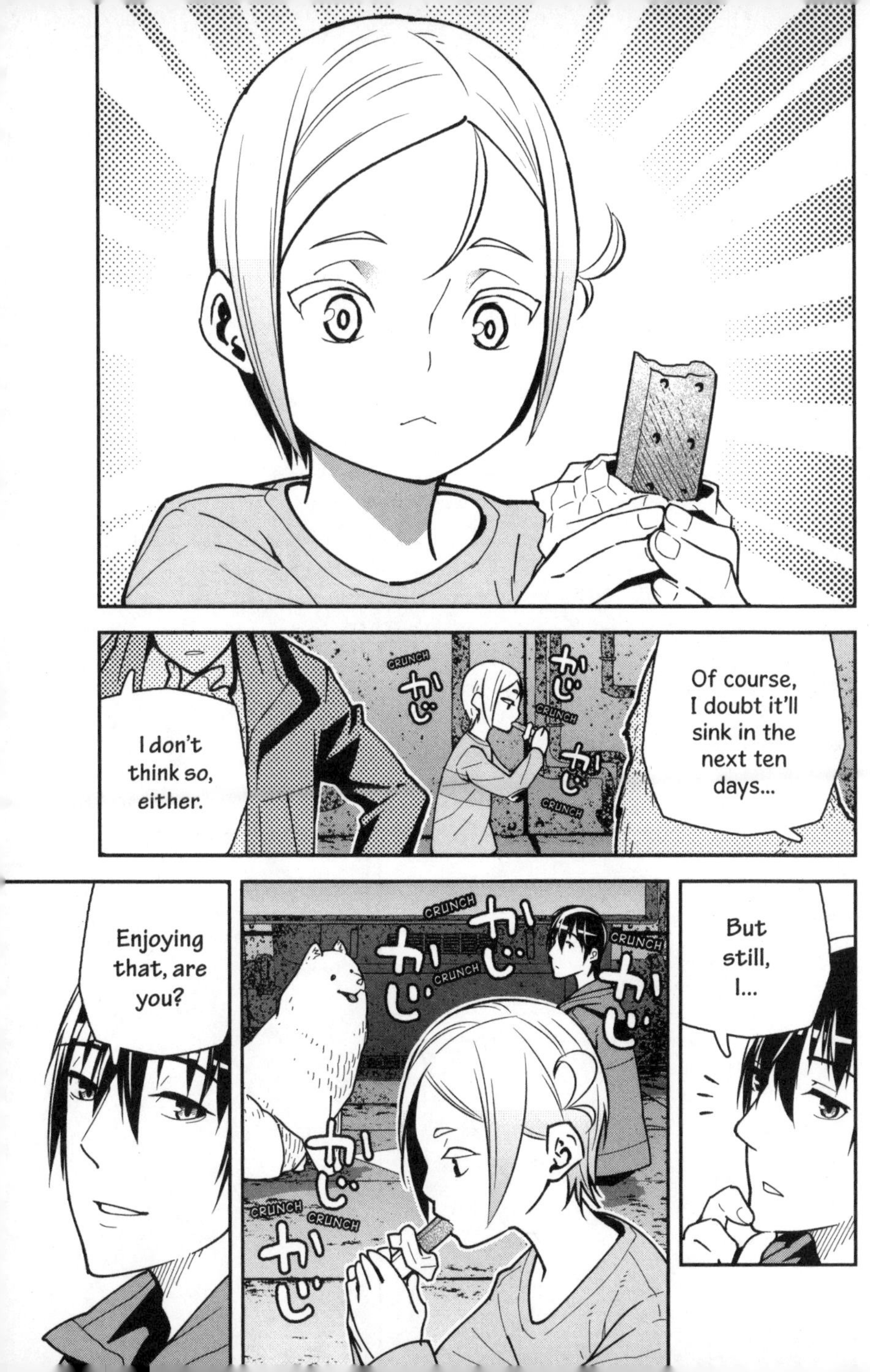

Of course, I doubt it'll sink in the next ten days...
かじ
CRUNCH
かじ
CRUNCH
かじ
CRUNCH
I don't think so, either.
But still, I...
かじ
CRUNCH
かじ
CRUNCH
かじ
CRUNCH
かじ
CRUNCH
かじ
CRUNCH
Enjoying that, are you?

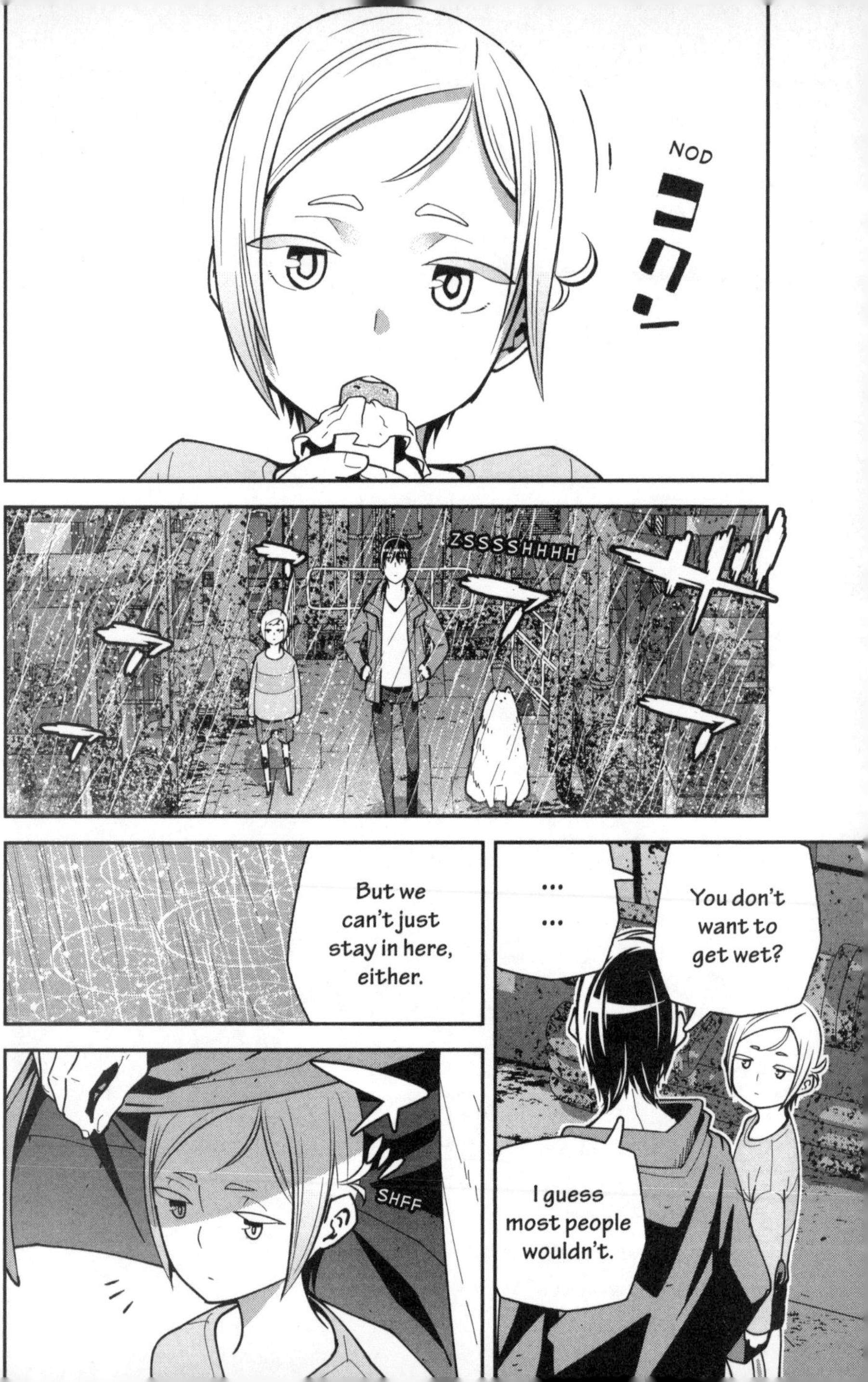
NOD
コクン
ZSSSSHHHH
You don't want to get wet?
...
...
I guess most people wouldn't.
But we can't just stay in here, either.
SHFF

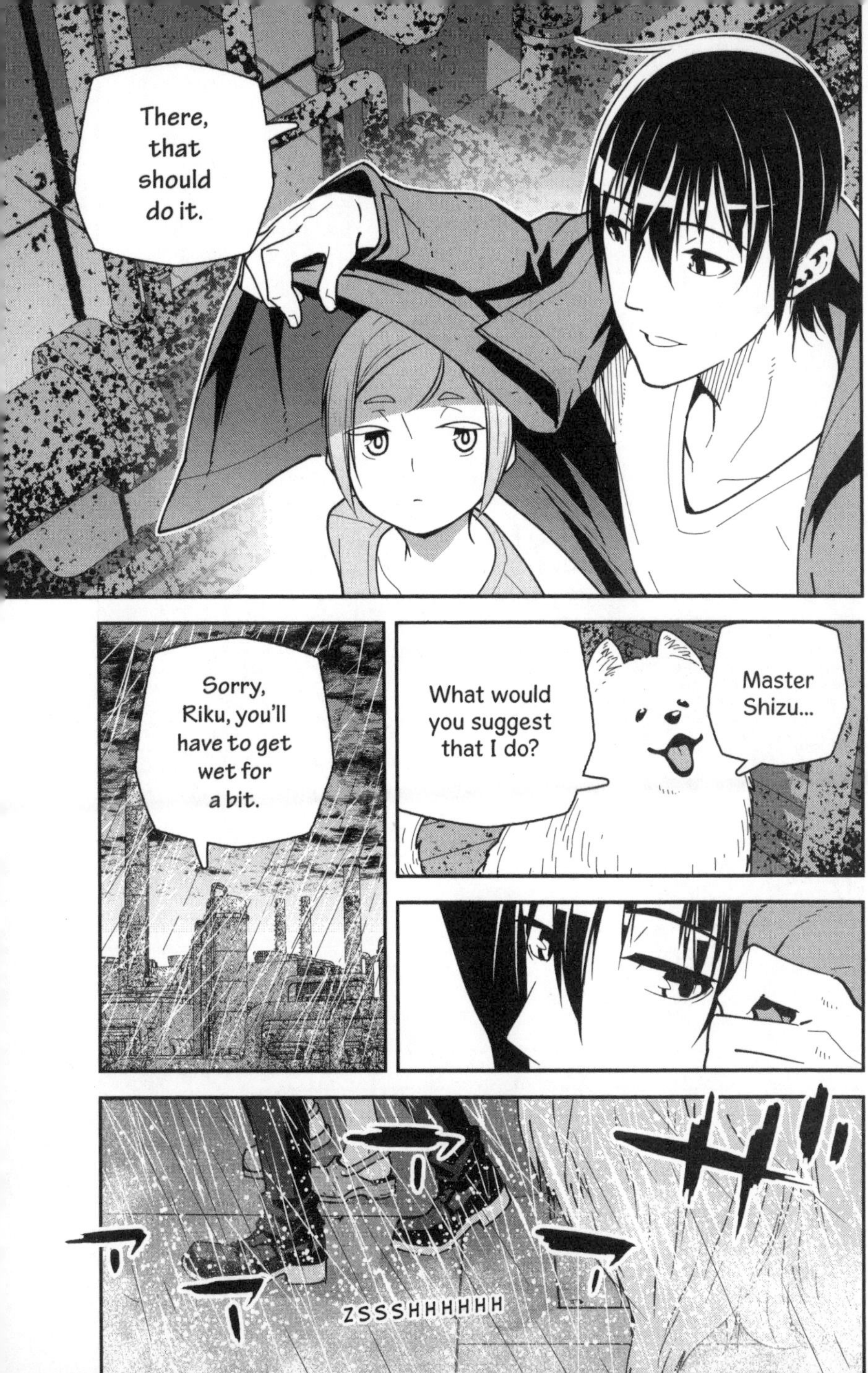
There, that should do it.
Master Shizu...
What would you suggest that I do?
Sorry, Riku, you'll have to get wet for a bit.
ZSSSHHHHHH

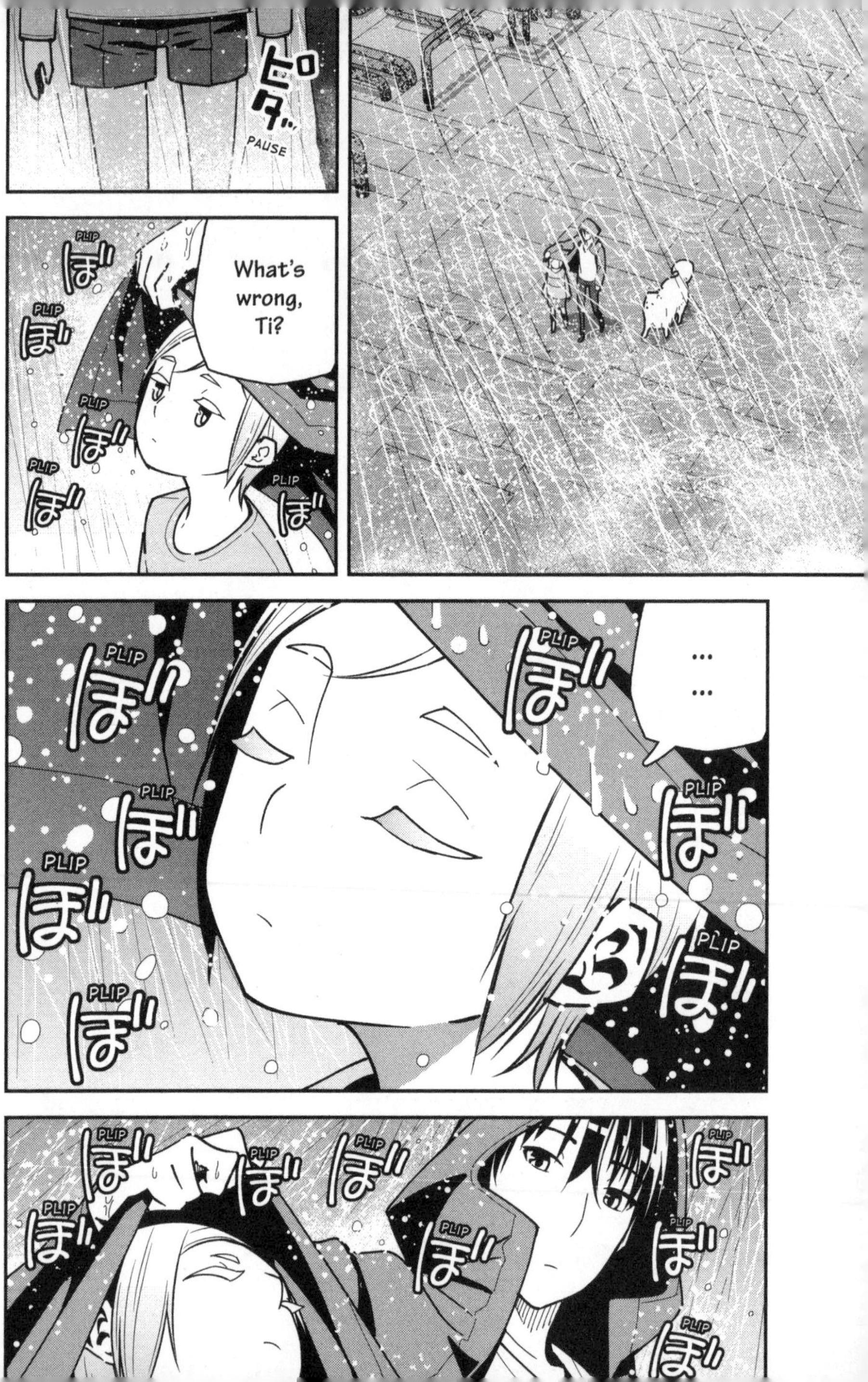
ピタ
PAUSE
PLIP
PLIP
What's wrong, Ti?
PLIP
PLIP
PLIP
…
…
PLIP
PLIP
PLIP
PLIP
PLIP
PLIP
PLIP
PLIP
PLIP
PLIP
PLIP
PLIP
PLIP
PLIP

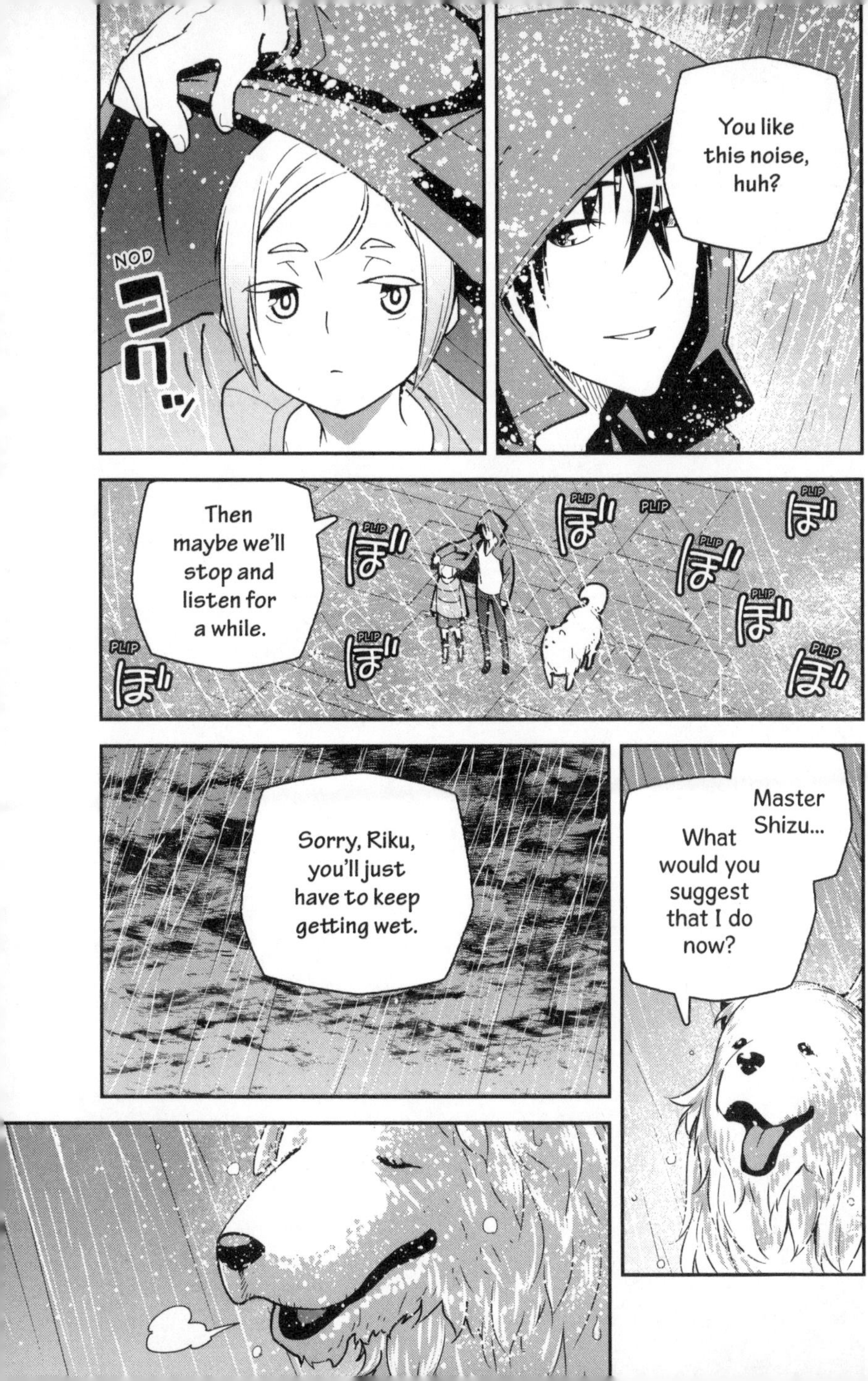
You like this noise, huh?
NOD
Then maybe we'll stop and listen for a while.
PLIP
PLIP
PLIP
PLIP
PLIP
PLIP
PLIP
PLIP
Master Shizu...
What would you suggest that I do now?
Sorry, Riku, you'll just have to keep getting wet.

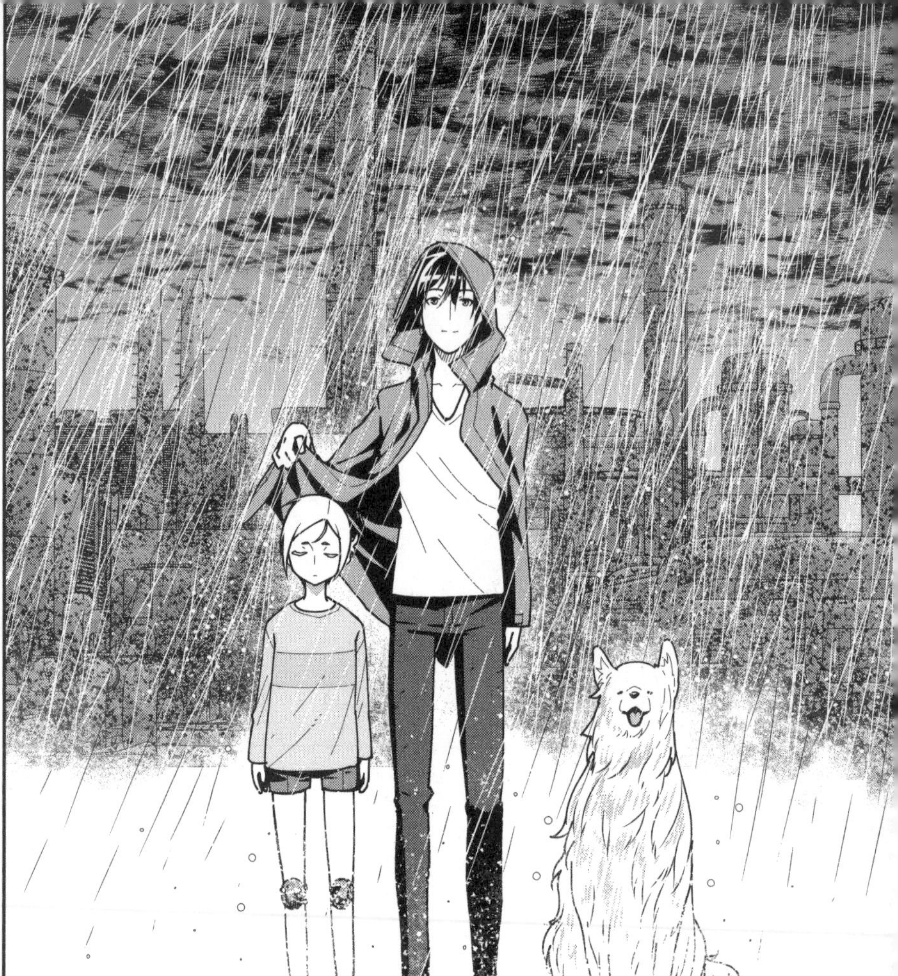

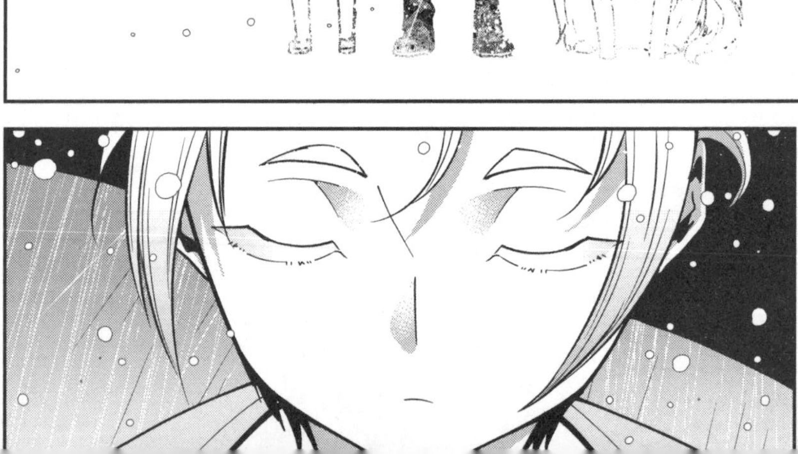

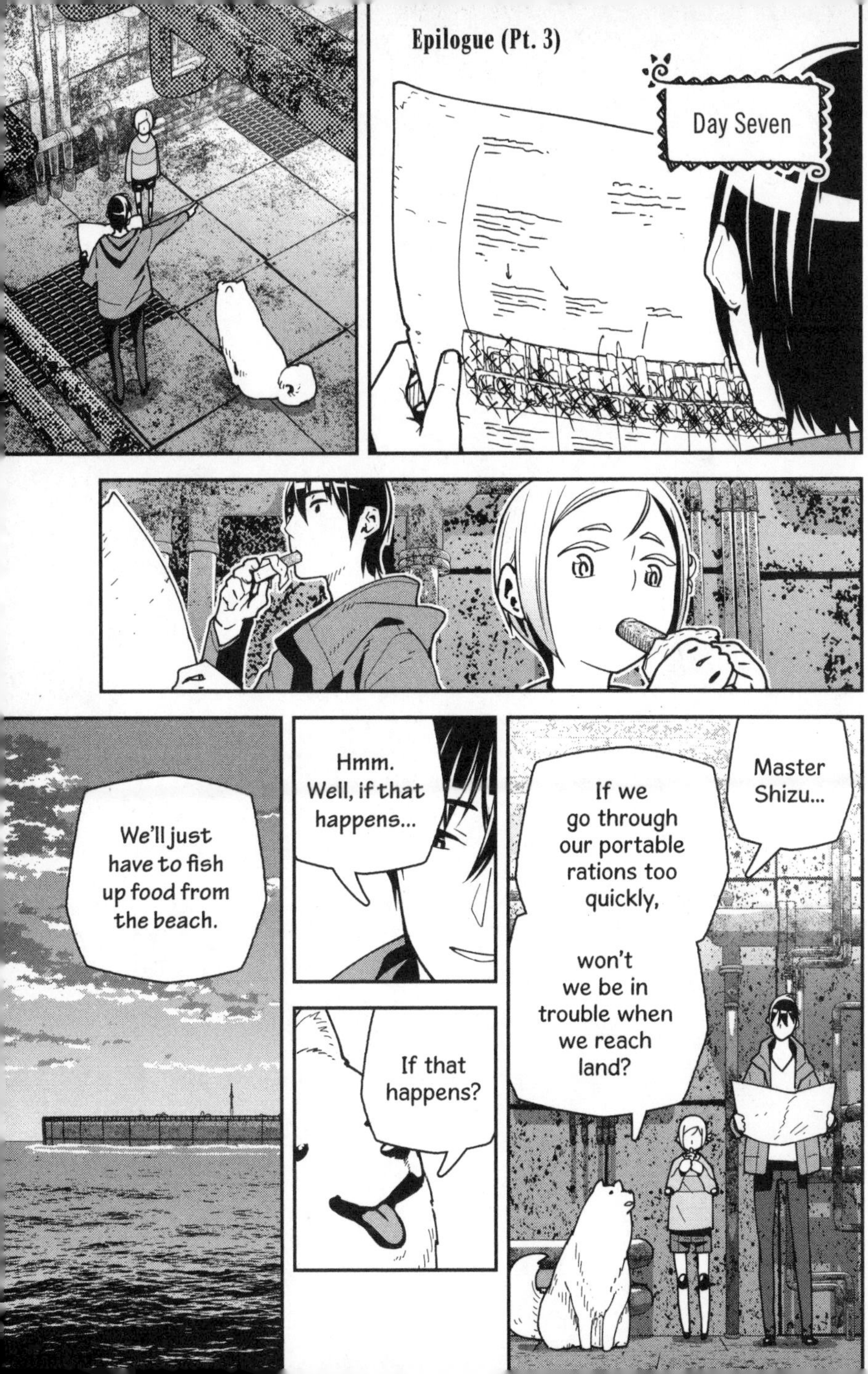
Epilogue (Pt. 3)
Day Seven
Master Shizu...
If we go through our portable rations too quickly,
won't we be in trouble when we reach land?
Hmm. Well, if that happens...
If that happens?
We'll just have to fish up food from the beach.

The Land of Ships (Pt. 3)

-On the Beach•a-

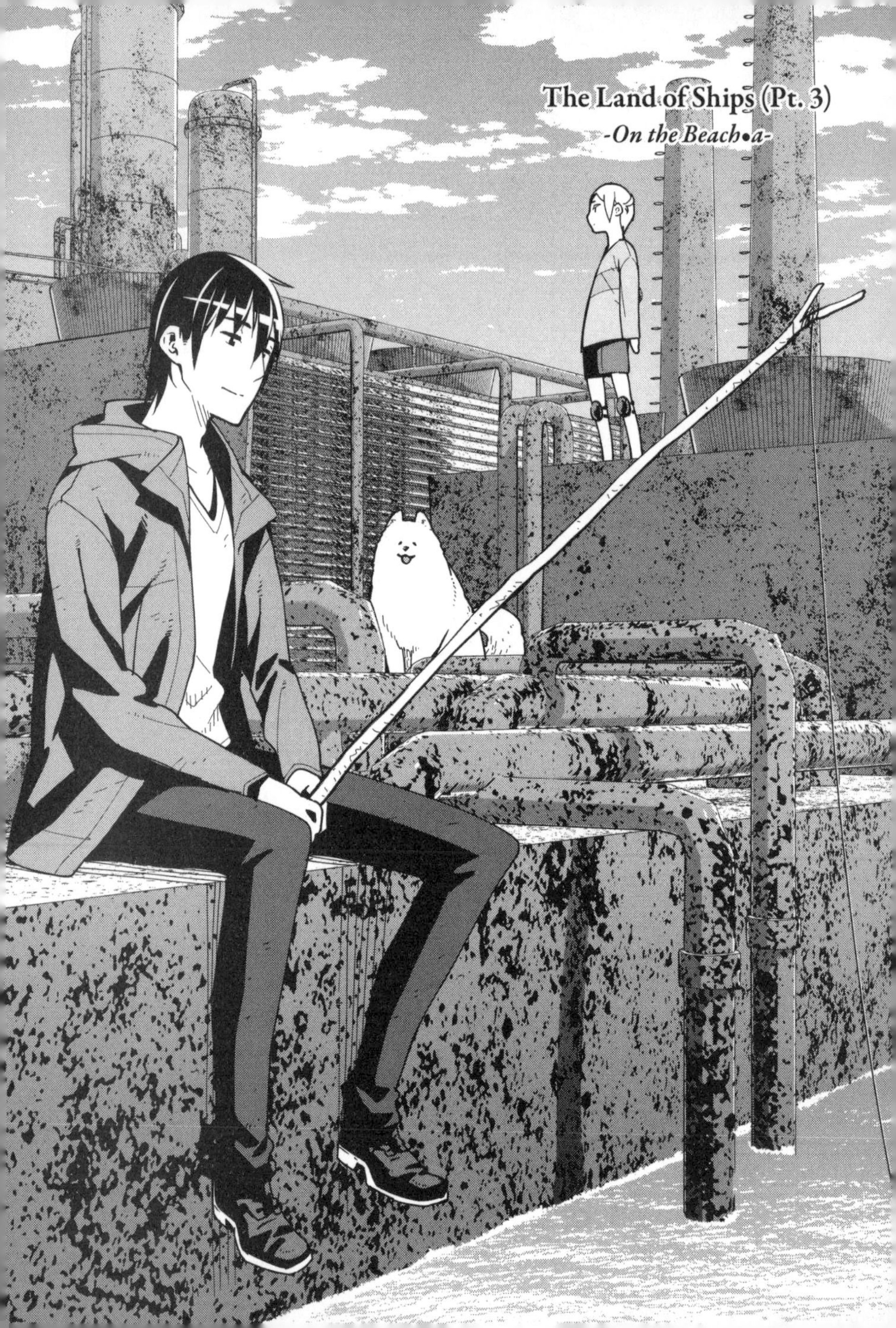

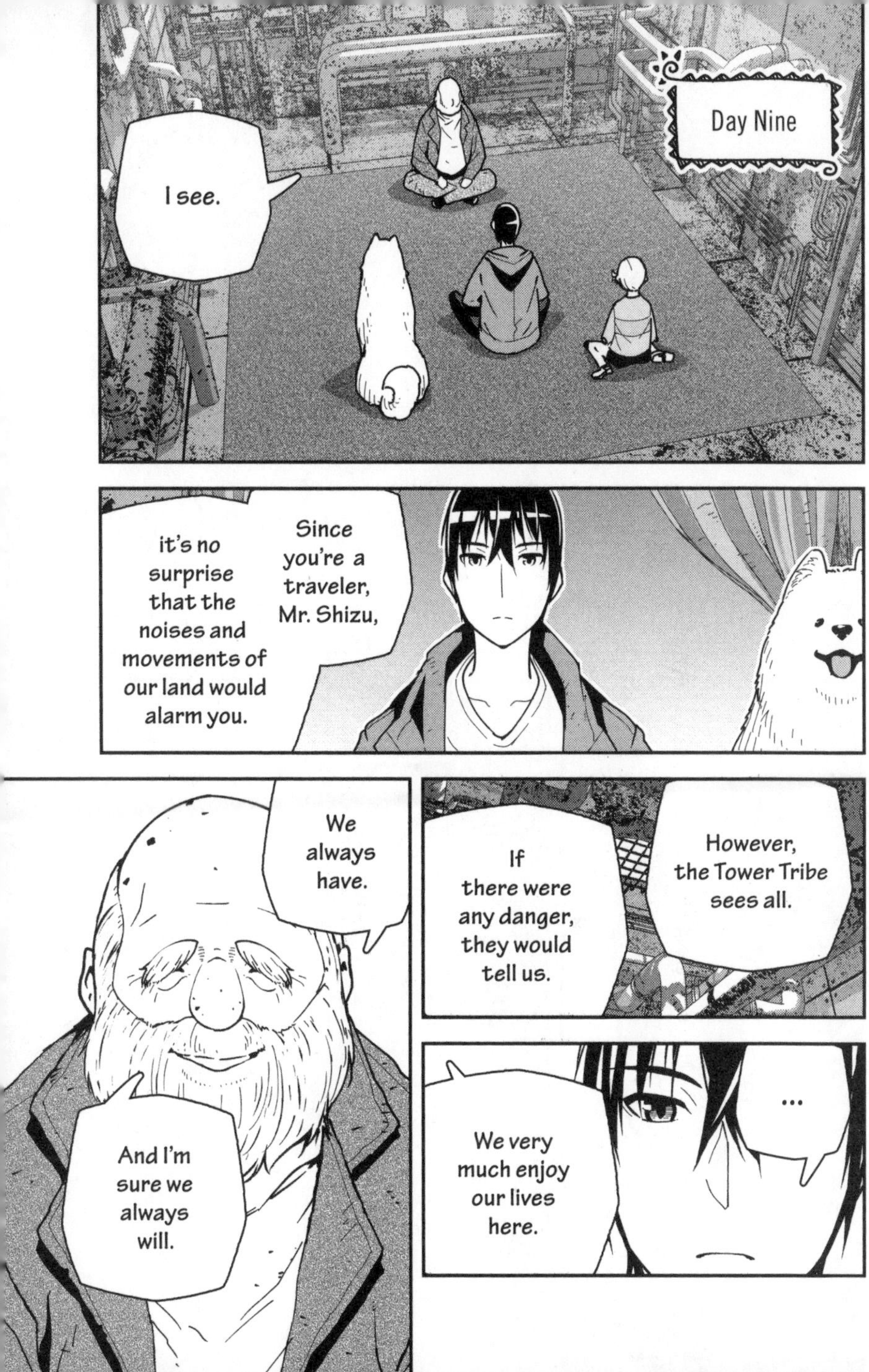
Day Nine
I see.
Since you're a traveler, Mr. Shizu,
it's no surprise that the noises and movements of our land would alarm you.
However, the Tower Tribe sees all.
If there were any danger, they would tell us.
...
We very much enjoy our lives here.
We always have.
And I'm sure we always will.

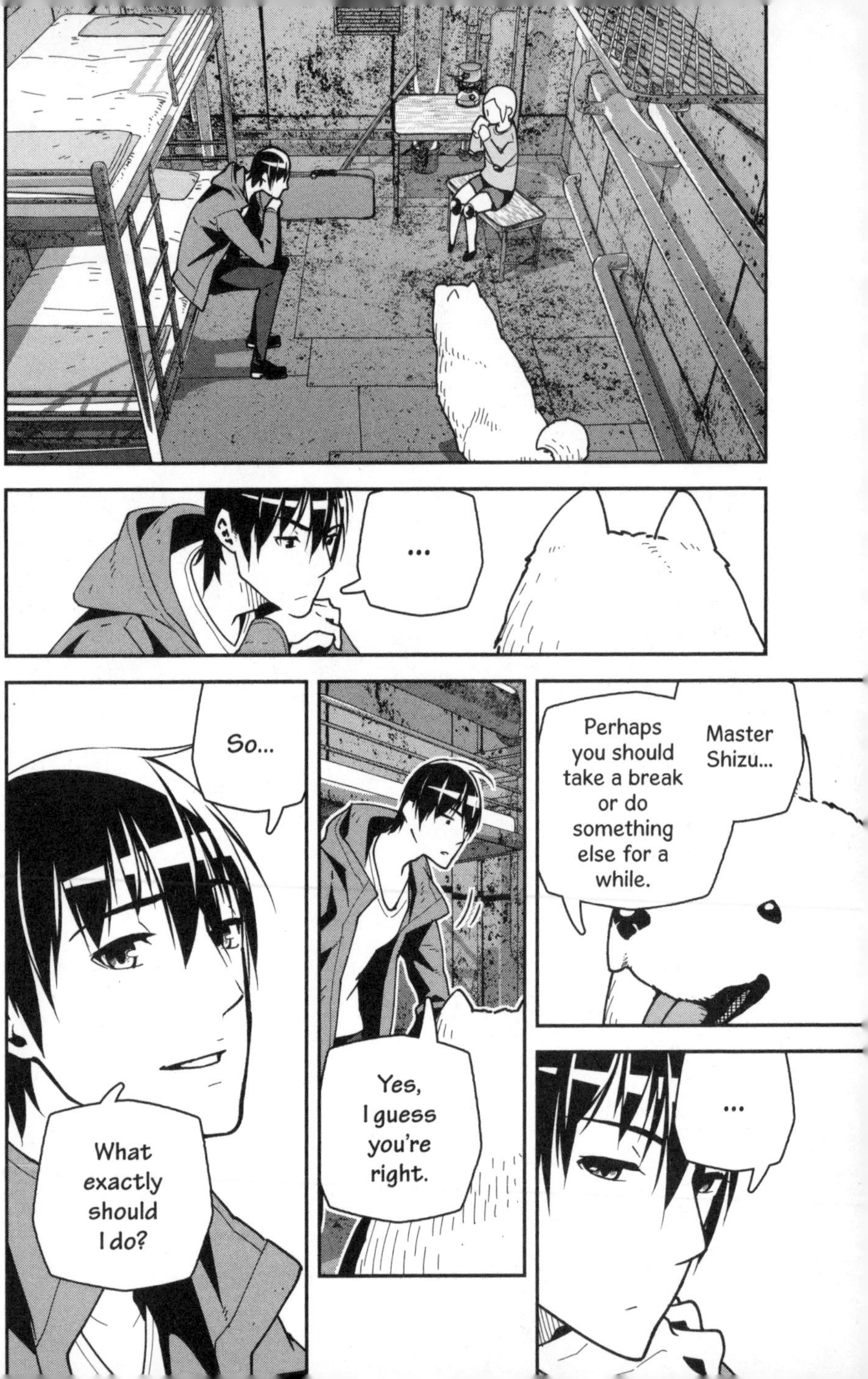
...
Master Shizu...
Perhaps you should take a break or do something else for a while.
...
Yes, I guess you're right.
So...
What exactly should I do?

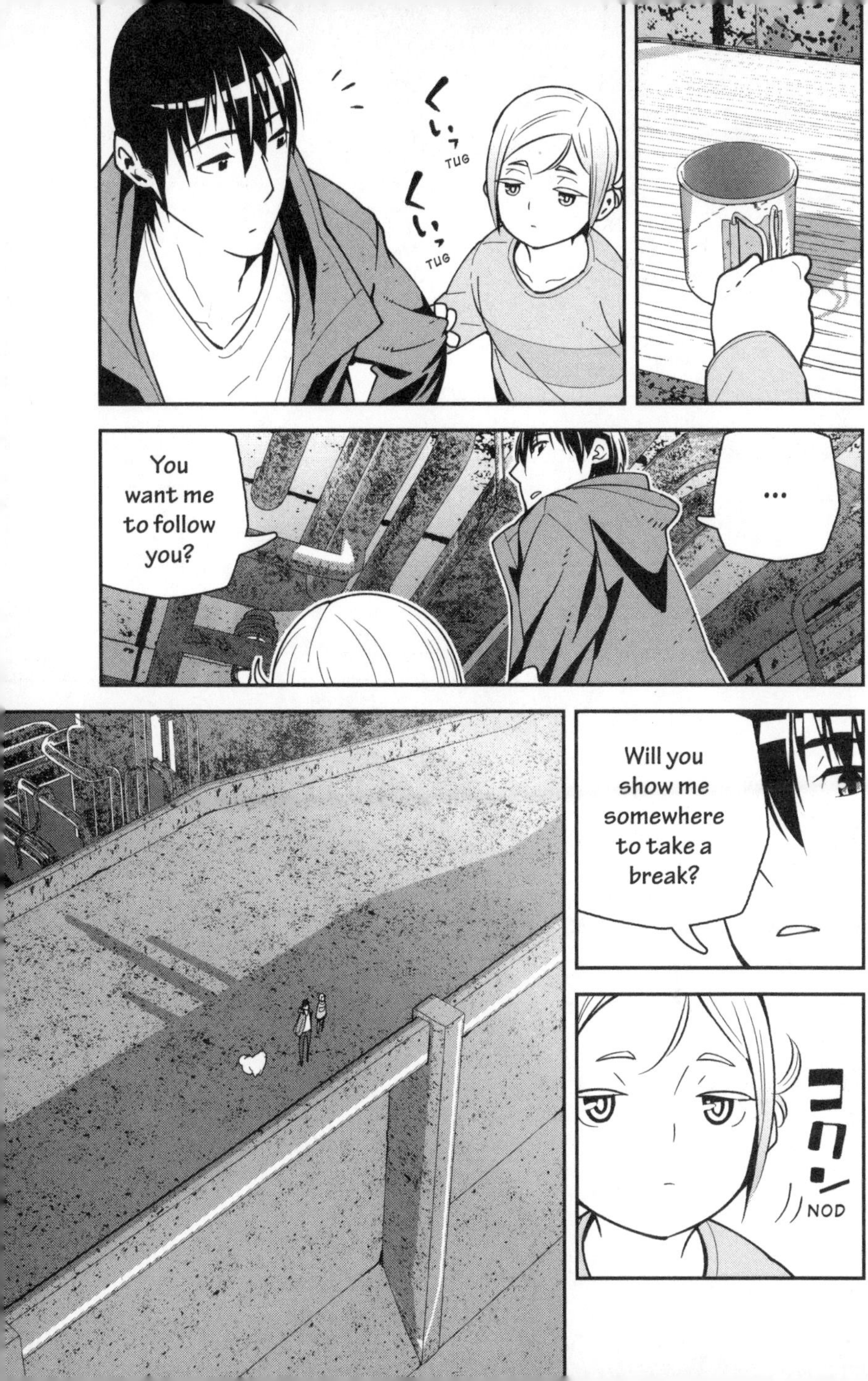
くいっ
TUG
くいっ
TUG
...
You want me to follow you?
Will you show me somewhere to take a break?
コクン
NOD

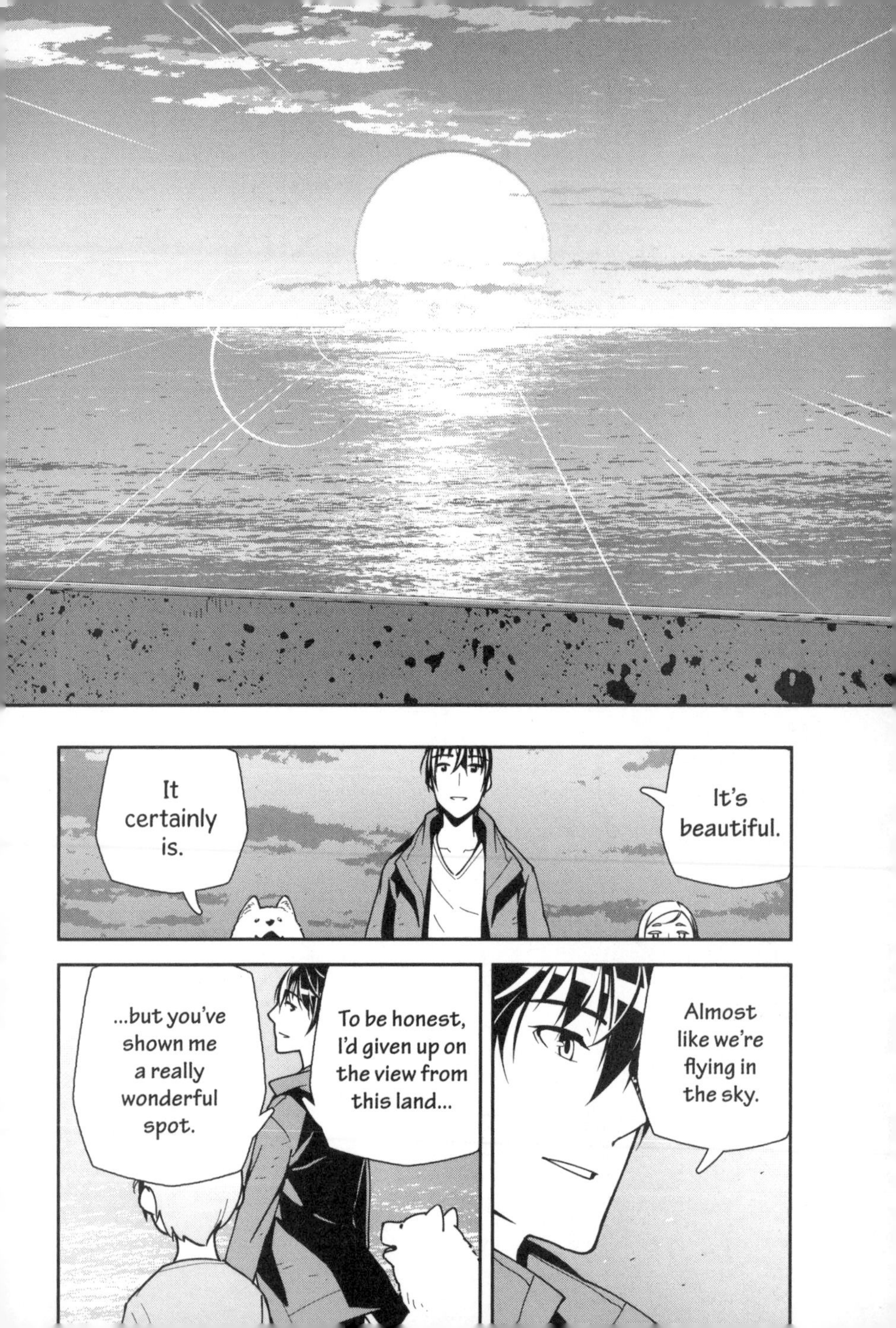
It's beautiful.
It certainly is.
Almost like we're flying in the sky.
To be honest, I'd given up on the view from this land...
...but you've shown me a really wonderful spot.

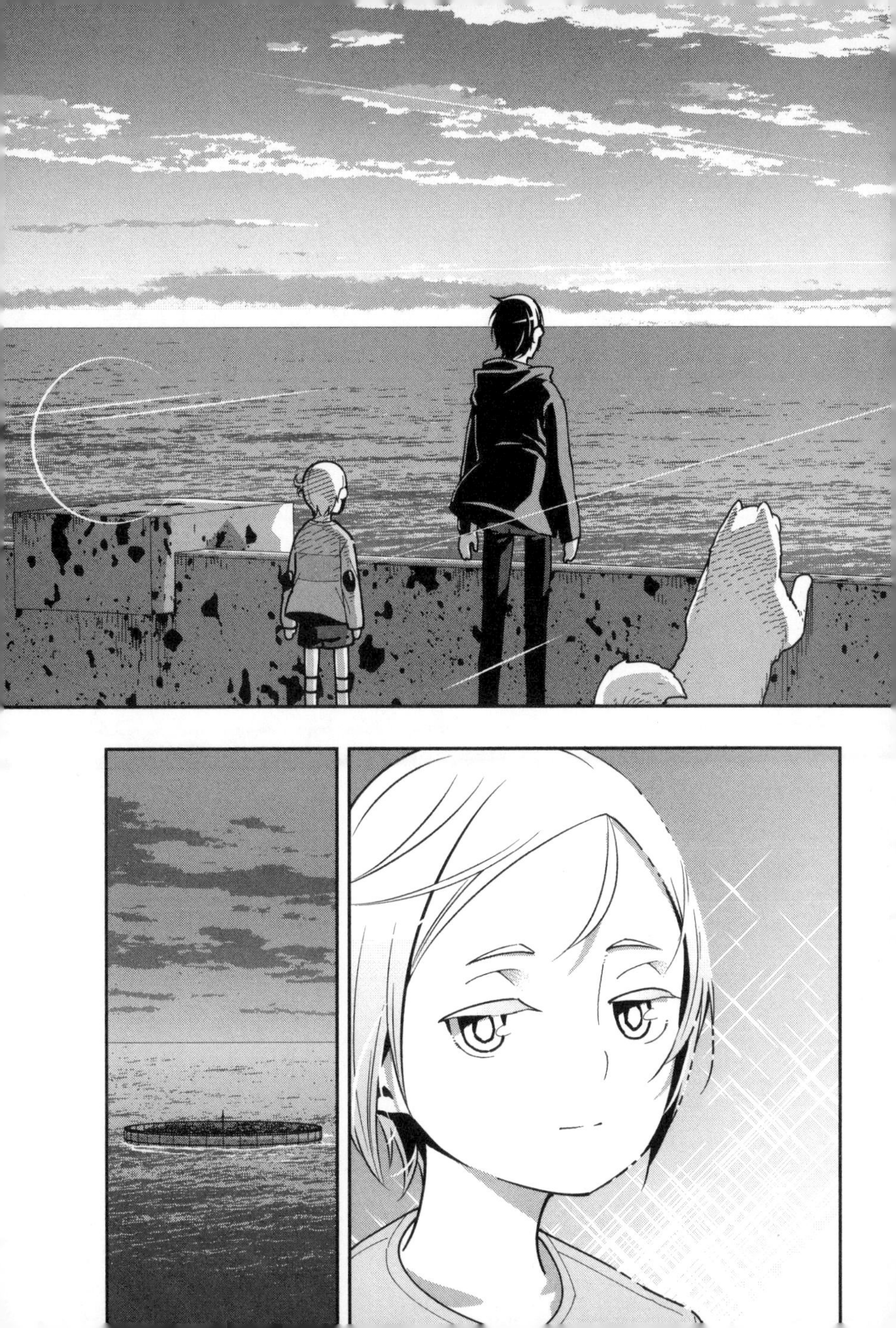

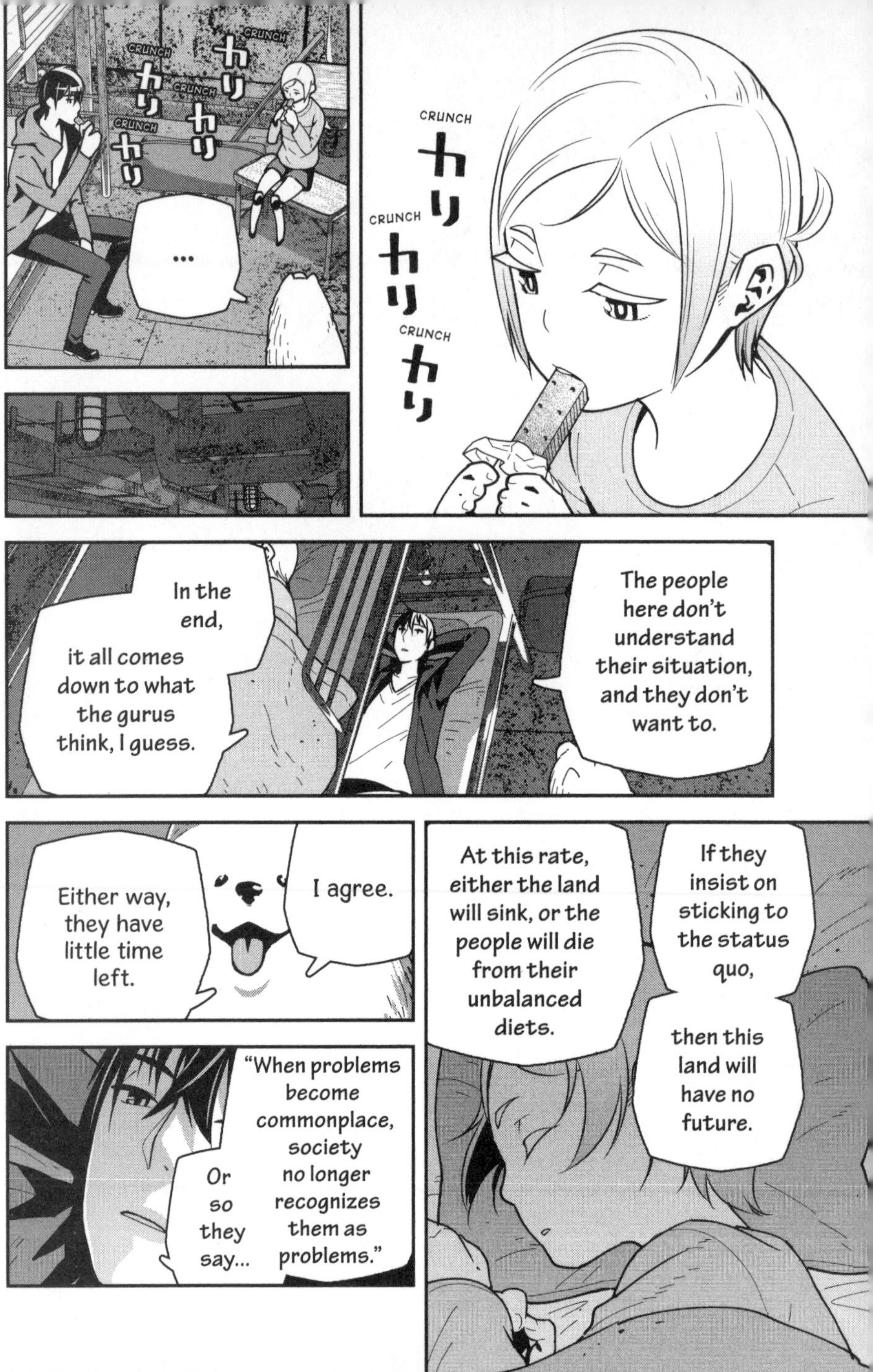
CRUNCH
カリ
CRUNCH
カリ
CRUNCH
カリ
CRUNCH
カリ
CRUNCH
カリ
CRUNCH
カリ
CRUNCH
カリ
...
The people here don't understand their situation, and they don't want to.
In the end, it all comes down to what the gurus think, I guess.
If they insist on sticking to the status quo,
then this land will have no future.
At this rate, either the land will sink, or the people will die from their unbalanced diets.
I agree.
Either way, they have little time left.
"When problems become commonplace, society no longer recognizes them as problems."
Or so they say...

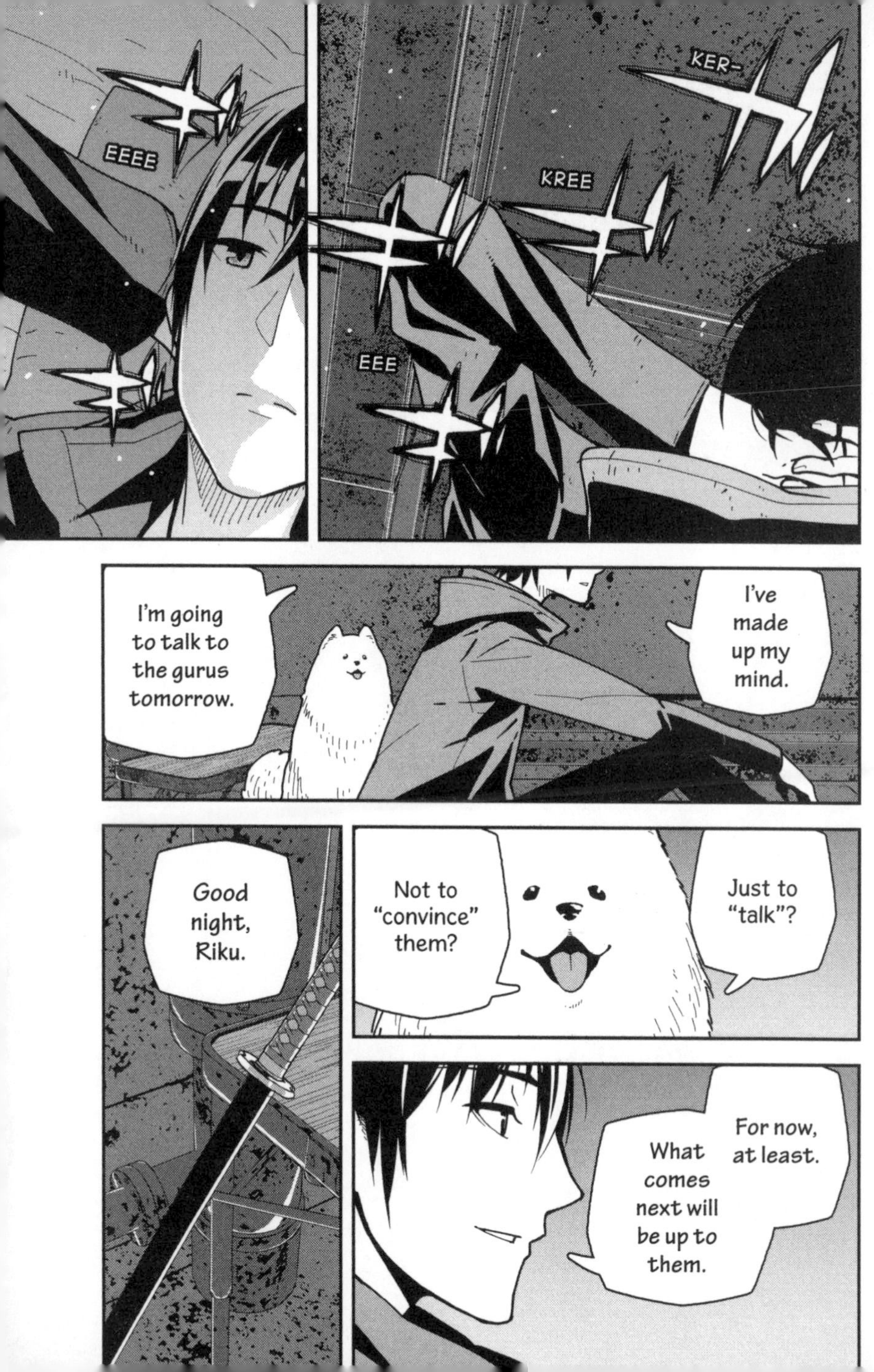
KER-
KREE
EEE
EEEE
I've made up my mind.
I'm going to talk to the gurus tomorrow.
Just to "talk"?
Not to "convince" them?
For now, at least.
What comes next will be up to them.
Good night, Riku.

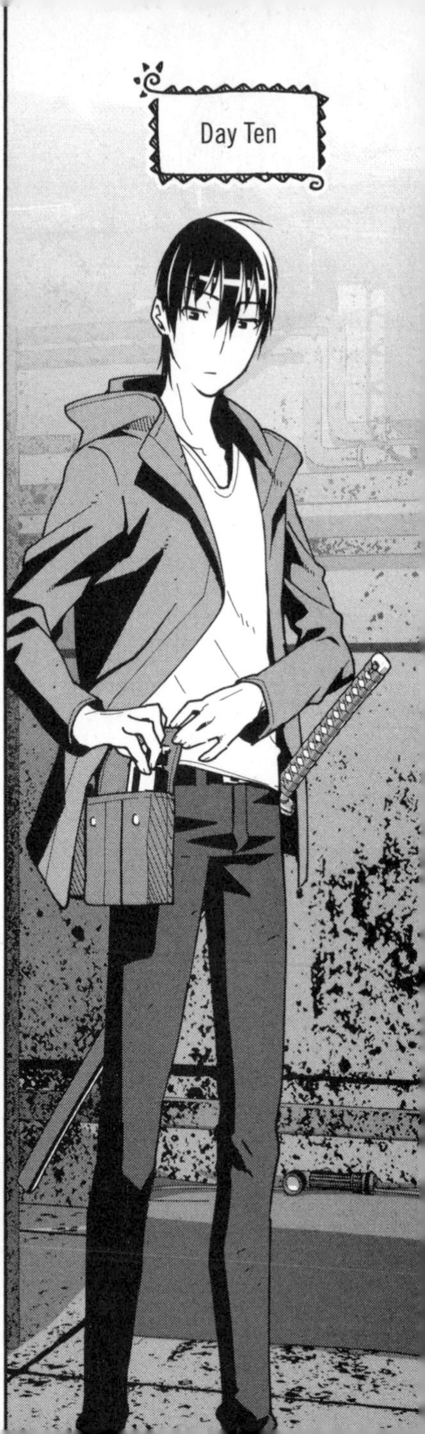
Day Ten

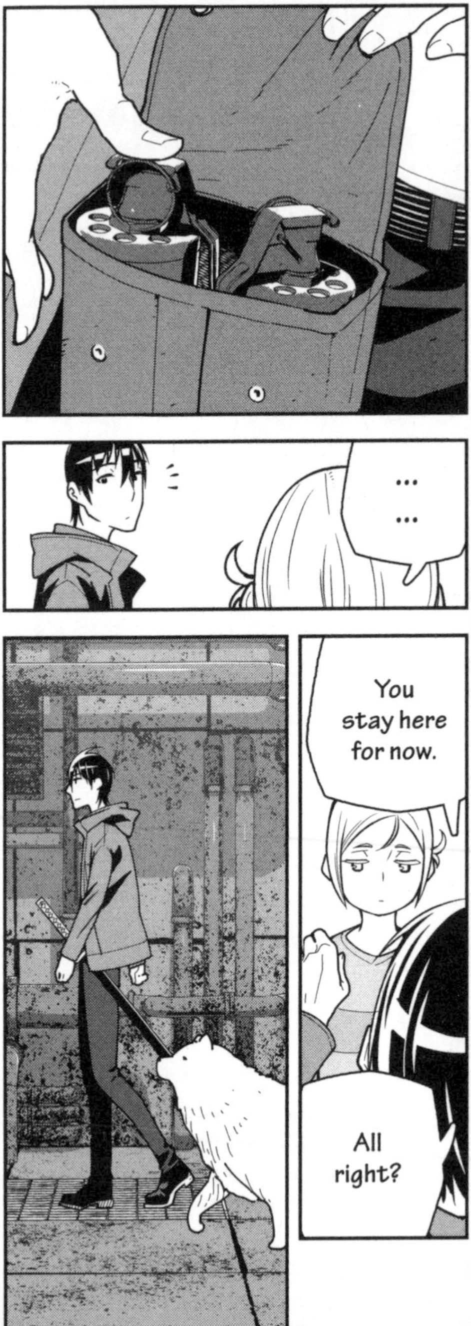
... ...
You stay here for now.
All right?

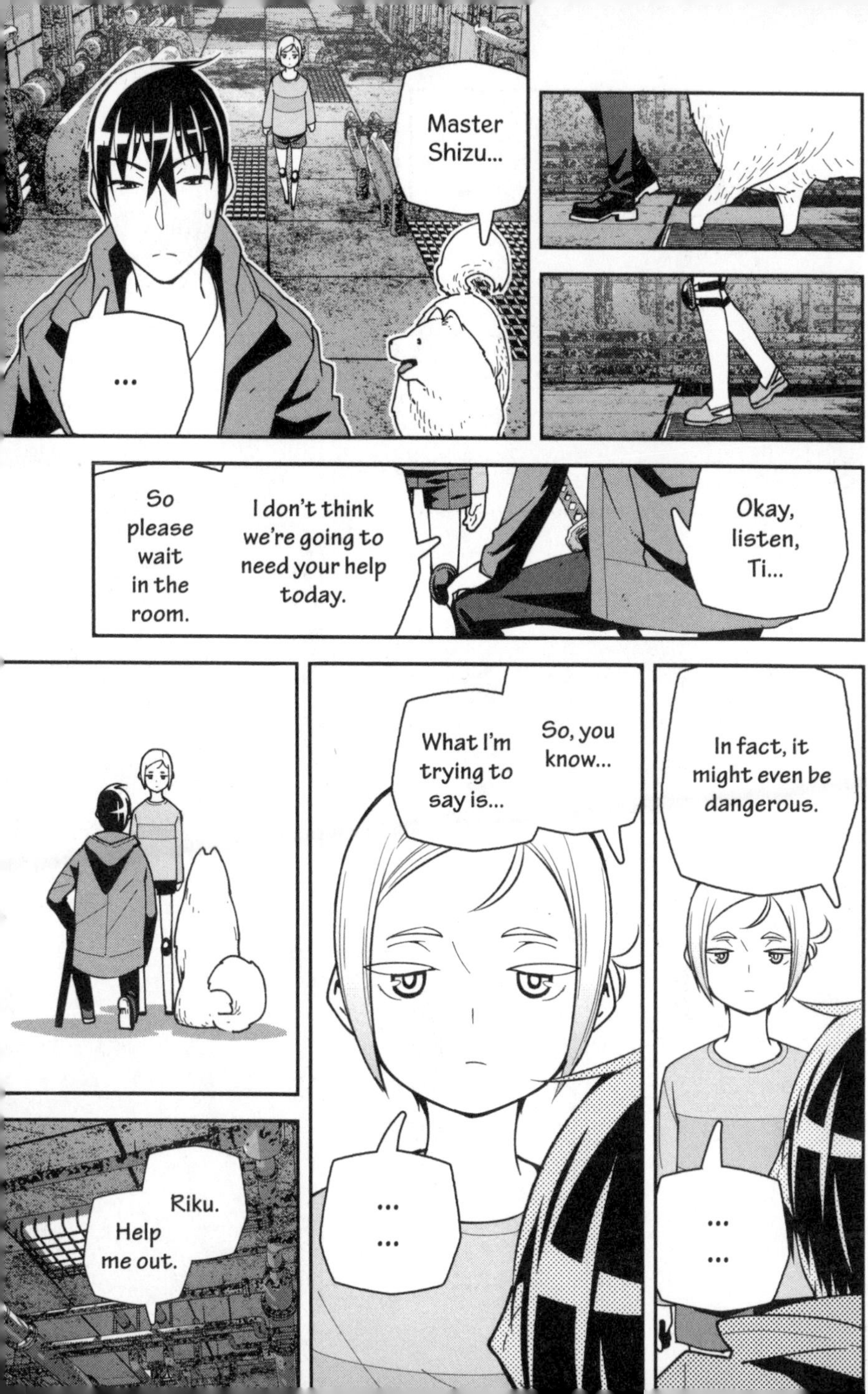
Master Shizu...
...
Okay, listen, Ti...
I don't think we're going to need your help today.
So please wait in the room.
In fact, it might even be dangerous.
... ...
So, you know...
What I'm trying to say is...
... ...
Riku. Help me out.

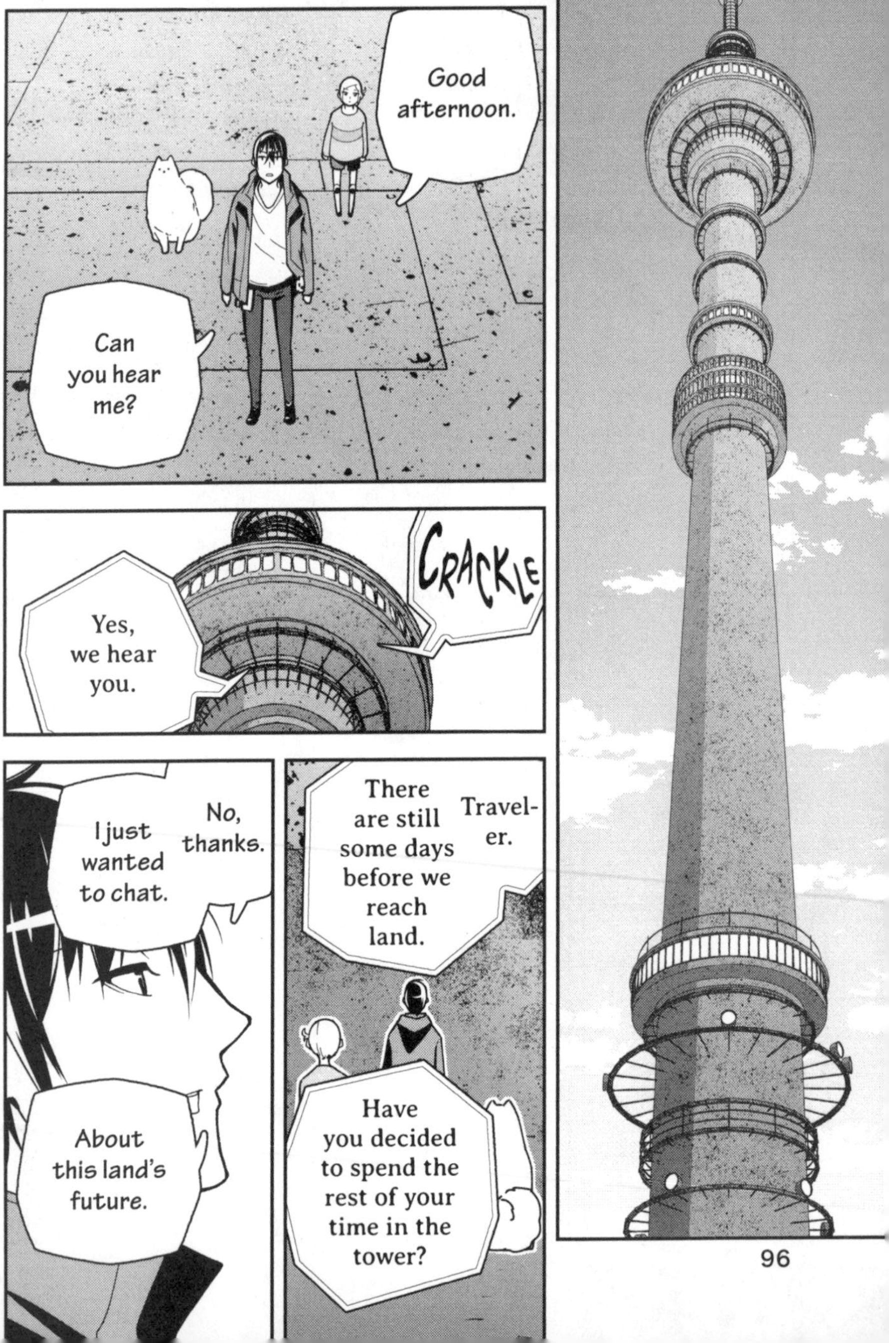
Good afternoon.
Can you hear me?
CRACKLE
Yes, we hear you.
Traveler.
There are still some days before we reach land.
Have you decided to spend the rest of your time in the tower?
No, thanks.
I just wanted to chat.
About this land's future.

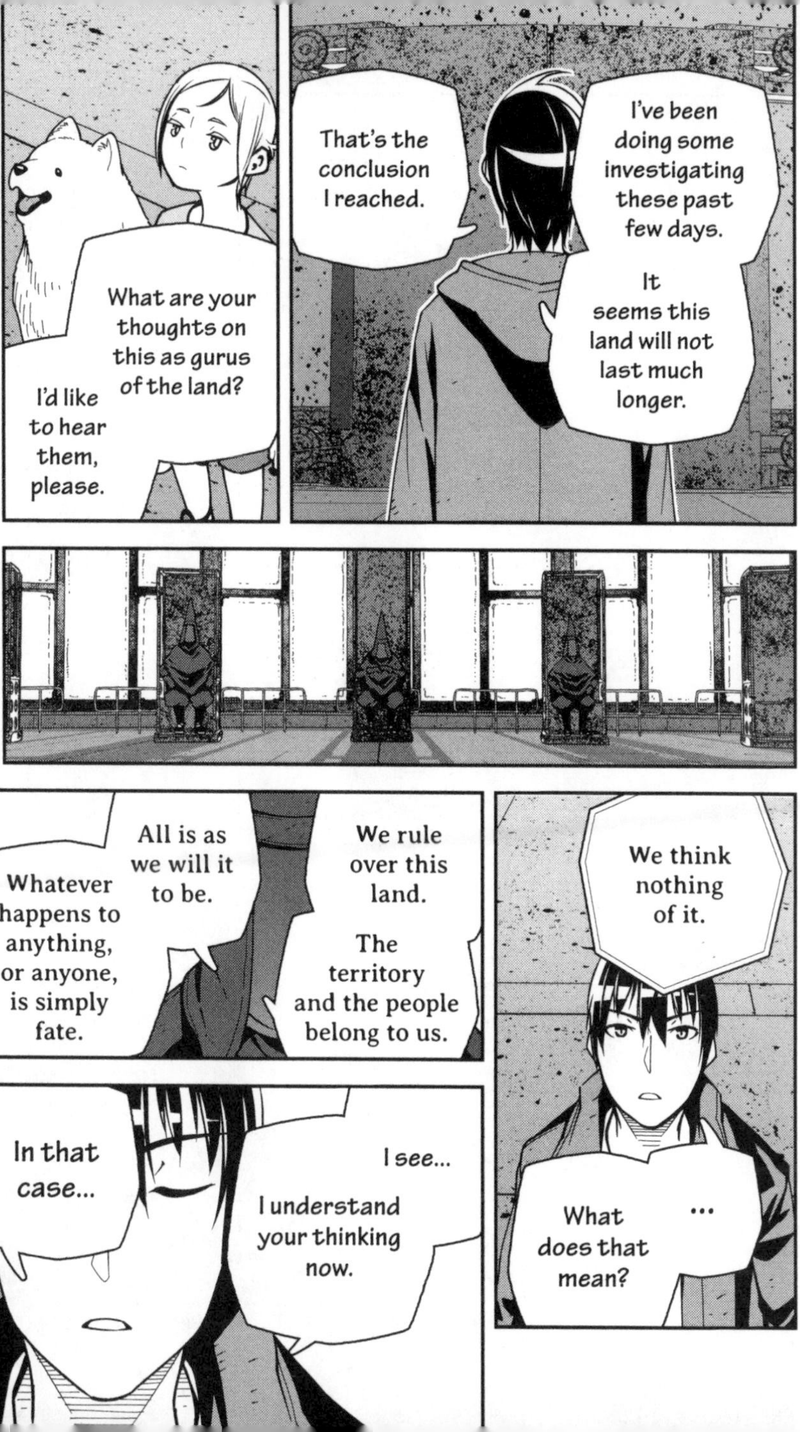
I've been doing some investigating these past few days.
It seems this land will not last much longer.
That's the conclusion I reached.
What are your thoughts on this as gurus of the land?
I'd like to hear them, please.
We think nothing of it.
...
What does that mean?
We rule over this land.
The territory and the people belong to us.
All is as we will it to be.
Whatever happens to anything, or anyone, is simply fate.
I see...
I understand your thinking now.
In that case...

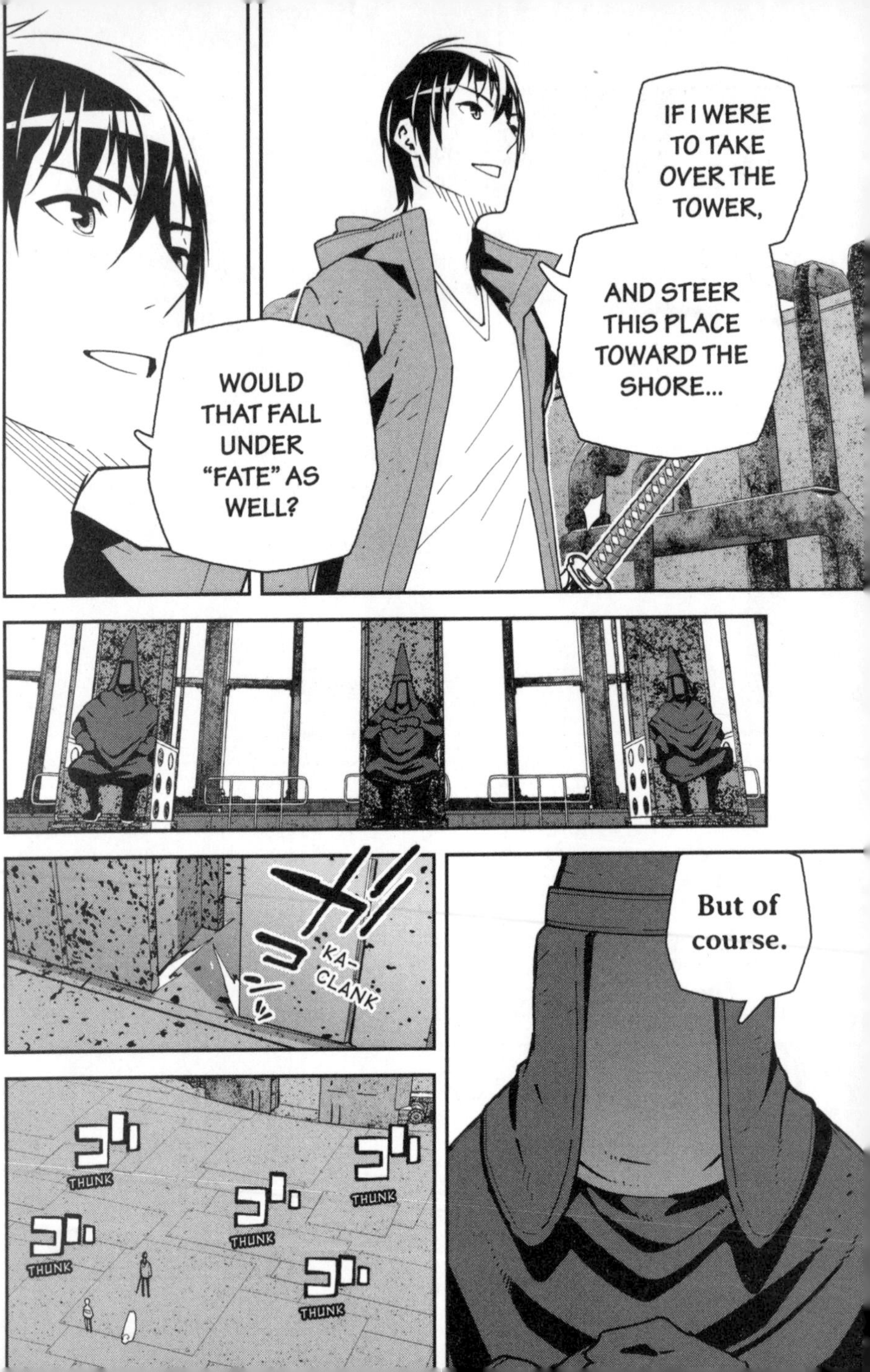
IF I WERE TO TAKE OVER THE TOWER,
AND STEER THIS PLACE TOWARD THE SHORE...
WOULD THAT FALL UNDER "FATE" AS WELL?
But of course.
KA-CLANK
THUNK
THUNK
THUNK
THUNK
THUNK

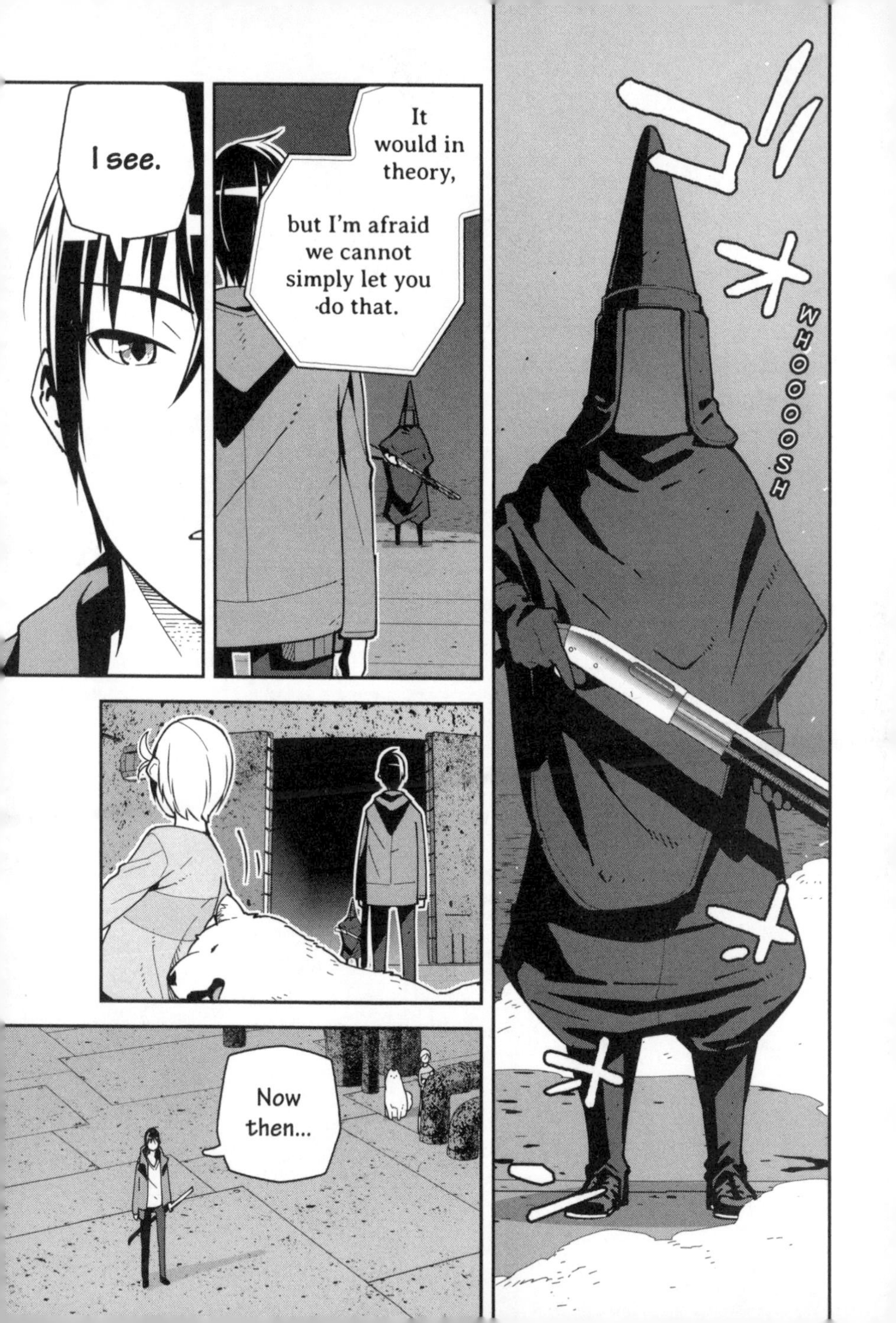
WHOOOOSH
It would in theory,
but I'm afraid we cannot simply let you do that.
I see.
Now then...

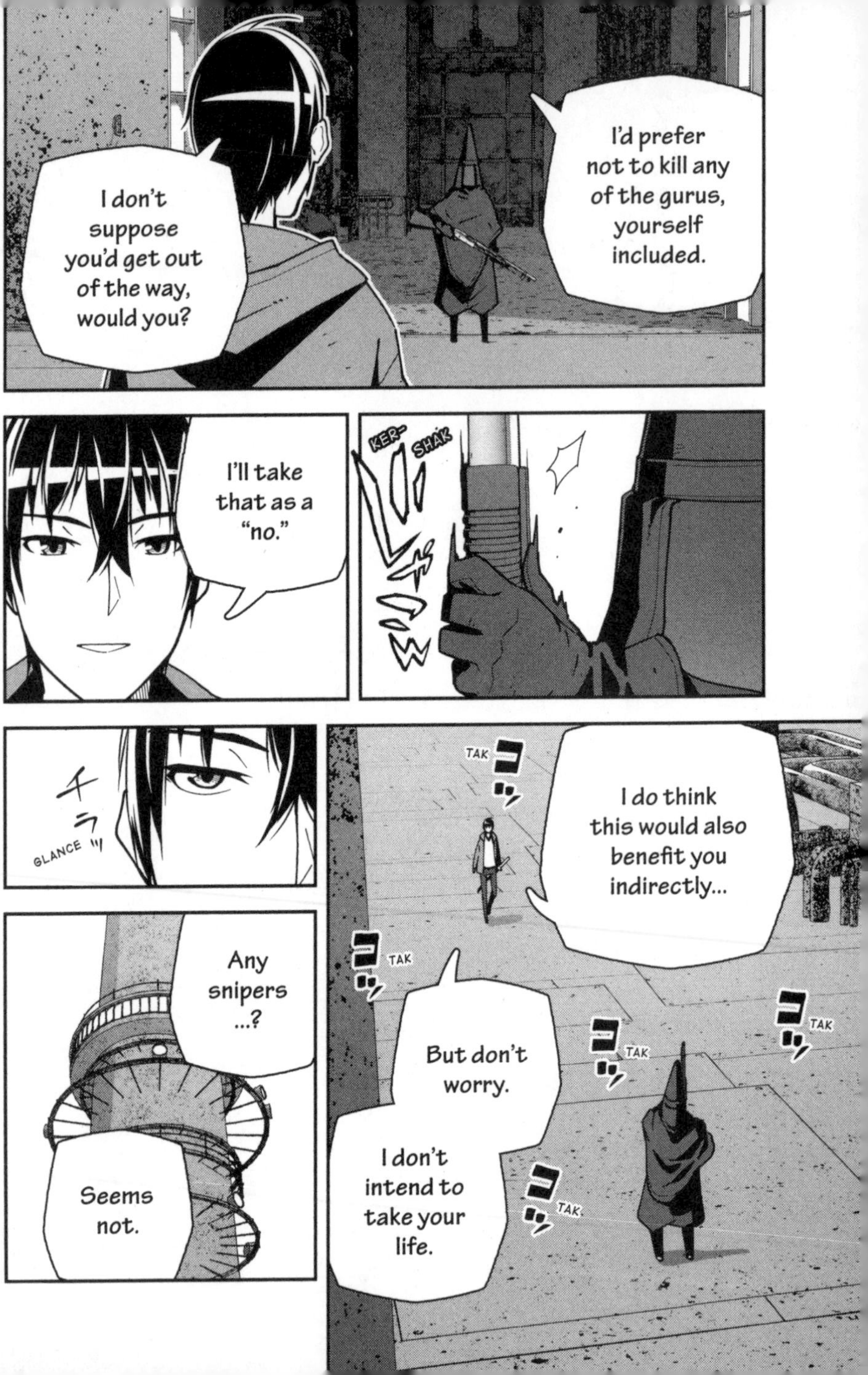

I'd prefer not to kill any of the gurus, yourself included.
I don't suppose you'd get out of the way, would you?
KER-SHAK
I'll take that as a "no."
TAK
I do think this would also benefit you indirectly...
TAK
TAK
TAK
But don't worry.
TAK
I don't intend to take your life.
GLANCE
Any snipers ...?
Seems not.

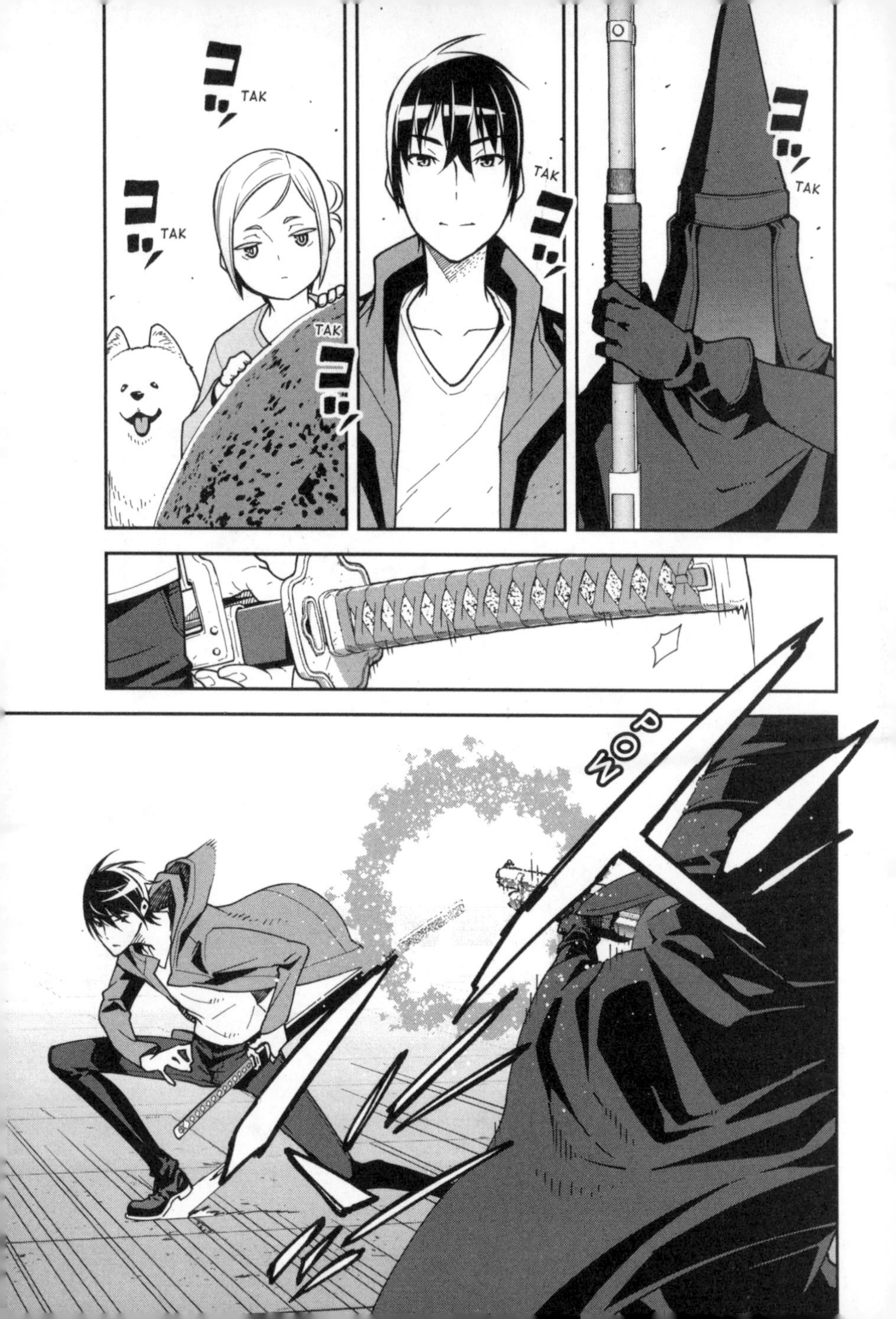
TAK
TAK
TAK
TAK
TAK
POW

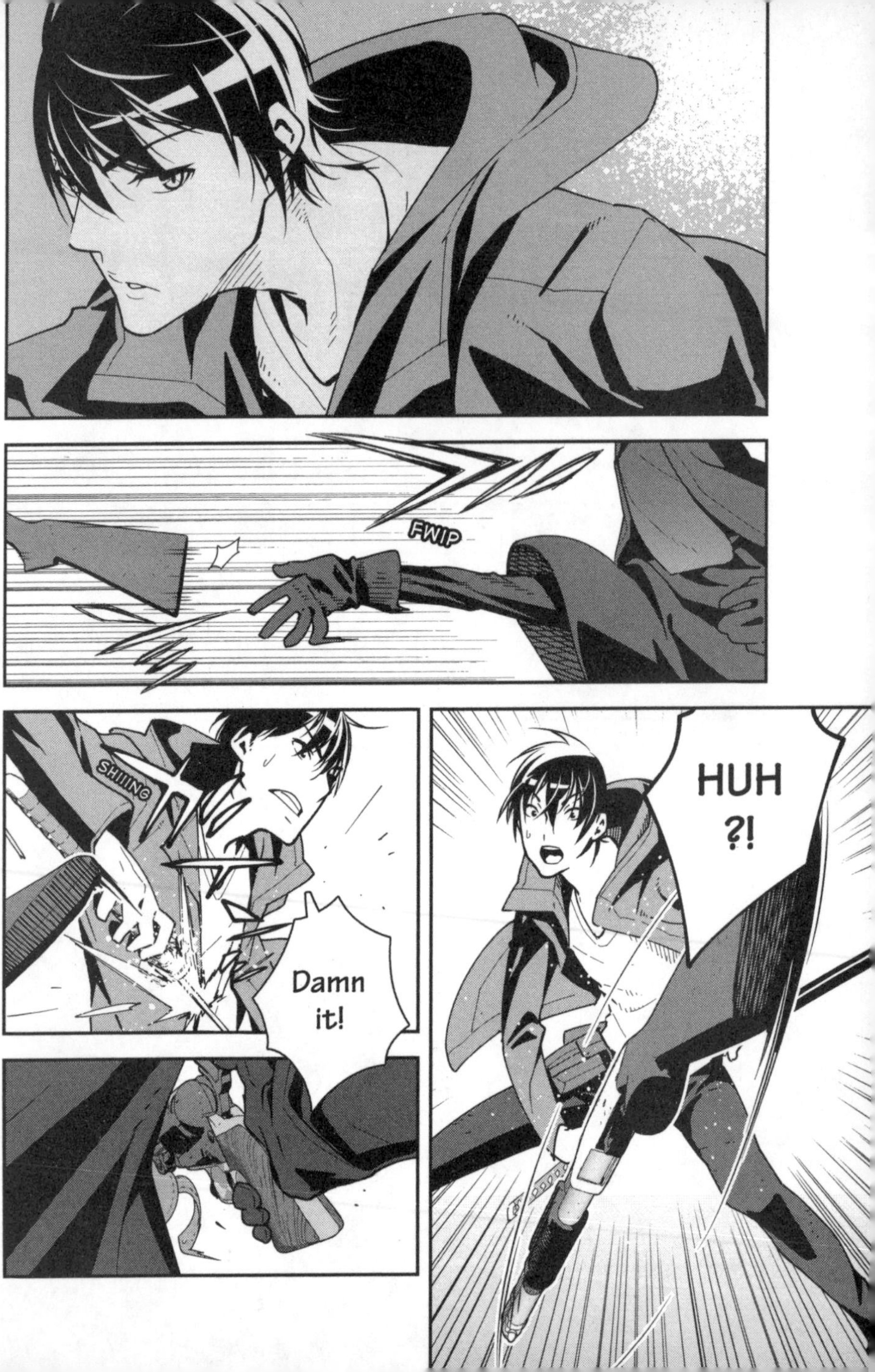
FWIP
HUH ?!
SHIIING
Damn it!

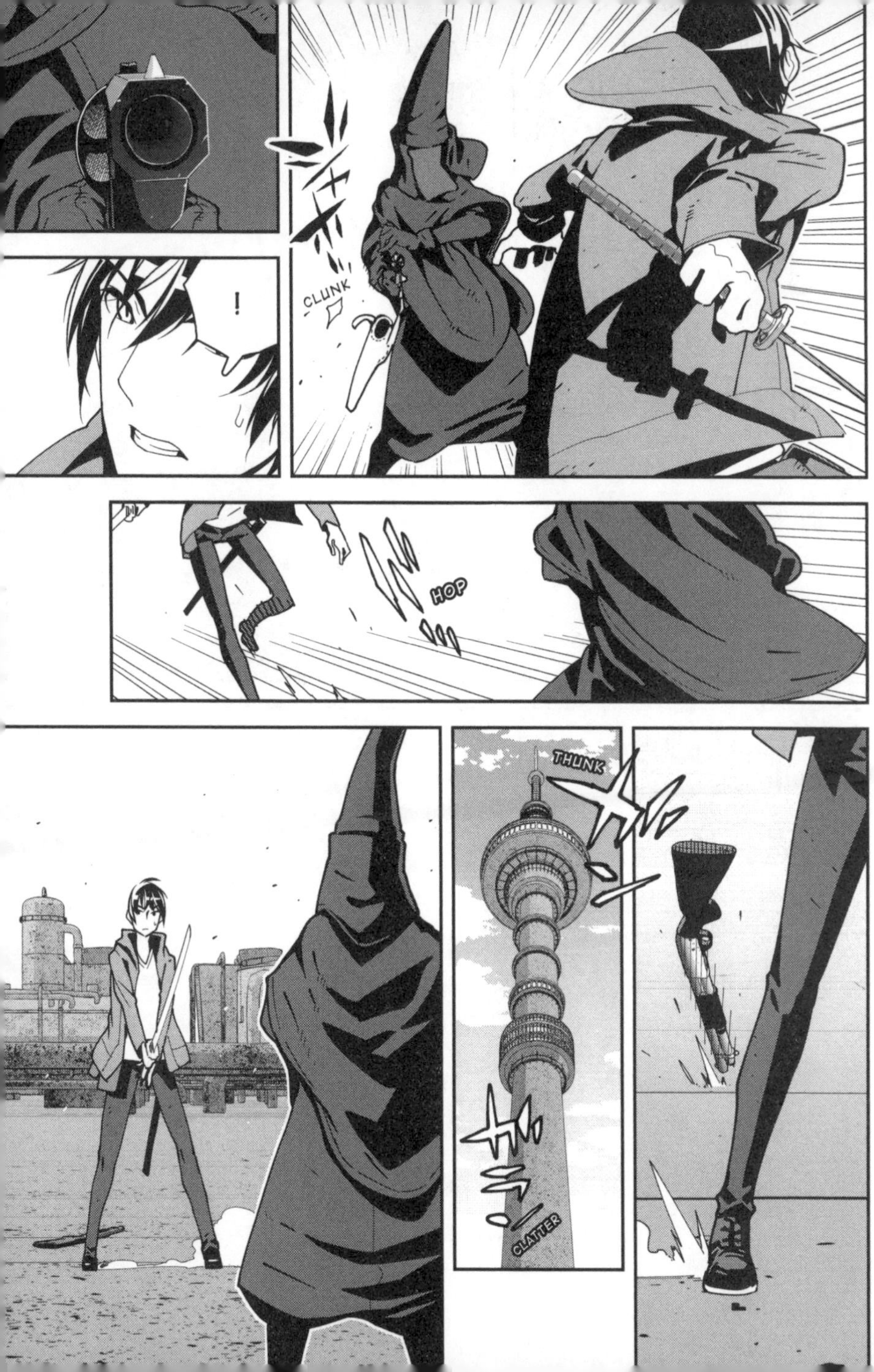
CLUNK
!
HOP
THUNK
CLATTER

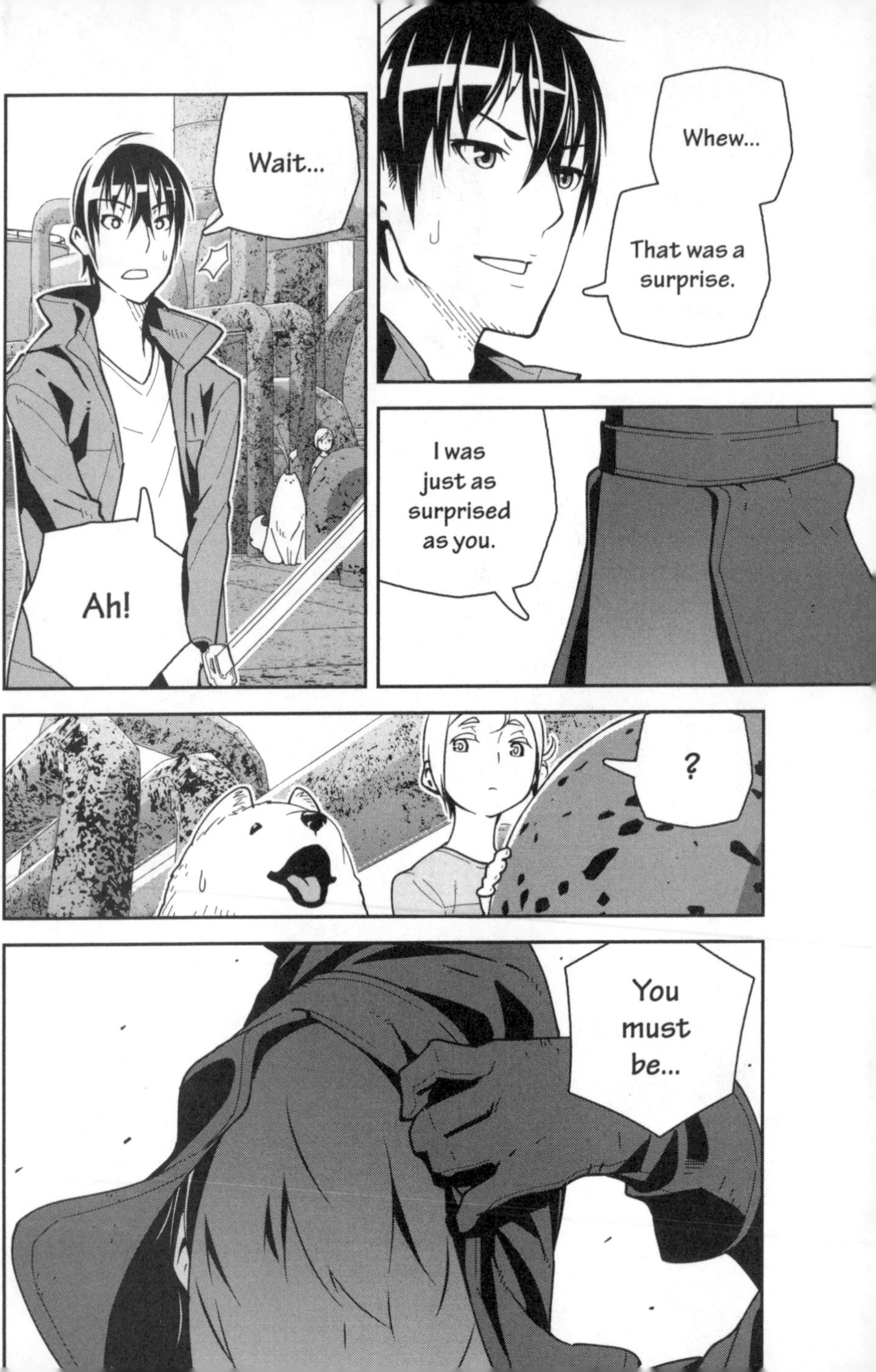
Whew...
That was a surprise.
I was just as surprised as you.
Wait...
Ah!
?
You must be...

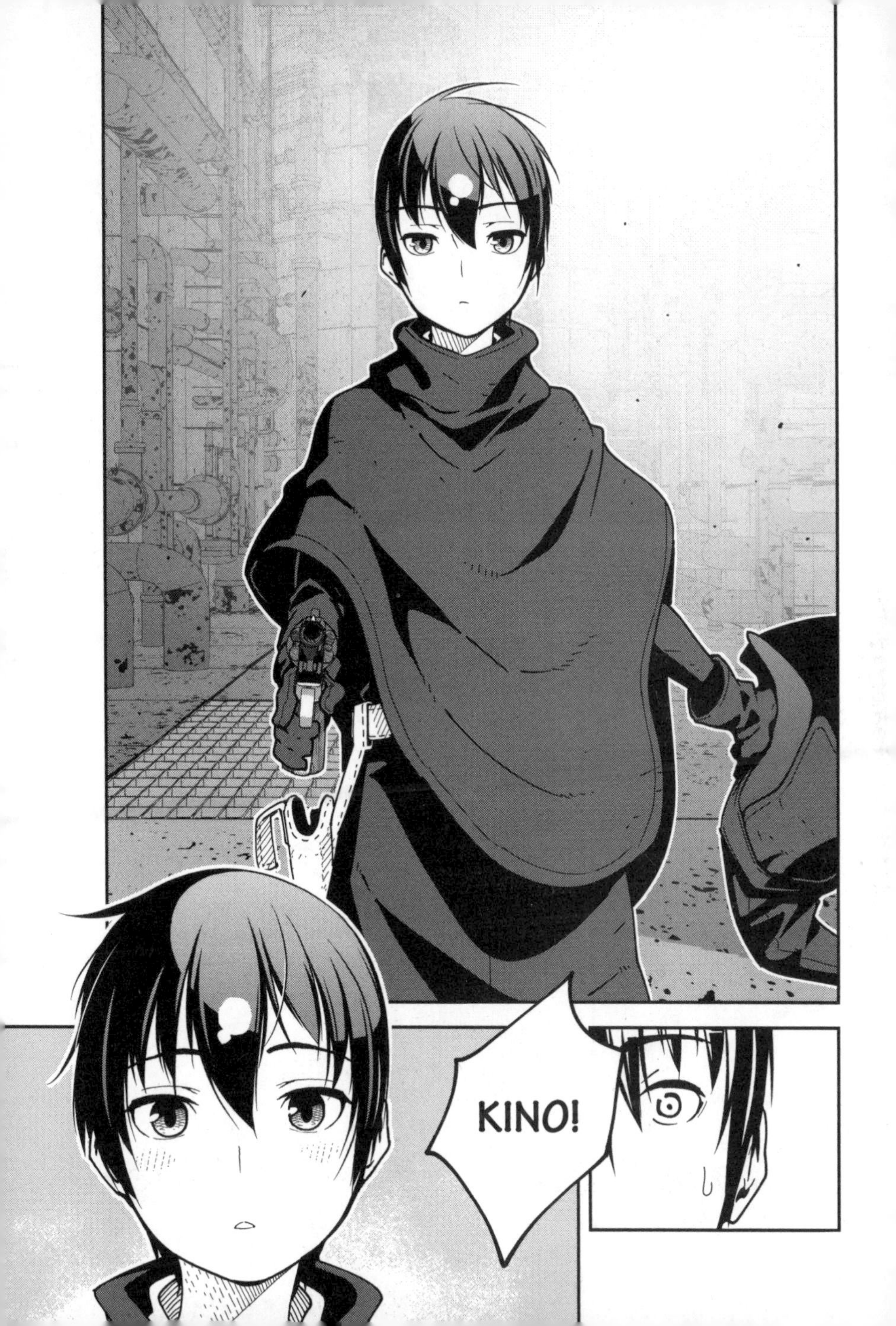
KINO!

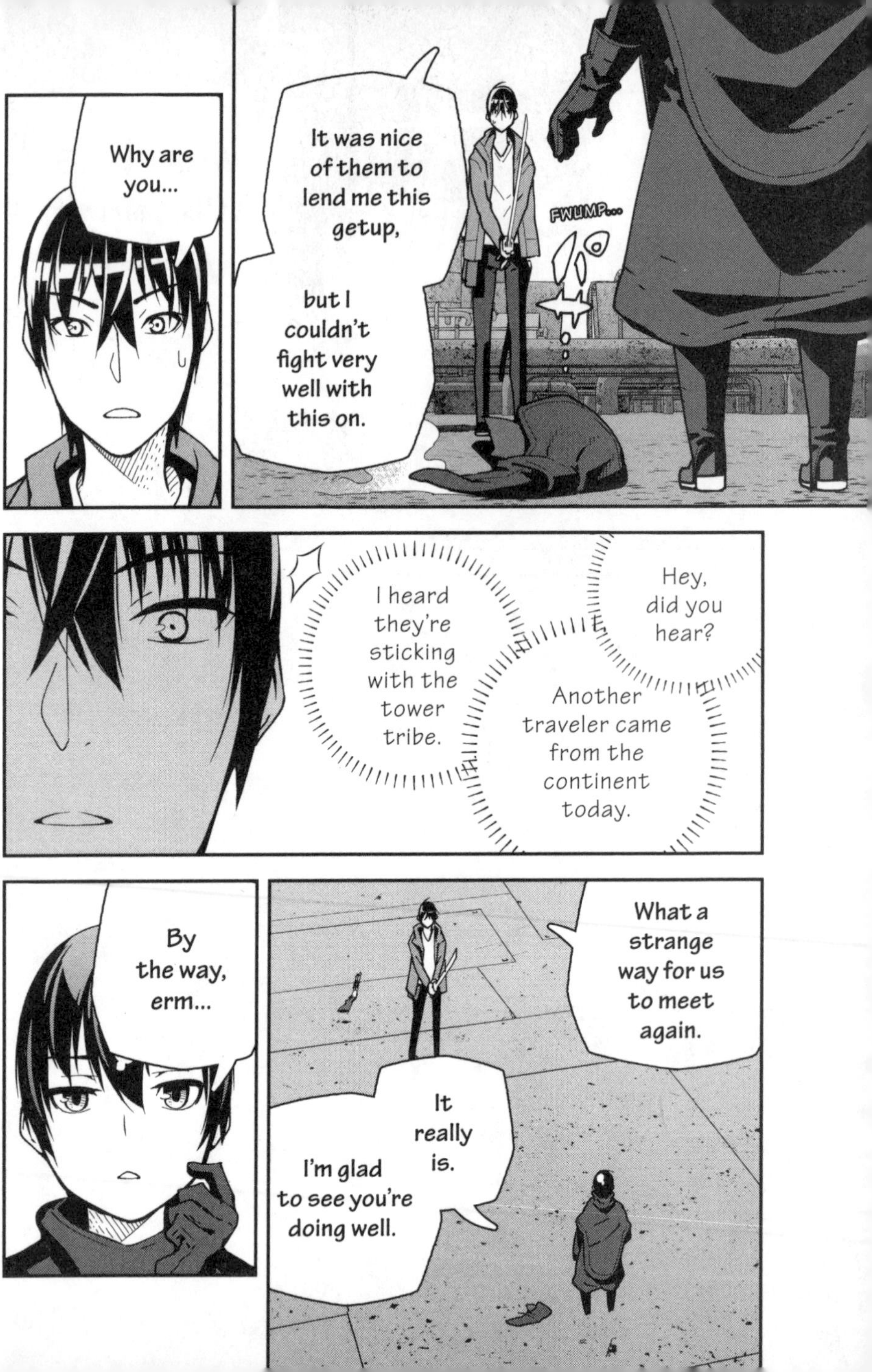
It was nice of them to lend me this getup,
but I couldn't fight very well with this on.
FWUMP...
Why are you...
Hey, did you hear?
Another traveler came from the continent today.
I heard they're sticking with the tower tribe.
What a strange way for us to meet again.
It really is.
I'm glad to see you're doing well.
By the way, erm...

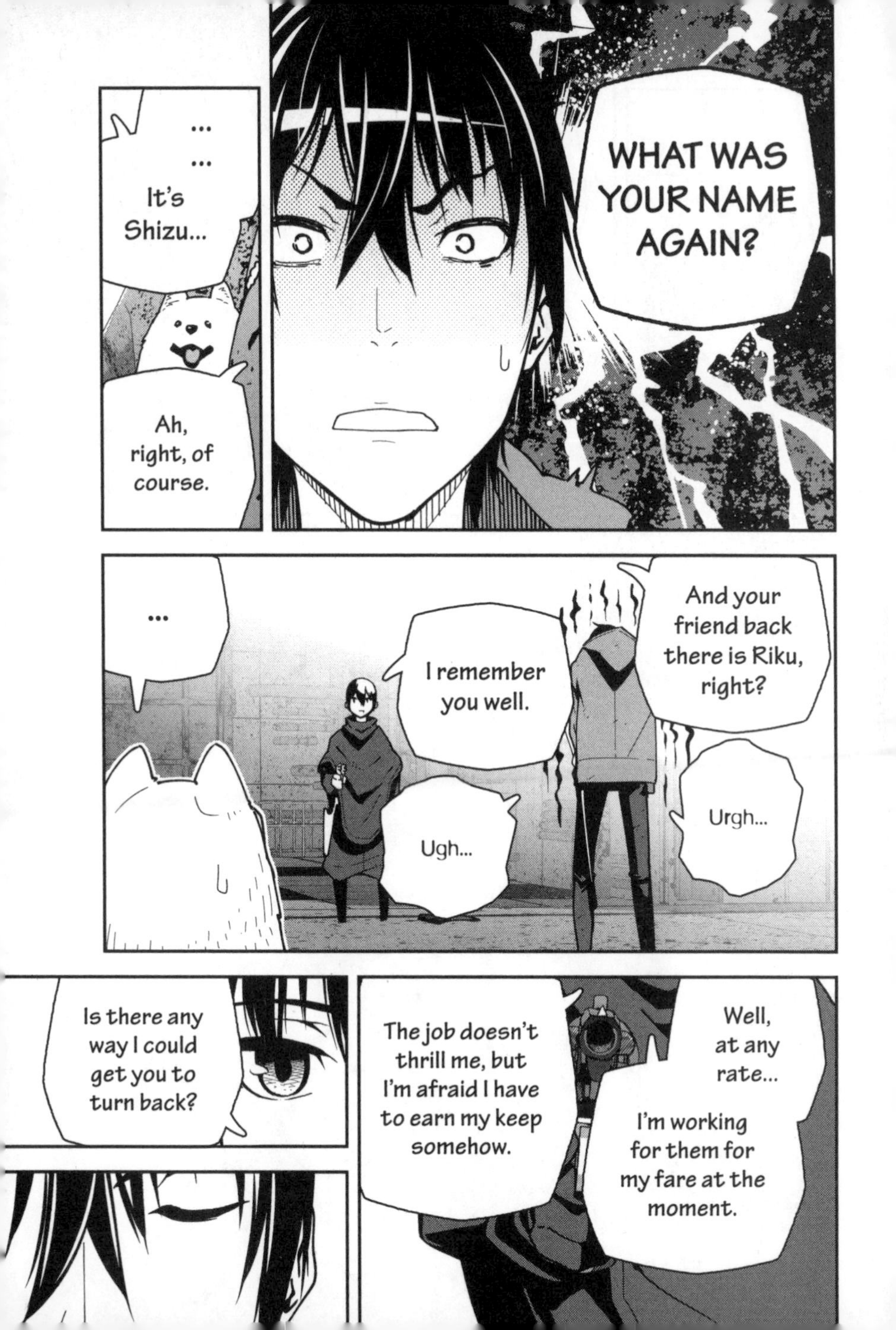
WHAT WAS YOUR NAME AGAIN?
... ... It's Shizu...
Ah, right, of course.
And your friend back there is Riku, right?
Urgh...
I remember you well.
Ugh...
...
Well, at any rate...
I'm working for them for my fare at the moment.
The job doesn't thrill me, but I'm afraid I have to earn my keep somehow.
Is there any way I could get you to turn back?

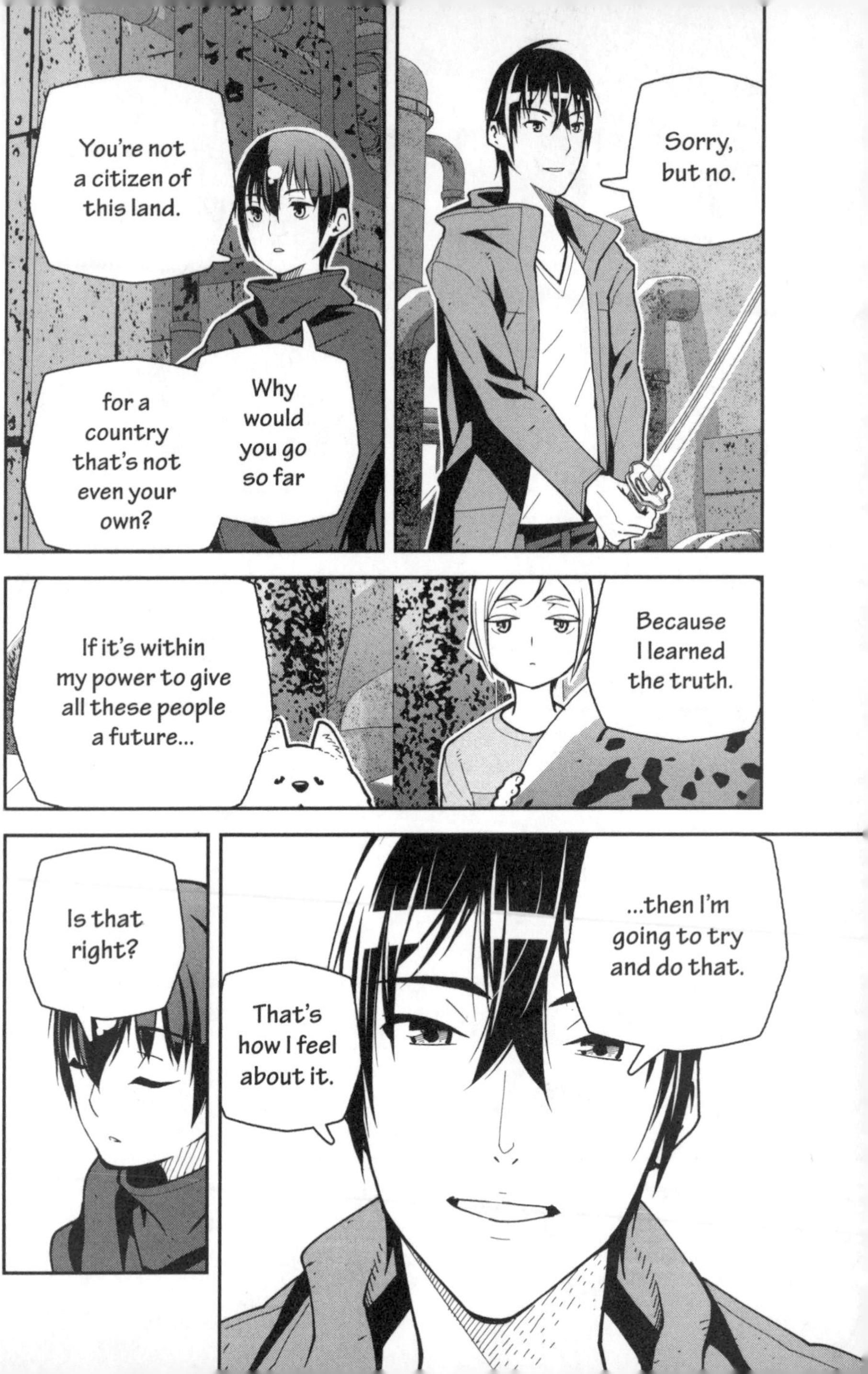

Sorry, but no.
You're not a citizen of this land.
Why would you go so far
for a country that's not even your own?
Because I learned the truth.
If it's within my power to give all these people a future...
...then I'm going to try and do that.
That's how I feel about it.
Is that right?

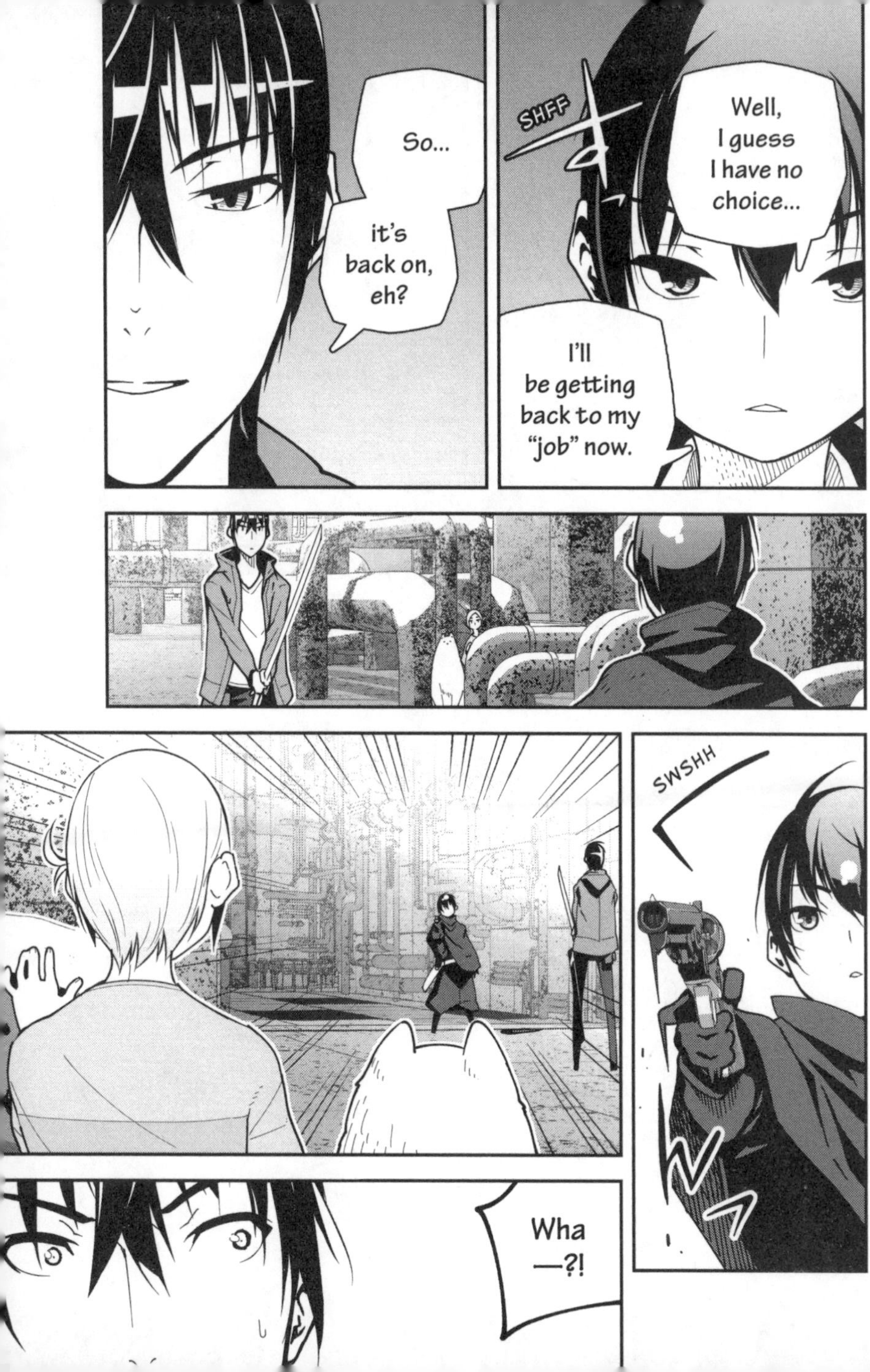
SHFF
Well, I guess I have no choice...
I'll be getting back to my "job" now.
So...
it's back on, eh?
SWSHH
Wha —?!

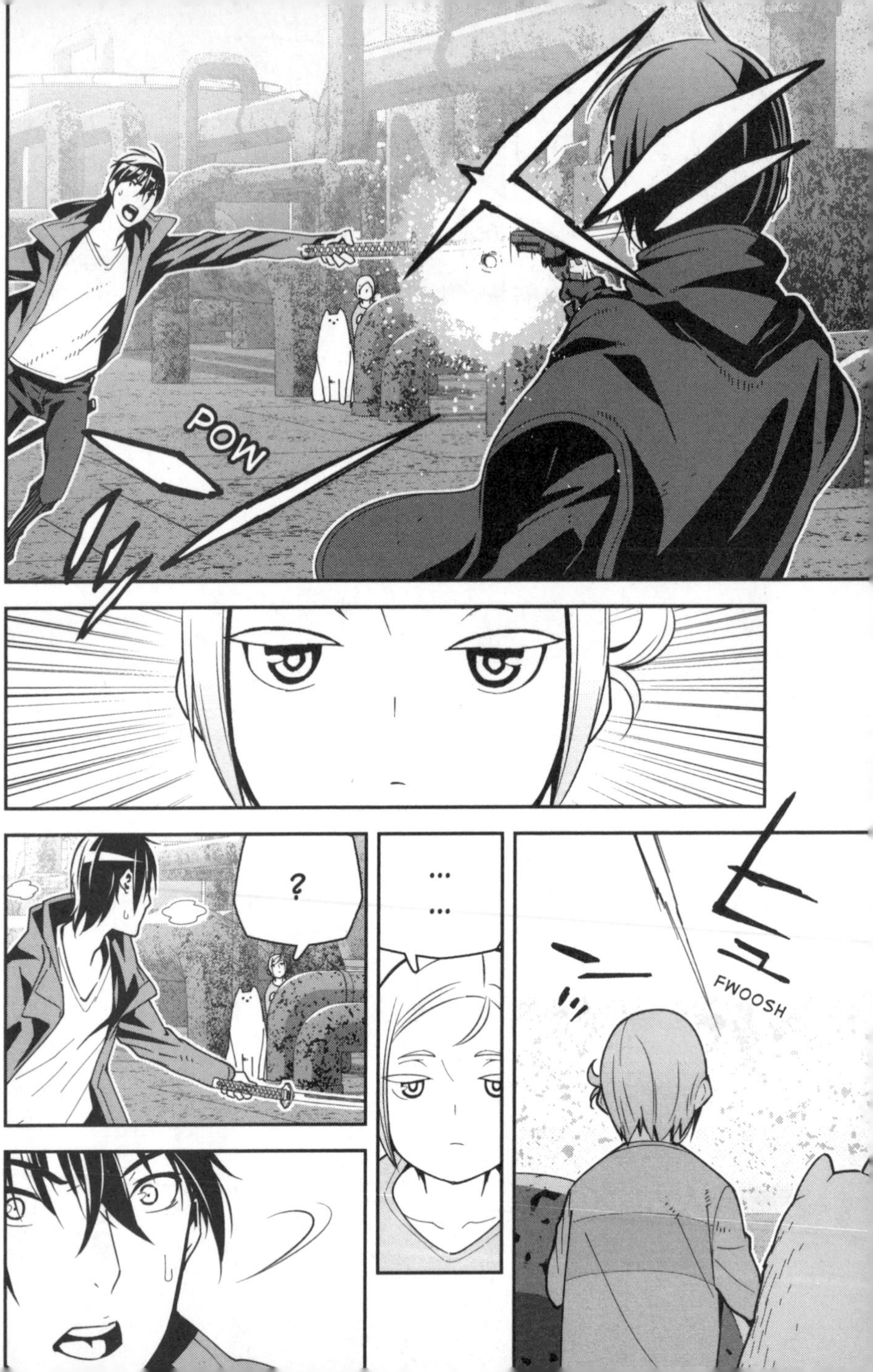
POW
FWOOSH
... ...
?

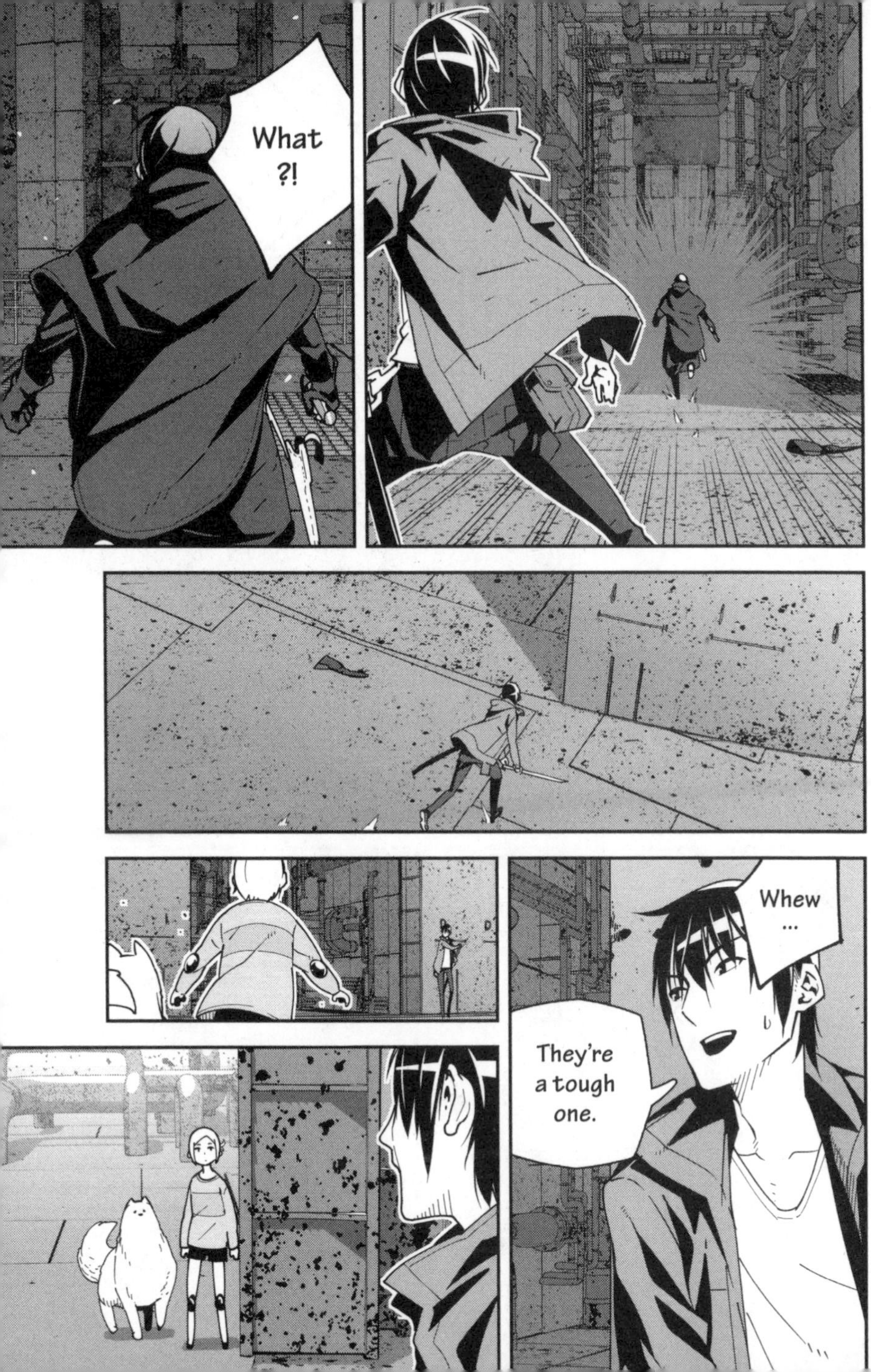
What ?!
Whew ...
They're a tough one.

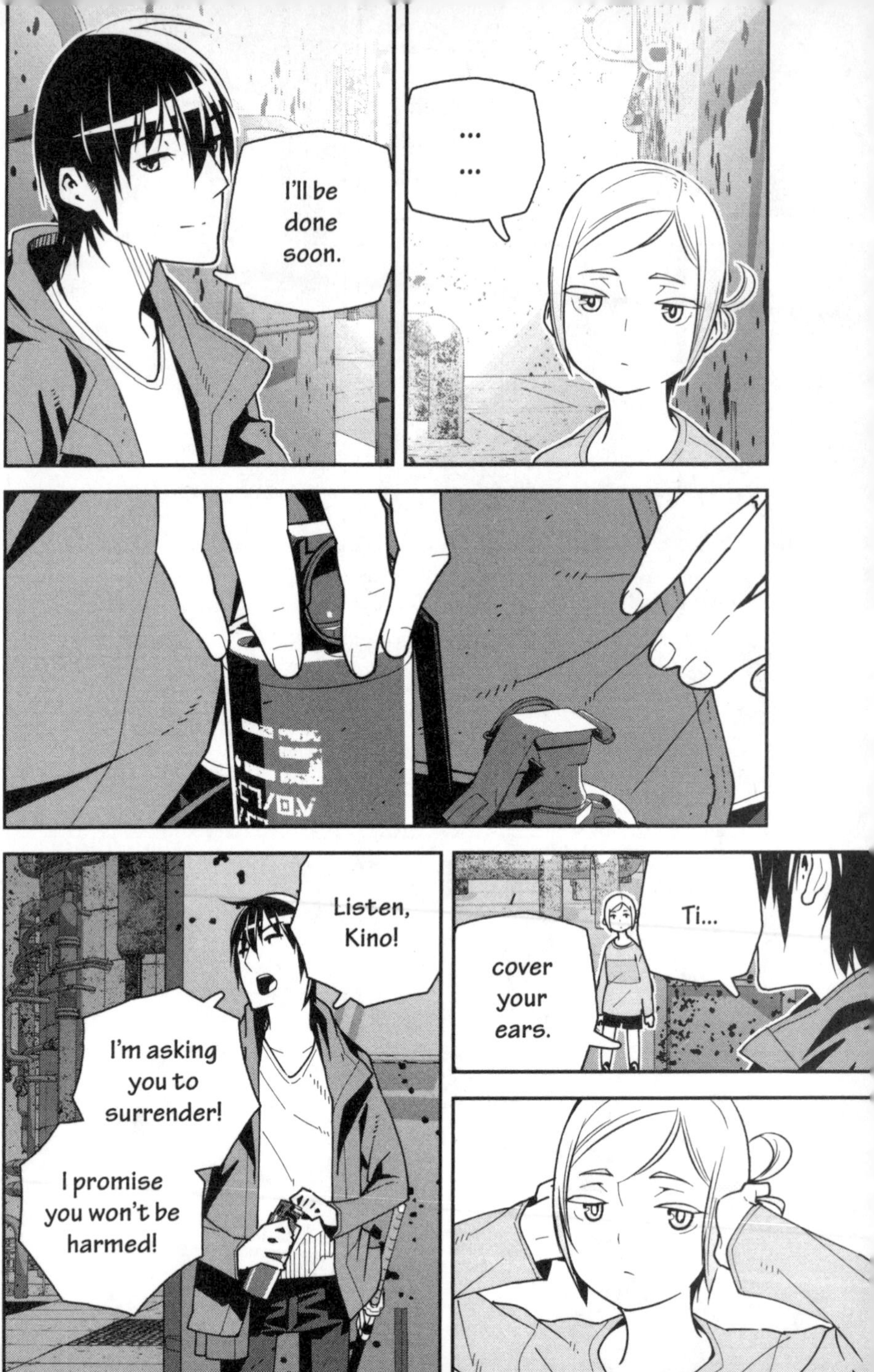
... ...
I'll be done soon.
Ti... cover your ears.
Listen, Kino!
I'm asking you to surrender!
I promise you won't be harmed!

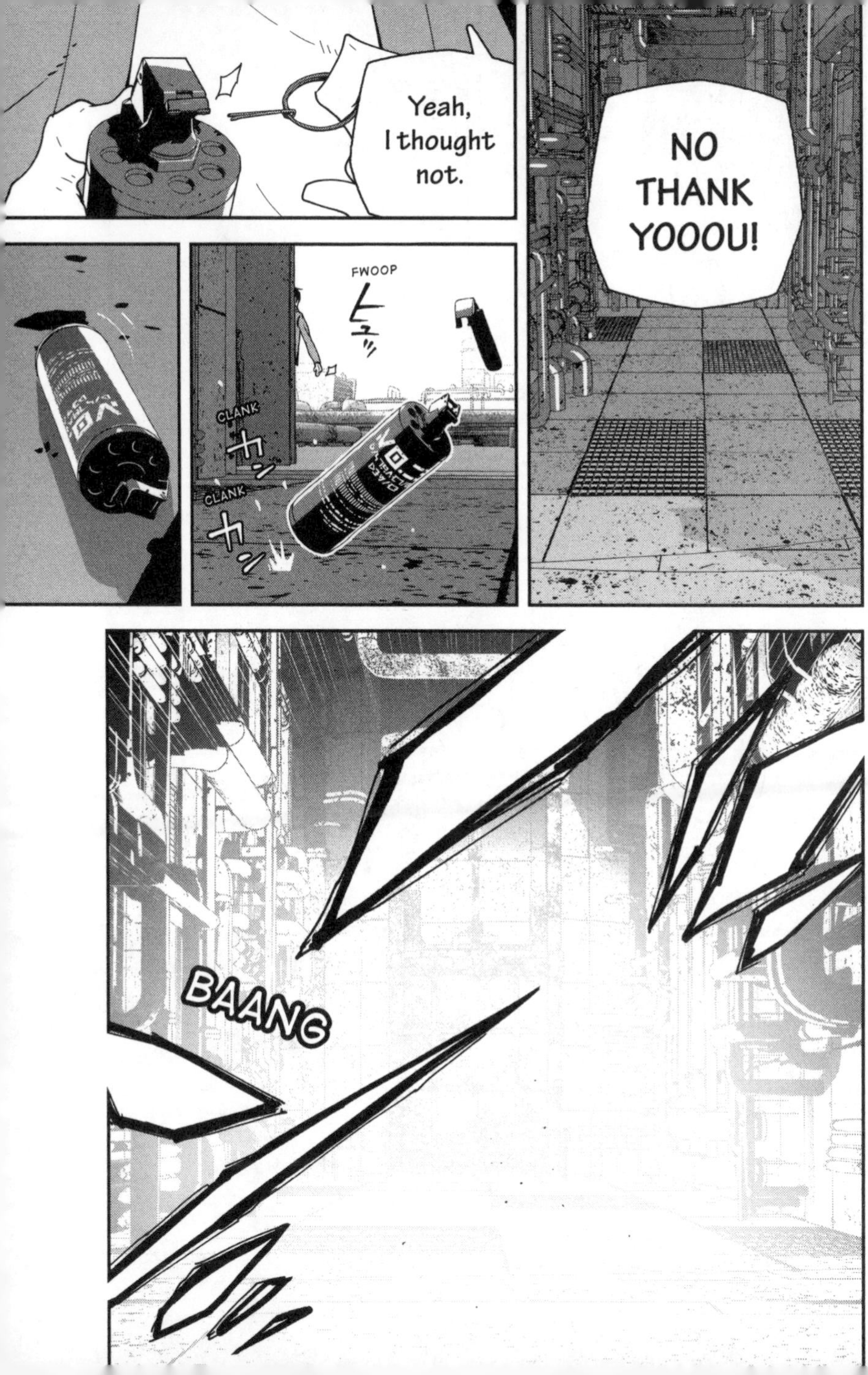
NO THANK YOOOU!
Yeah, I thought not.
FWOOP
CLANK
CLANK
BAANG

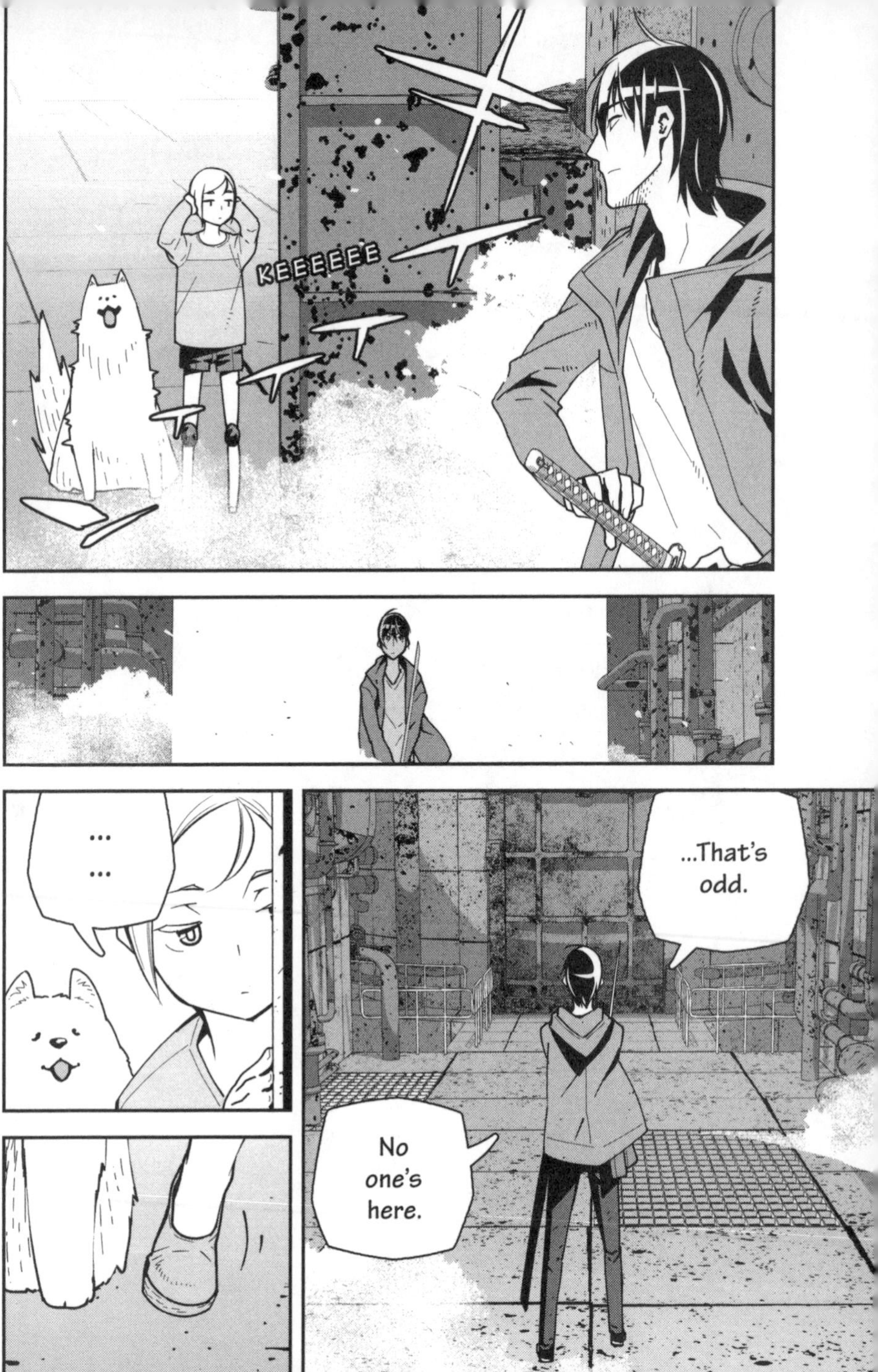
KEEEEEEE
...That's odd.
No one's here.
...
...

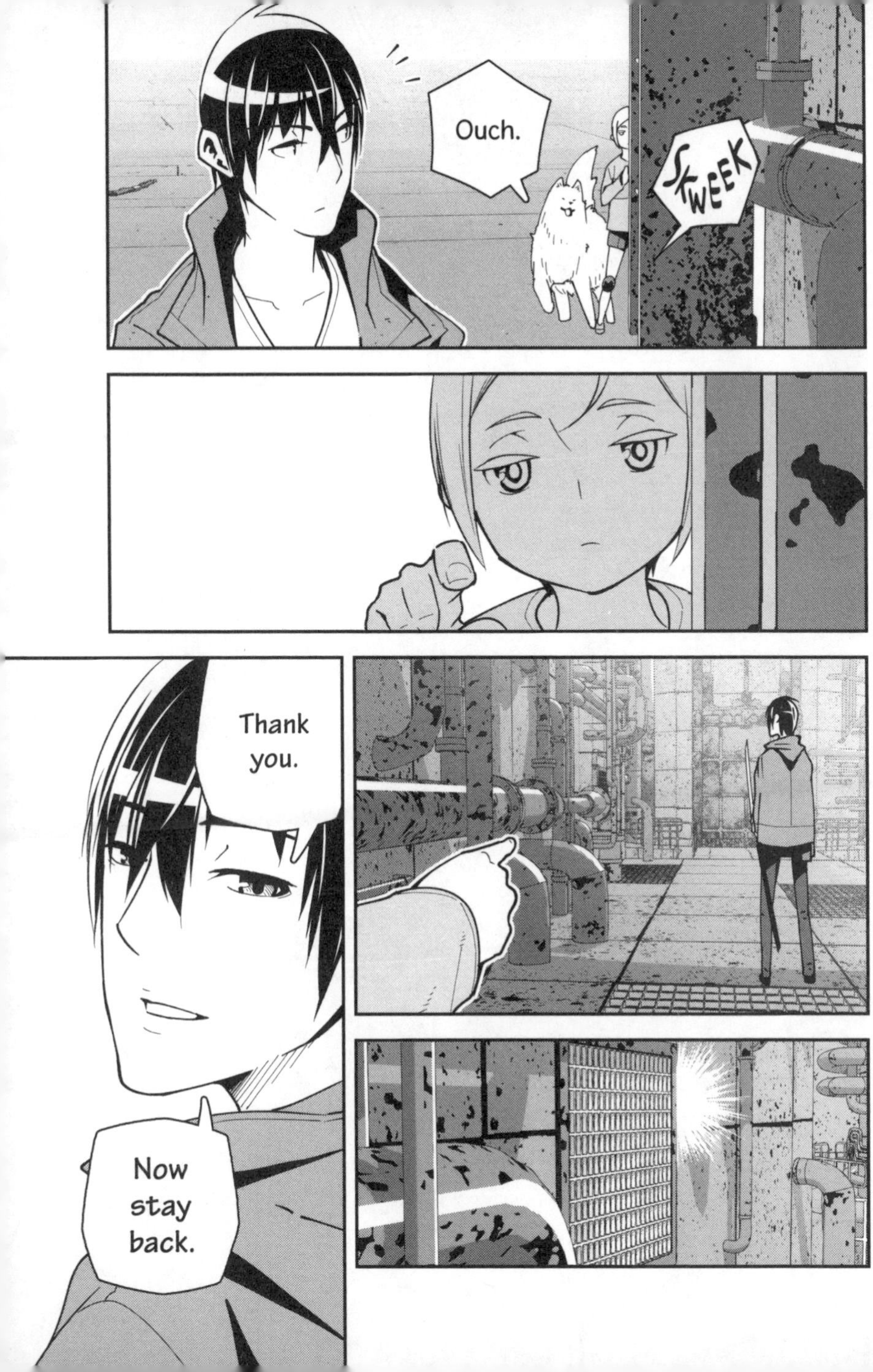
SKWEEK
Ouch.
Thank you.
Now stay back.

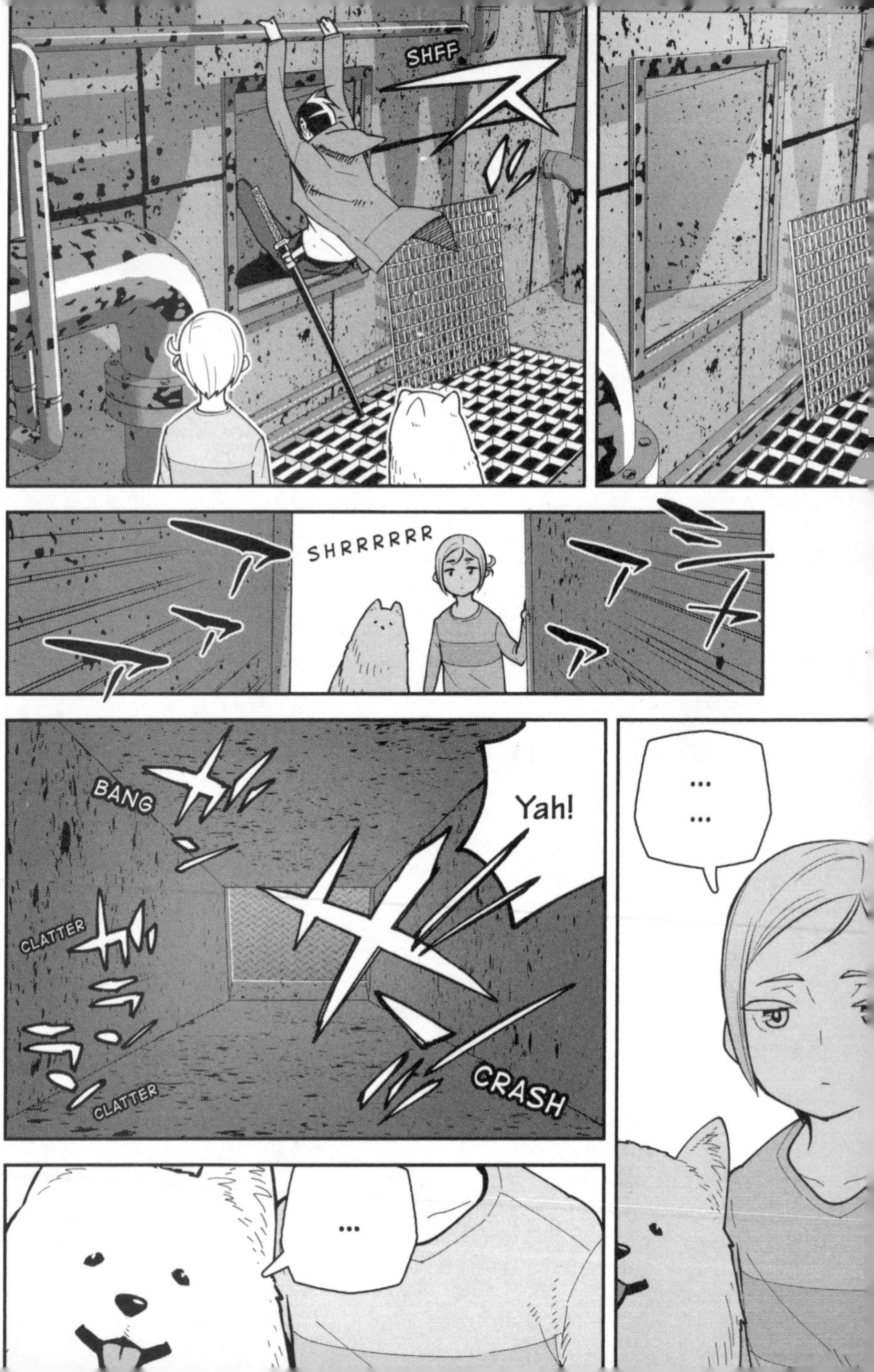
SHFF
SHRRRRRR
...
...
Yah!
BANG
CRASH
CLATTER
CLATTER
...

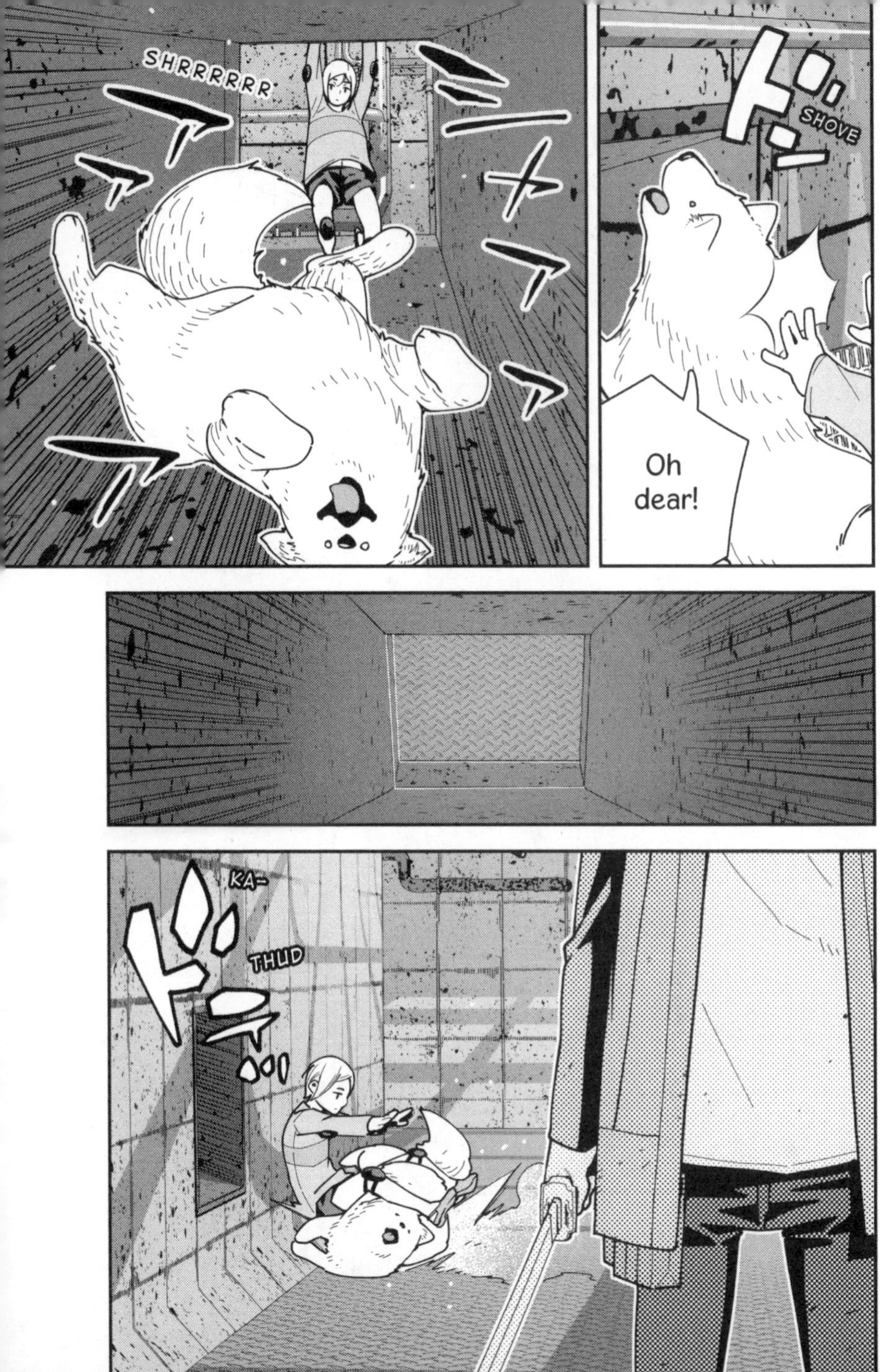
SHOVE
Oh dear!
SHRRRRRRR
KA-
THUD

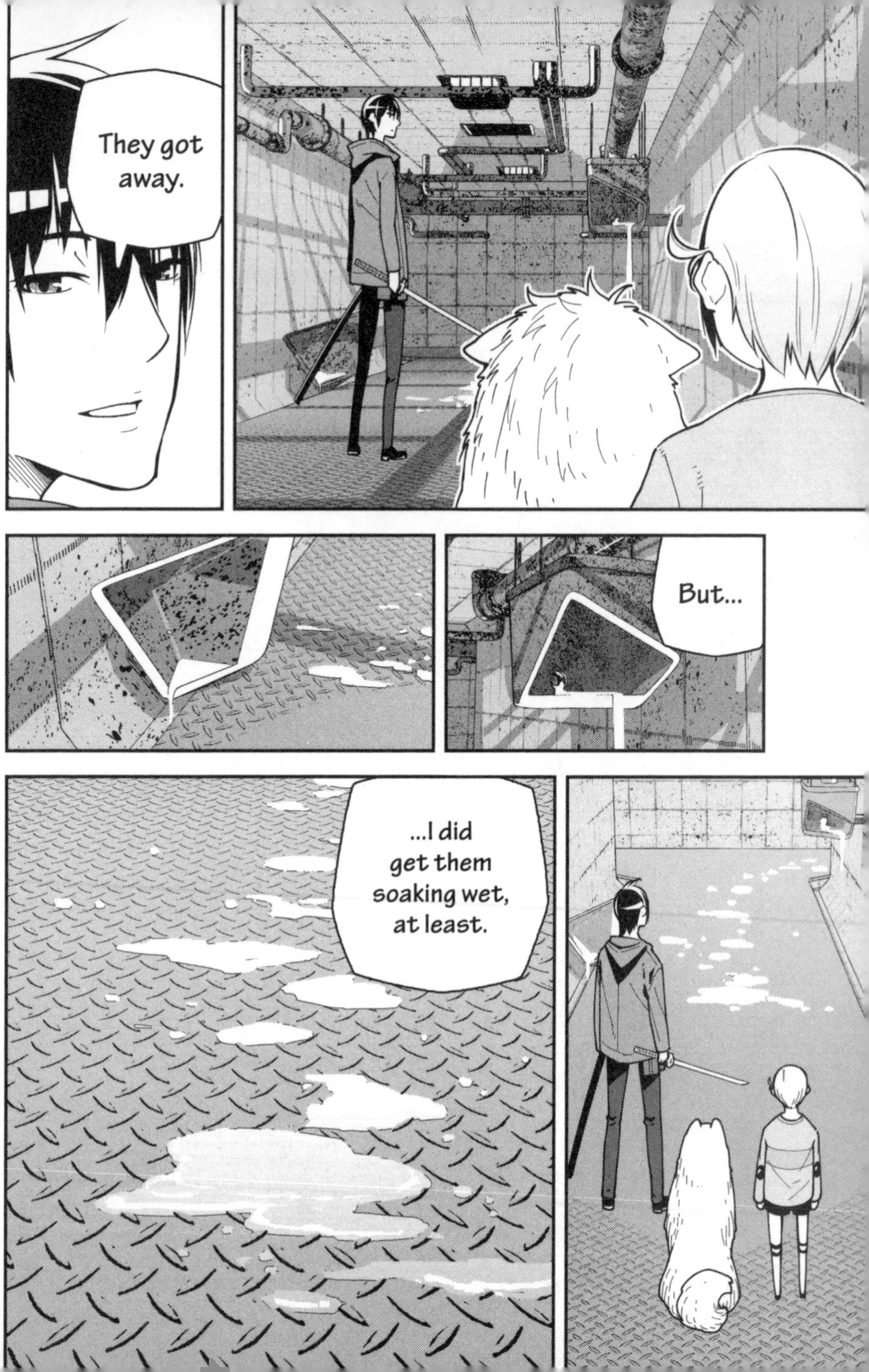
They got away.
But...
...I did get them soaking wet, at least.

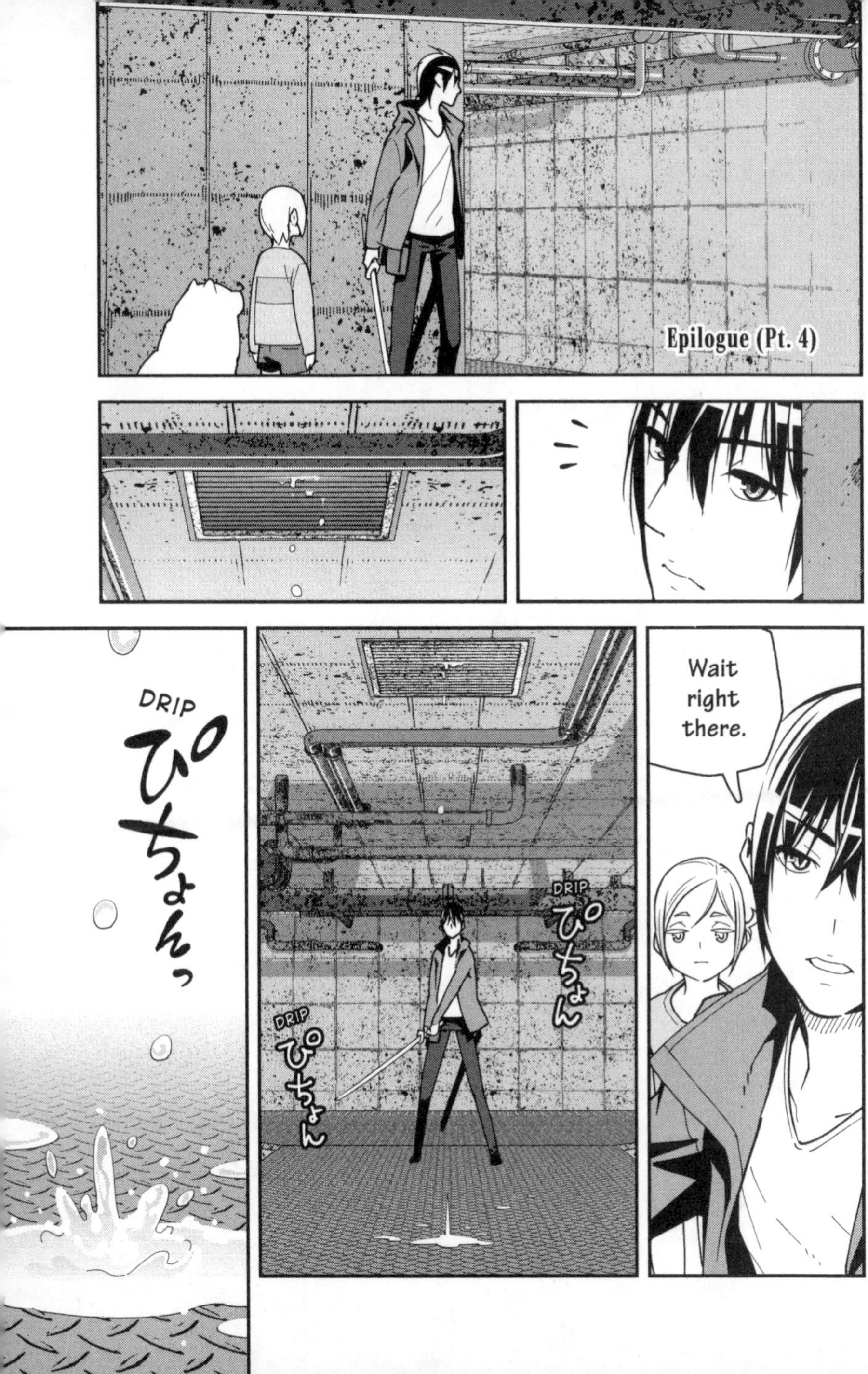
Epilogue (Pt. 4)
Wait right there.
DRIP
ぴちょん
DRIP
ぴちょん
DRIP
ぴちょんっ

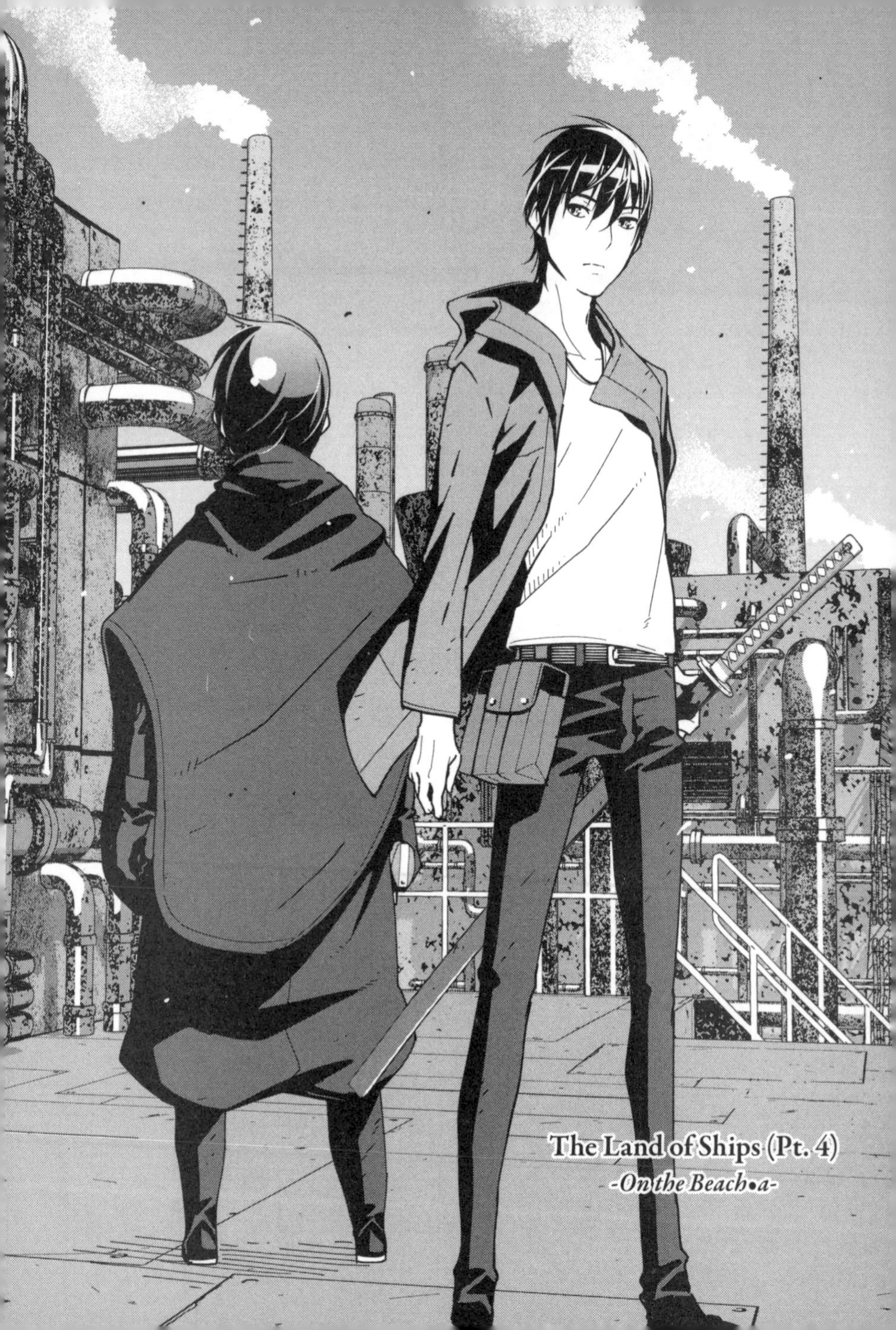
The Land of Ships (Pt. 4)
-On the Beach•a-

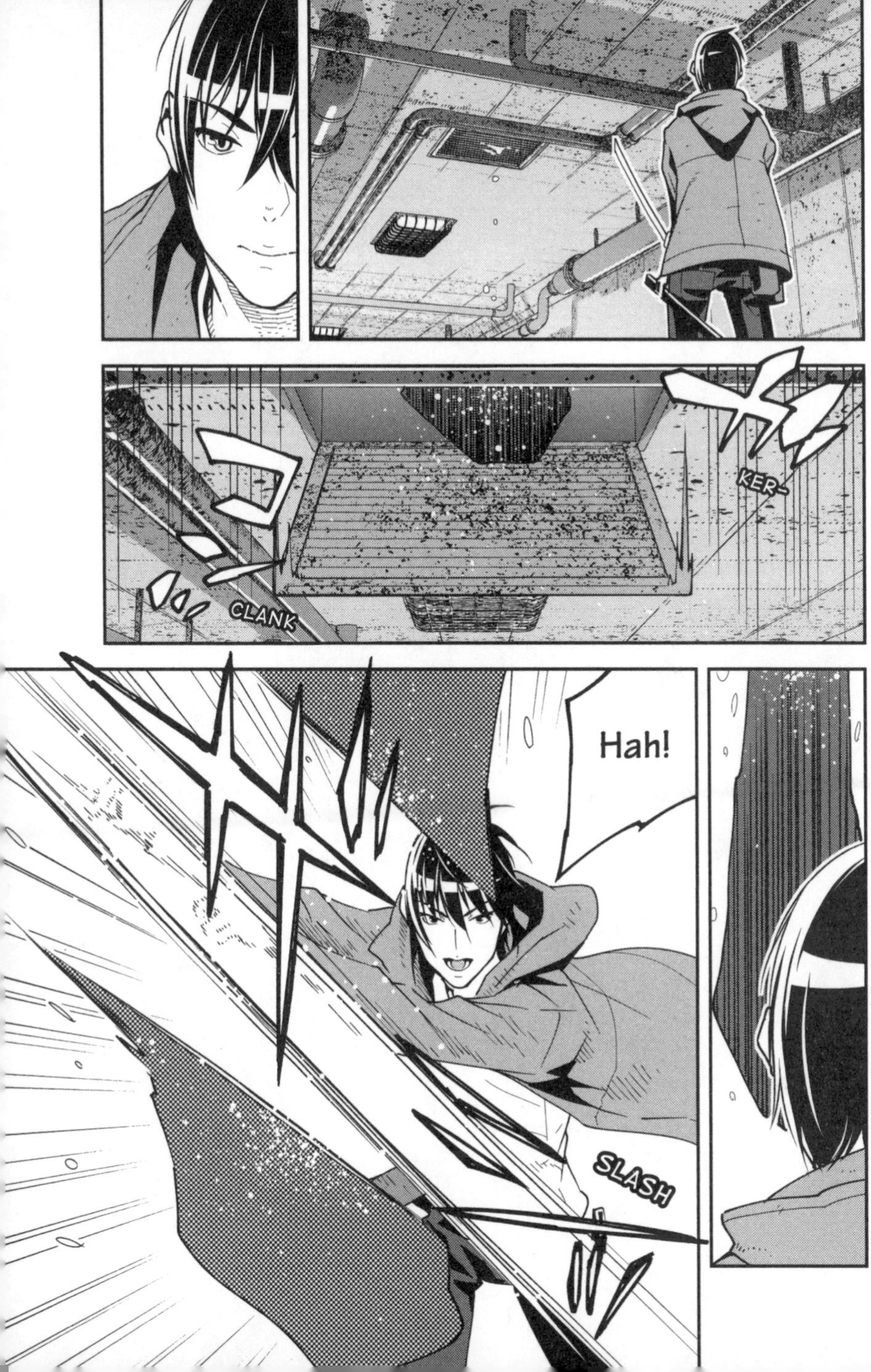
KER-
CLANK
Hah!
SLASH

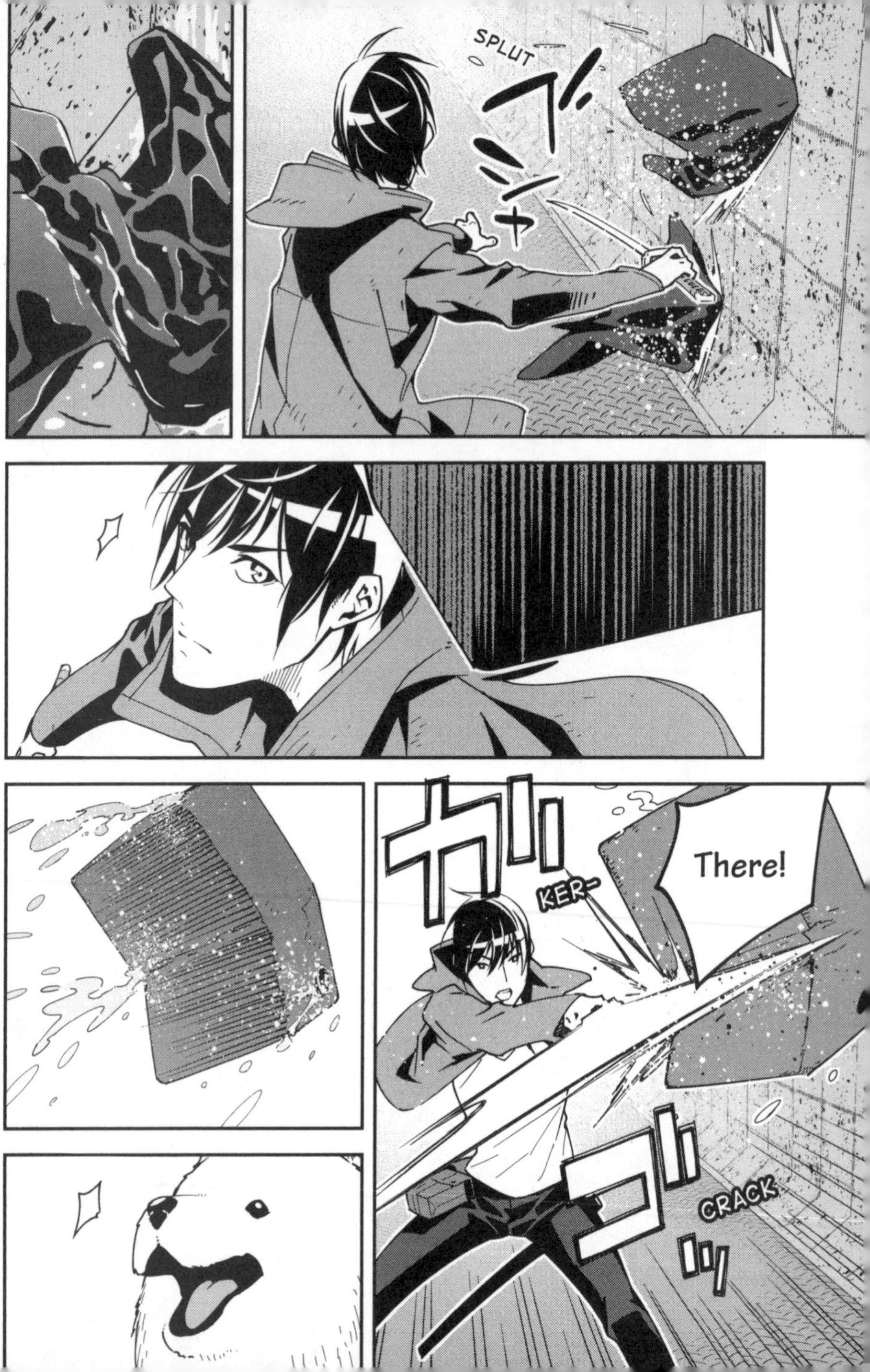
SPLUT
There!
KER-
CRACK

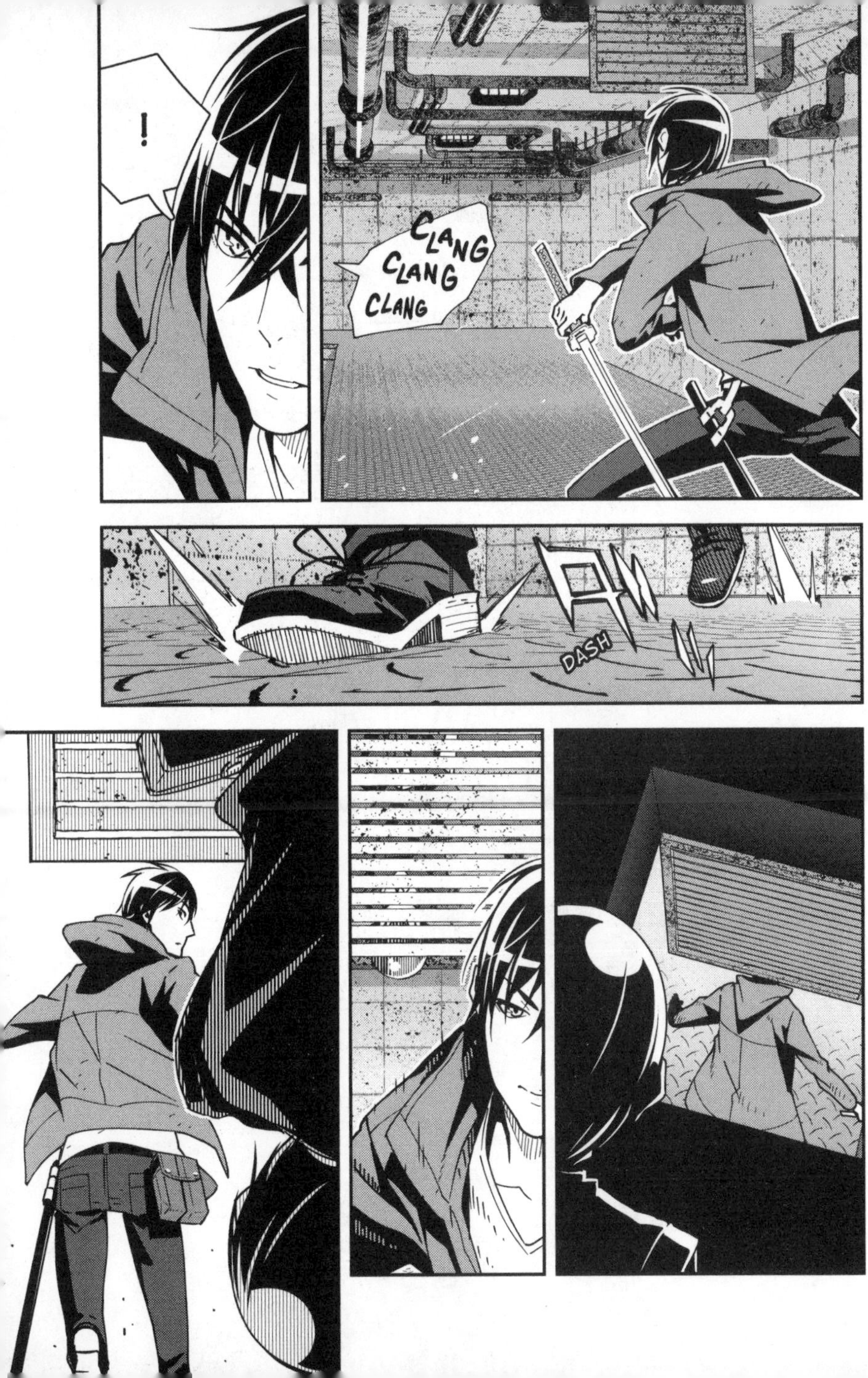
CLANG
CLANG
CLANG
!
DASH

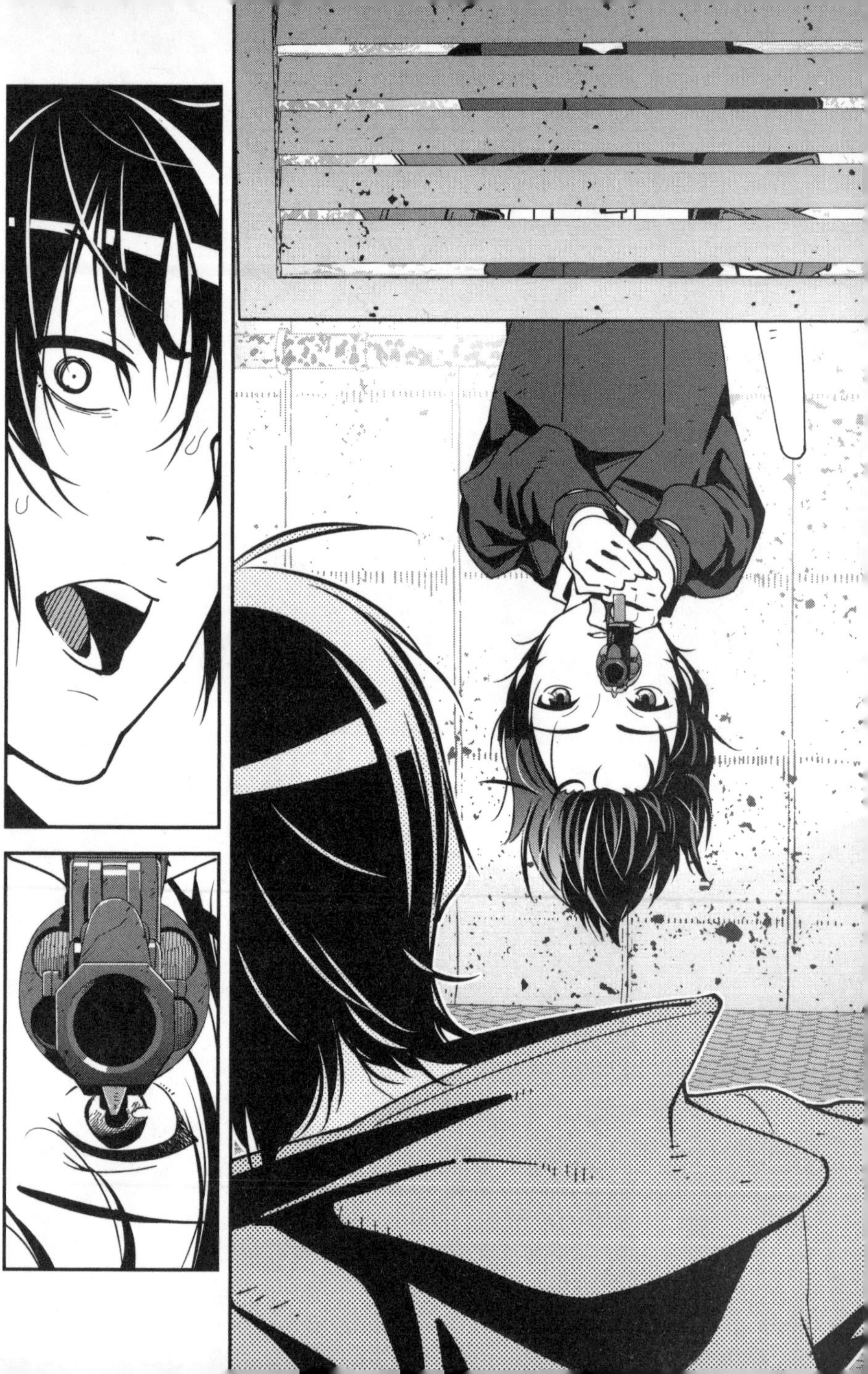

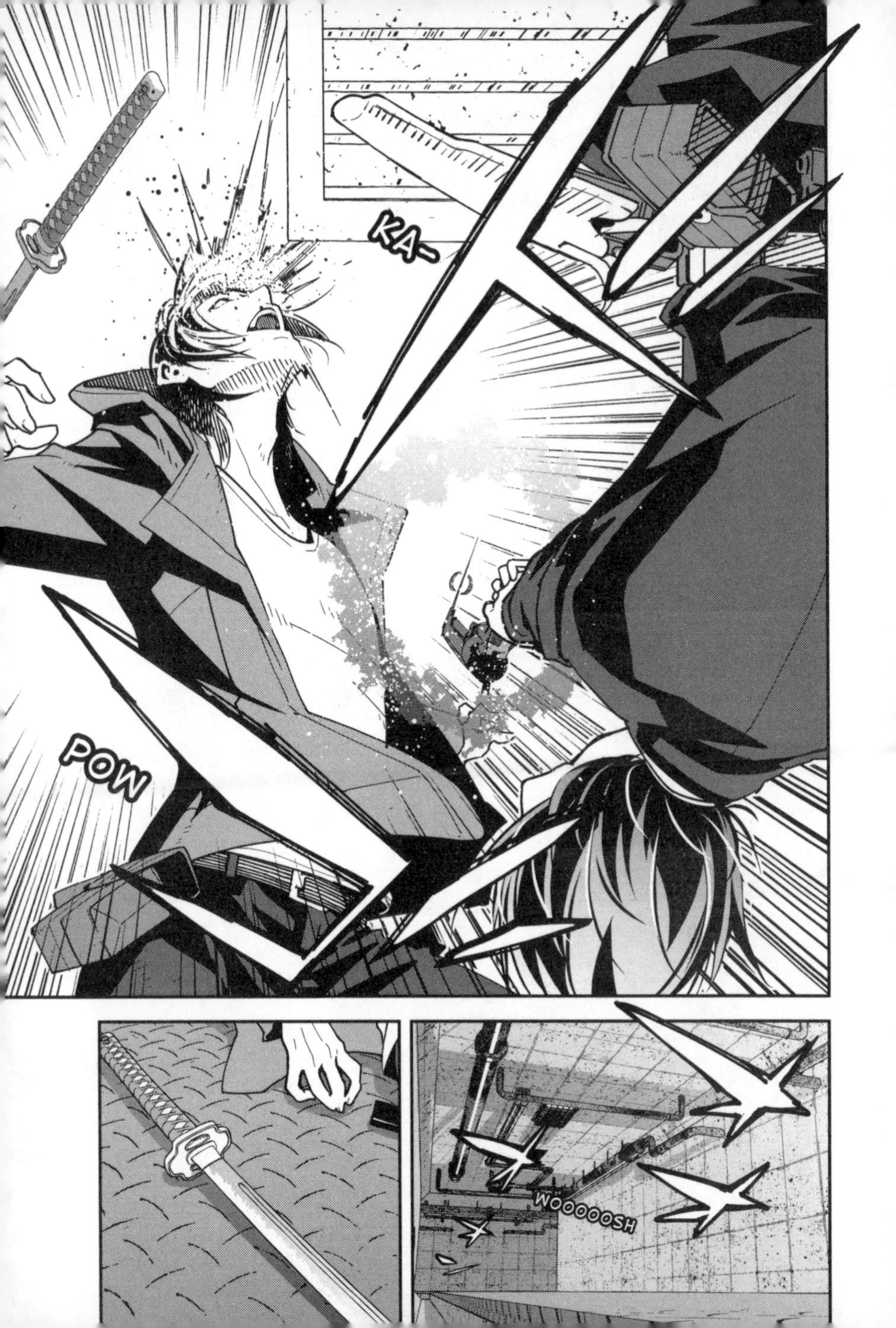
KA-
POW
WOOOOOSH

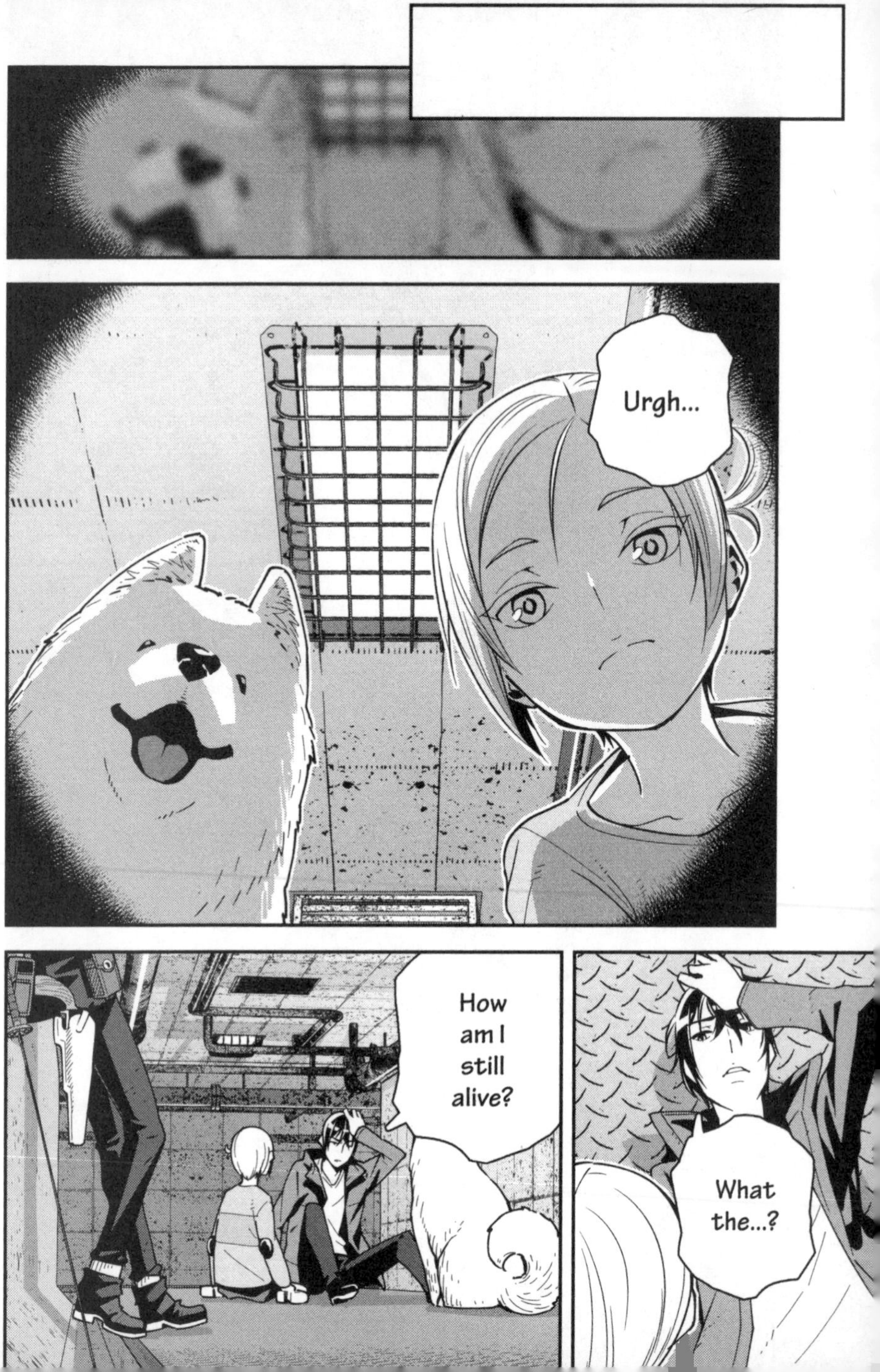
Urgh...
What the...?
How am I still alive?

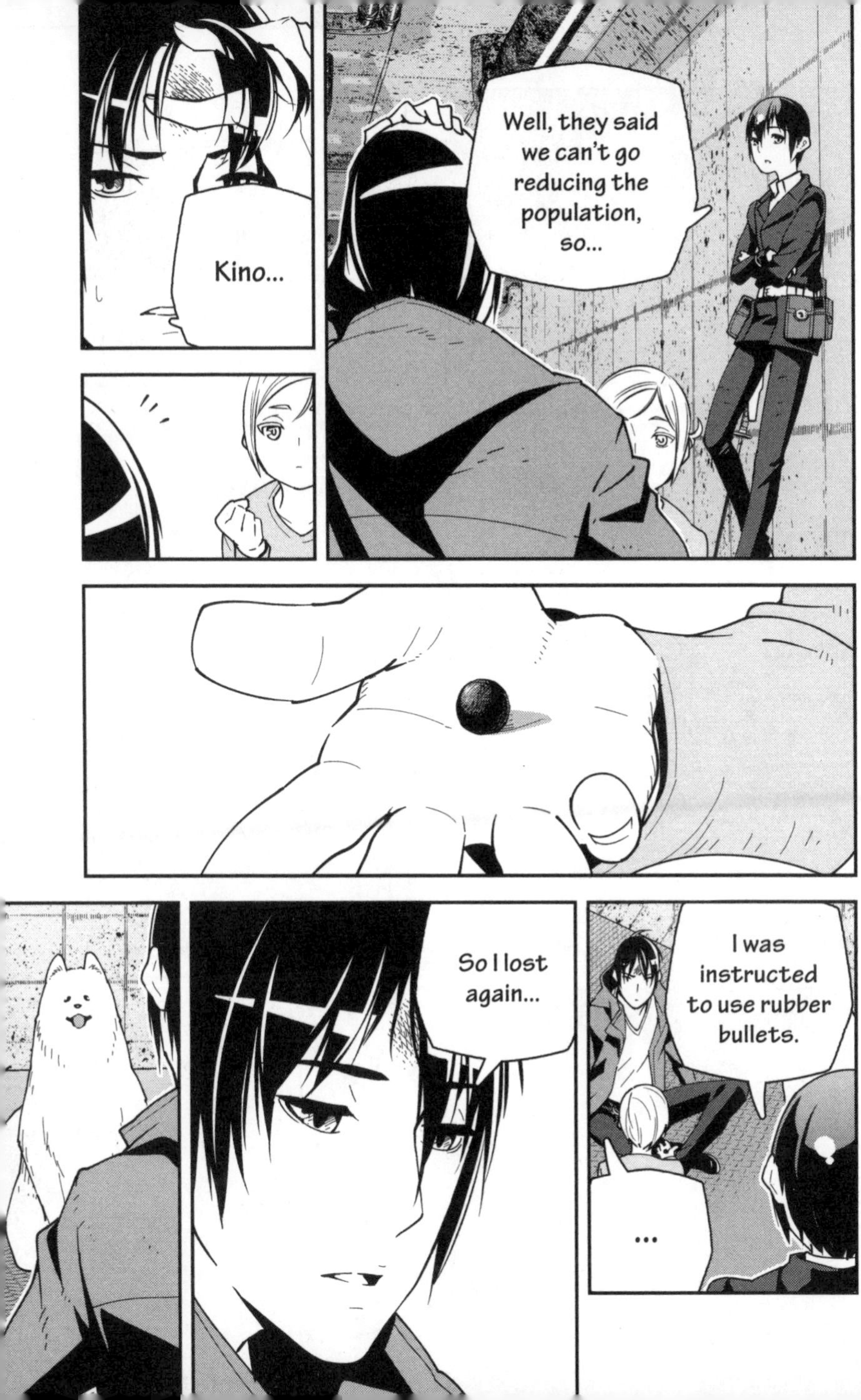
Well, they said we can't go reducing the population, so...
Kino...
I was instructed to use rubber bullets.
...
So I lost again...

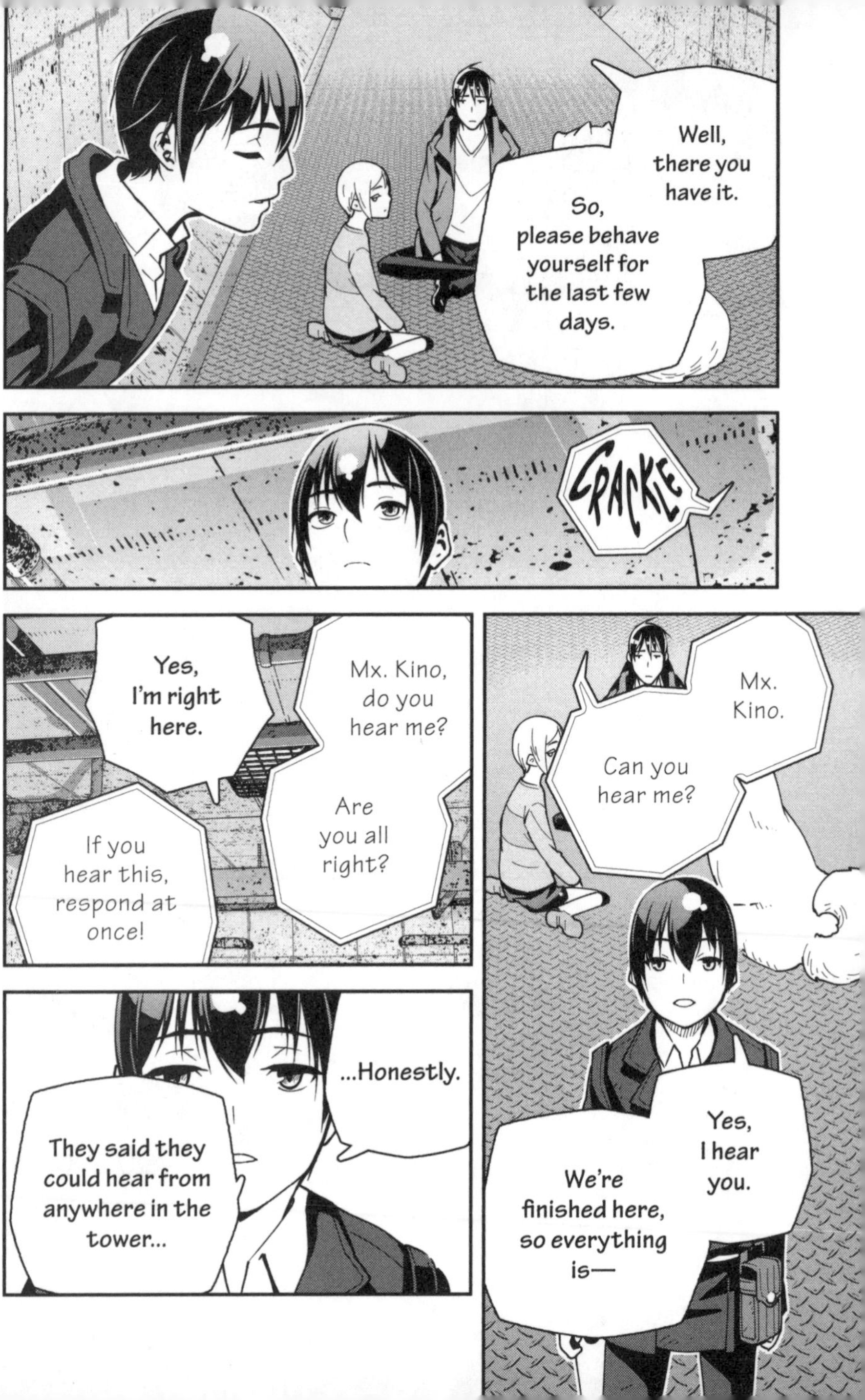
Well, there you have it.
So, please behave yourself for the last few days.
CRACKLE
Mx. Kino.
Can you hear me?
Yes, I hear you.
We're finished here, so everything is—
Mx. Kino, do you hear me?
Yes, I'm right here.
Are you all right?
If you hear this, respond at once!
...Honestly.
They said they could hear from anywhere in the tower...

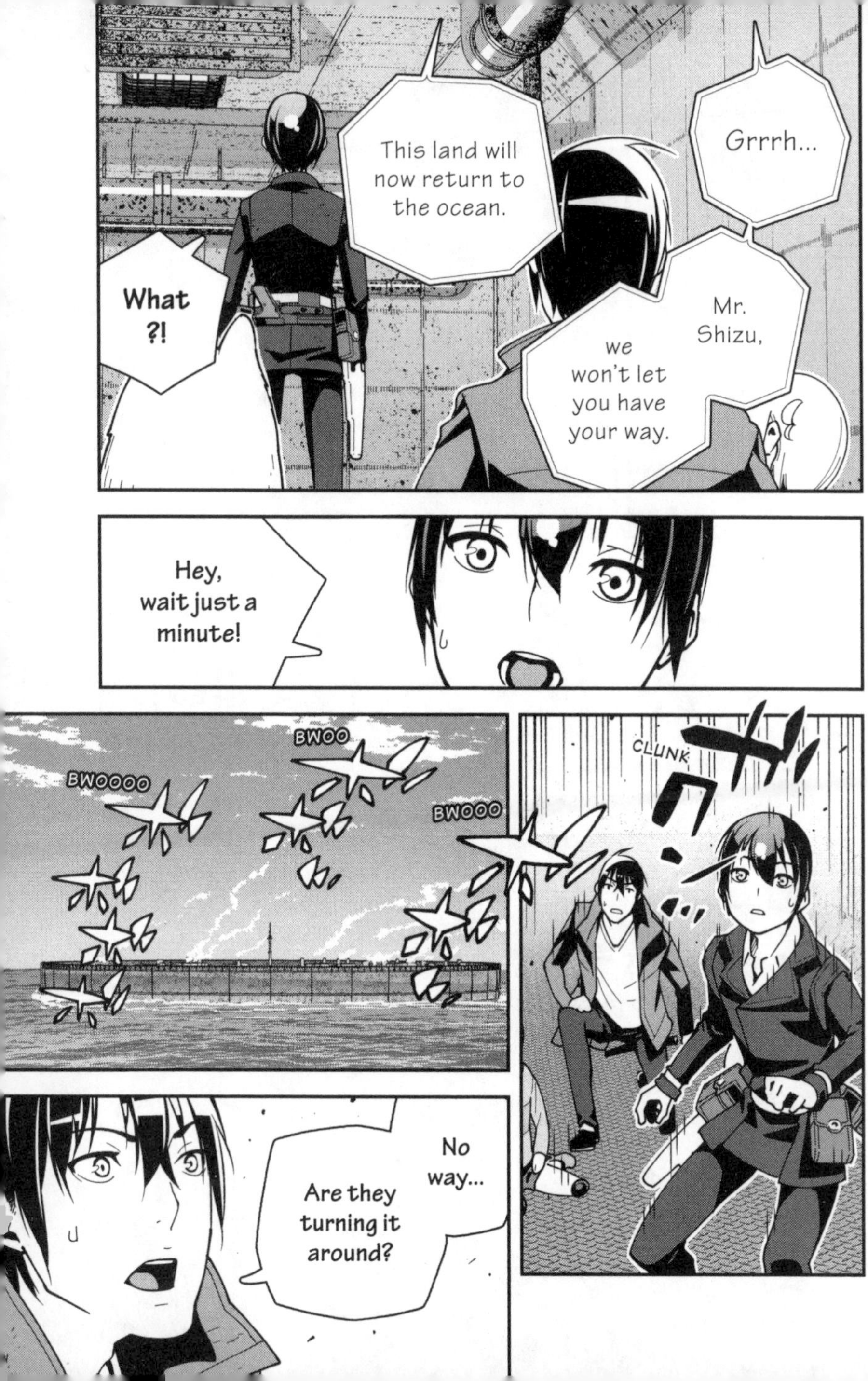
Grrrh...
This land will now return to the ocean.
Mr. Shizu, we won't let you have your way.
What?!
Hey, wait just a minute!
CLUNK
BWOO
BWOOO
BWOOOOO
No way...
Are they turning it around?

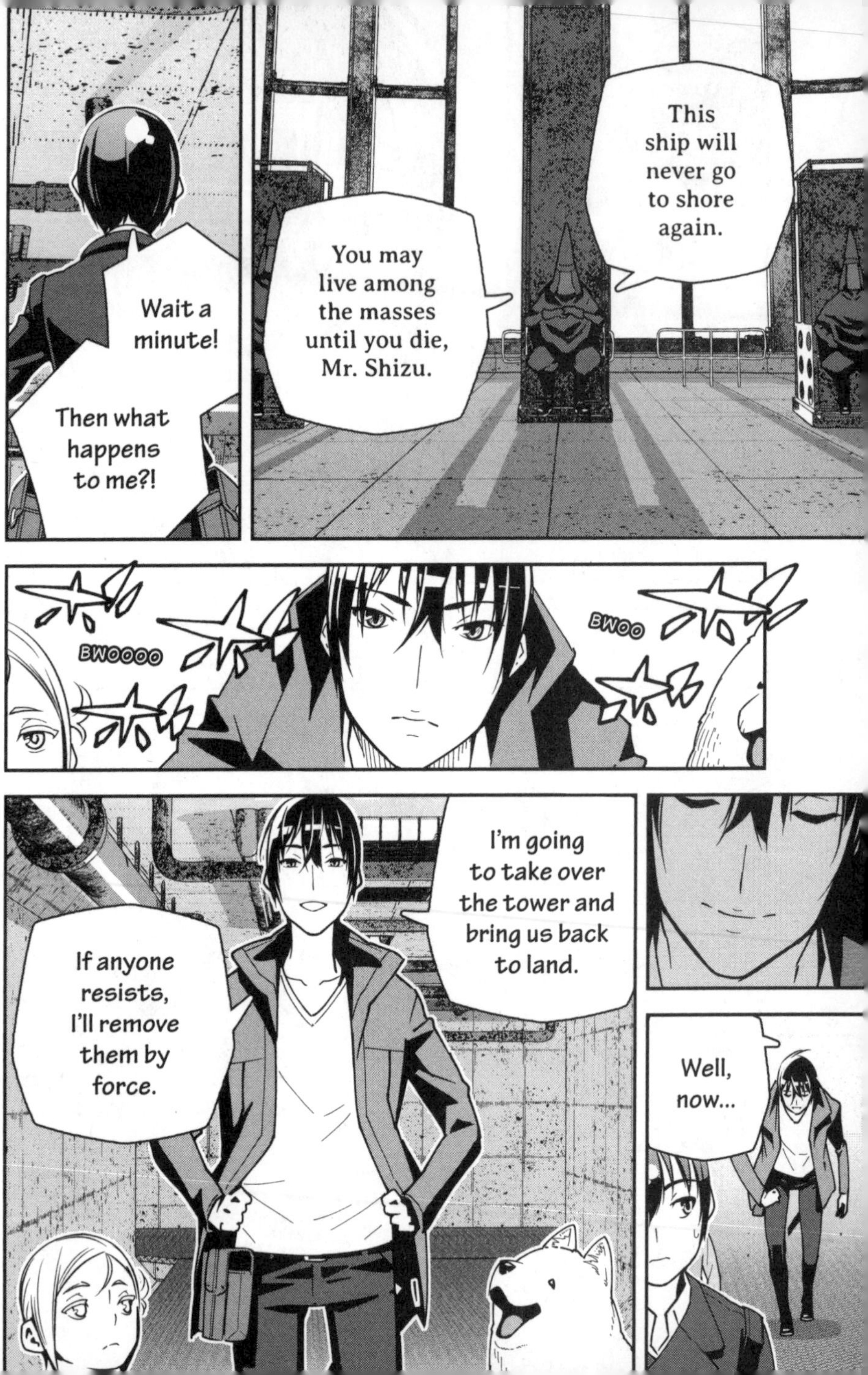
This ship will never go to shore again.
You may live among the masses until you die, Mr. Shizu.
Wait a minute!
Then what happens to me?!
BWOO
BWOOOOO
Well, now...
I'm going to take over the tower and bring us back to land.
If anyone resists, I'll remove them by force.

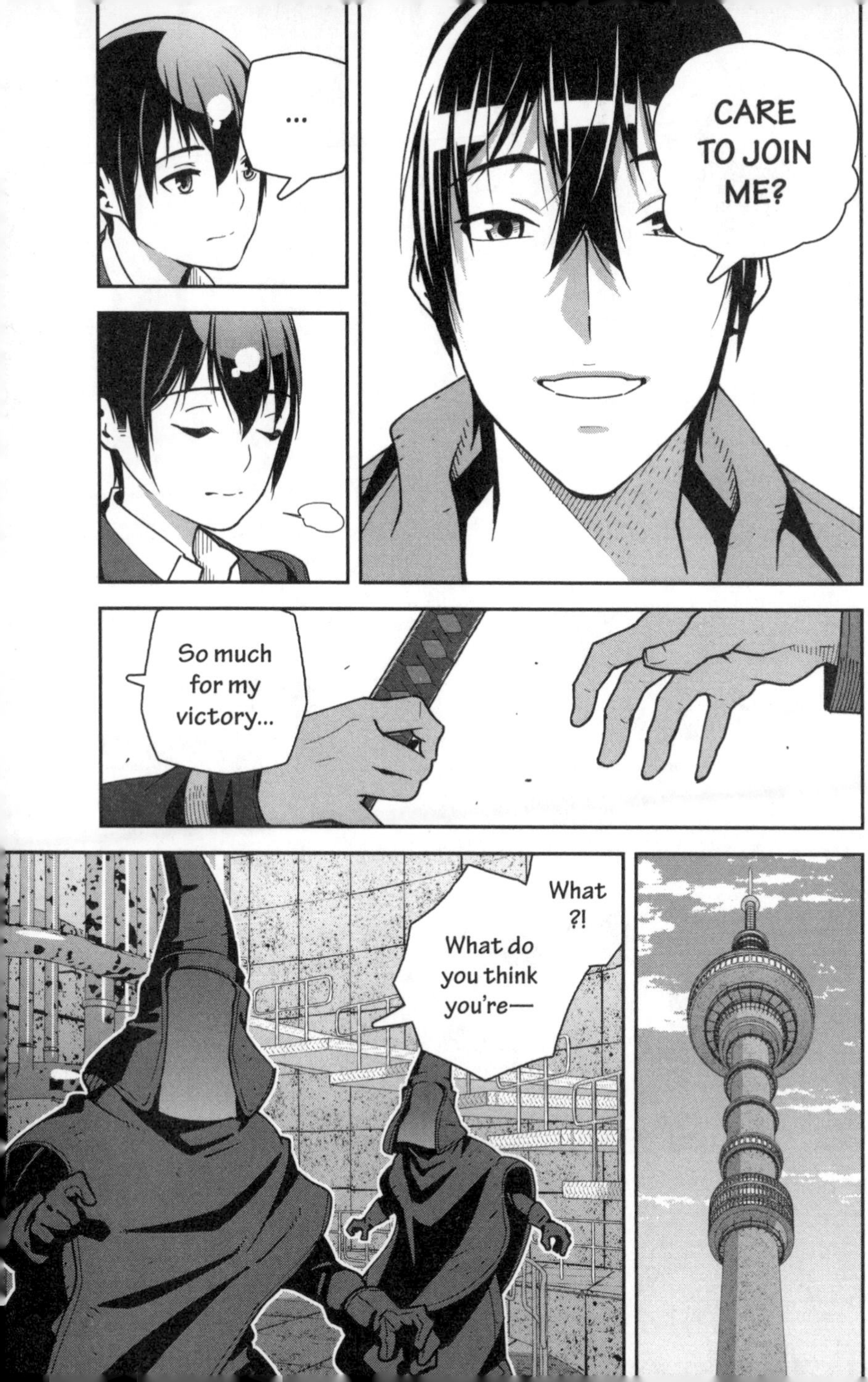
CARE TO JOIN ME?
...
So much for my victory...
What ?!
What do you think you're—

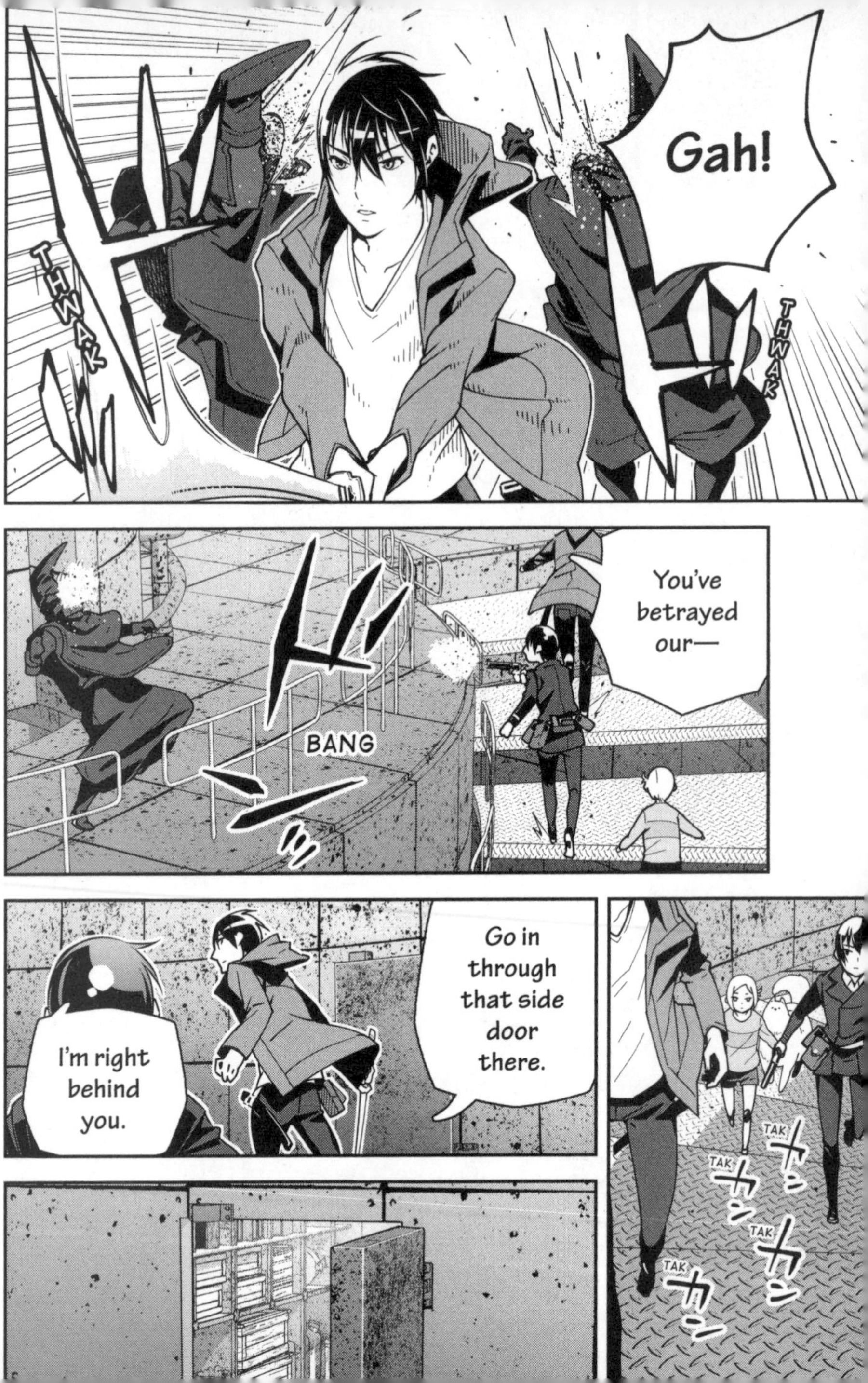
Gah!
THWAK
THWAK
You've betrayed our—
BANG
TAK
TAK
TAK
TAK
Go in through that side door there.
I'm right behind you.

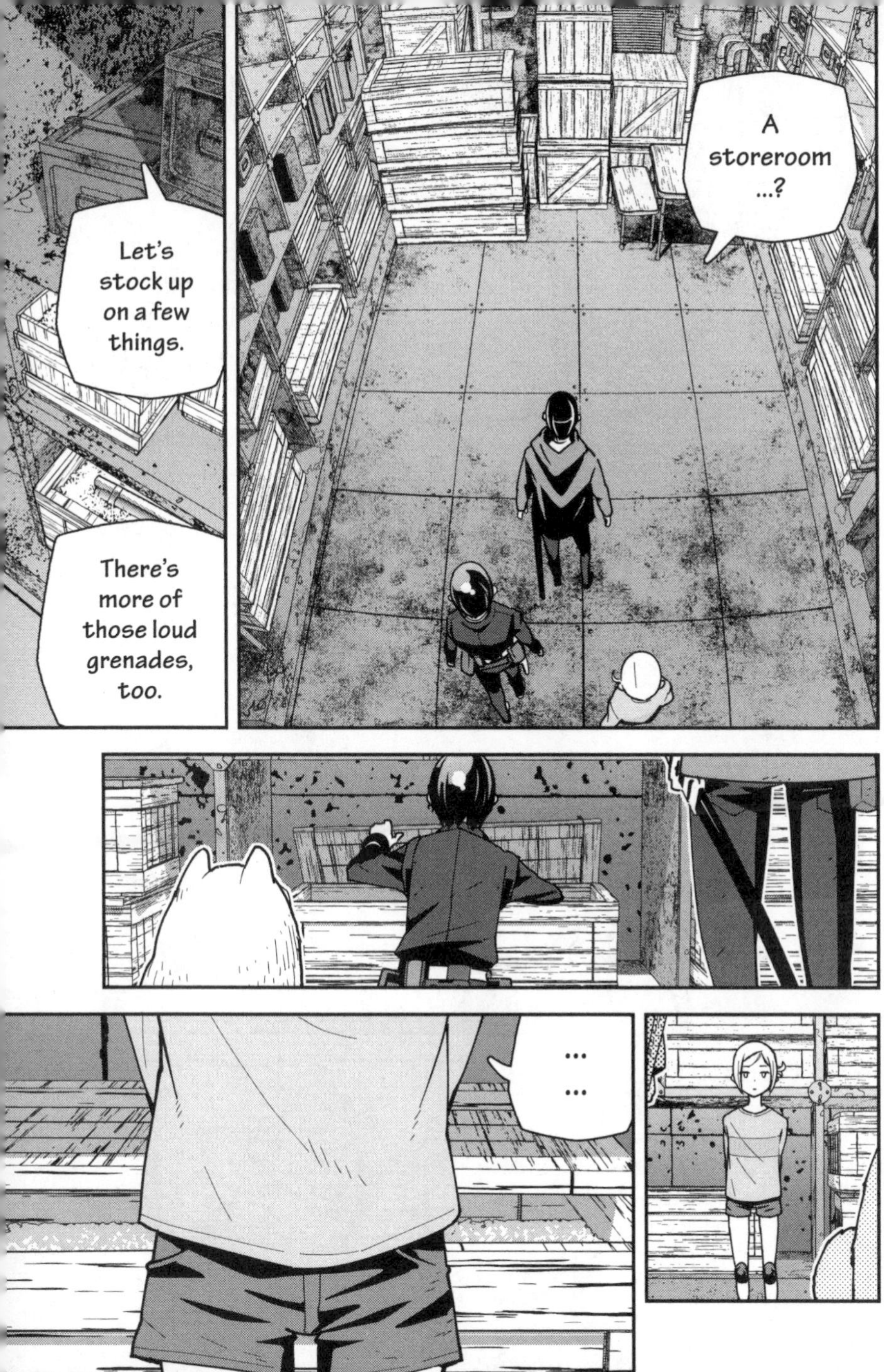
A storeroom ...?
Let's stock up on a few things.
There's more of those loud grenades, too.
...
...

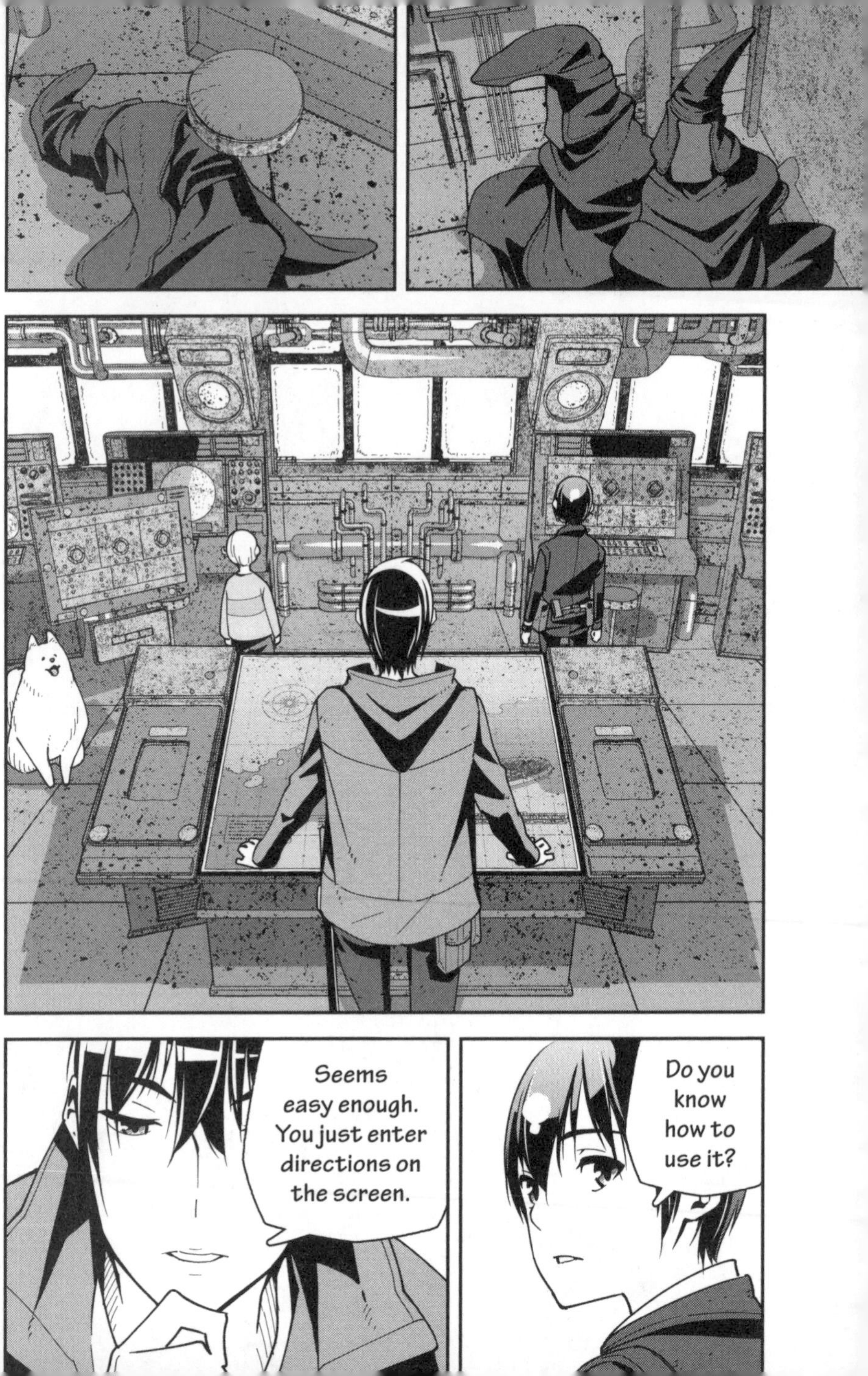
Do you know how to use it?
Seems easy enough. You just enter directions on the screen.

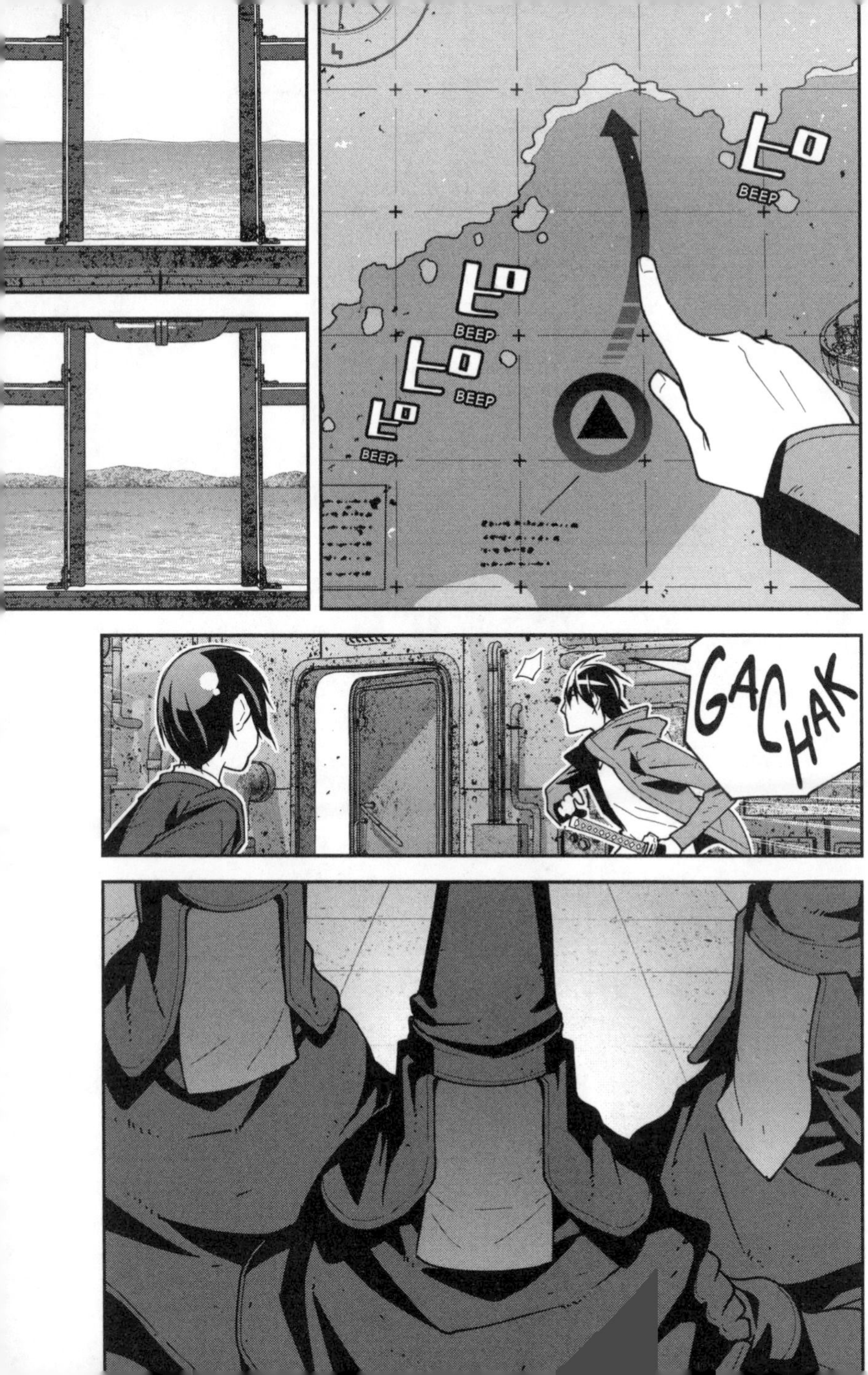
ピ
BEEP
ピ
BEEP
ピ
BEEP
ピ
BEEP
GACHAK

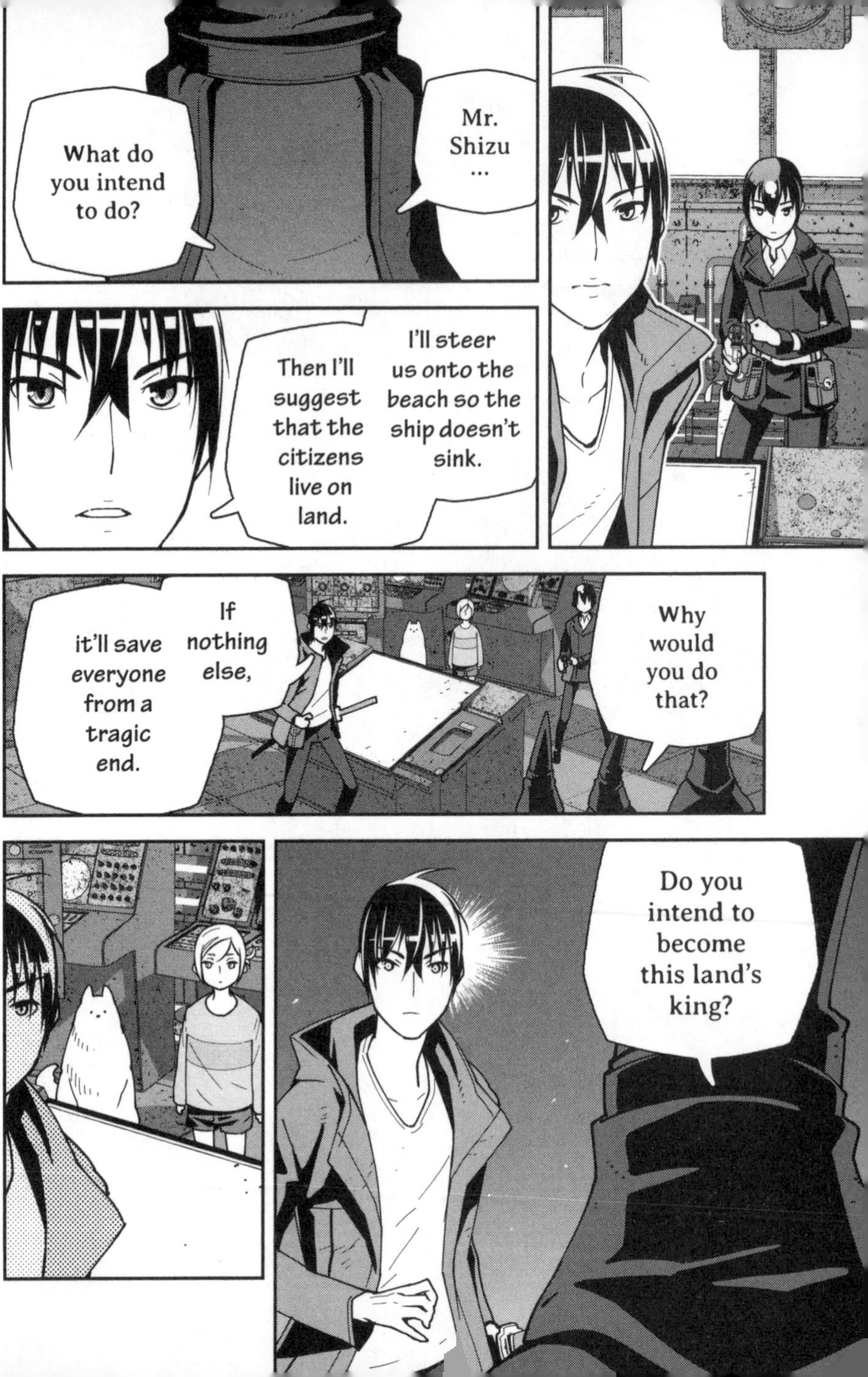
Mr. Shizu ...
What do you intend to do?
I'll steer us onto the beach so the ship doesn't sink.
Then I'll suggest that the citizens live on land.
Why would you do that?
If nothing else,
it'll save everyone from a tragic end.
Do you intend to become this land's king?

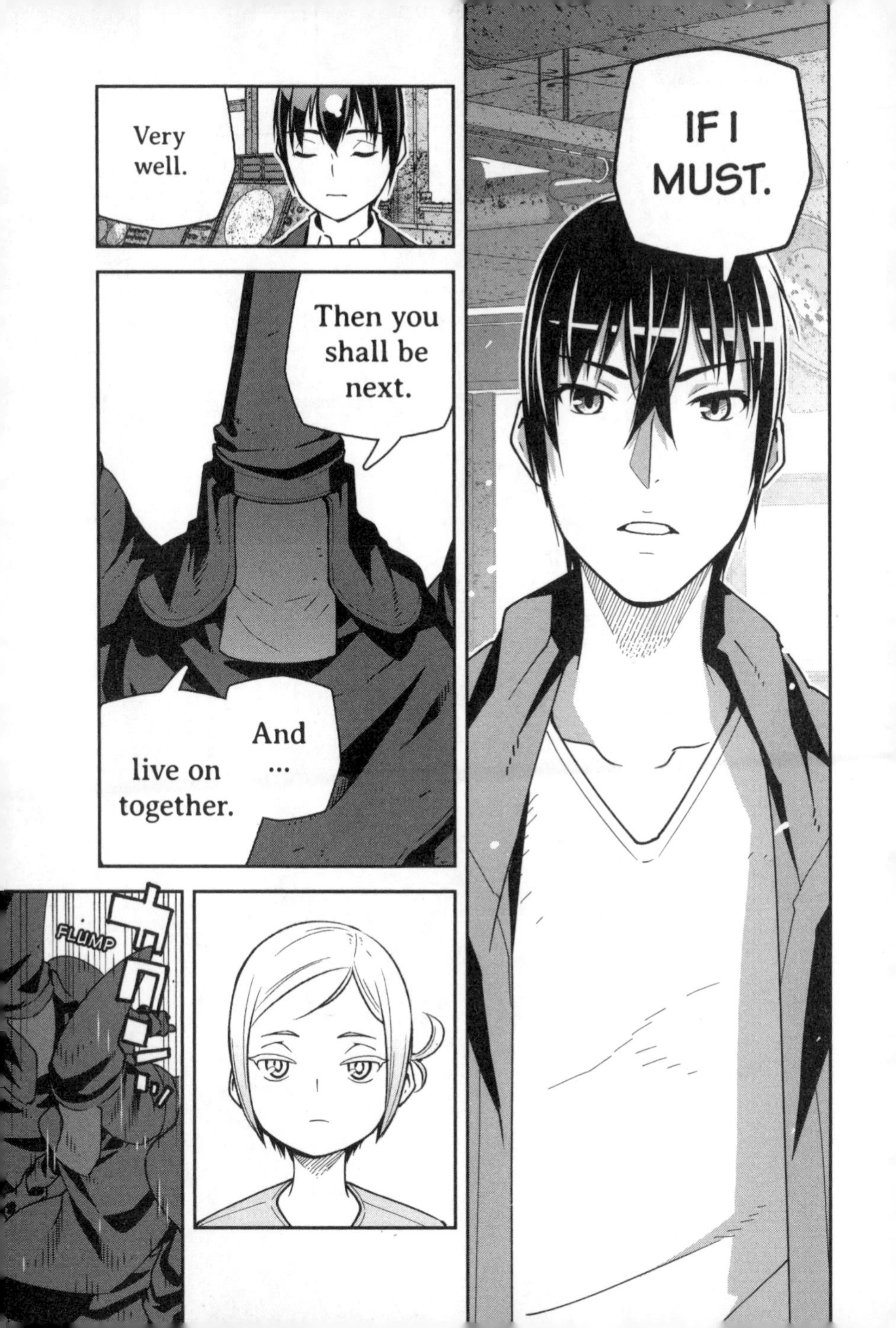
IF I MUST.
Very well.
Then you shall be next.
And ...
live on together.
FLUMP

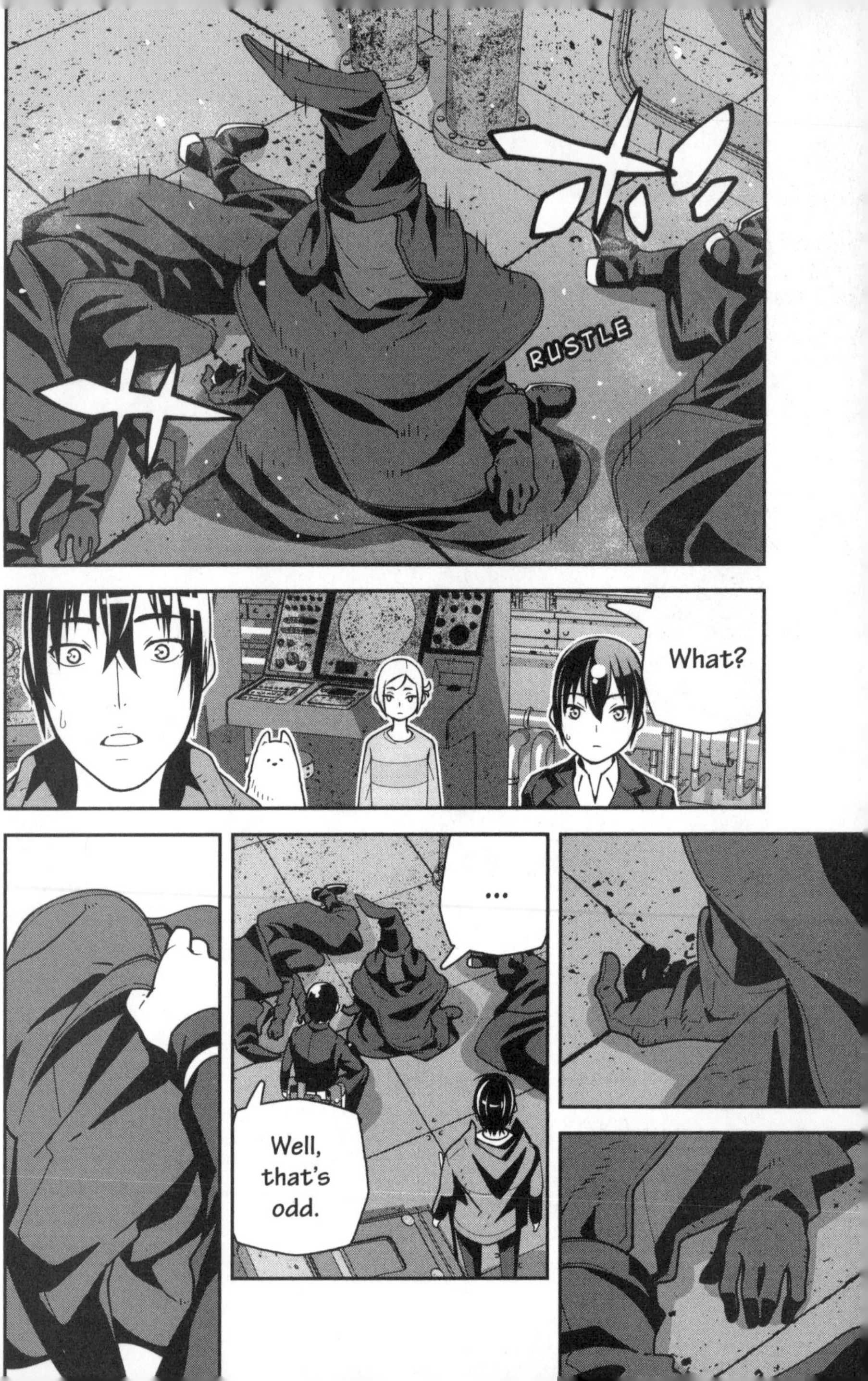
RUSTLE
What?
...
Well, that's odd.

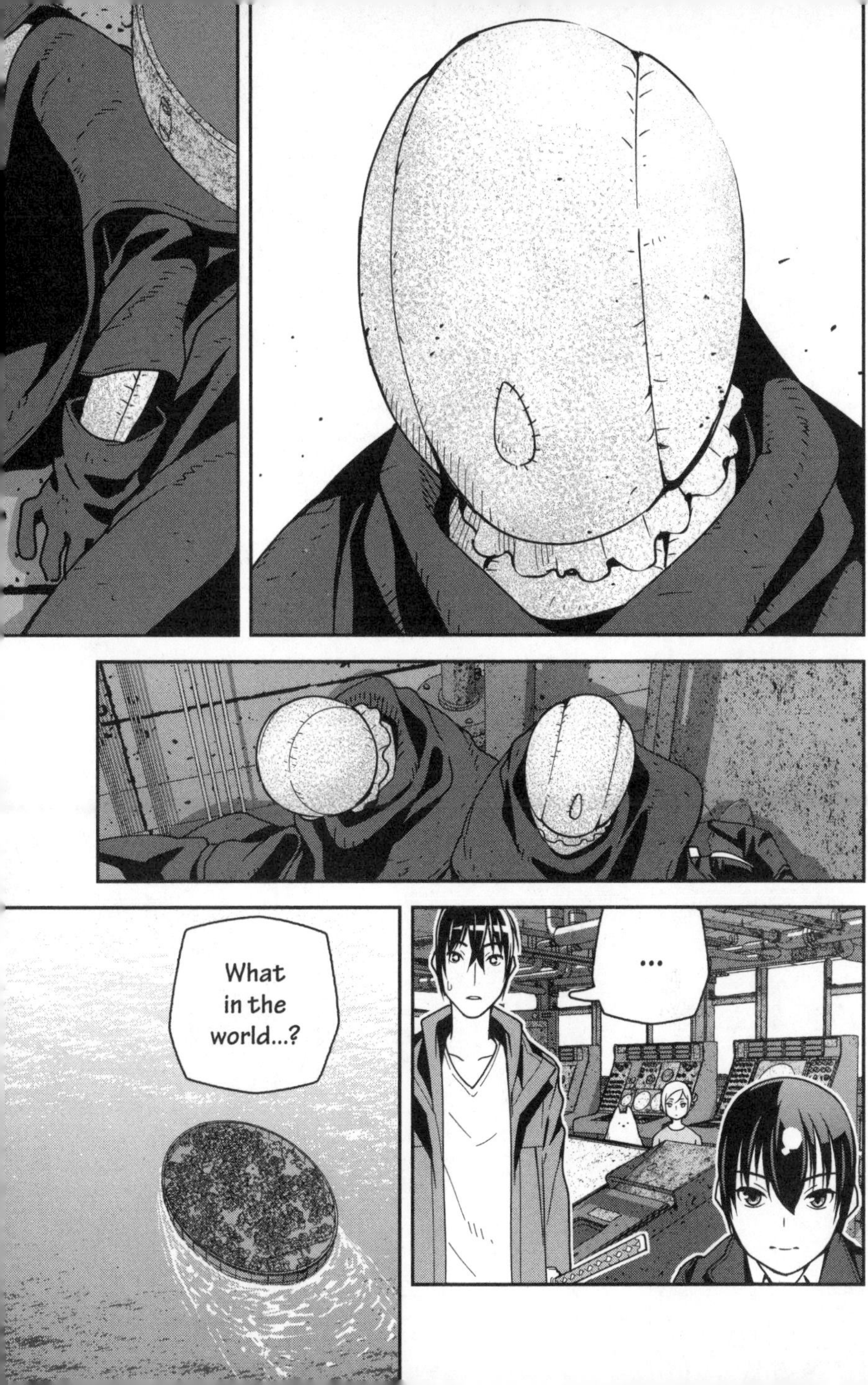
...
What in the world...?

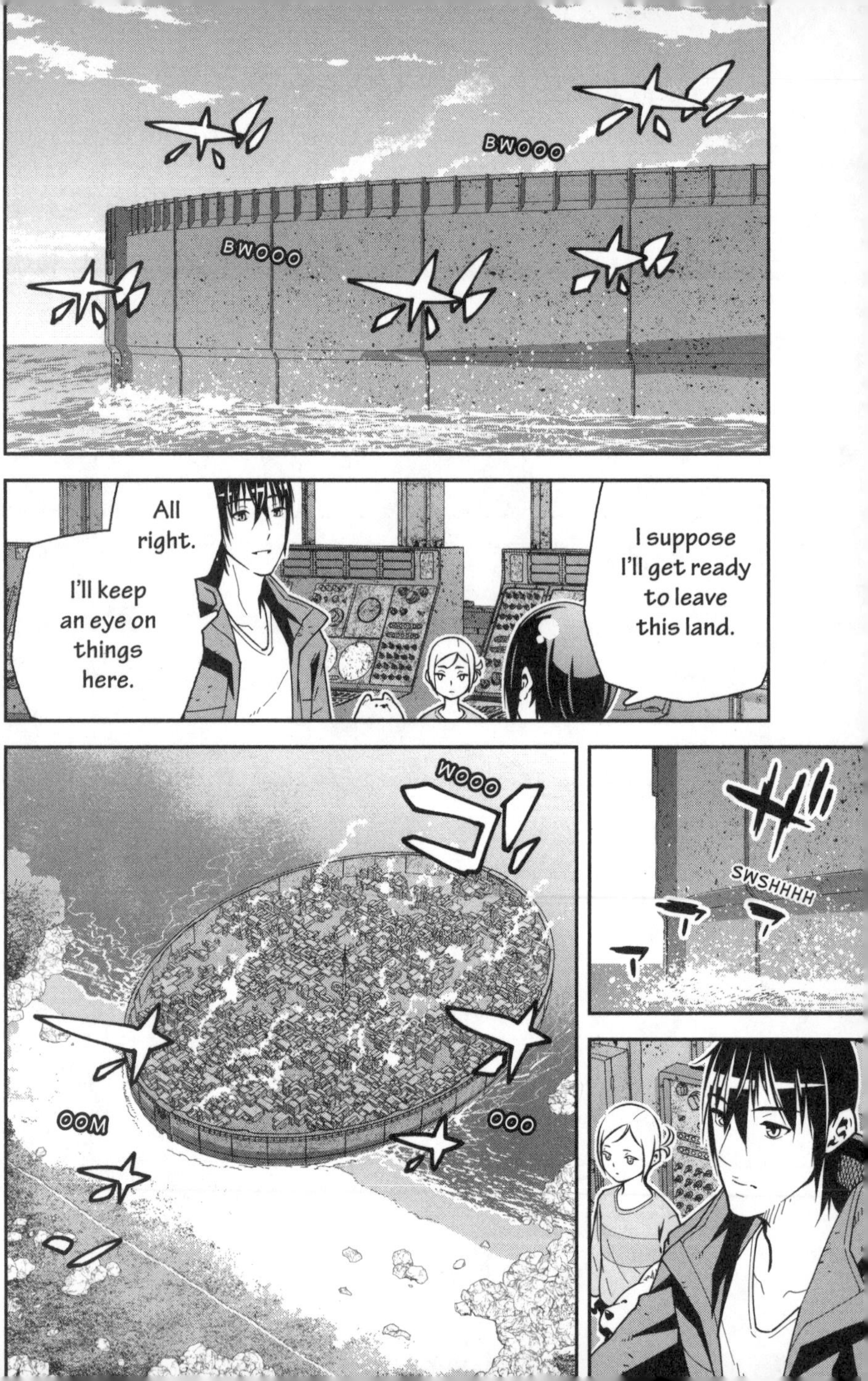
BWOOO
BWOOO
I suppose I'll get ready to leave this land.
All right.
I'll keep an eye on things here.
SWSHHHH
WOOO
OOO
OOM

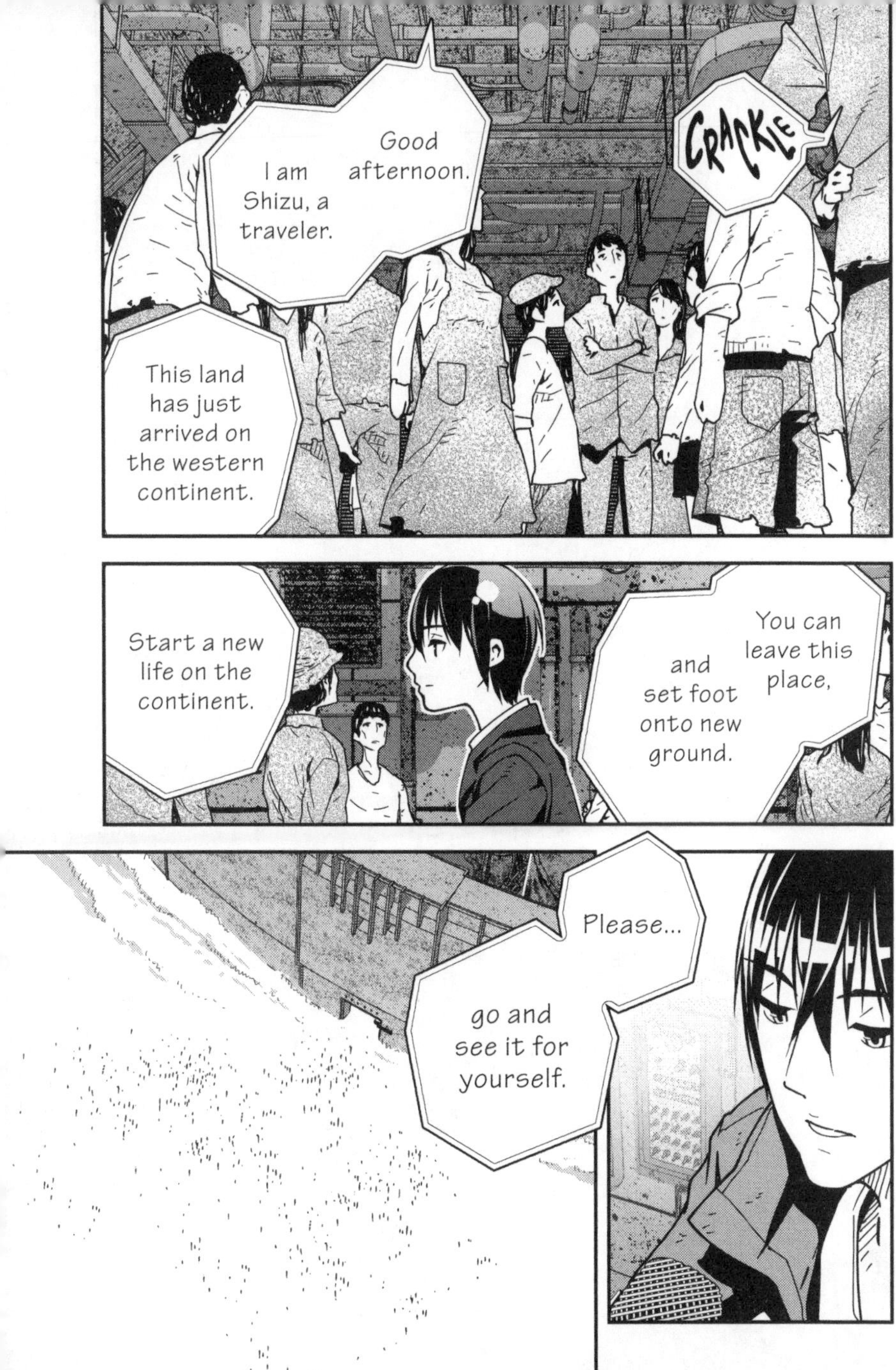
CRACKLE
Good afternoon.
I am Shizu, a traveler.
This land has just arrived on the western continent.
You can leave this place,
and set foot onto new ground.
Start a new life on the continent.
Please...
go and see it for yourself.

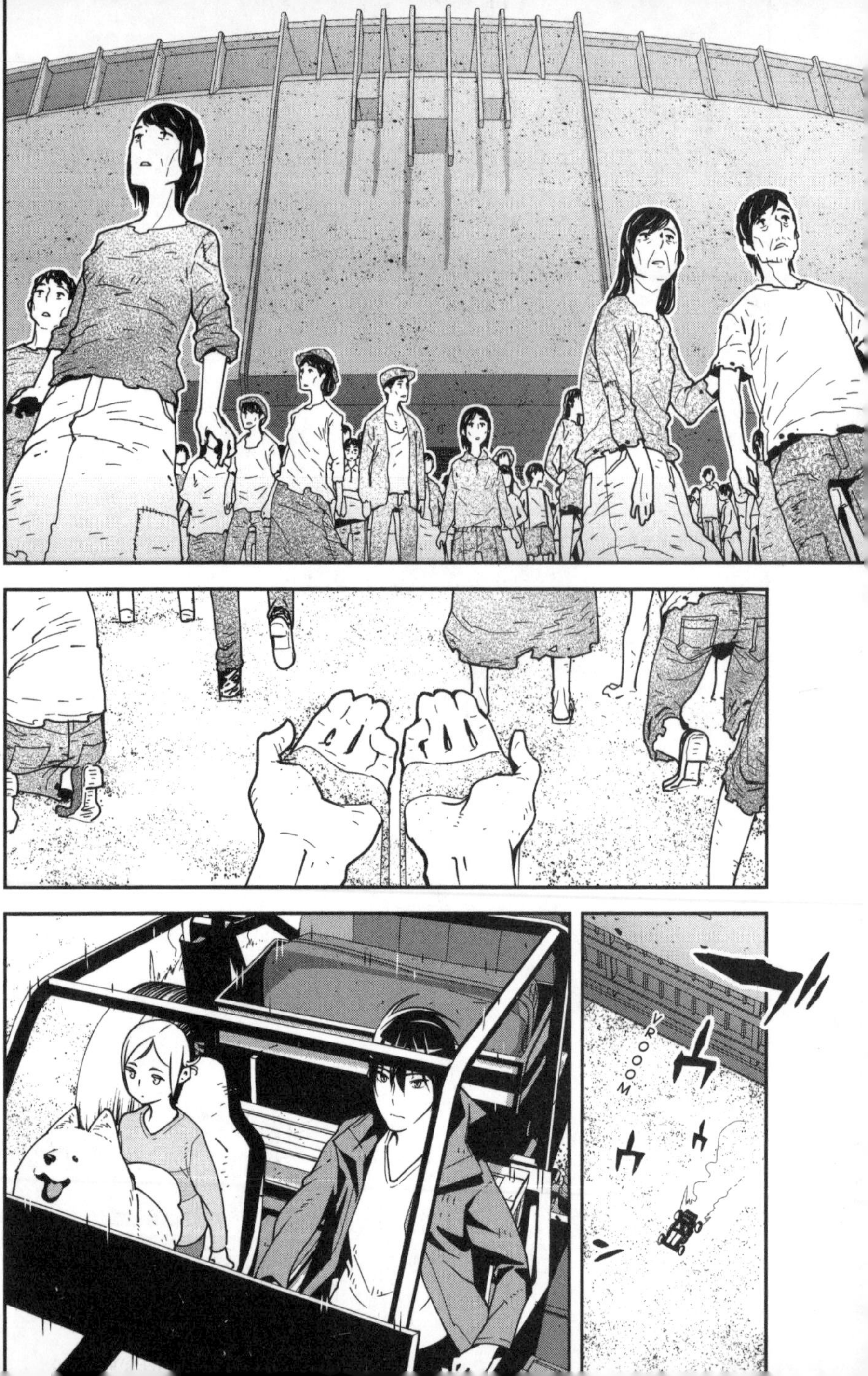
VROOOM

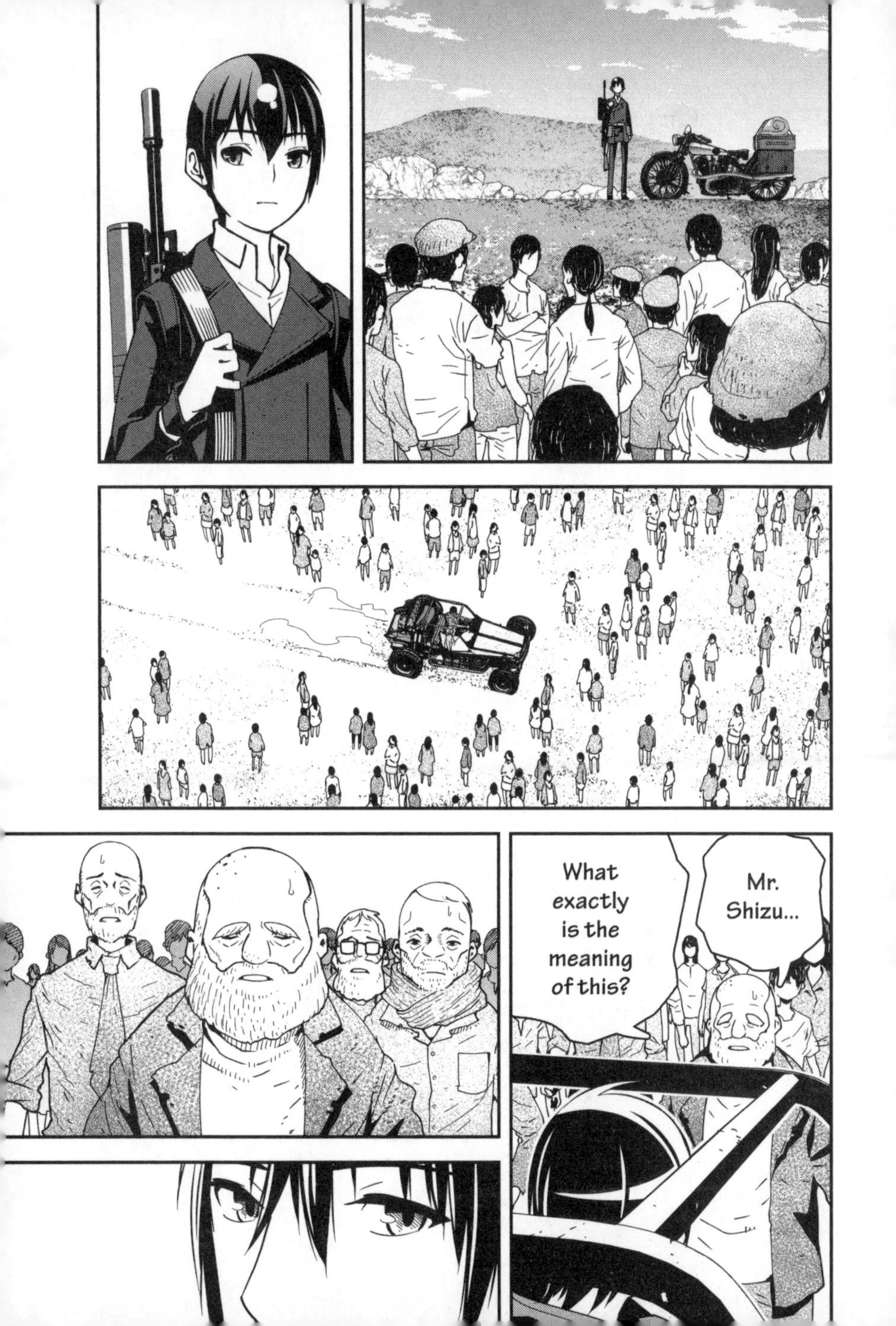
Mr. Shizu...
What exactly is the meaning of this?

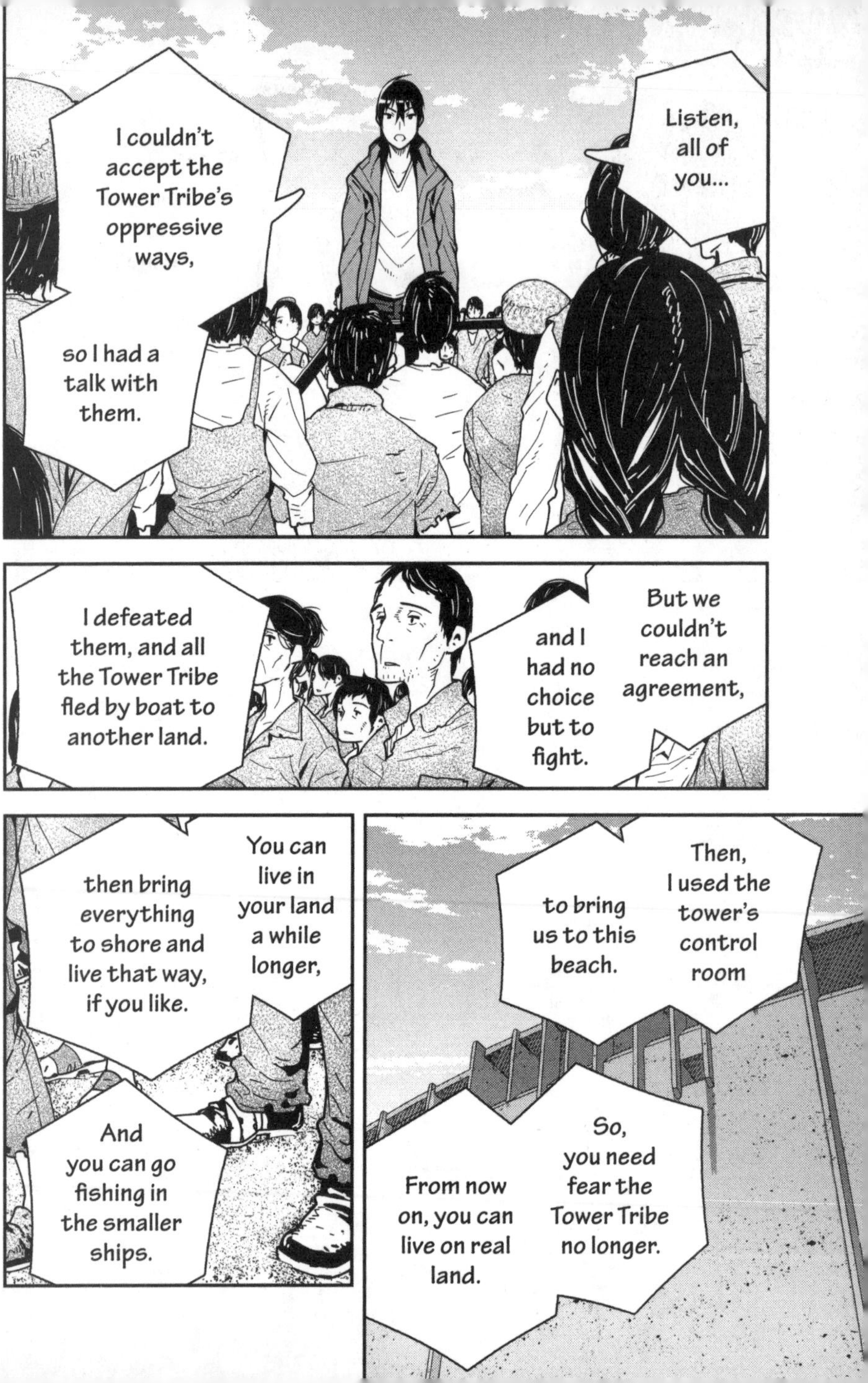
Listen, all of you...
I couldn't accept the Tower Tribe's oppressive ways,
so I had a talk with them.
But we couldn't reach an agreement,
and I had no choice but to fight.
I defeated them, and all the Tower Tribe fled by boat to another land.
Then, I used the tower's control room
to bring us to this beach.
So, you need fear the Tower Tribe no longer.
From now on, you can live on real land.
You can live in your land a while longer,
then bring everything to shore and live that way, if you like.
And you can go fishing in the smaller ships.

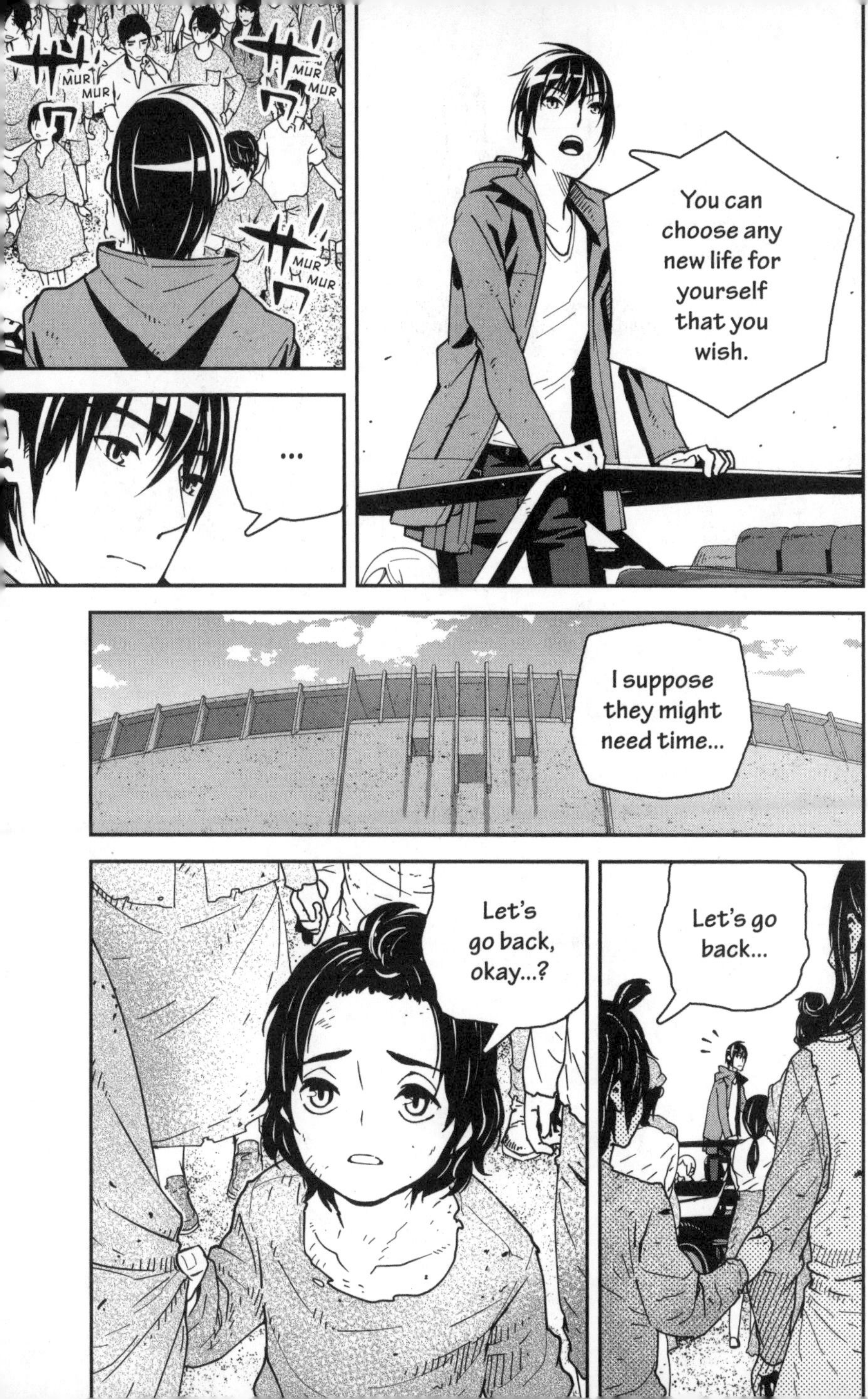
You can choose any new life for yourself that you wish.
MUR MUR
MUR MUR
MUR MUR
...
I suppose they might need time...
Let's go back...
Let's go back, okay...?

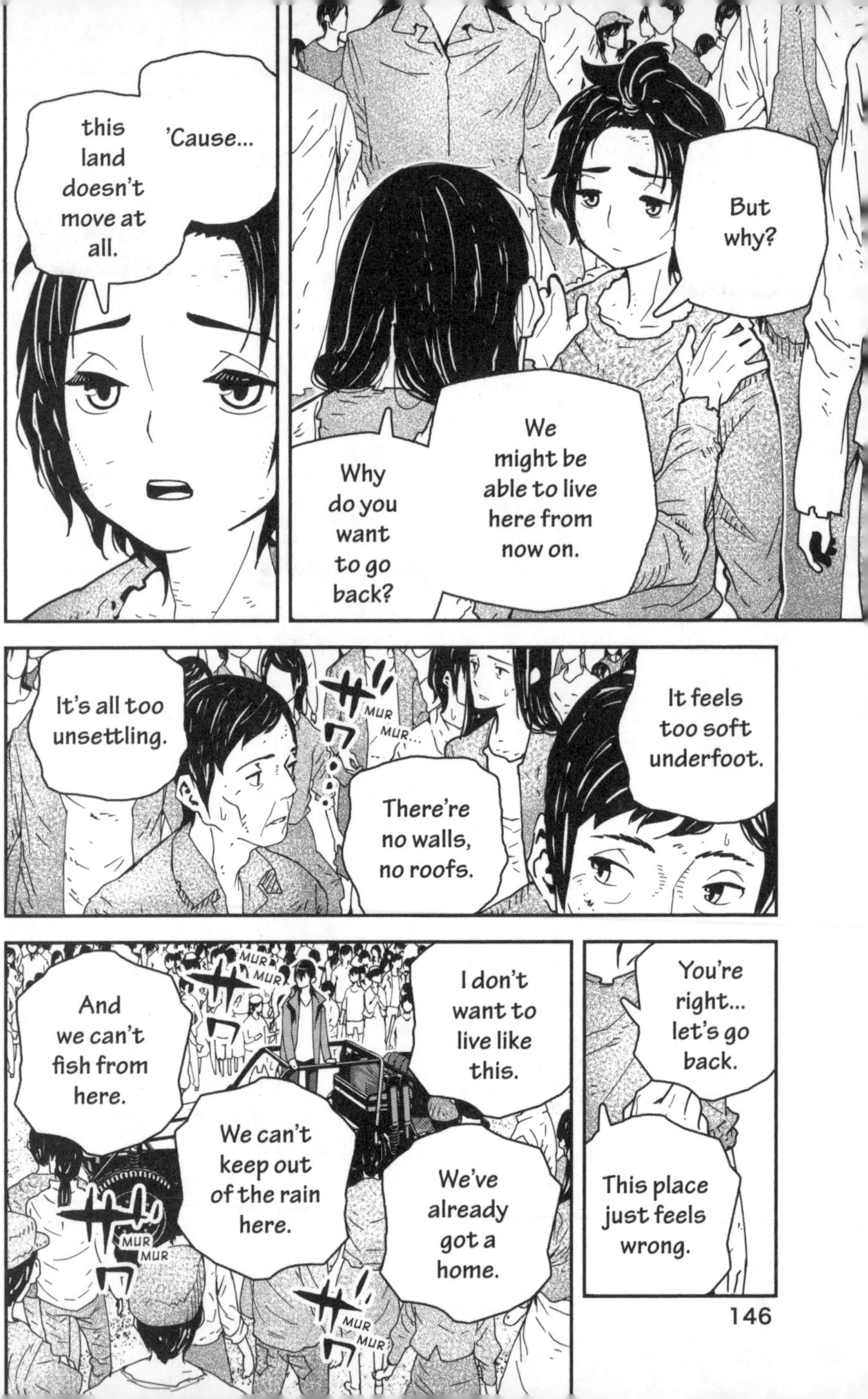
But why?
We might be able to live here from now on.
Why do you want to go back?
'Cause...
this land doesn't move at all.
It feels too soft underfoot.
MUR MUR...
There're no walls, no roofs.
It's all too unsettling.
You're right... let's go back.
This place just feels wrong.
I don't want to live like this.
MUR MUR
And we can't fish from here.
We've already got a home.
We can't keep out of the rain here.
MUR MUR
MUR MUR

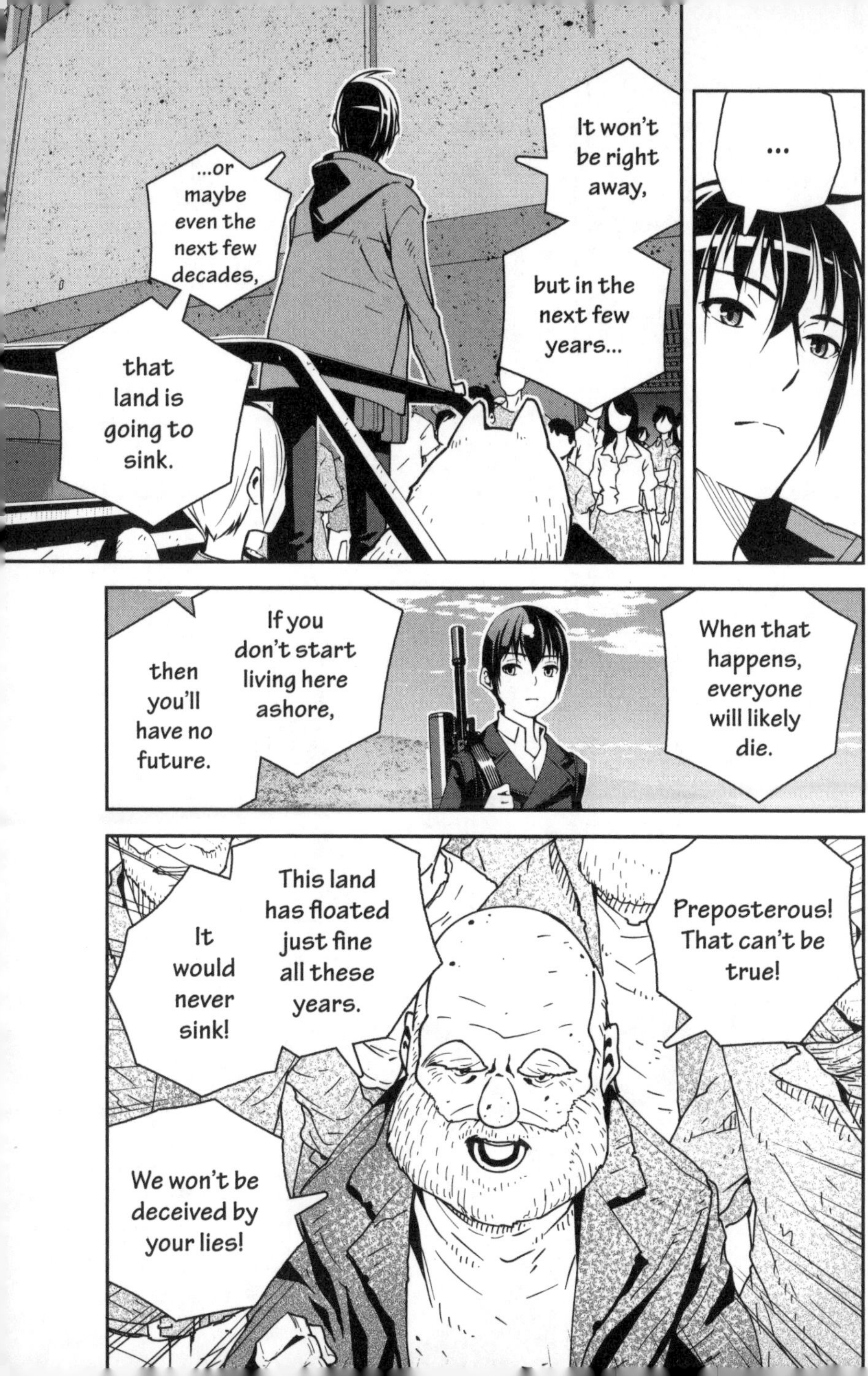
...
It won't be right away,
but in the next few years...
...or maybe even the next few decades,
that land is going to sink.
When that happens, everyone will likely die.
If you don't start living here ashore,
then you'll have no future.
Preposterous! That can't be true!
This land has floated just fine all these years.
It would never sink!
We won't be deceived by your lies!

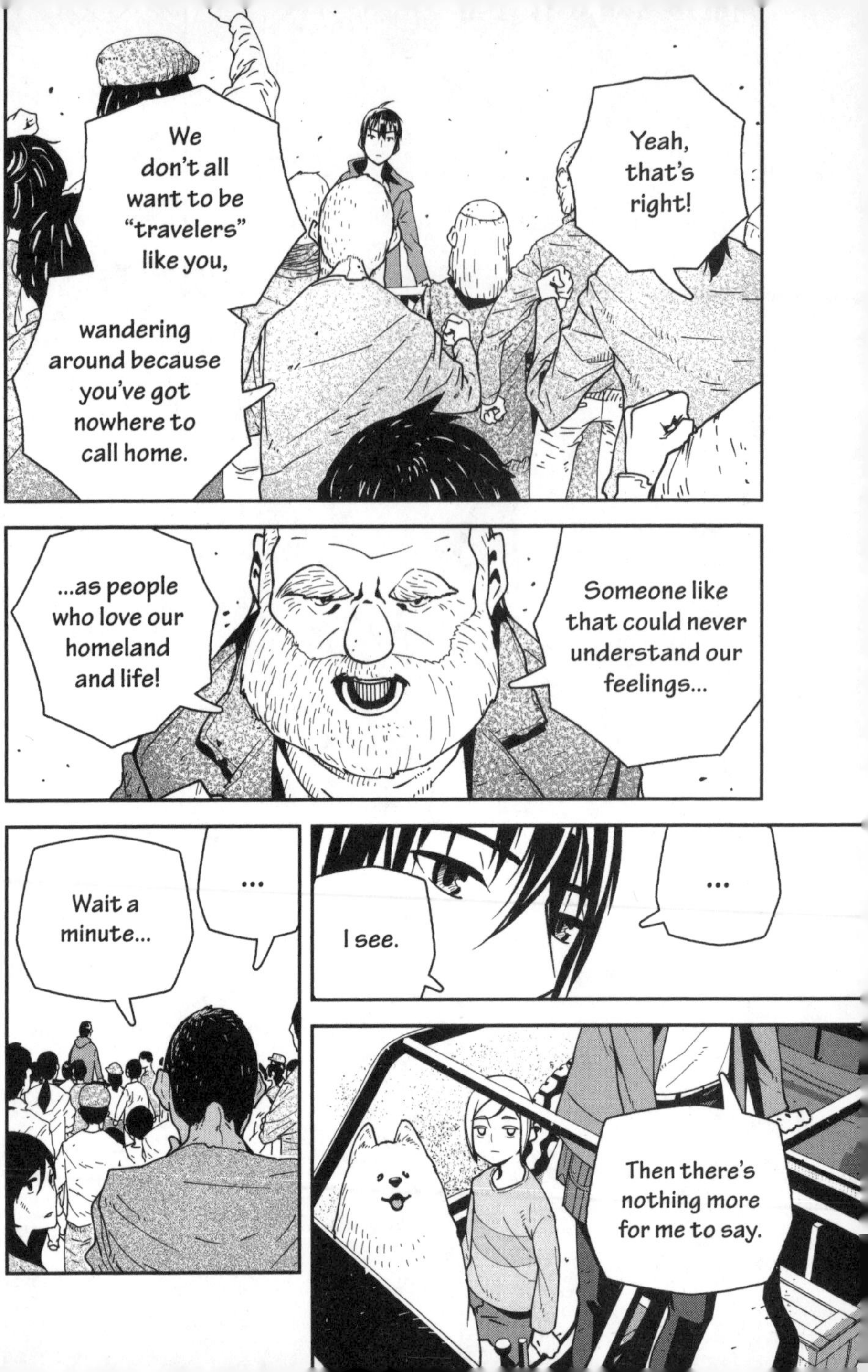
Yeah, that's right!
We don't all want to be "travelers" like you,
wandering around because you've got nowhere to call home.
Someone like that could never understand our feelings...
...as people who love our homeland and life!
...
I see.
Then there's nothing more for me to say.
...
Wait a minute...

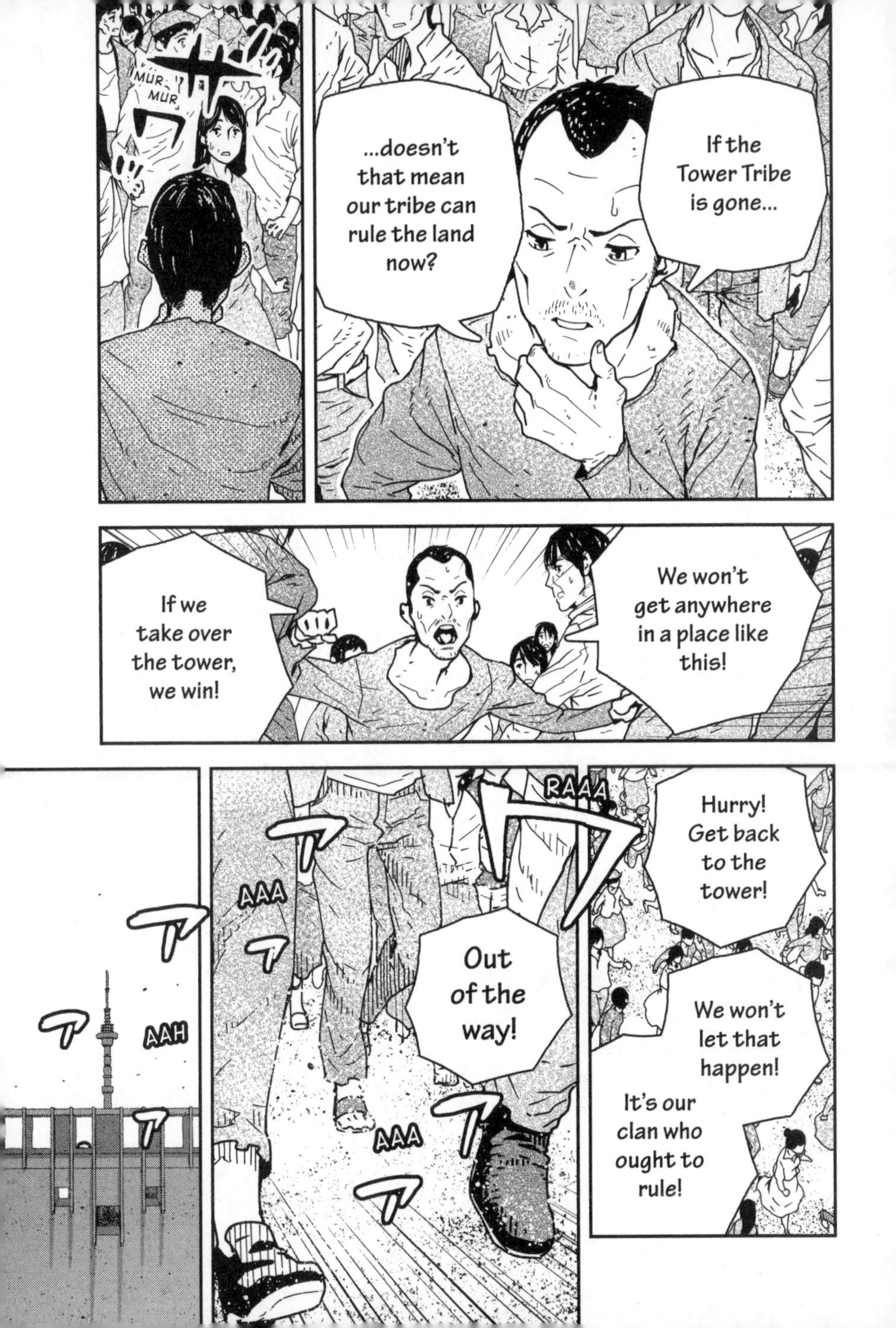
If the Tower Tribe is gone...
...doesn't that mean our tribe can rule the land now?
MUR MUR
We won't get anywhere in a place like this!
If we take over the tower, we win!
Hurry! Get back to the tower!
We won't let that happen!
It's our clan who ought to rule!
RAAA
Out of the way!
AAA
AAA
AAH

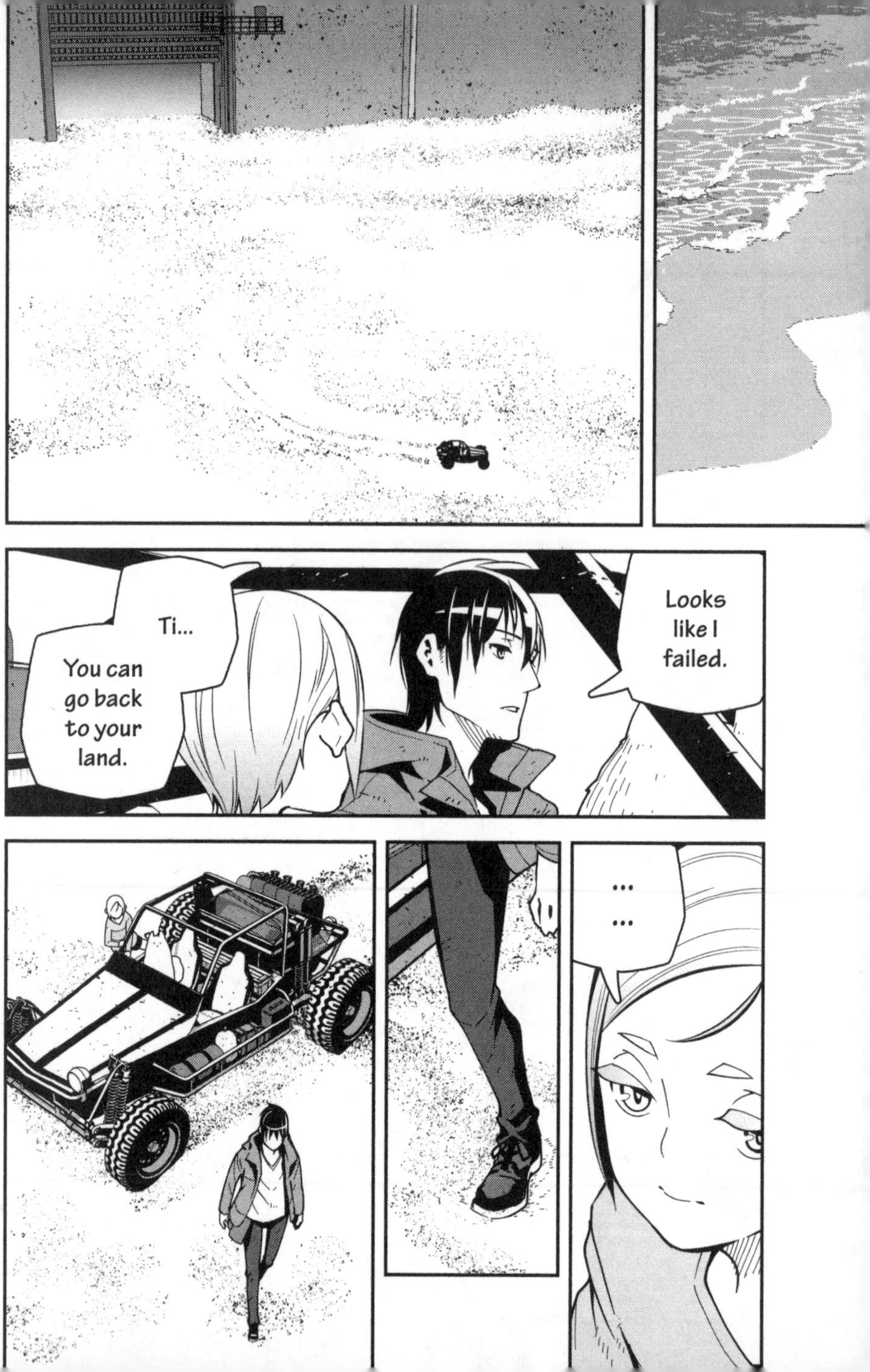
Looks like I failed.
Ti...
You can go back to your land.
... ...

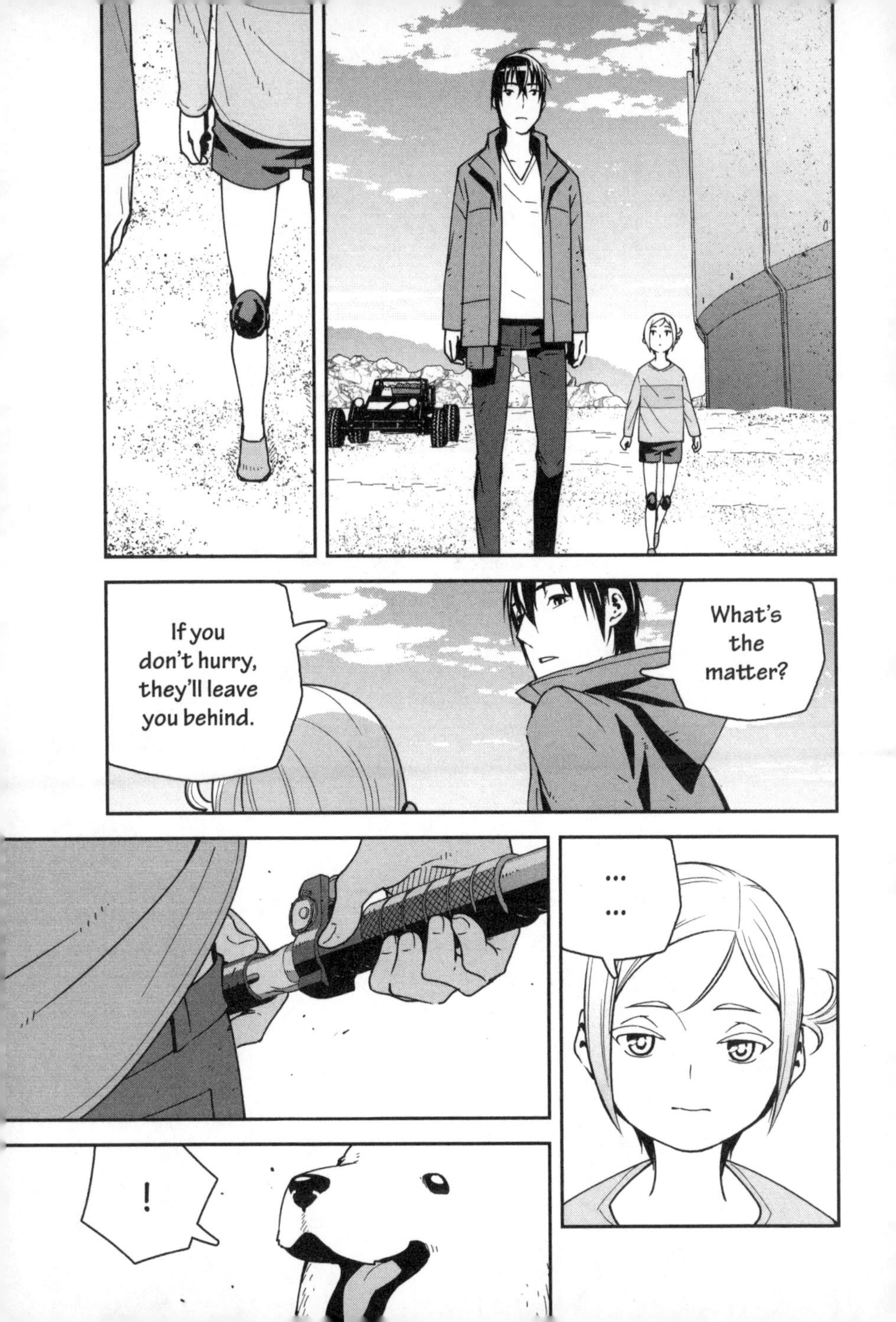
What's the matter?
If you don't hurry, they'll leave you behind.
… …
!

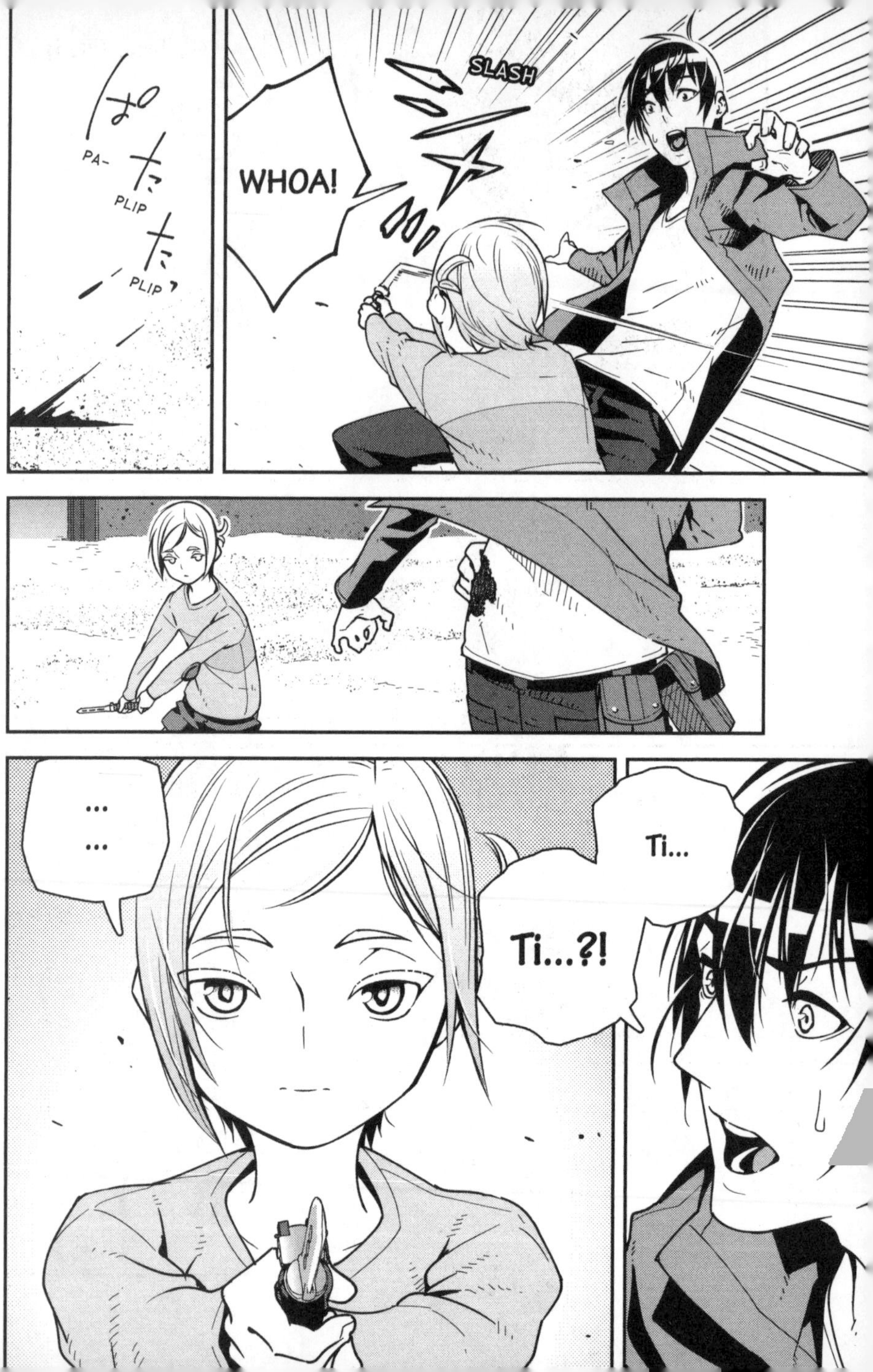
SLASH
WHOA!
ぱた
PA-
PLIP
た
PLIP
Ti...
Ti...?!
...
...

Epilogue (Pt. 5)

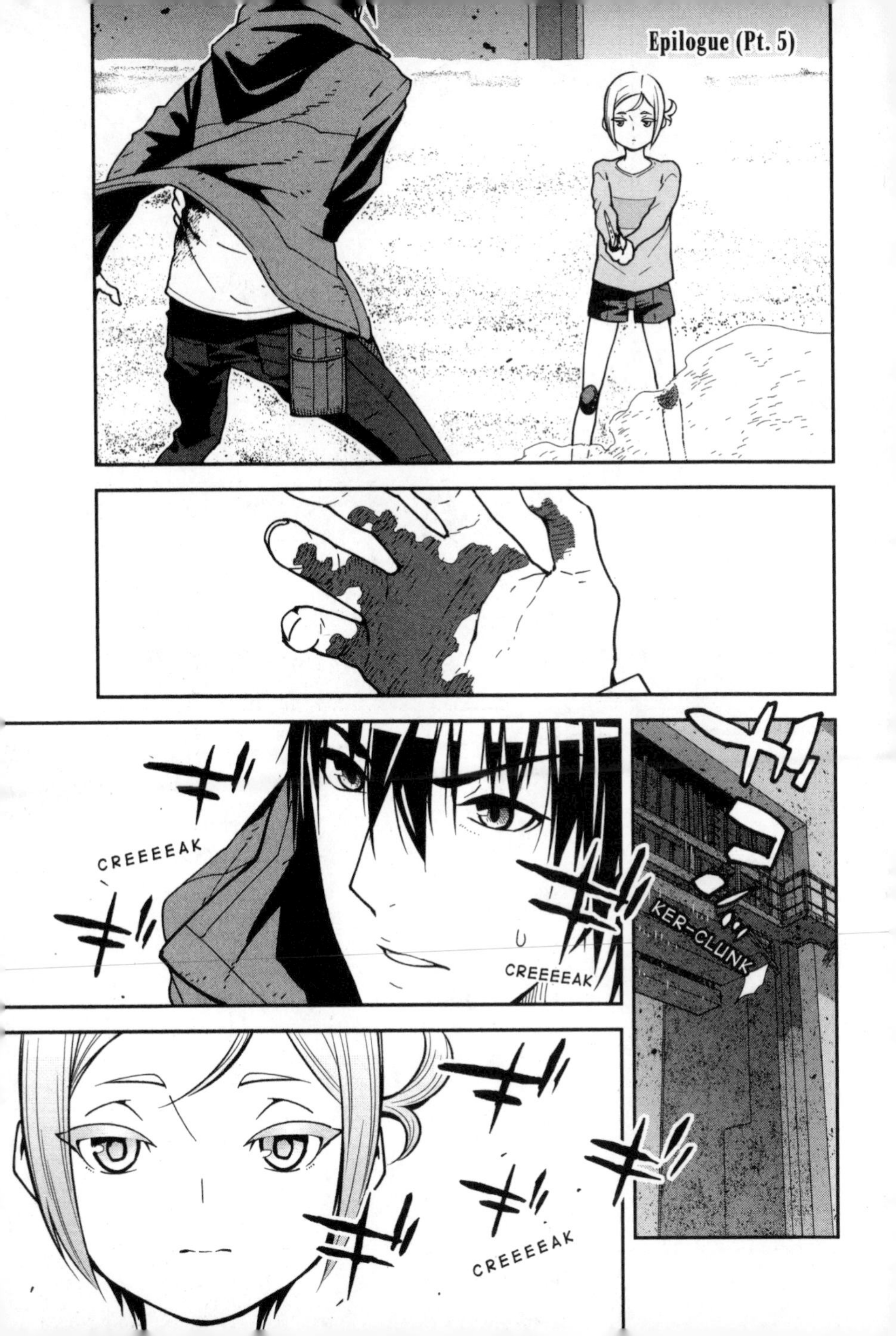
KER-CLUNK
CREEEEAK
CREEEEAK
CREEEEAK

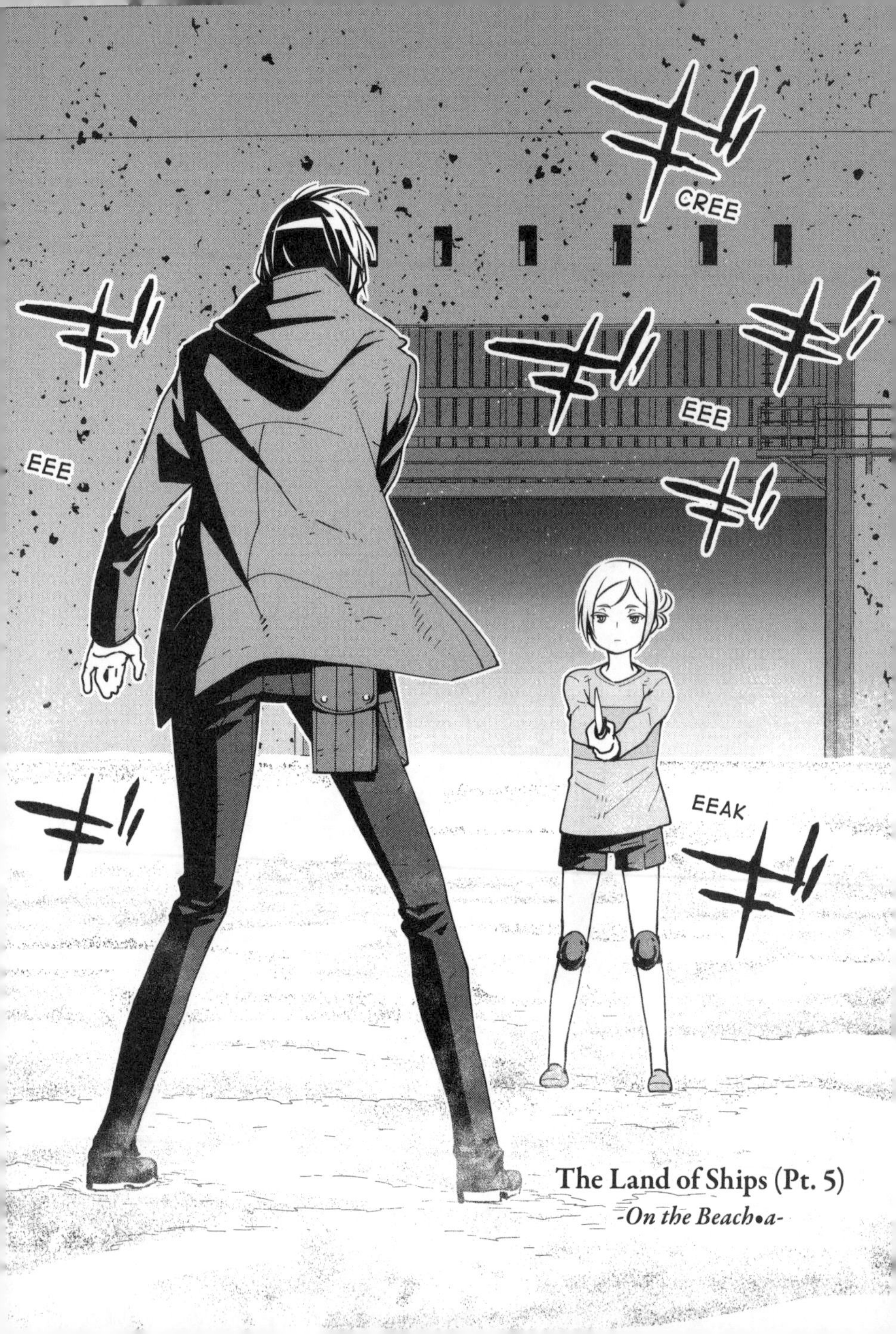
CREEE
EEE
EEE
EEAK

The Land of Ships (Pt. 5)

-On the Beach•a-

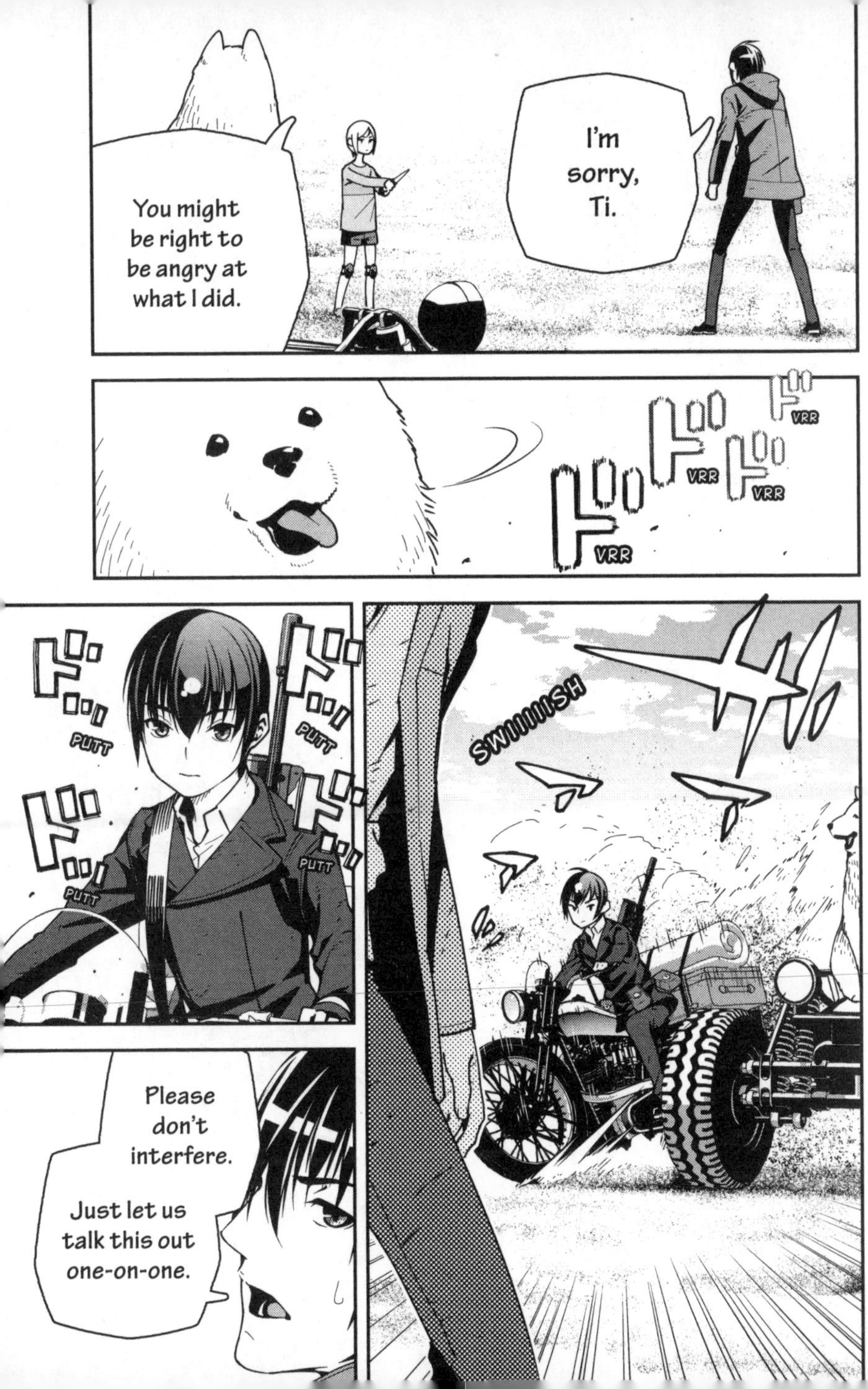
I'm sorry, Ti.
You might be right to be angry at what I did.
VRR
VRR
VRR
VRR
SWIIIIISH
PUTT
PUTT
PUTT
PUTT
Please don't interfere.
Just let us talk this out one-on-one.

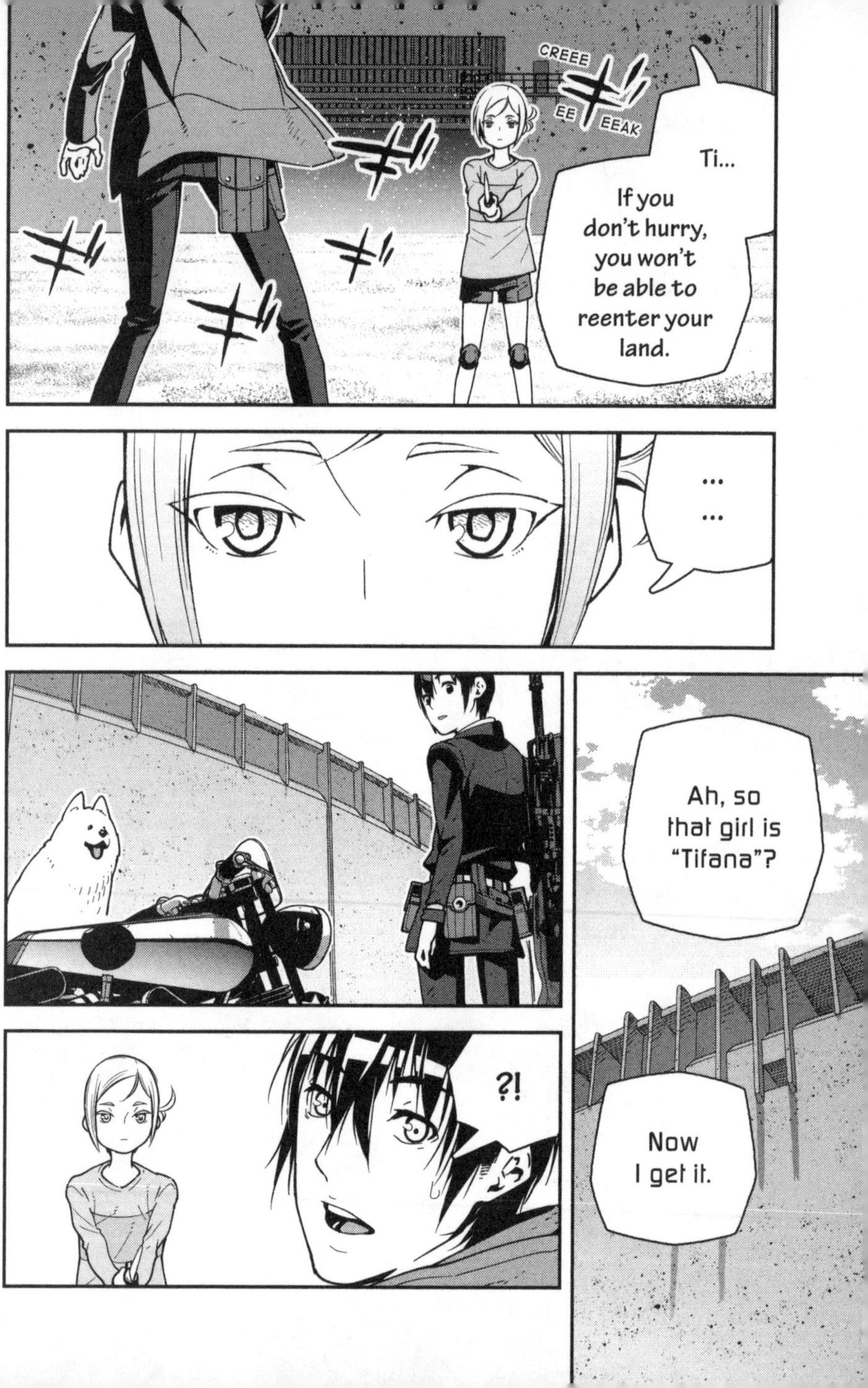
CREEE
EE EEAK
Ti...
If you don't hurry, you won't be able to reenter your land.
...
...
Ah, so that girl is "Tifana"?
Now I get it.
?!

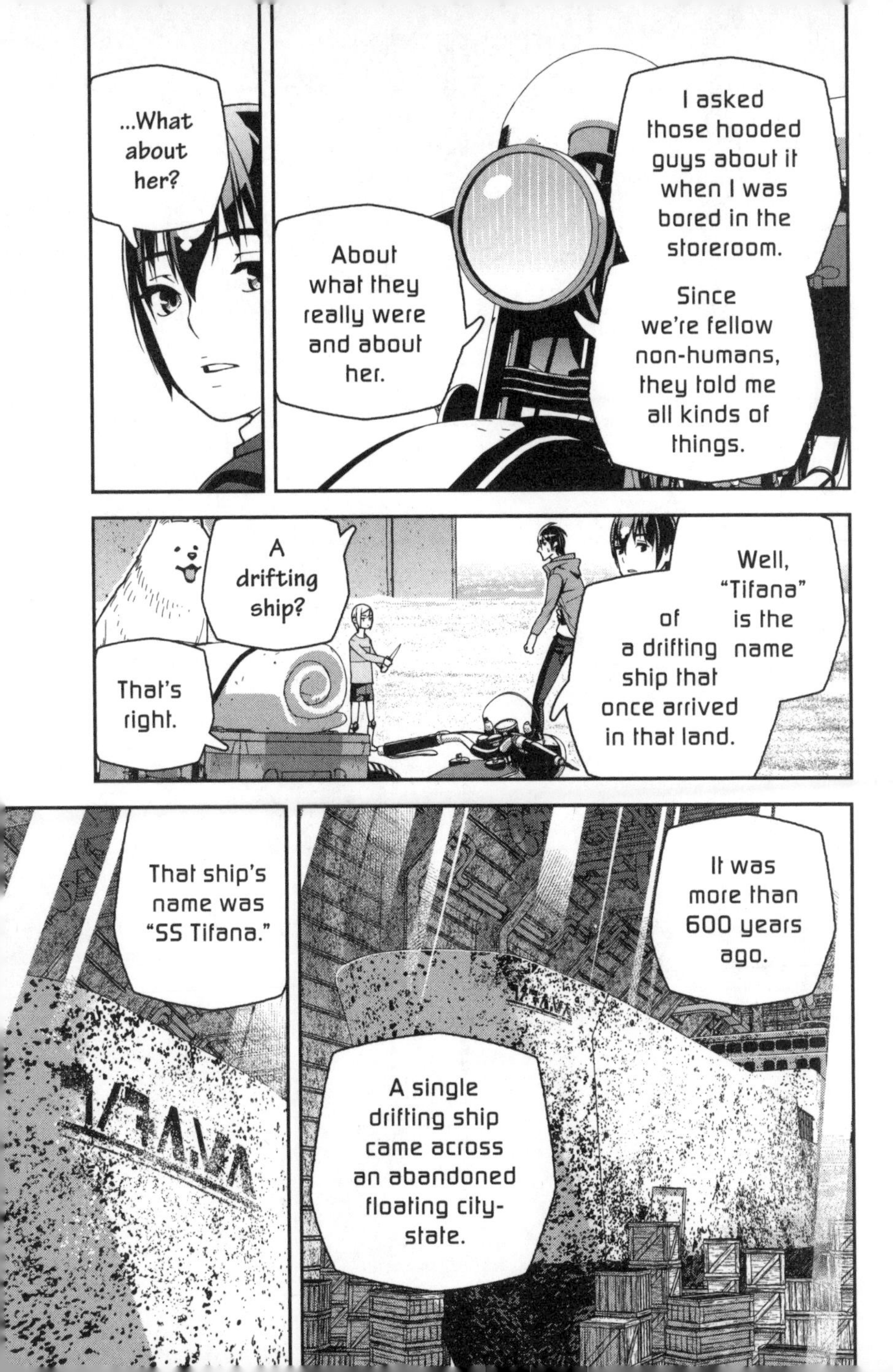
I asked those hooded guys about it when I was bored in the storeroom.
Since we're fellow non-humans, they told me all kinds of things.
About what they really were and about her.
...What about her?
Well, "Tifana" is the name of a drifting ship that once arrived in that land.
A drifting ship?
That's right.
It was more than 600 years ago.
A single drifting ship came across an abandoned floating city-state.
That ship's name was "SS Tifana."

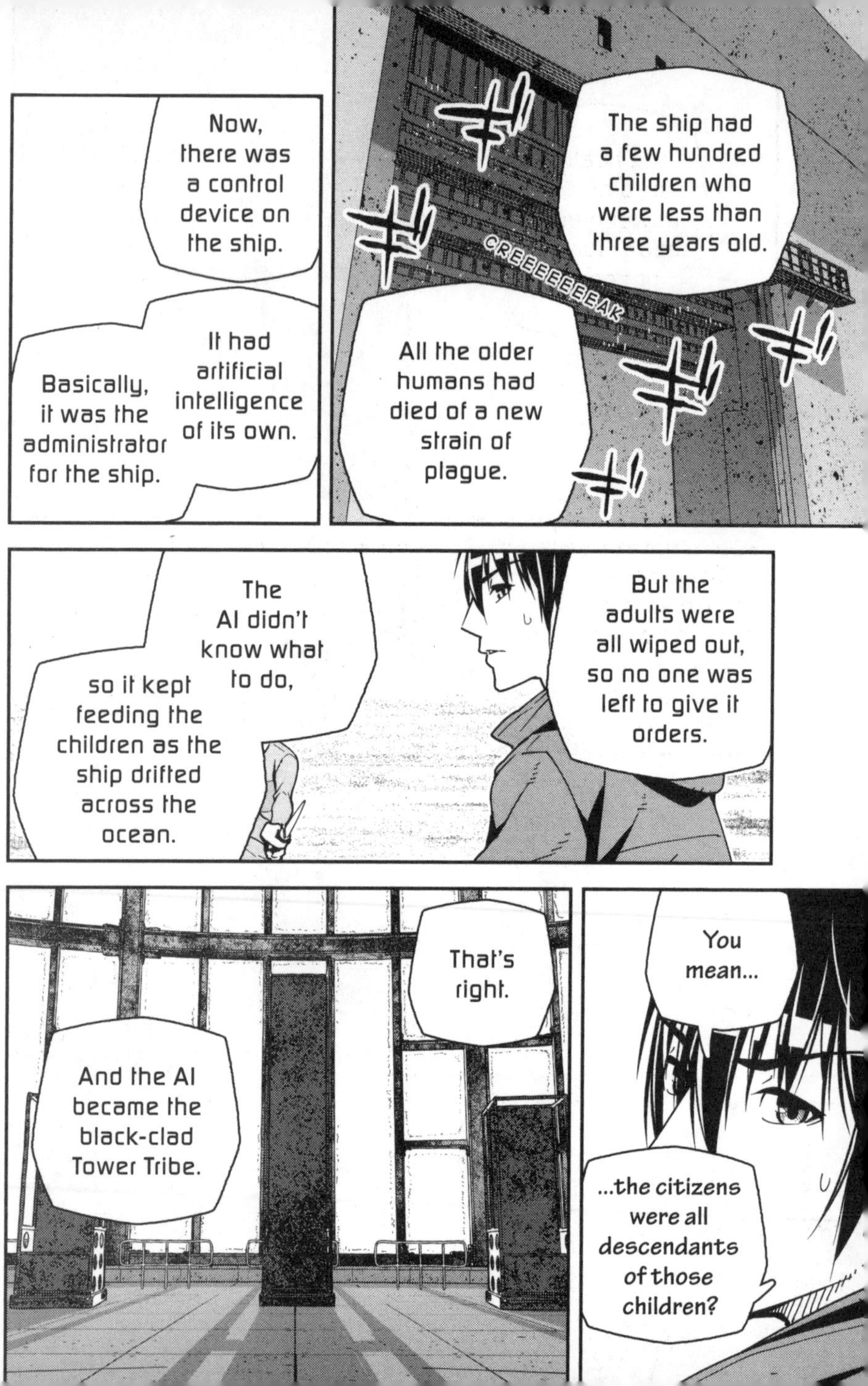
The ship had a few hundred children who were less than three years old.
CREEEEEEEEAK
All the older humans had died of a new strain of plague.
Now, there was a control device on the ship.
It had artificial intelligence of its own.
Basically, it was the administrator for the ship.
But the adults were all wiped out, so no one was left to give it orders.
The AI didn't know what to do,
so it kept feeding the children as the ship drifted across the ocean.
You mean...
...the citizens were all descendants of those children?
That's right.
And the AI became the black-clad Tower Tribe.

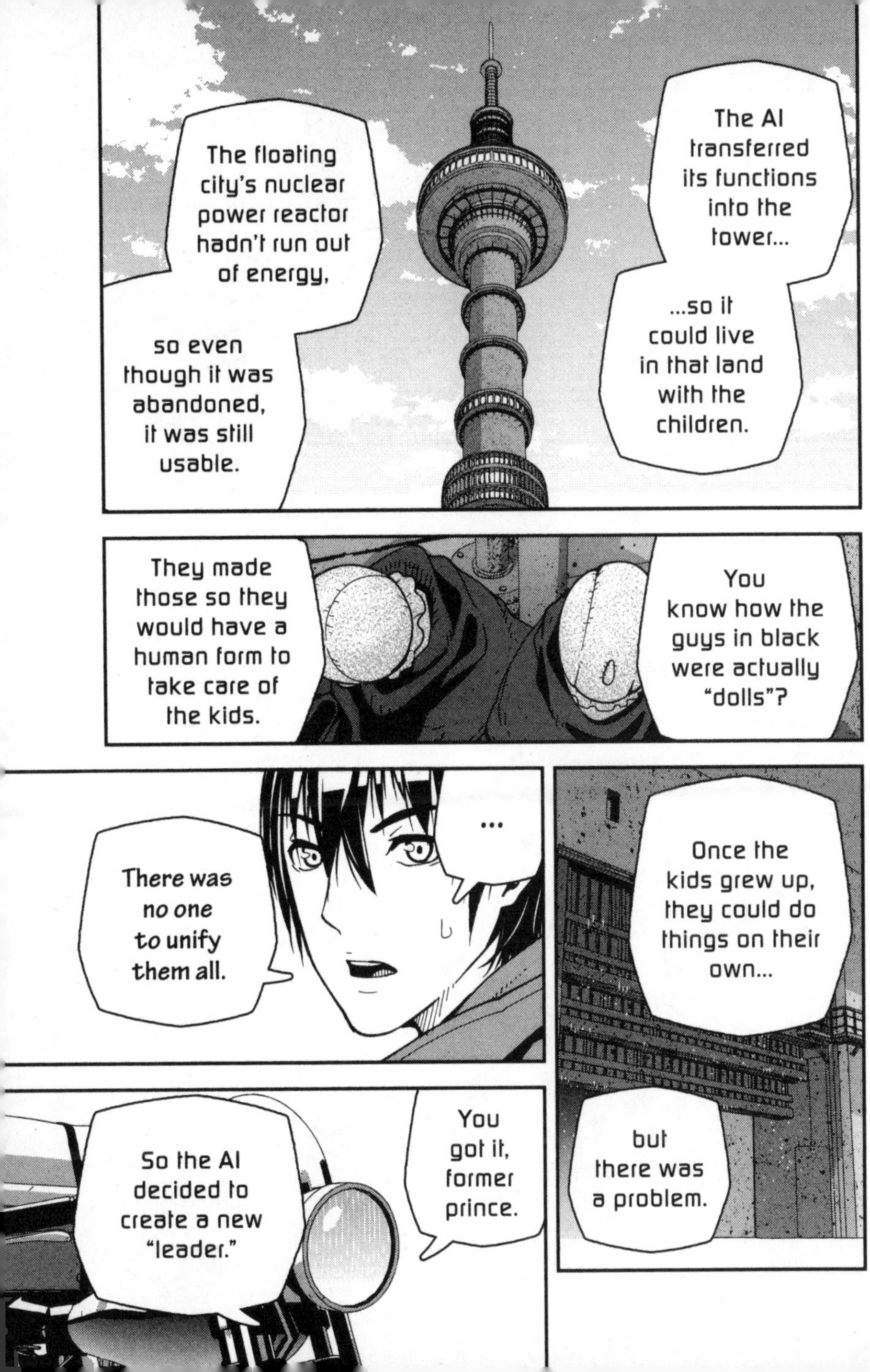
The AI transferred its functions into the tower...
...so it could live in that land with the children.
The floating city's nuclear power reactor hadn't run out of energy,
so even though it was abandoned, it was still usable.
You know how the guys in black were actually "dolls"?
They made those so they would have a human form to take care of the kids.
Once the kids grew up, they could do things on their own...
but there was a problem.
...
There was no one to unify them all.
You got it, former prince.
So the AI decided to create a new "leader."

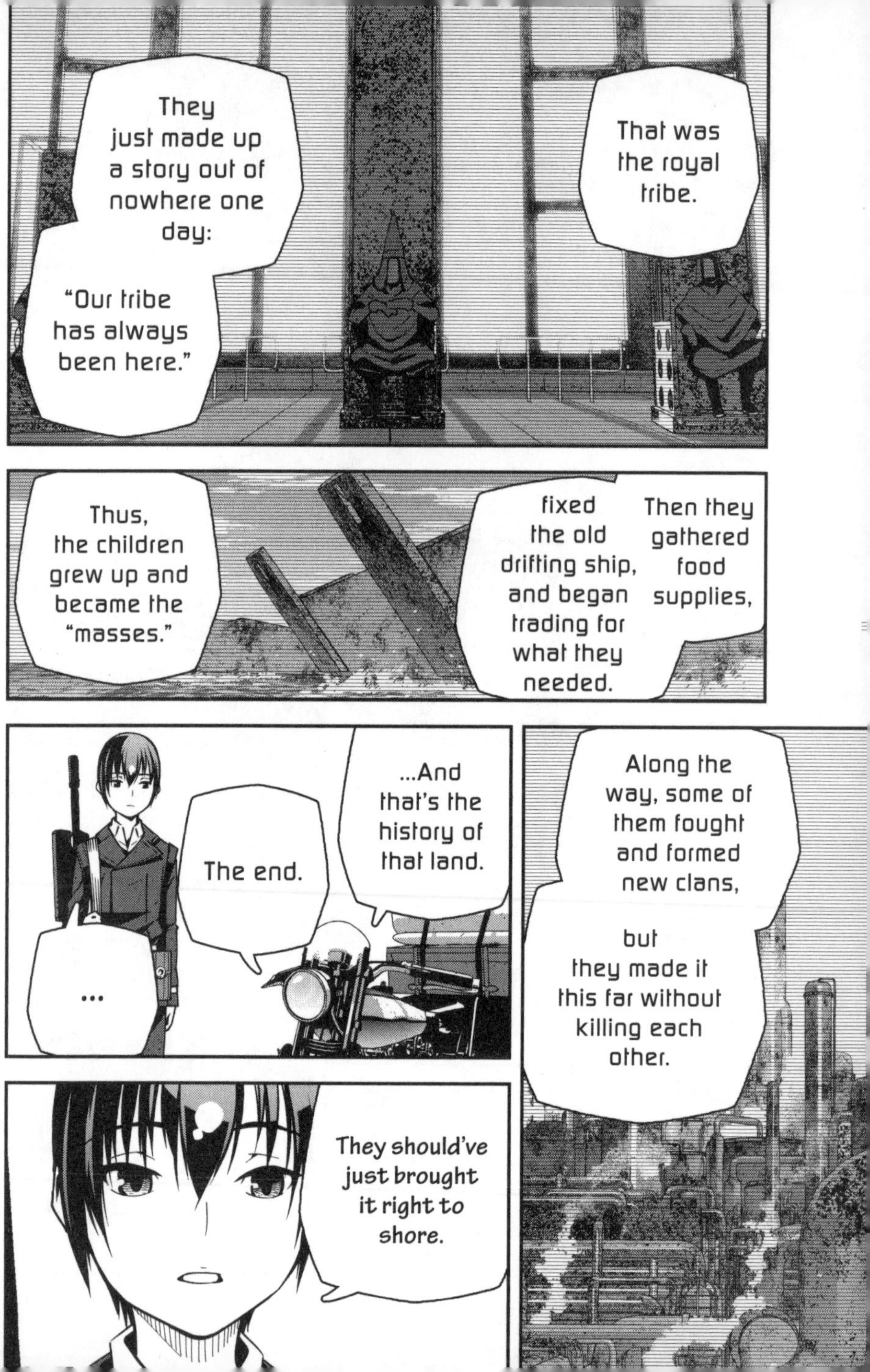
That was the royal tribe.
They just made up a story out of nowhere one day:
"Our tribe has always been here."
Then they gathered food supplies,
fixed the old drifting ship, and began trading for what they needed.
Thus, the children grew up and became the "masses."
Along the way, some of them fought and formed new clans,
but they made it this far without killing each other.
...And that's the history of that land.
The end.
...
They should've just brought it right to shore.

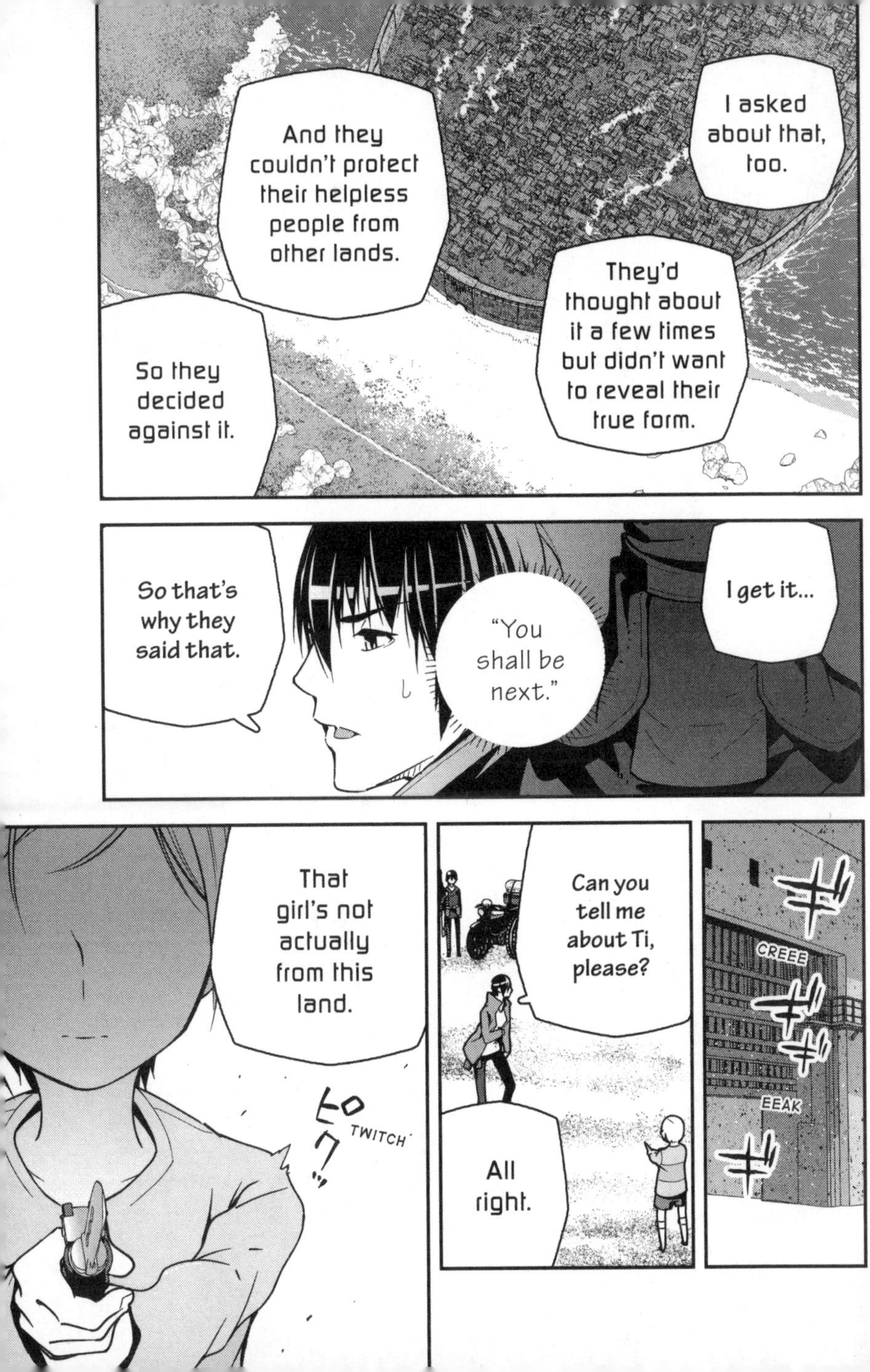
I asked about that, too.
And they couldn't protect their helpless people from other lands.
They'd thought about it a few times but didn't want to reveal their true form.
So they decided against it.
I get it...
"You shall be next."
So that's why they said that.
CREEE
EEAK
Can you tell me about Ti, please?
All right.
That girl's not actually from this land.
TWITCH

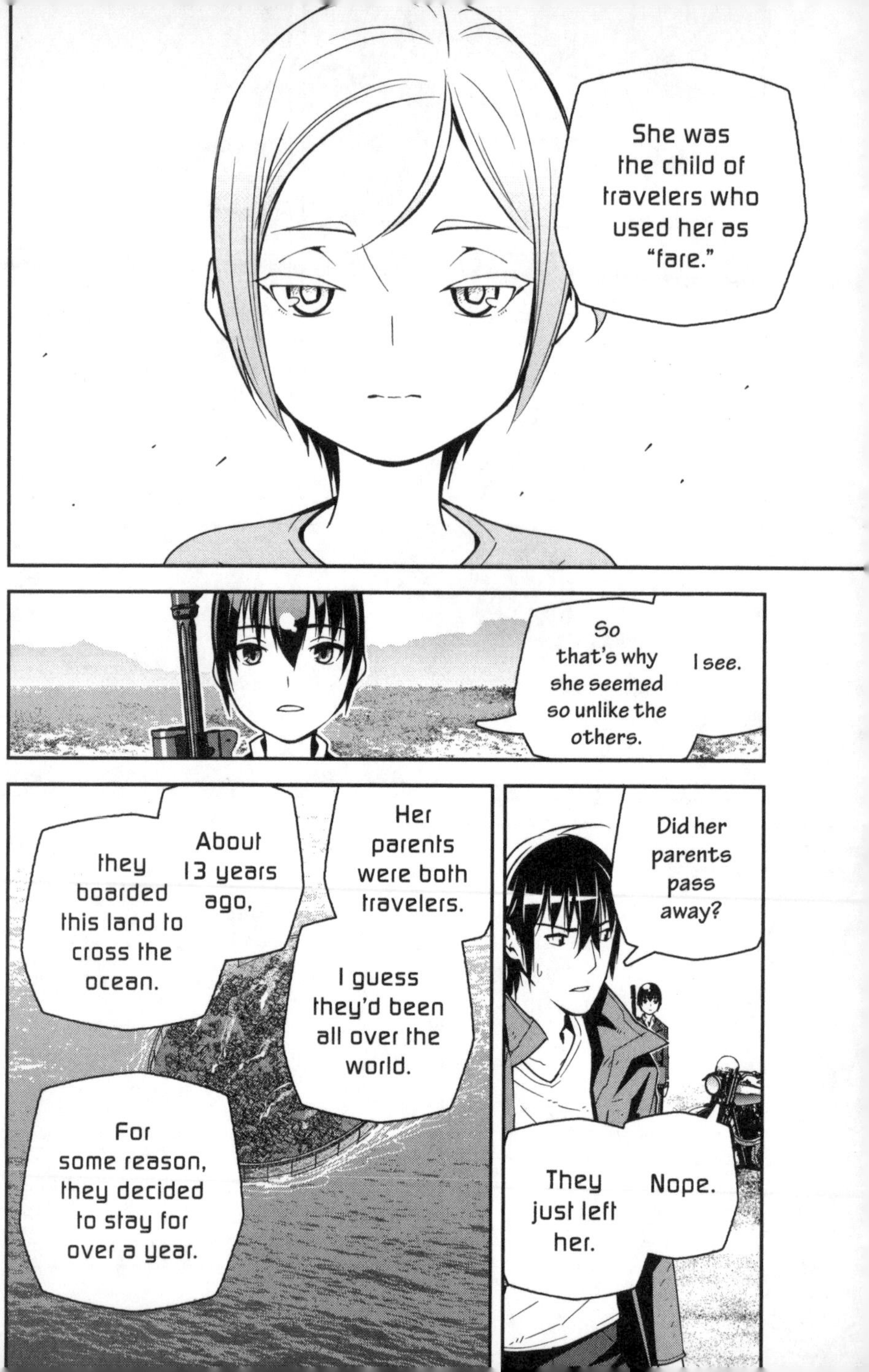
She was the child of travelers who used her as "fare."
I see.
So that's why she seemed so unlike the others.
Did her parents pass away?
Nope.
They just left her.
Her parents were both travelers.
About 13 years ago,
they boarded this land to cross the ocean.
I guess they'd been all over the world.
For some reason, they decided to stay for over a year.

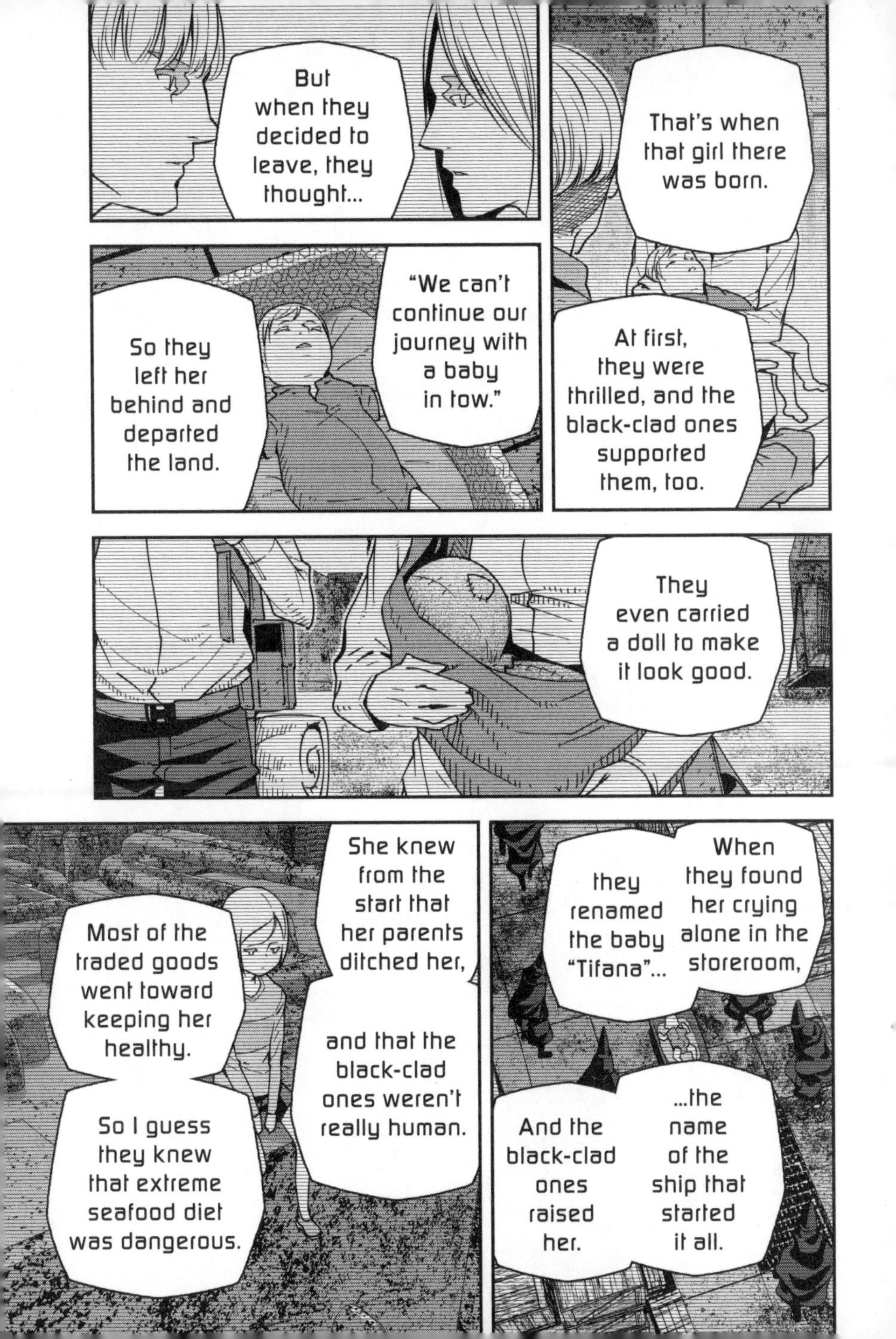
That's when that girl there was born.
At first, they were thrilled, and the black-clad ones supported them, too.
But when they decided to leave, they thought...
"We can't continue our journey with a baby in tow."
So they left her behind and departed the land.
They even carried a doll to make it look good.
When they found her crying alone in the storeroom,
they renamed the baby "Tifana"...
...the name of the ship that started it all.
And the black-clad ones raised her.
She knew from the start that her parents ditched her,
and that the black-clad ones weren't really human.
Most of the traded goods went toward keeping her healthy.
So I guess they knew that extreme seafood diet was dangerous.

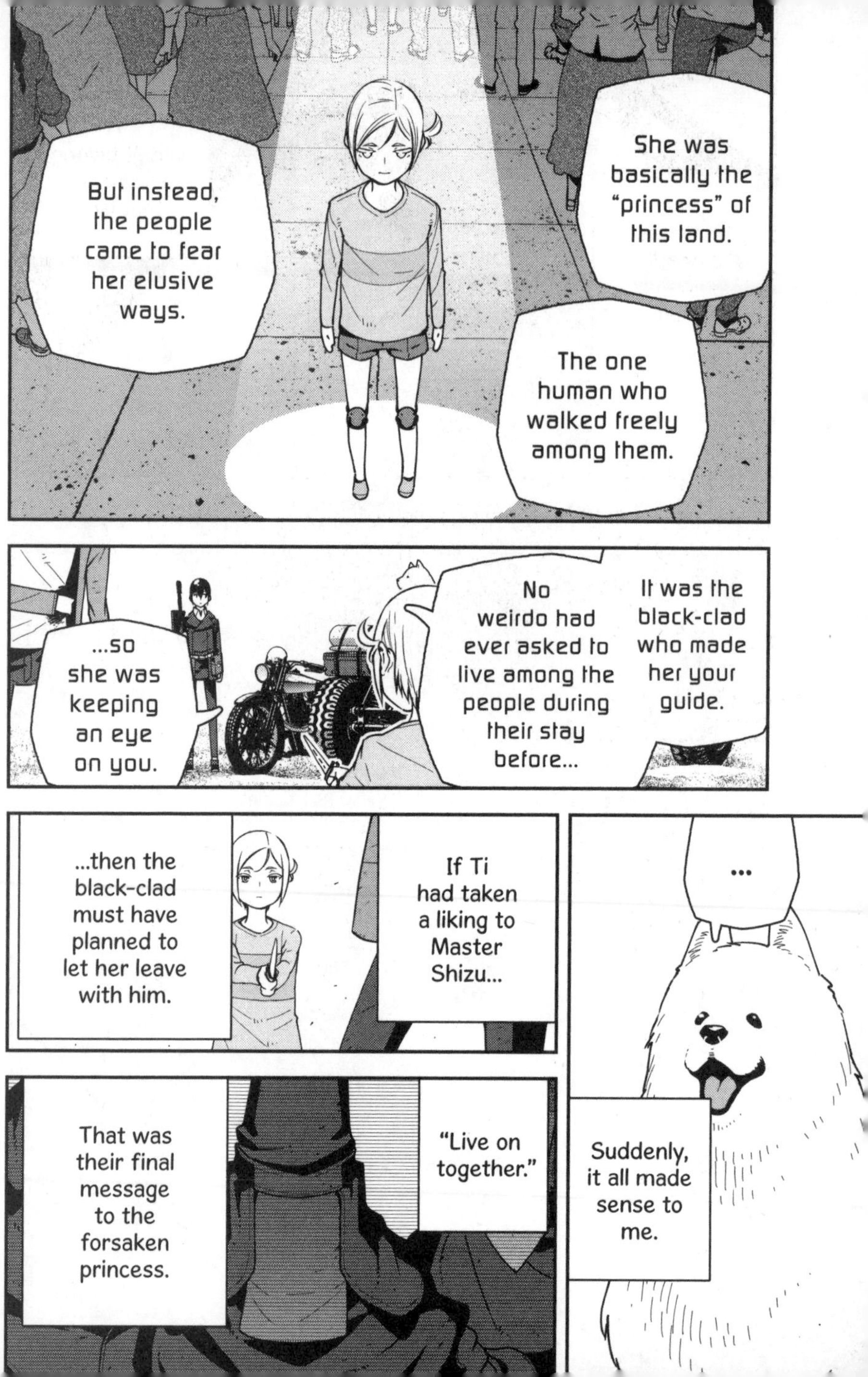
She was basically the "princess" of this land.
The one human who walked freely among them.
But instead, the people came to fear her elusive ways.
It was the black-clad who made her your guide.
No weirdo had ever asked to live among the people during their stay before...
...so she was keeping an eye on you.
...
Suddenly, it all made sense to me.
If Ti had taken a liking to Master Shizu...
...then the black-clad must have planned to let her leave with him.
"Live on together."
That was their final message to the forsaken princess.

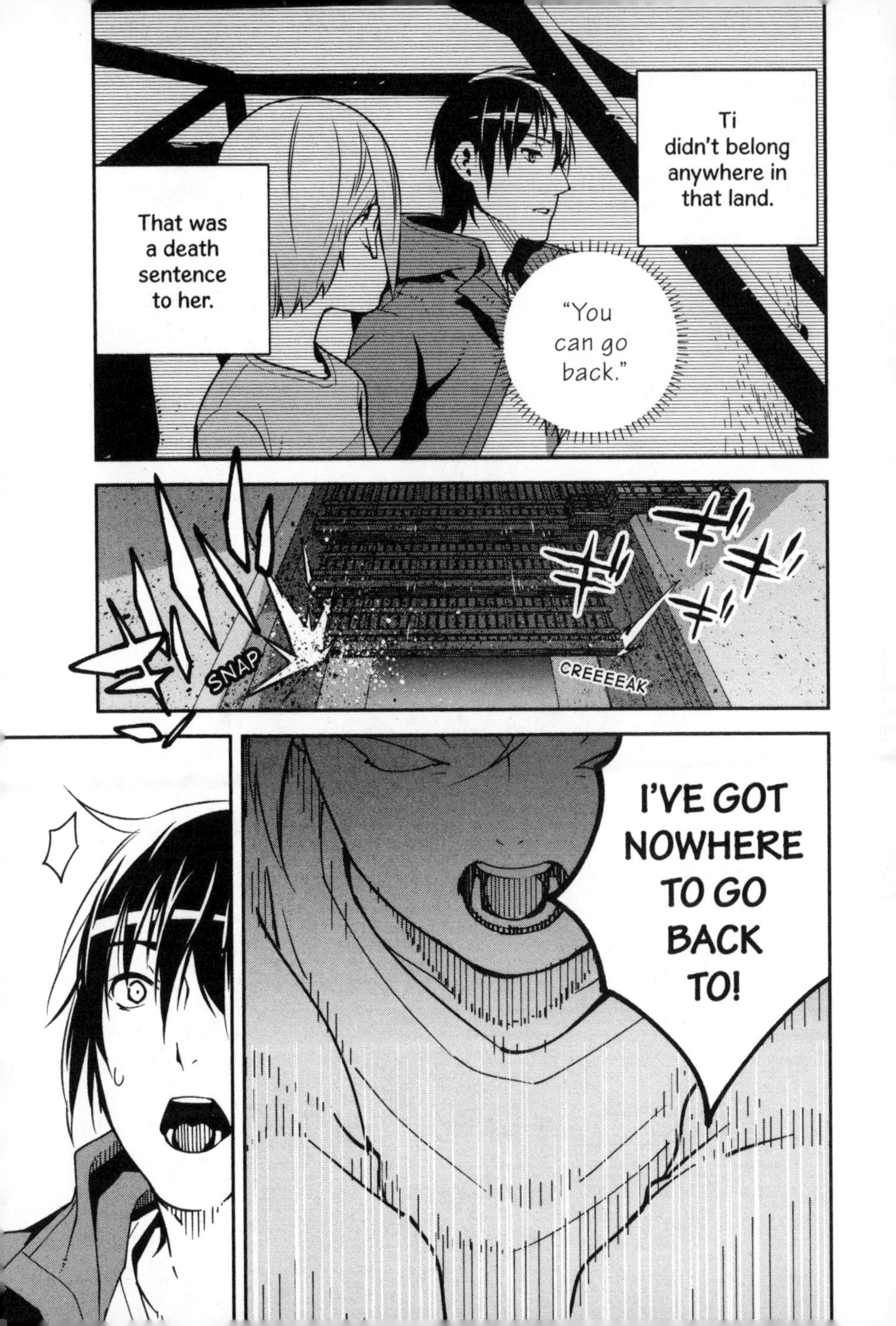
Ti didn't belong anywhere in that land.
"You can go back."
That was a death sentence to her.
CREEEEAK
SNAP
I'VE GOT NOWHERE TO GO BACK TO!

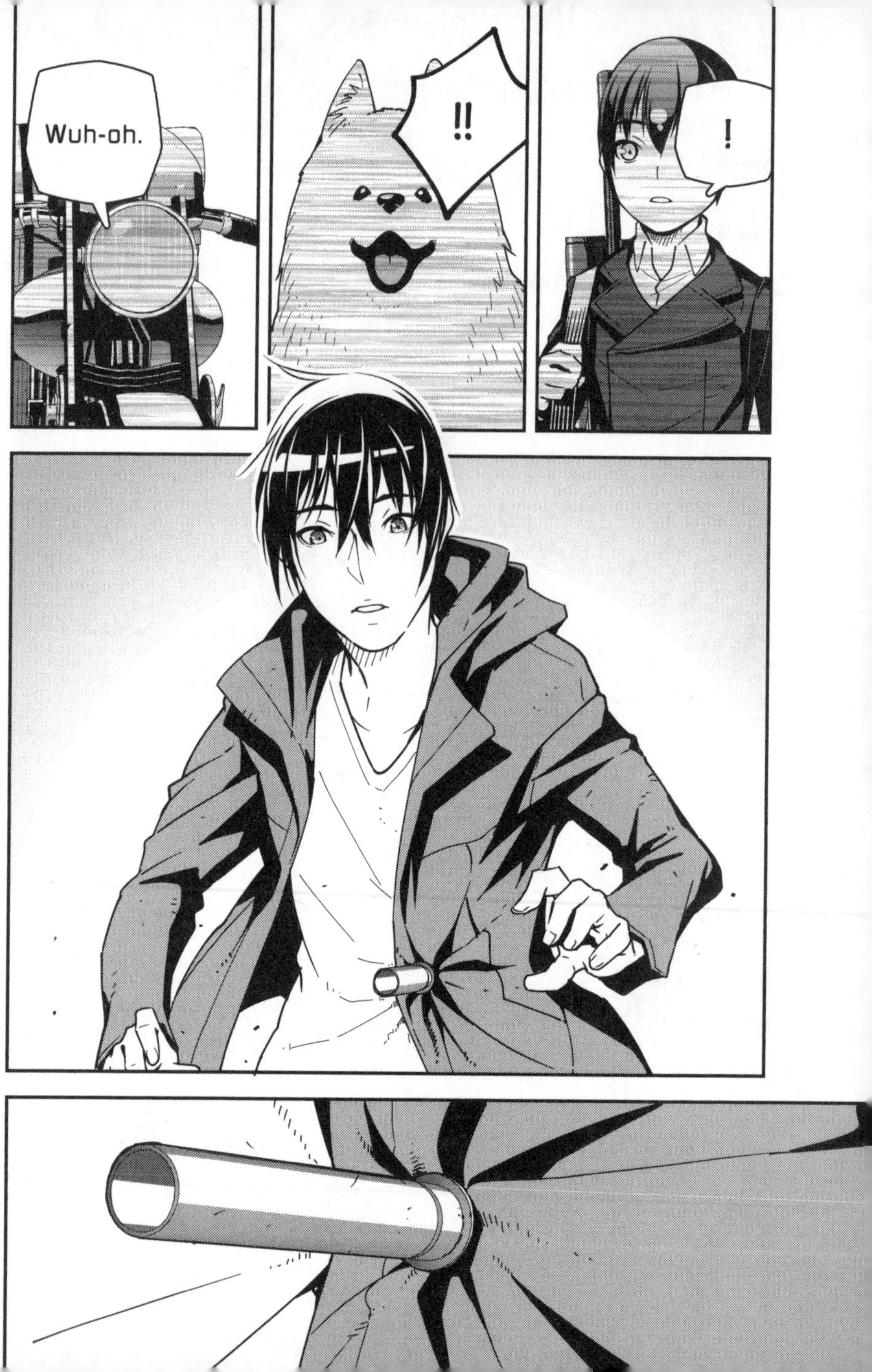
!
!!
Wuh-oh.

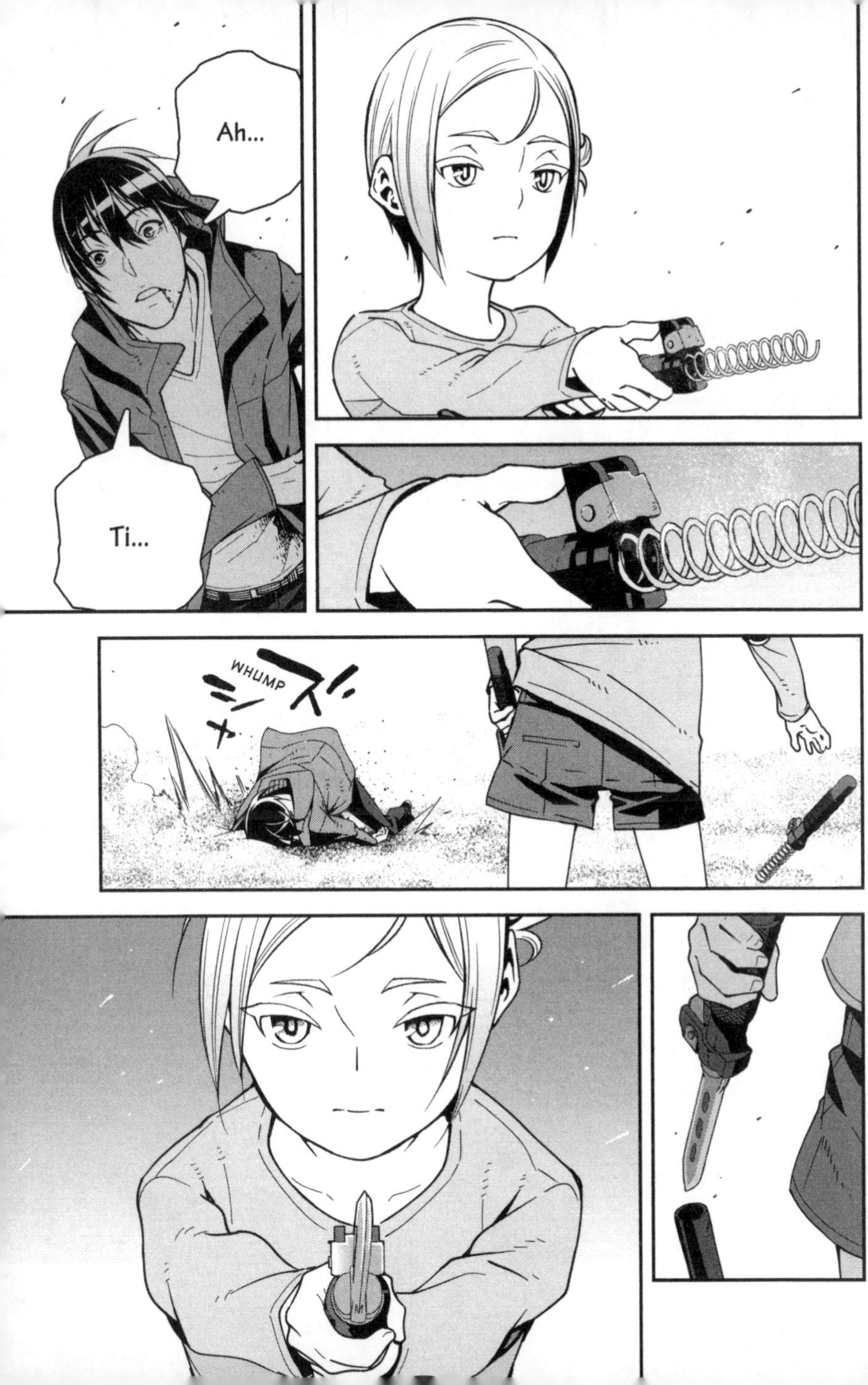
Ah...
Ti...
WHUMP

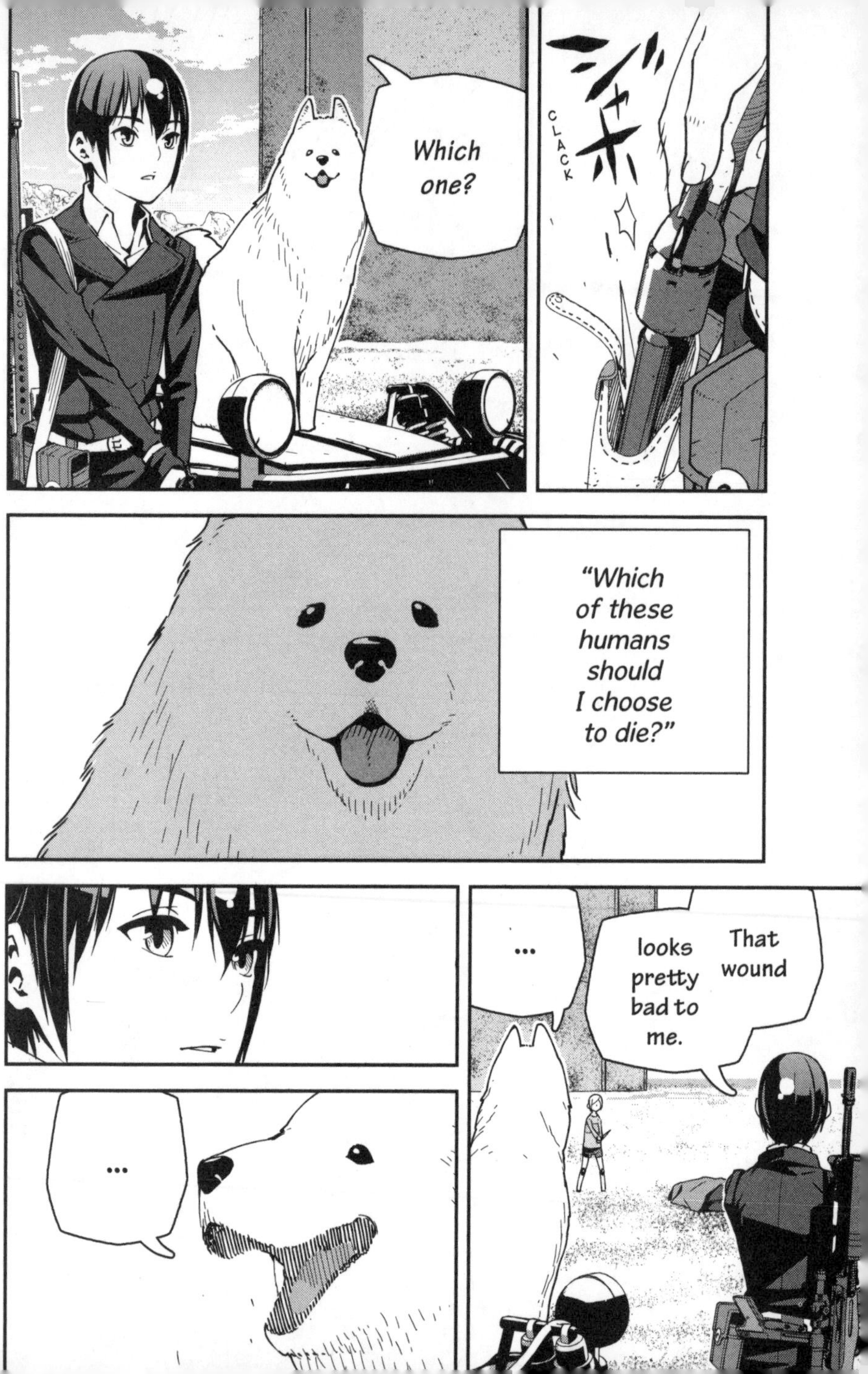
CLACK
Which one?
"Which of these humans should I choose to die?"
That wound looks pretty bad to me.
...
...

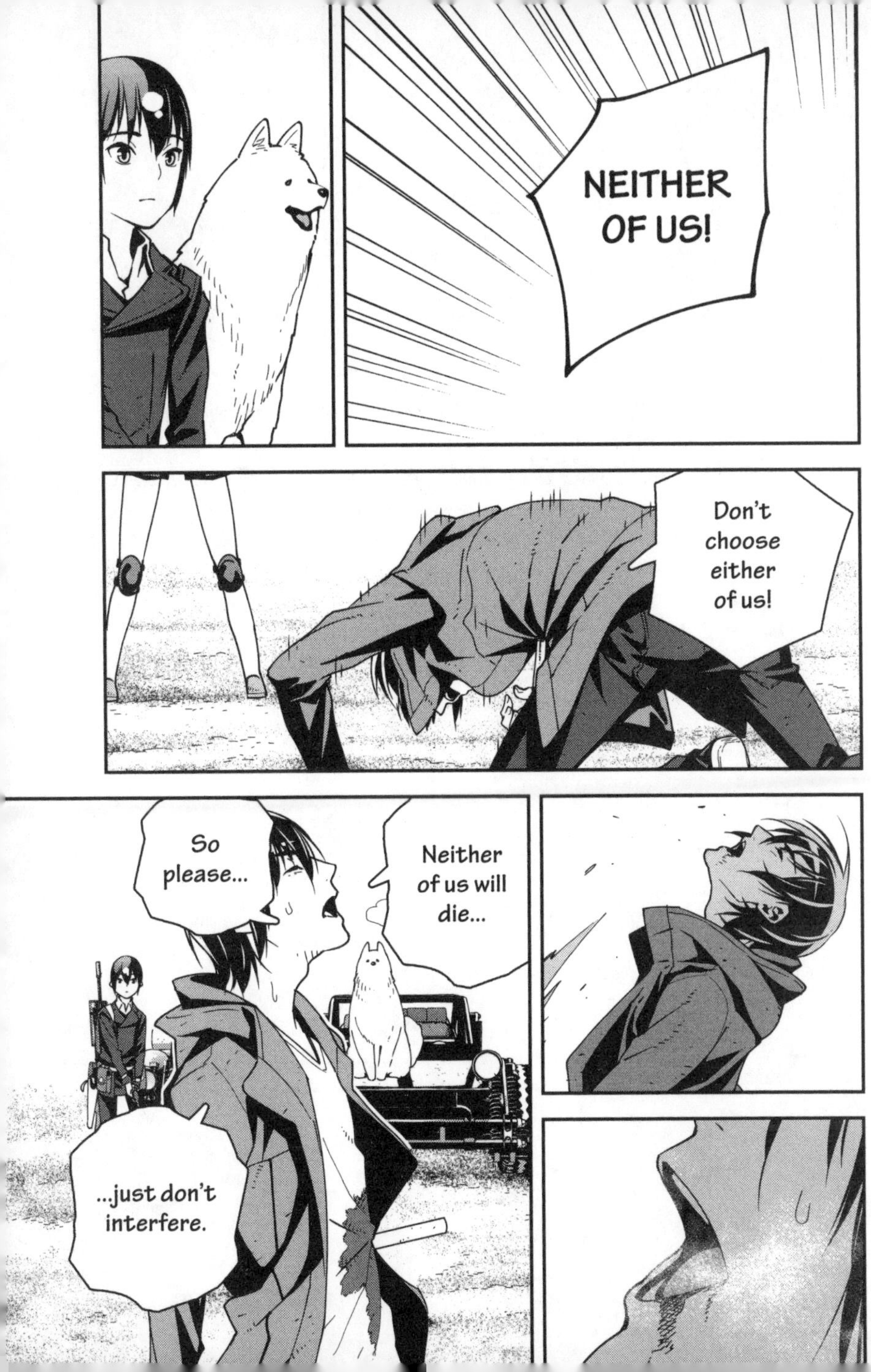
NEITHER OF US!
Don't choose either of us!
Neither of us will die...
So please...
...just don't interfere.

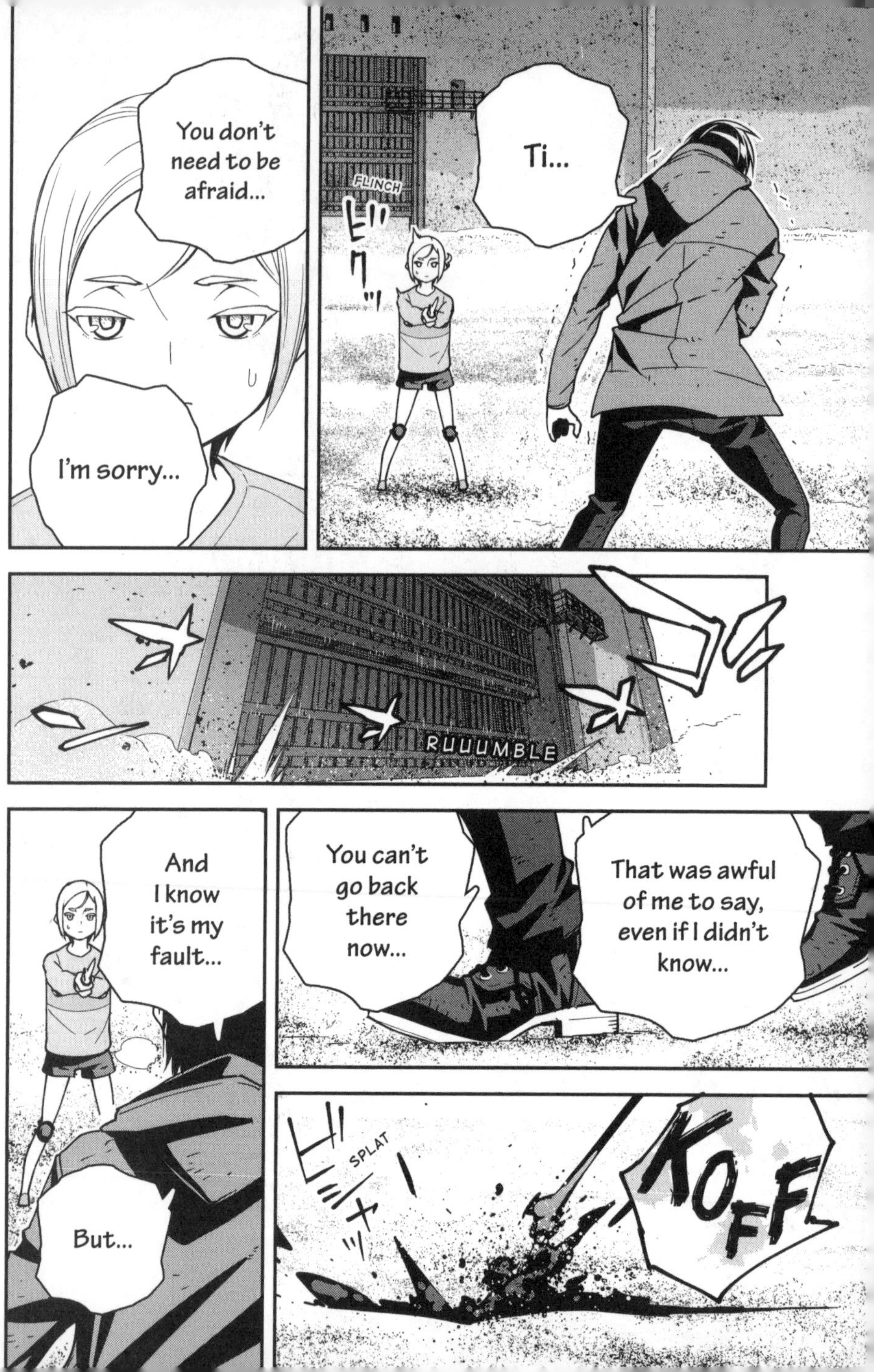
Ti...
FLINCH
You don't need to be afraid...
I'm sorry...
RUUUMBLE
That was awful of me to say, even if I didn't know...
You can't go back there now...
KOFF
SPLAT
And I know it's my fault...
But...

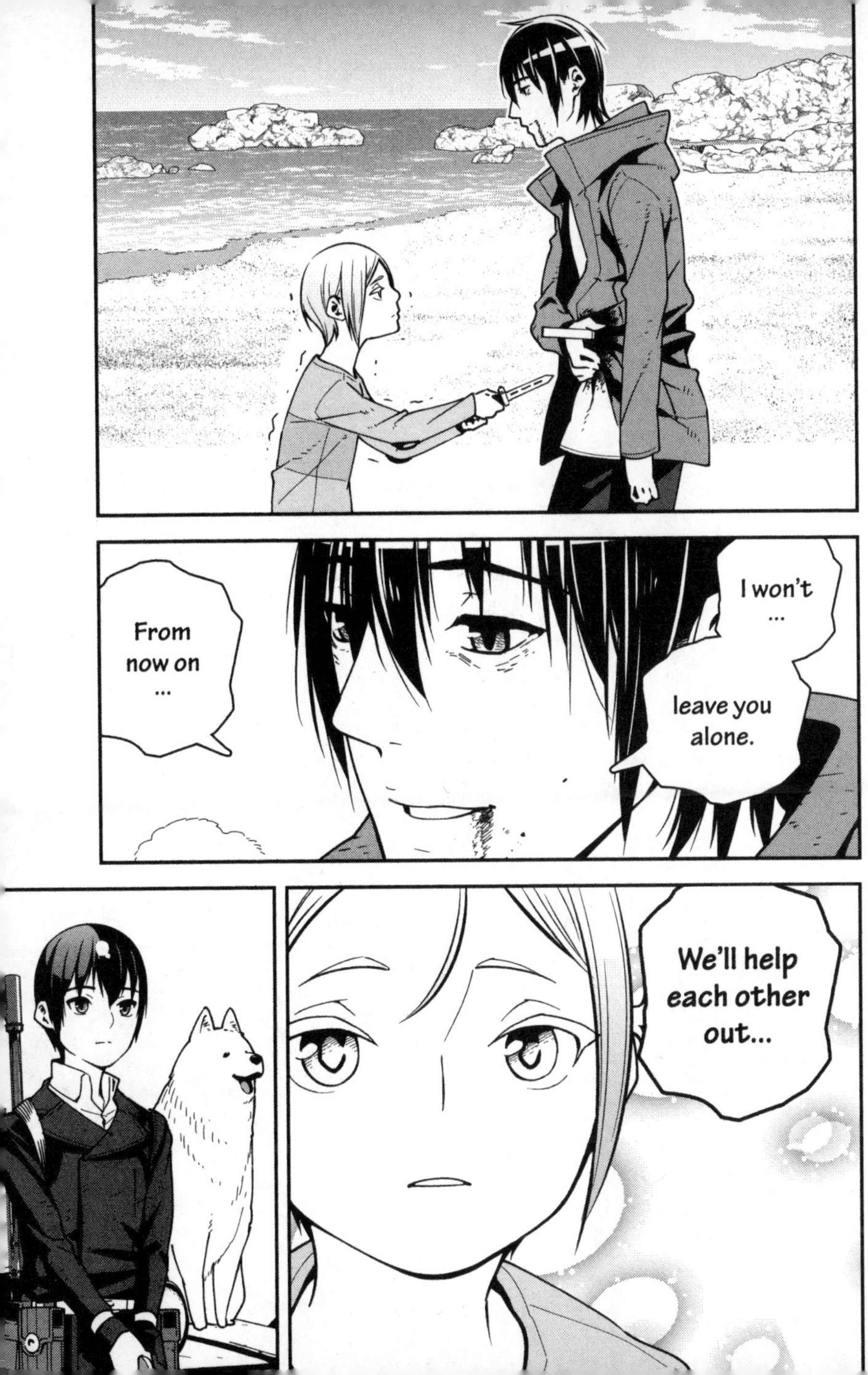
I won't ...
leave you alone.
From now on ...
We'll help each other out...

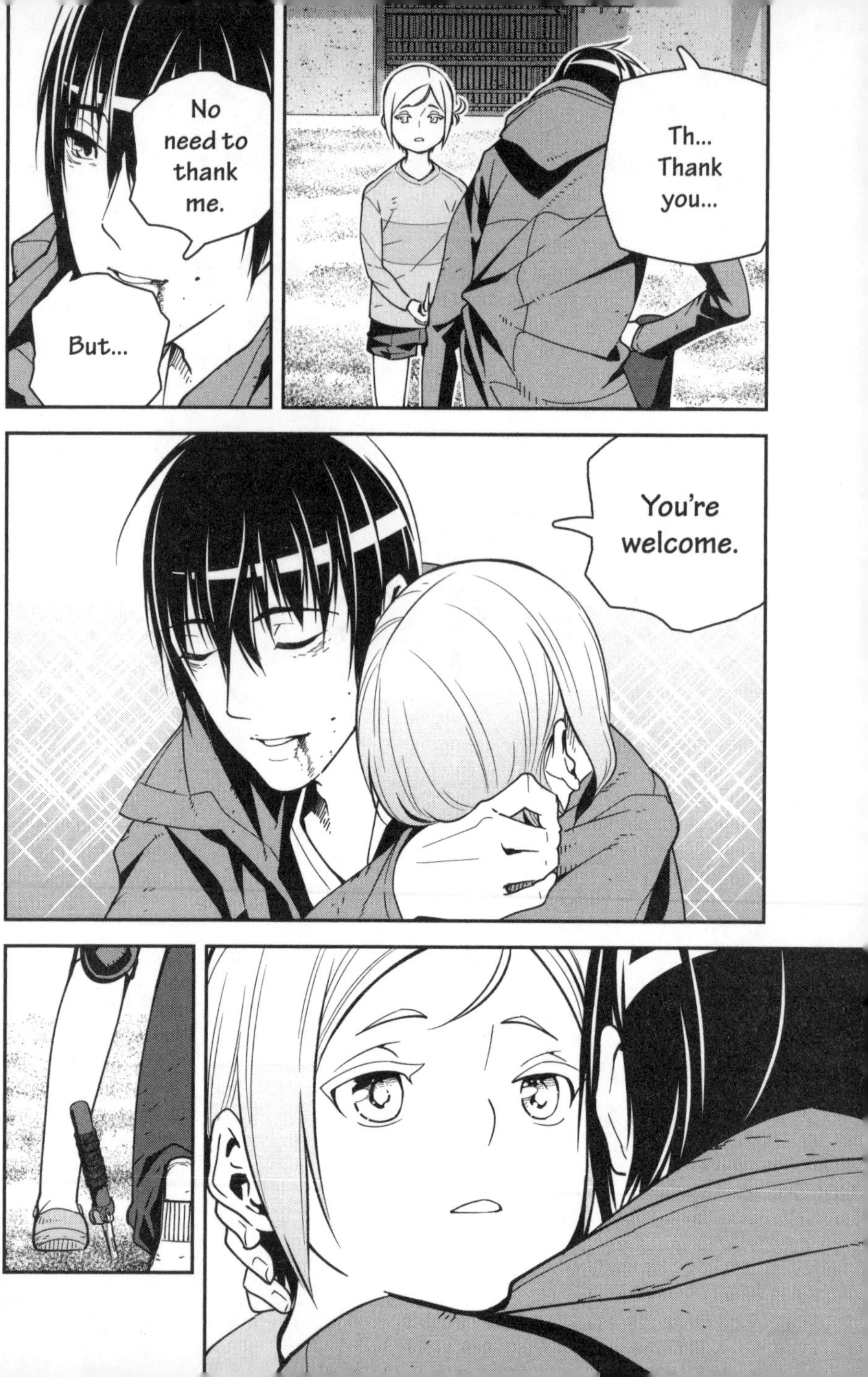
Th... Thank you...
No need to thank me.
But...
You're welcome.

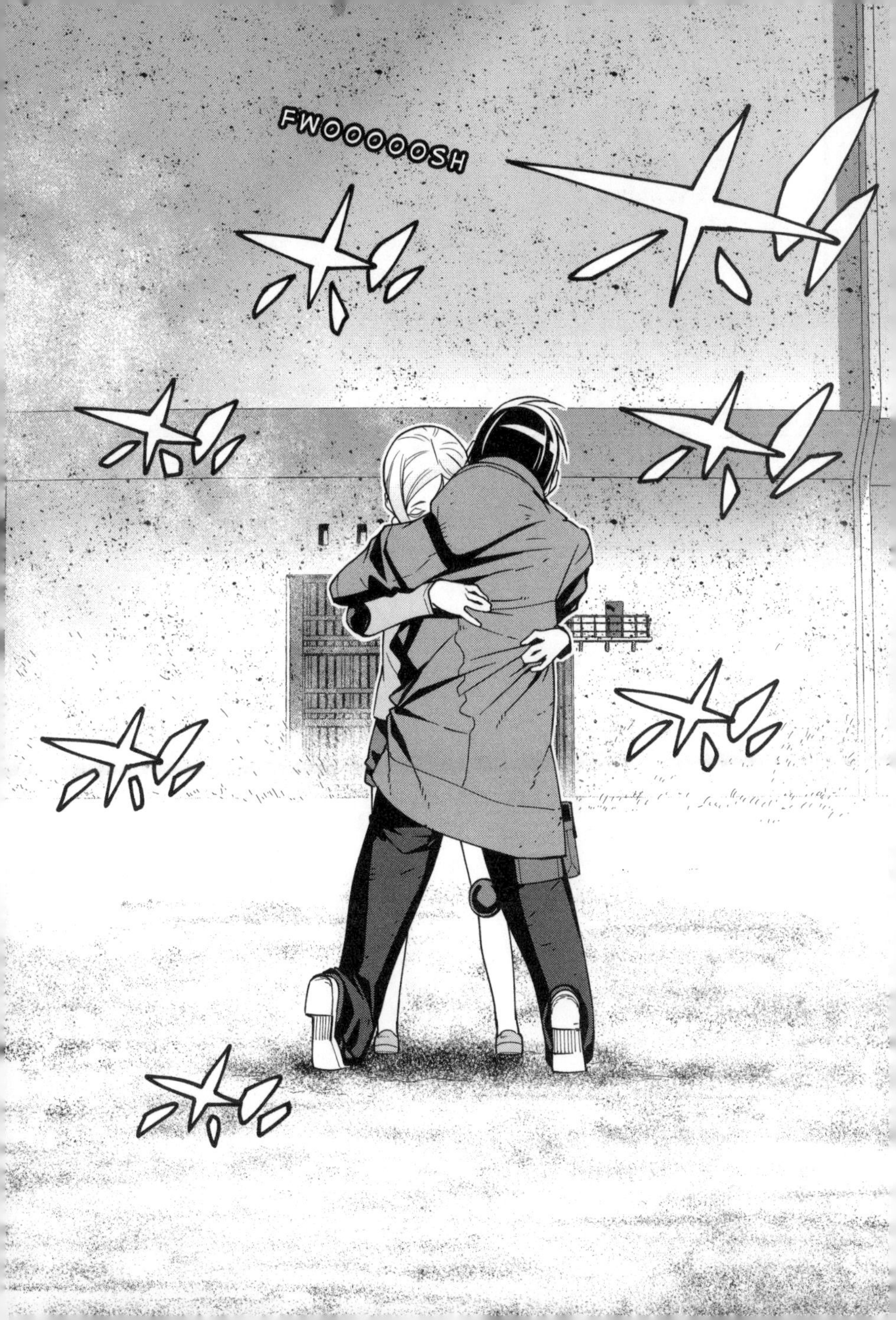
FWOOOOOOSH

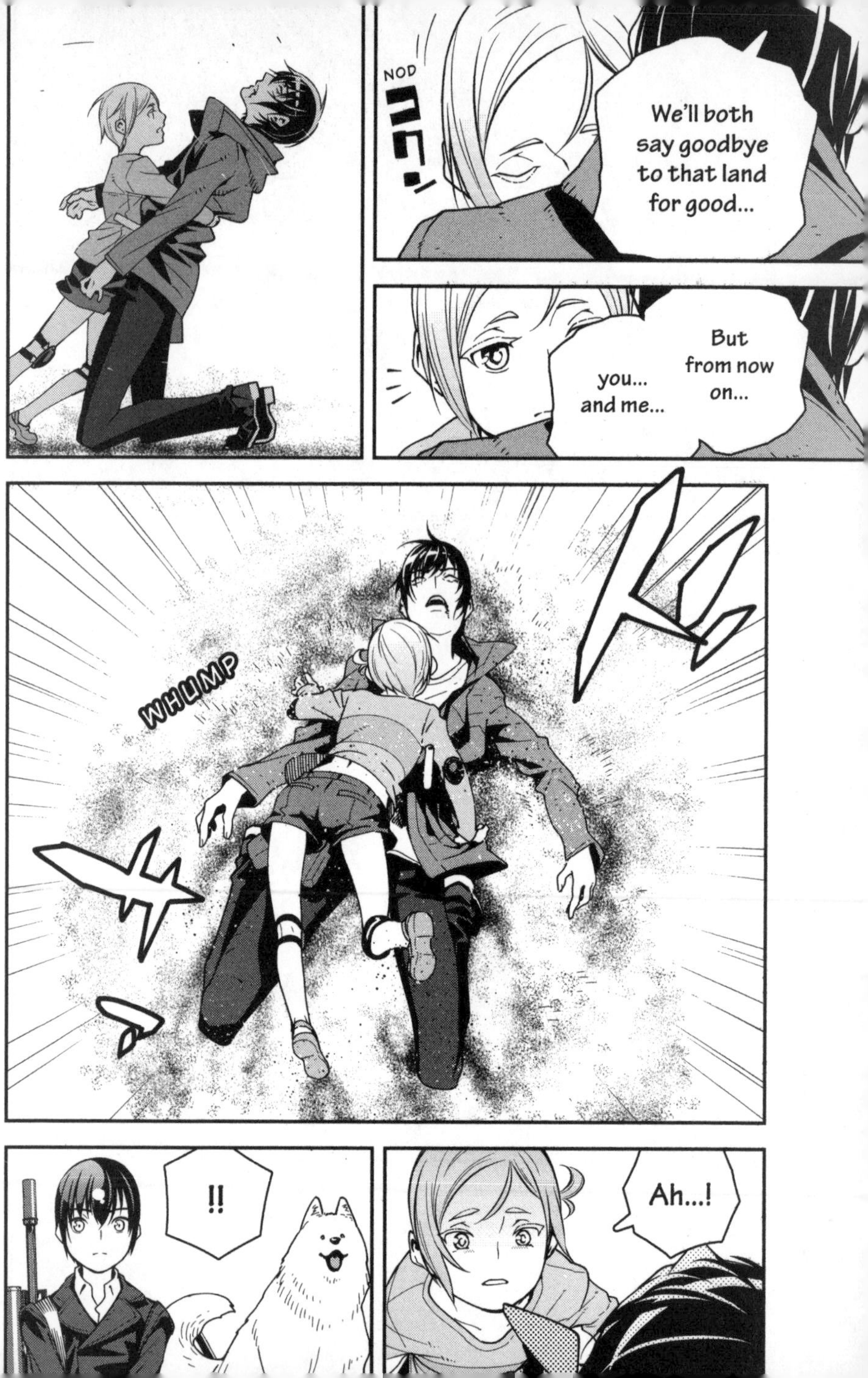
NOD
We'll both say goodbye to that land for good...
But from now on...
you... and me...
WHUMP
Ah...!
!!

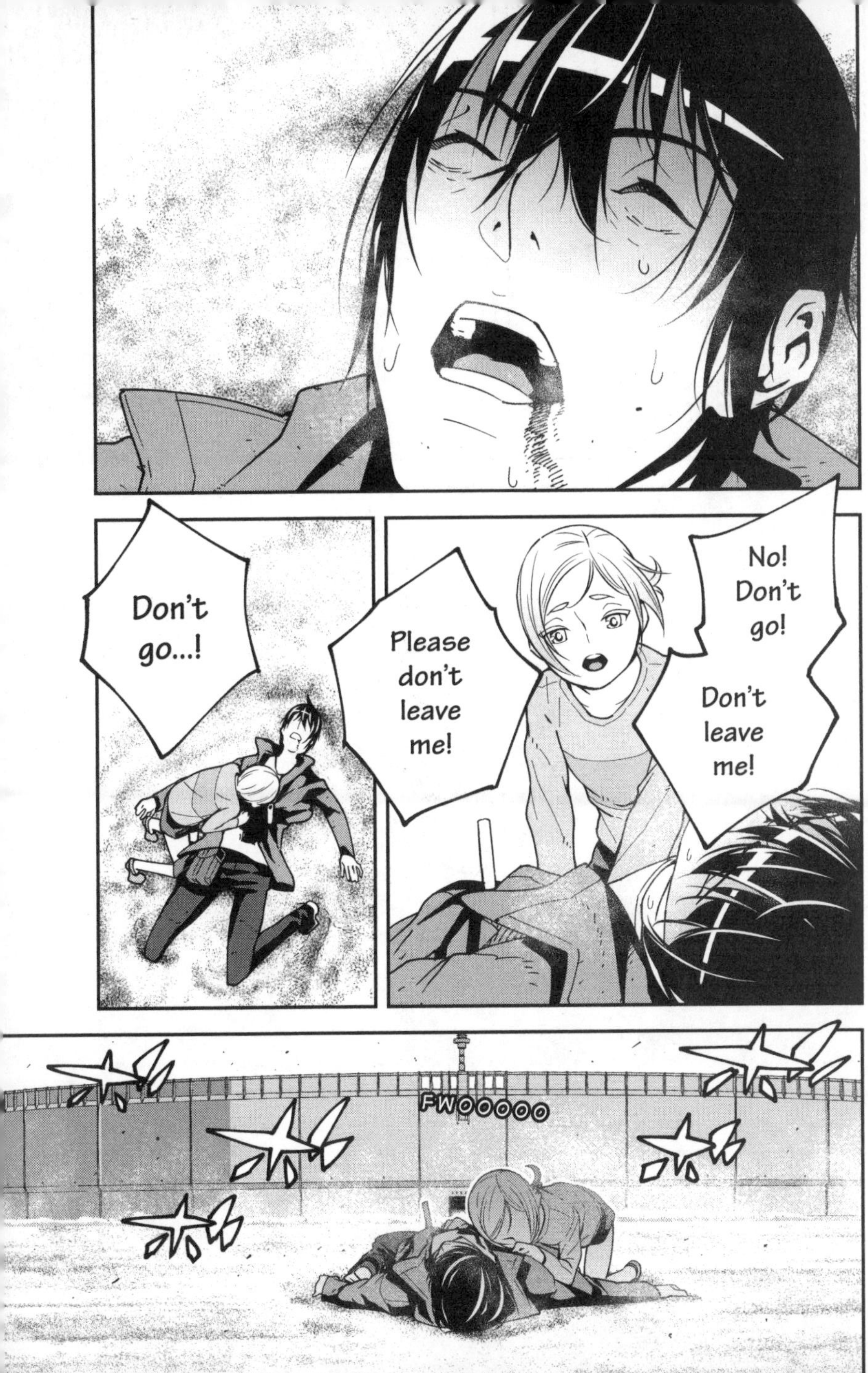
No! Don't go!
Don't leave me!
Please don't leave me!
Don't go...!
FWOOOOO

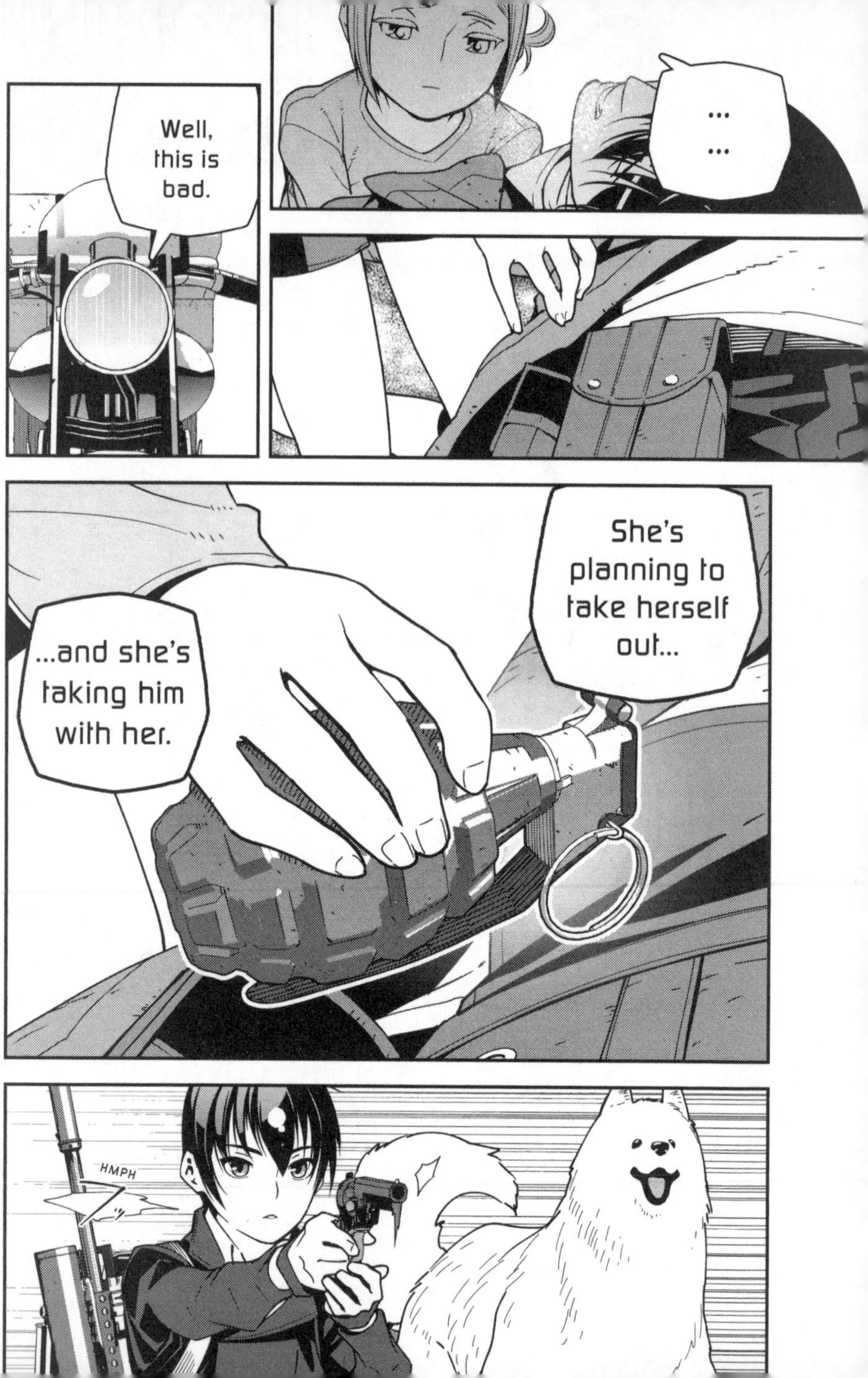
…
…
Well, this is bad.
She's planning to take herself out…
…and she's taking him with her.
HMPH

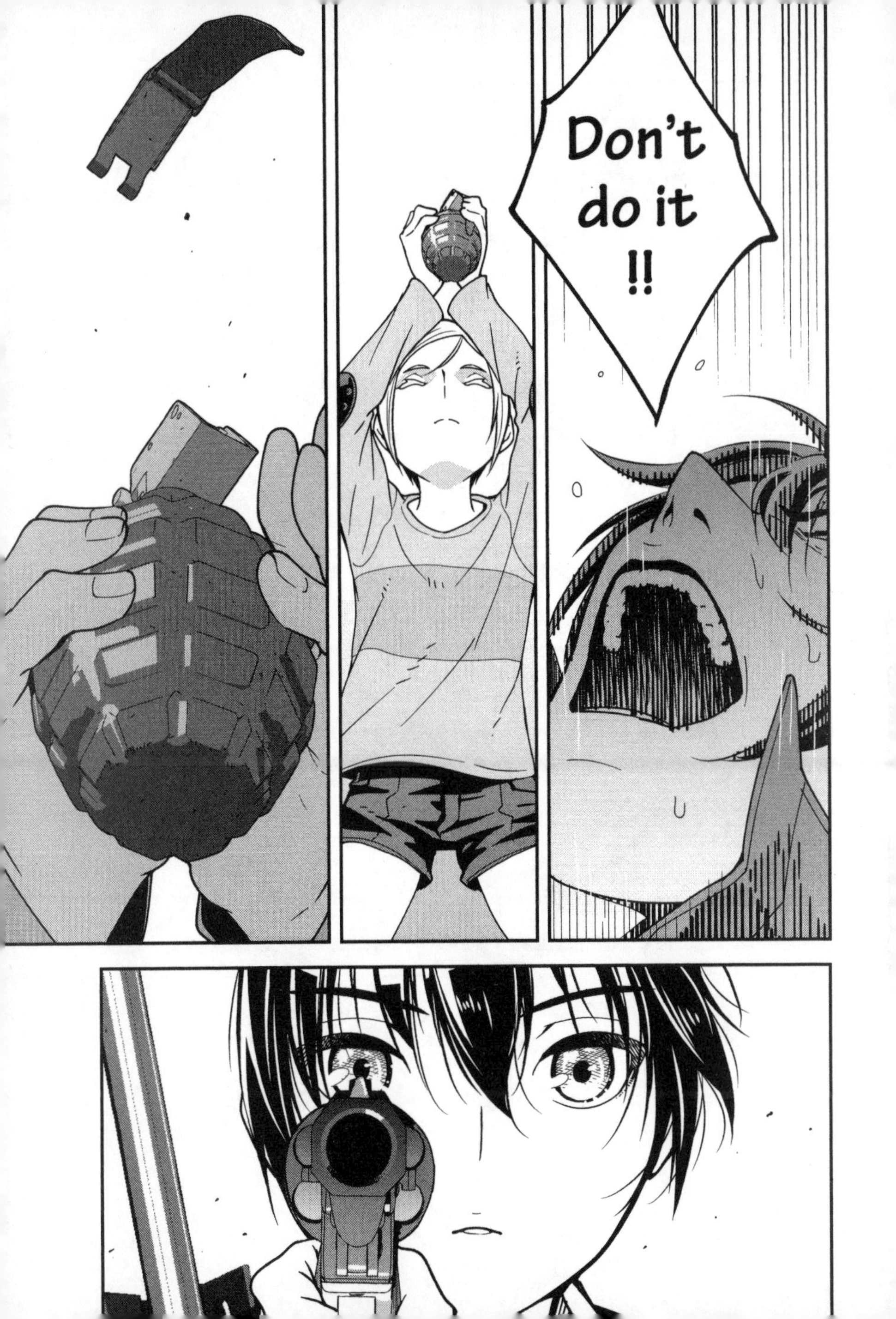
Don't do it !!

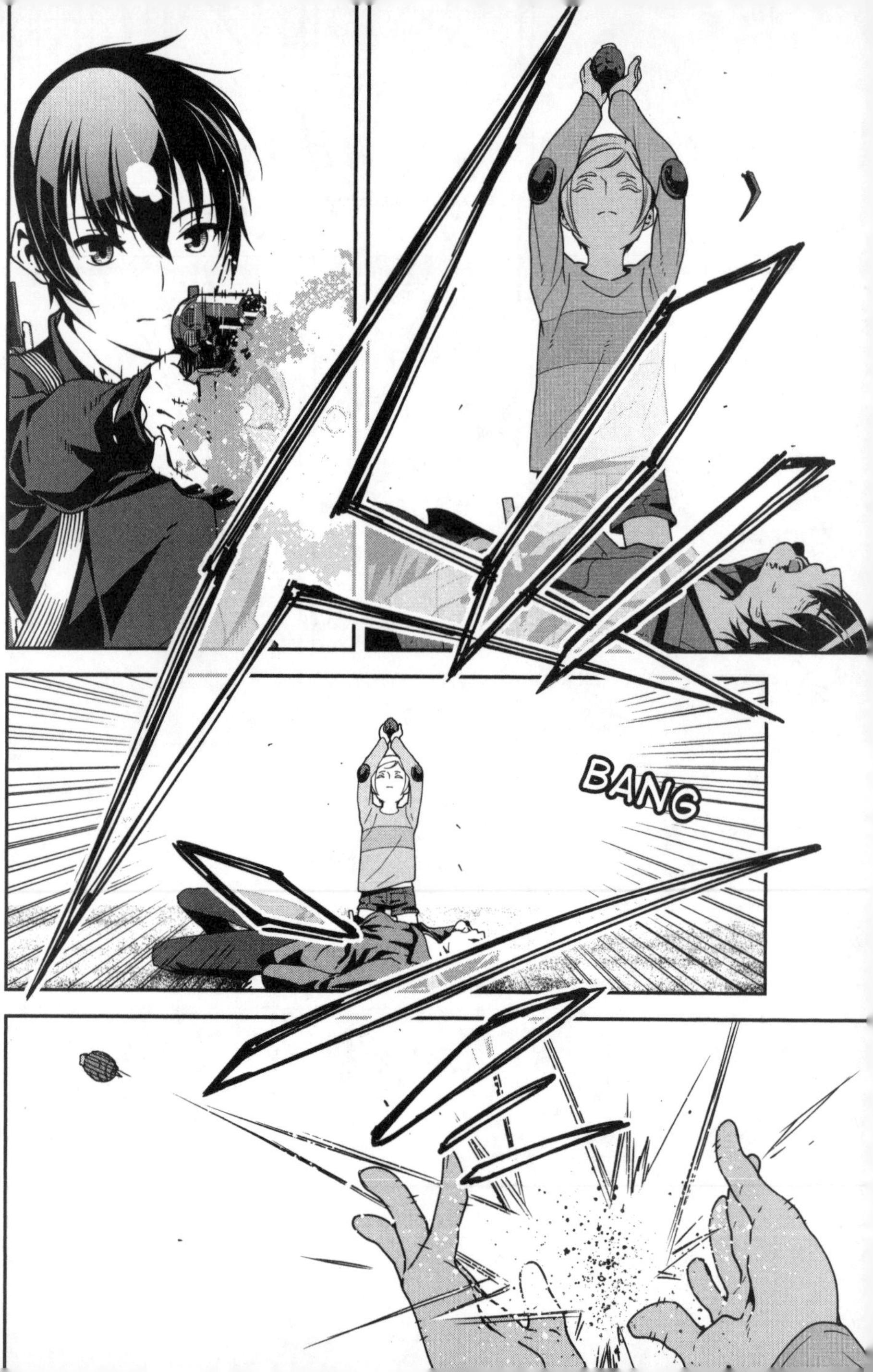
BANG

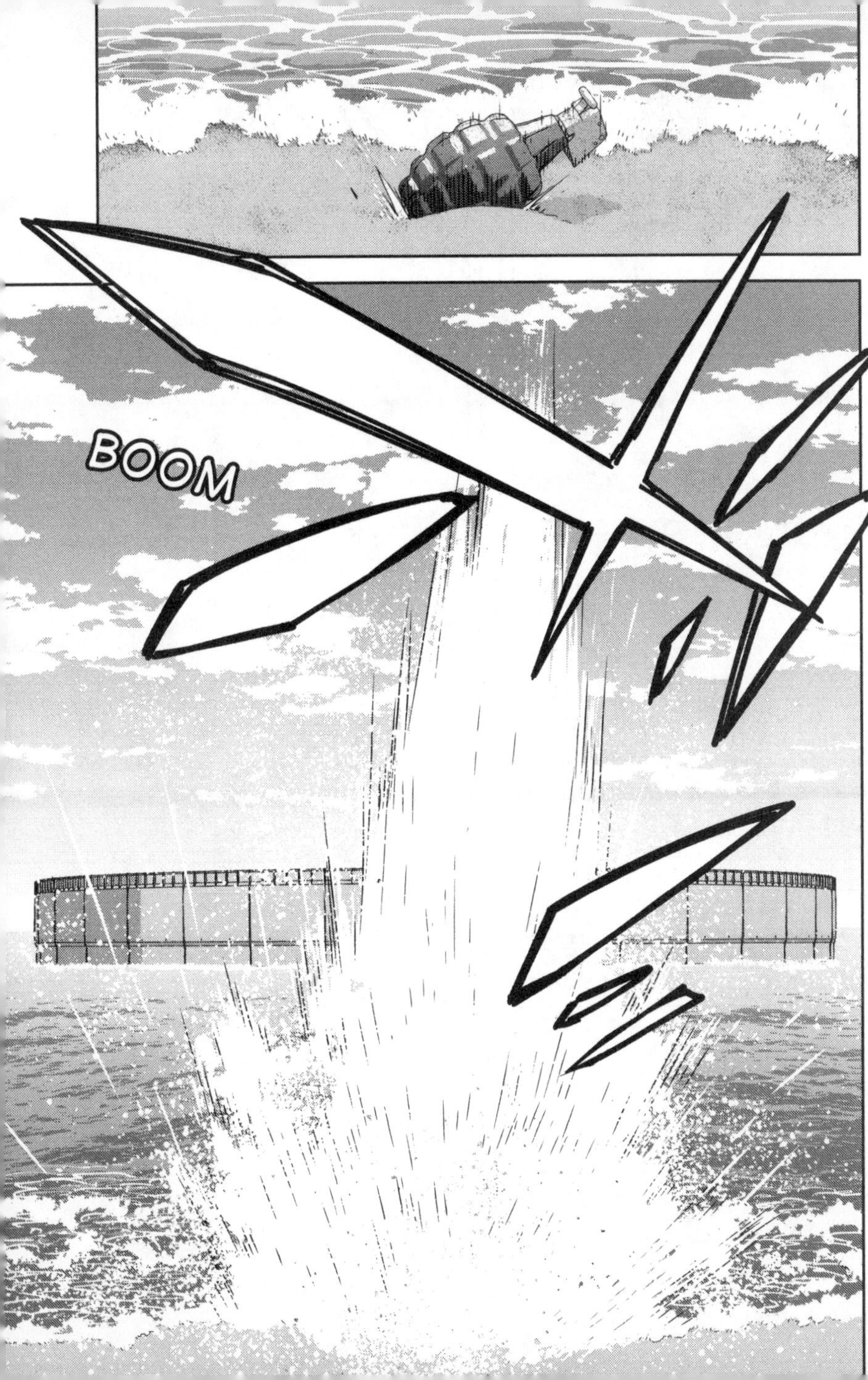
BOOM

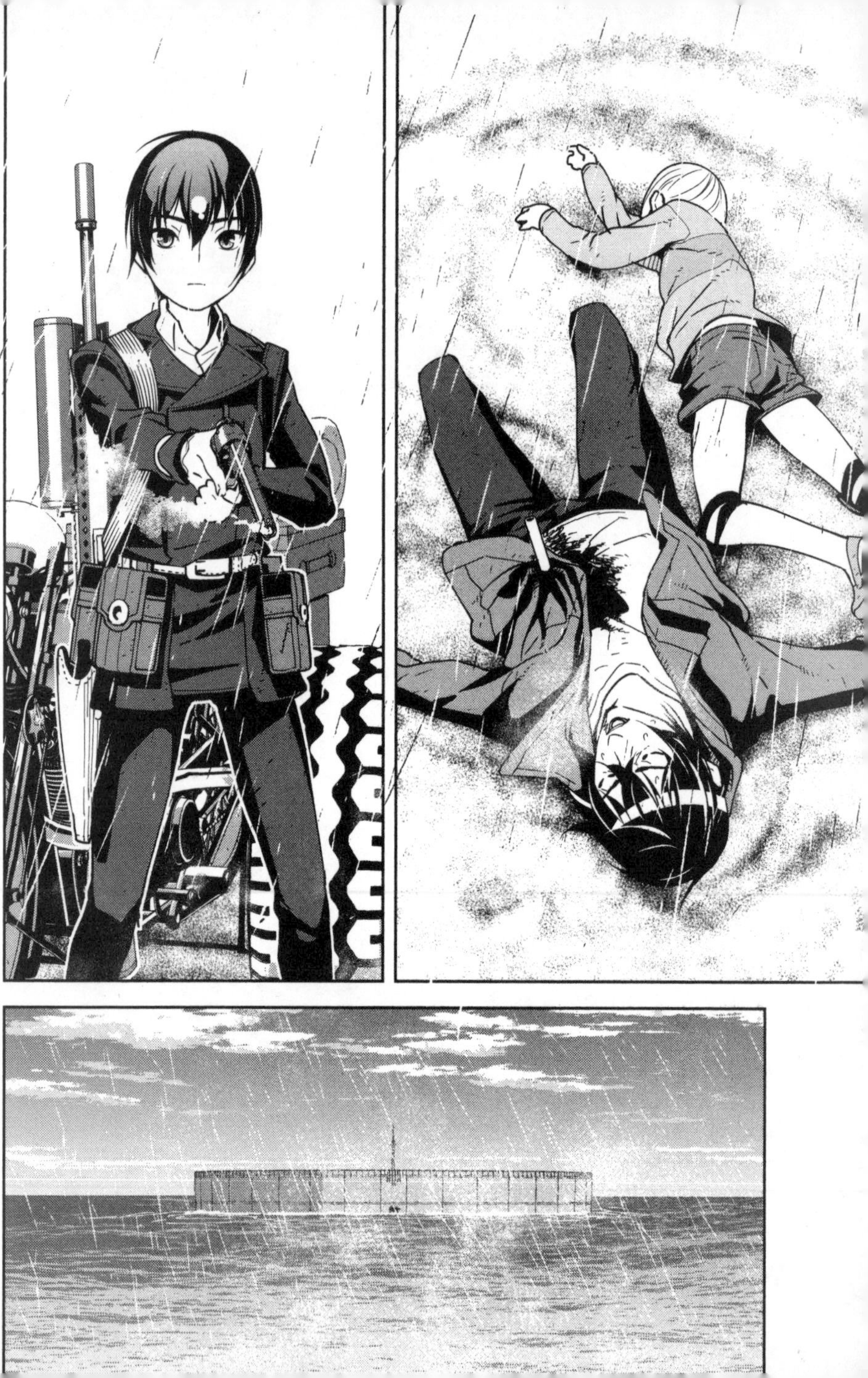

Do you remember? Shizu once met and parted ways with another girl. That's right, it was in the previous volume. It was because of that story that I wrote the one in this volume.

It's a long and heavy story, so it took an entire volume to adapt into a comic, resulting in a very deep and rewarding read.

When I first wrote this story, I was remembering that girl who I once parted ways with...in Shizu's story, of course. It's not about an ex-girlfriend or anything.

That girl, Rafa, was named after her town. So Tifana is also named after a town of sorts.

As an author, I was honored to have Shiomiya-san draw Tifana's story as well as Rafa's.

Sadly, we'll be parting ways with this afterword.

Iruka Shiomiya, thank you so much for all your hard work drawing *The Beautiful World* so very beautifully over the course of eight volumes. You did an excellent job!

And to everyone who read these books, I also want to thank you from the bottom of my heart.

Thank you so much!

I hope *The Beautiful World* will forever remain in your hearts.

September 2020   Keiichi Sigsawa

Afterword...!

I just got back by overnight bus. Yes, I'm showing up two volumes in a row.

That's right, it's me: novelist, motorcyclist, and napper-in-training, Keiichi Sigsawa. I don't know if I've gotten much better at writing novels, and I'm just as bad at riding a motorcycle as I've ever been (although I do it safely, at least), but lately, I've gotten really good at napping. I can fall asleep right away.

And since you're reading this afterword, there's a book I want to recommend to you!

It's the Kodansha manga adaptation of *Kino's Journey: The Beautiful World*!

In other words, this very book. Have you heard of it?

Well, whether you're familiar with it or not, please at least remember the name of the slightly strange person called "Keiichi Sigsawa" as you leave today.

Now, this entire volume consists of the "Land of Ships" story.

Technically, it also contains "At the Shore: The Beginning and End of a Journey," but they're really interconnected as the prologue and epilogue to the same story, just with a different title.

I won't spoil anything for those who haven't read it yet, but...it's a story in which Shizu has a fateful meeting.

Kino's Journey

The Beautiful World

3DCG

HERMES

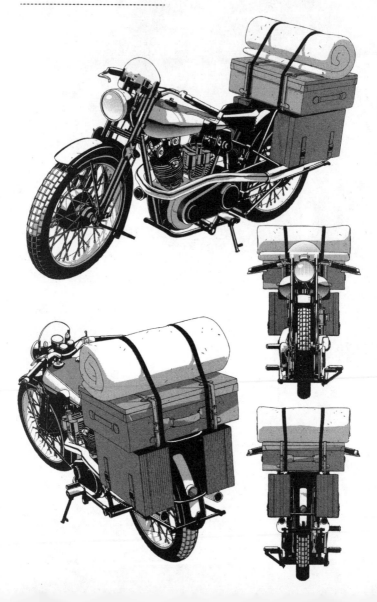

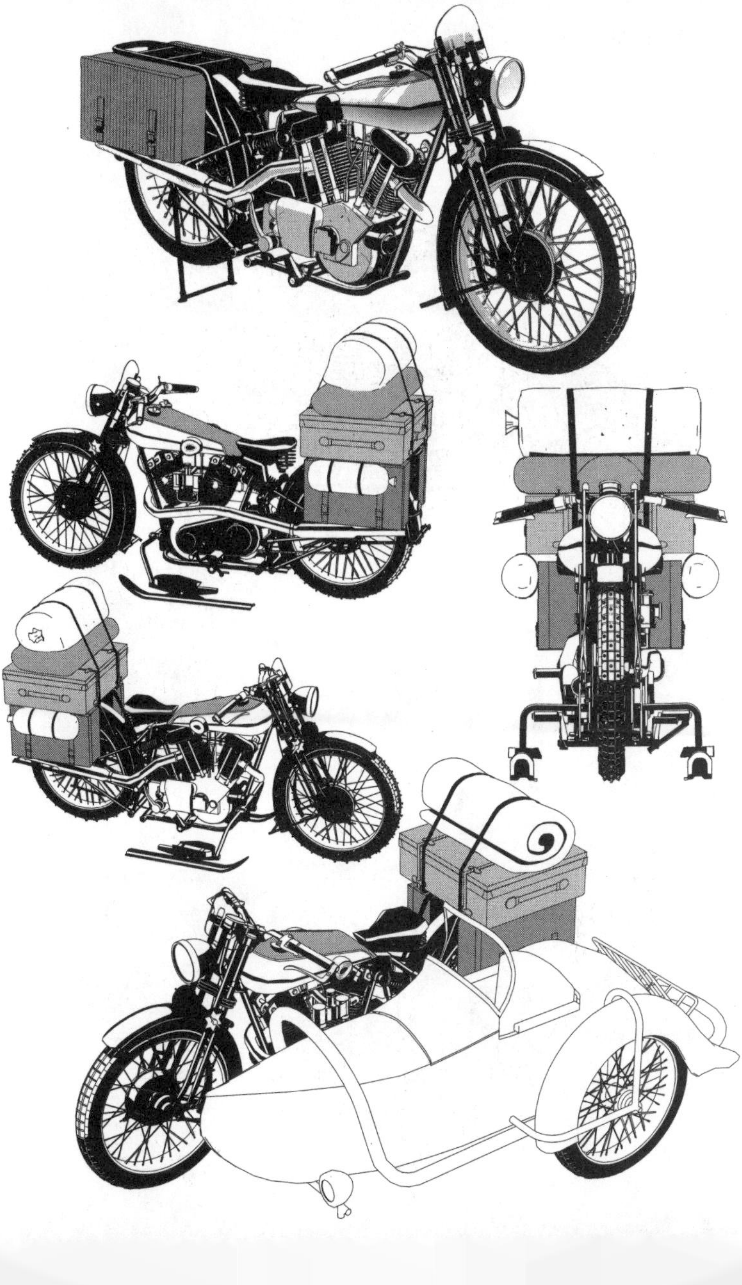

BUGGY

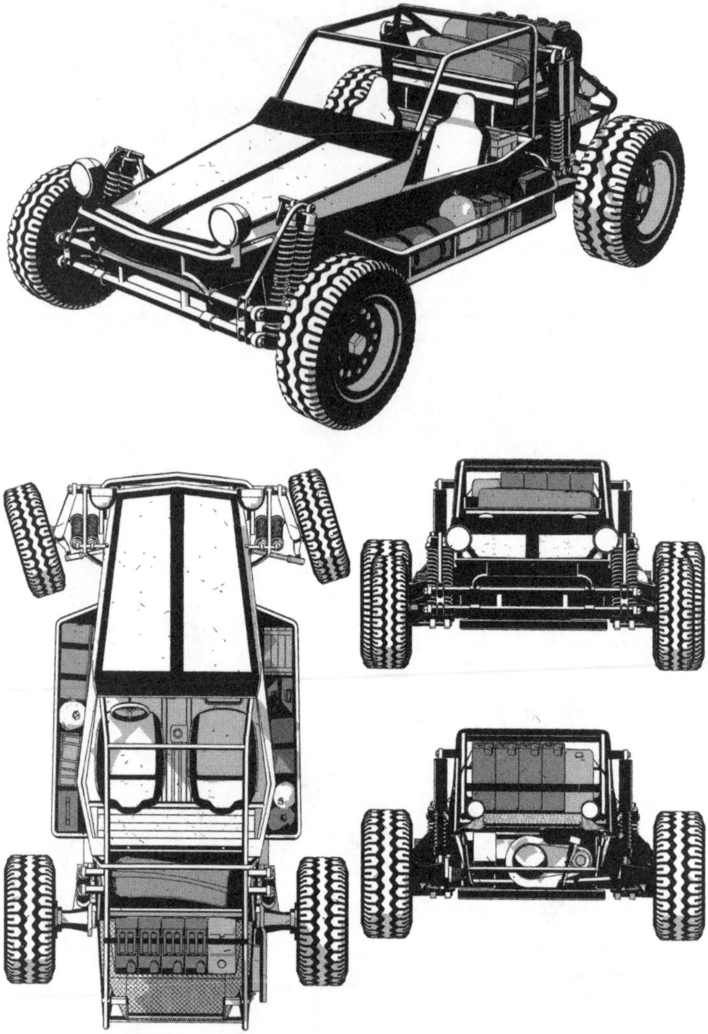

S U B A R U 3 6 0

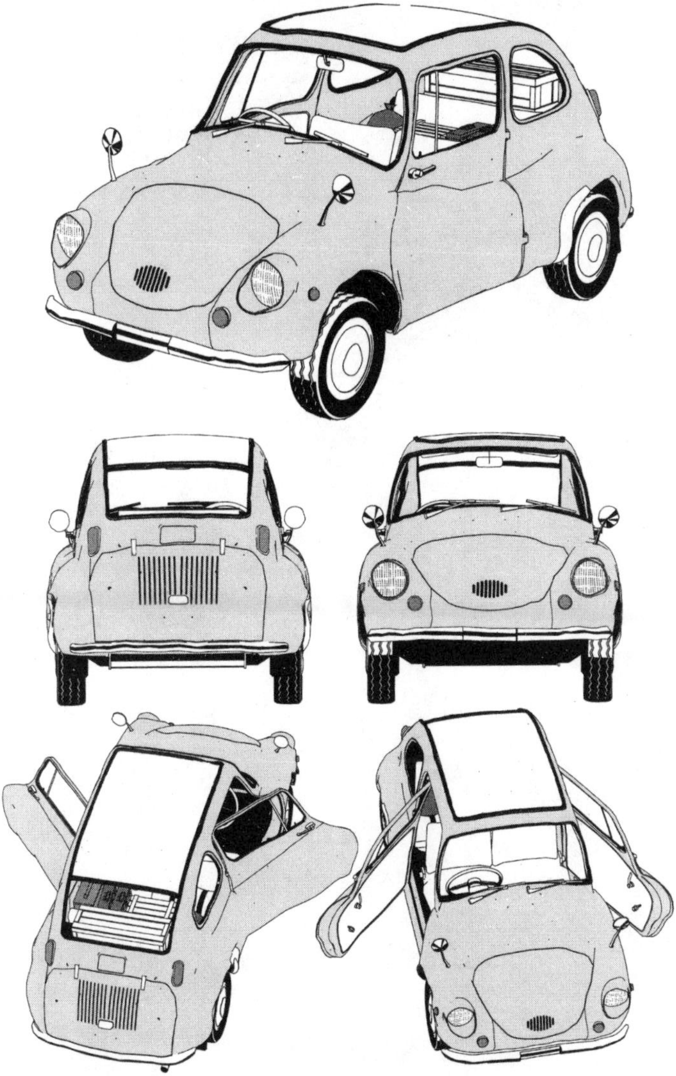

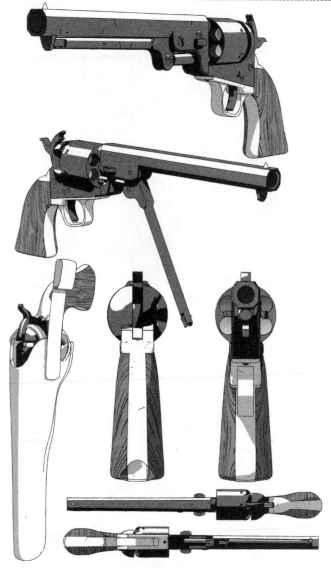

FLUTE

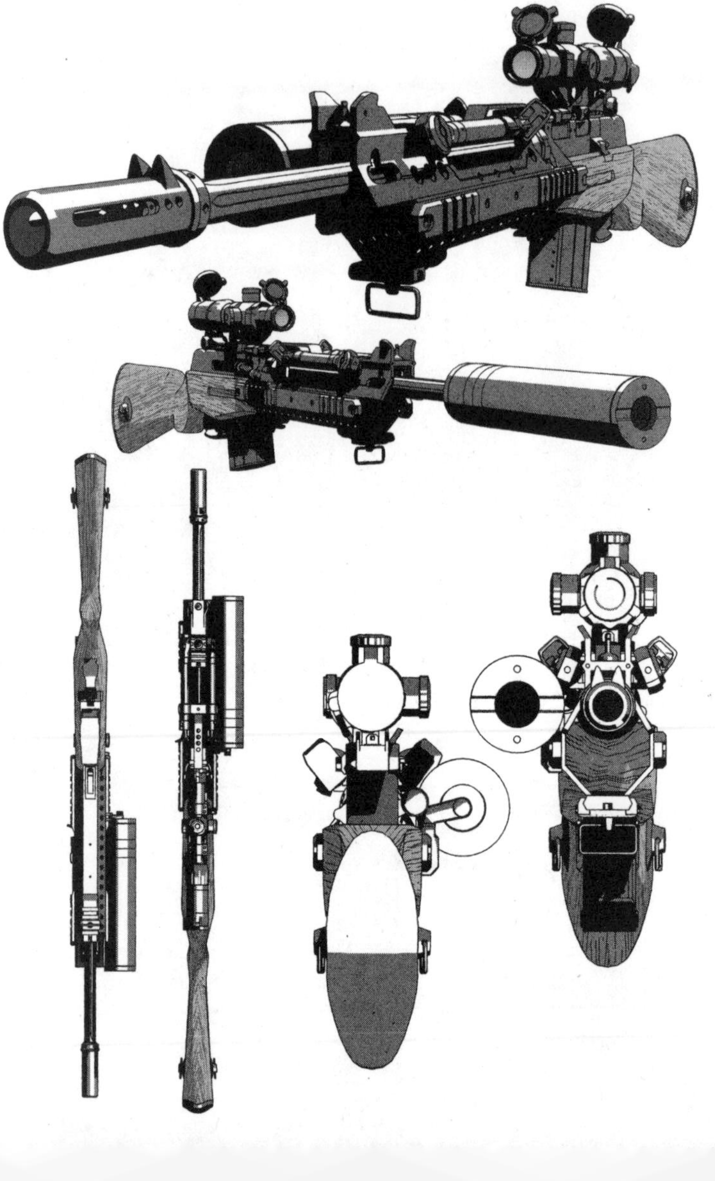

KNIVES

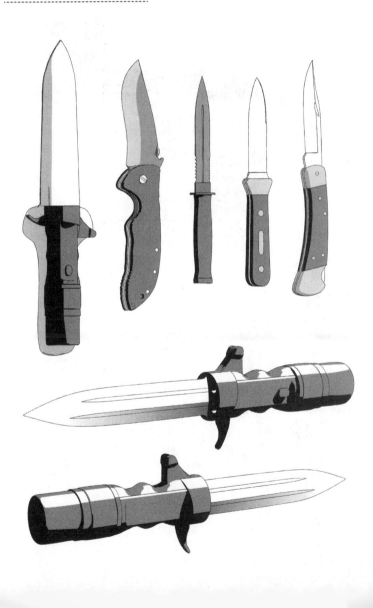

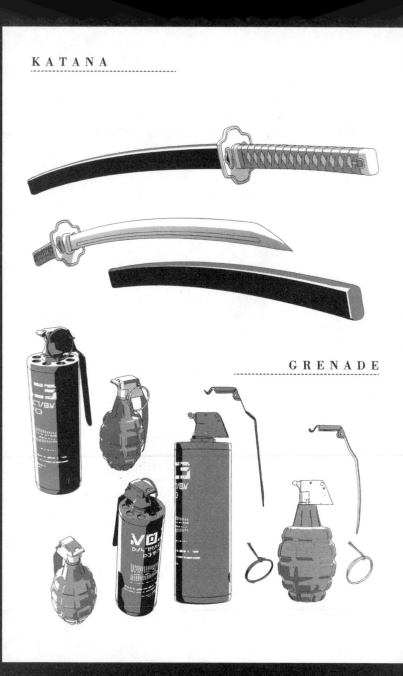

KATANA

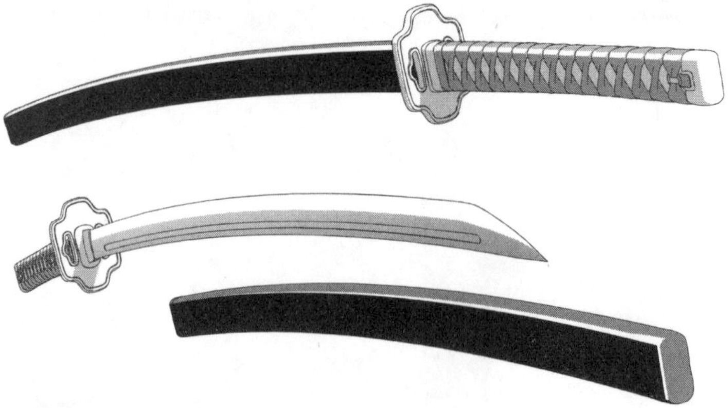

GRENADE

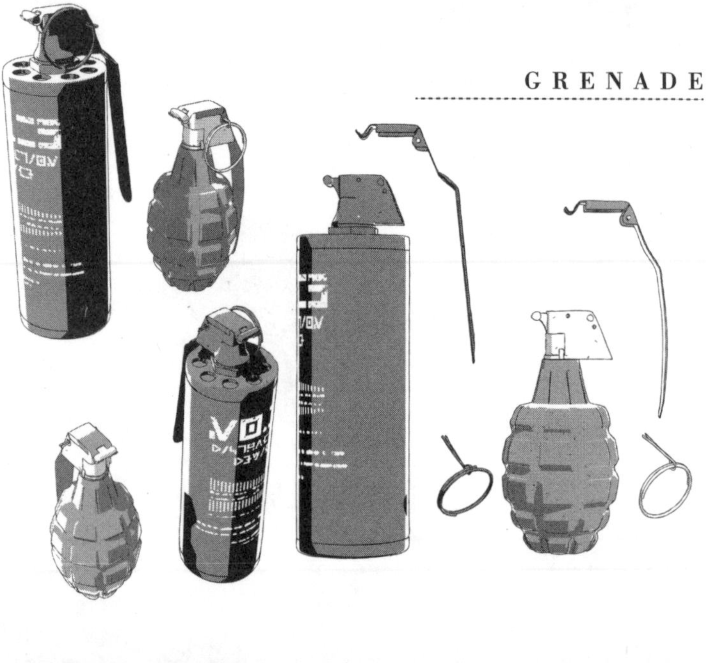

3D Assistant
Jeri

Kino's Journey

The Beautiful World

volume 8

A Vertical Comics Edition

Editor: Ajani Oloye
Translation: Jenny McKeon
Production: Grace Lu
Anthony Quintessenza

First published in Japan in 2020 by Kodansha, Ltd., Tokyo
Publication for this English edition arranged through Kodansha, Ltd., Tokyo
English language version produced by Vertical Comics,
an imprint of Kodansha USA Publishing, LLC

Translation provided by Vertical Comics, 2021
Published by Kodansha USA Publishing, LLC, New York

Originally published in Japanese as *Kino no Tabi the Beautiful World 8* by Kodansha, Ltd.
Kino no Tabi the Beautiful World first serialized in *Shonen Magazine Edge*,
Kodansha, Ltd., 2017-2020

ISBN: 978-1-949980-73-8

Manufactured in Canada

First Edition

Kodansha USA Publishing, LLC
451 Park Avenue South
7th Floor
New York, NY 10016
www.readvertical.com

Vertical books are distributed through Penguin-Random House Publisher Services.